Explaining Law

International Studies in Sociology and Social Anthropology

VOLUME 124

The titles published in this series are listed at *brill.com/issa*

Explaining Law

Macrosociological Theory and Empirical Evidence

By

Larry D. Barnett

BRILL

LEIDEN | BOSTON

Cover illustration: The Picture of Law. Design by Larry and Linda Barnett.

Library of Congress Cataloging-in-Publication Data

Barnett, Larry D., author.
Explaining law : macrosociological theory and empirical evidence / by Larry D. Barnett.
pages cm. — (International studies in sociology and social anthropology ; v. 124)
Includes bibliographical references and index.
ISBN 978-90-04-28120-2 (hardback : alk. paper) — ISBN 978-90-04-28121-9 (e-book) 1. Law—Social aspects—United States. 2. Sociological jurisprudence. 3. Macrosociology. 4. Social change. I. Title.

KF380.B35 2015
340'.115--dc23

2015020783

This publication has been typeset in the multilingual "Brill" typeface. With over 5,100 characters covering Latin, IPA, Greek, and Cyrillic, this typeface is especially suitable for use in the humanities.
For more information, please see www.brill.com/brill-typeface.

ISSN 0074-8684
ISBN 978-90-04-28120-2 (hardback)
ISBN 978-90-04-28121-9 (e-book)

This book is printed on acid-free paper.

Contents

PART 2
Macrosociology, Law, and Societal Problems

PART 3
Final Comments

Preface

> The progress of science requires more than new data; it needs novel frameworks and contexts.[1]

Humans make sense of the world in which they live by employing assumptions, and when an assumption leads to unsuccessful adaptations, it is replaced. Regrettably, the mortality rate of assumptions over the course of history is unknown. However, if the rate could be ascertained, it would probably be found to have been very high, because the social and physical world invariably undergoes change to which human thought responds. During the twentieth century, law schools in the United States assumed that the social sciences offered them little of value, but the assumption has been rendered obsolete by advances in the data sources and statistical methods of the social sciences. Put simply, the social sciences have moved into an entirely new league, and given the changes that are now taking place in the profession of law,[2] a large number of lawyers in training (through courses in law schools) as well as a large number of lawyers in practice (through programs of continuing education) will probably have no choice but to learn about the uses that can be made of the social sciences.[3] The handwriting is on the wall, although as usually happens in human societies, reading it will take time.

I came to a law school setting in the early 1970s, and not surprisingly my introduction to law was through conventional analyses of its concepts and doctrines. That pedagogical approach was justifiable for two reasons—law schools prepare their students to practice law, and in the 1960s and 1970s, the social sciences were just starting to make the gains that have since taken them

---

1 Stephen Jay Gould, The Flamingo's Smile: Reflections in Natural History 138 (1985).

2 Richard Susskind, Tomorrow's Lawyers: An Introduction to Your Future (2013).

3 *See id.* at 113 (predicting that many lawyers in the future will also be educated in other disciplines). Professor Susskind also expects that numerous lawyers will be engaged in assessing, and hence anticipating, risks that law poses for clients. *Id.* at 117–18. The anticipation of law-related client problems will necessarily include the prediction of changes in law. Such changes will be accurately predicted more often and farther in advance to the extent that well-designed studies have been conducted on the jurisdiction conditions that shape the content of law. Research to date indicates that the macro-level factors responsible for changes in law usually evolve slowly rather than change abruptly, permitting data on trends in the factors to be used to forecast the changes.

so far. Fortunately, before entering the domain of law, I had spent a decade involved in sociology and demography, an involvement that allowed me to become familiar with premises and research resources quite different from those in the world of law. As I sought to understand the origin of society-salient law and the not-infrequent shifts that this law undergoes, familiarity with sociology and demography proved of immense value. Such an understanding, I eventually concluded, was not possible with the assumptions about law that prevailed in law schools. My thinking thus shifted toward the paradigm of the social sciences and away from the paradigm of law schools.

Journals published by law schools are generally the principal home for mainstream analyses of law in the United States. Notably, articles in the journals, when attempting to account for the substance of and change in law, tend to assume, explicitly or implicitly, that law is a self-contained institution. This assumption, of course, is not universally accepted by scholars[4] and is rejected by the framework for law that I propose. In particular, the assumption conflicts with writings in the sociology of law, while a corollary assumption—that law is the master, rather than the servant, of the society in which it exists—is rendered of dubious accuracy by the findings of the quantitative social science research that I discuss in Part 1 of *infra* Chapter 1. For me, therefore, sociology and demography have provided tools that allowed a critical assessment of common beliefs found in U.S. law schools, and they are responsible for the present book.[5] Hopefully, the book will encourage academic lawyers and social scientists to focus on the societal substructure of law and to do so with quantitative data and studies.

The framework for law around which *Explaining Law* has been organized is concerned with concepts and doctrines that appear in documents such as statutes, government-agency rules and rulings, and court opinions. These concepts and doctrines are the stuff of law in the United States—they are what law school professors teach and write about, and what law school students read and learn. While I appreciate that the foregoing focus is essential for the practice of law, I believe that it misses an important aspect of law, namely, the roots

---

4 *E.g.*, Roger Cotterrell, *Subverting Orthodoxy, Making Law Central: A View of Sociolegal Studies*, 29 J. L. & Soc'y 632, 640, 643 (2002) (proposing that law be considered "normative ideas embedded in social practices" and "an expression and support of community").

5 U.S. law schools harbor reservations about sociology, a situation for which sociologists must bear some responsibility. *Infra* Chapter 6, at notes 28–30 and accompanying text. However, the reservations that exist about sociology do not exist about demography. The principal bar to the use of demography in law school scholarship appears to be the highly quantitative nature of demographic work. Members of the professional staff of law schools are generally unable or unwilling to utilize large amounts of numerical data.

in society that give rise to the content of law. The framework I advocate will hopefully help to overcome this failure. Its propositions are enumerated in Part 1-b of *infra* Chapter 1 and are the basis of the studies reported in Chapters 2 through 5. By focusing on macro-level factors that mold what law says, the studies add to a line of research that is central to uncovering the societal origins of law.[6]

Explaining Law, like each of my two earlier books on the sociology of law,[7] has historical roots in macrosociological theory. Specifically, the three books can be traced to the theory that sociologists label functionalism (also known as structural functionalism),[8] although at least one of the propositions of my framework departs from traditional applications of this theory to law.[9] The latter conflict may exist partially because current quantitative data and statistical techniques did not become available until long after the theory of functionalism developed, but even recent sociological theory on the institution of law seems to make minimal use of quantitative social science data and research. As a consequence, current thinking about law includes the assumption that the proscriptions and prescriptions of law in a modern nation have a permanent, substantial impact on the incidence of social activities that are important in a modern society. Based on a review and analysis of quantitative social science studies, I believe that the assumption is wrong and that law seldom if ever has an enduring, large effect on the society-important social activities it addresses.[10] I may be mistaken, of course, and I acknowledge that my position is subject to challenge. However, the challenge will almost certainly need to extend to the faith that social (and other) scientists have placed in tests of statistical significance and in the maximum but arbitrary criteria of these tests (the 0.10 and 0.05 significance levels) that are applied when deciding whether to reject the null hypothesis, i.e., the hypothesis that an independent variable such as law is unrelated to a dependent variable such as activity incidence. Because the tests are pervasive in quantitative research today, any challenge to their use faces formidable obstacles. The tests are convenient—they are built into current data-analysis software, offer investigators an easy criterion for reaching conclusions, and reduce subjectivity. In addition, the tests benefit

---

6 Known studies in the line are listed in Appendix A to *infra* Chapter 1.

7 Larry D. Barnett, The Place of Law: The Role and Limits of Law in Society (2011) [hereinafter The Place of Law]; Larry D. Barnett, Legal Construct, Social Concept: A Macrosociological Perspective on Law (1993).

8 The Place of Law, *supra* note 7, at 21–23, 302–07.

9 See notes 12 & 143 in *infra* Chapter 1.

10 In Part 1-b of *infra* Chapter 1, see proposition #6 and the text and notes that elaborate on it.

from a lack of competition; simply put, there is as yet no generally appealing alternative to them.

Tests of statistical significance thus will be difficult to dislodge from social science studies, but if the belief that the tests are legitimate tools is not justified for many if not most of the studies—a belief that is certainly within the realm of possibility—much of what we have concluded from scientific research, including research on the impact of law, may be wrong. However, while the role of tests of statistical significance in analyzing quantitative data raises a question that must be addressed, few social scientists have done so[11] despite warnings that the tests have the potential to hamper the advance of knowledge[12] and misguide public policy.[13] "Orthodoxy," we should remember, "can be as stubborn in science as in religion."[14]

Setting aside questions about research procedure, what if, as I contend, the impact of law on core social behaviors in a modern society is negligible? My position is not unreasonable in light of available evidence, yet because the position is in conflict with conventional wisdom, it has profound implications for popular beliefs about the contributions that law makes to a modern nation. To be exact, the position, if correct, will force us to overhaul our assumptions about law, and when we do so, we will be compelled to acknowledge the following:

1. Law is generally not an effective cure for social problems that concern a modern society; solutions to these problems must be found outside of law.
2. The reasons that law is evidently a universal and persistent feature of modern nations have yet to be empirically demonstrated. Law exists in these nations presumably because it aids their operation, but law seems to do so in ways other than through the control of society-significant behaviors.
3. The popular and often-referenced concept of "the rule of law" requires a careful reassessment. The concept, by using the word "rule," implies that

11 Ruma Falk & Charles W. Greenbaum, *Significance Tests Die Hard: The Amazing Persistence of a Probabilistic Misconception*, 5 THEORY & PSYCHOL. 75, 75 (1995).

12 R. Murray Lindsay, *Reconsidering the Status of Tests of Significance: An Alternative Criterion of Adequacy*, 20 ACCT. ORGANIZATIONS & SOC'Y 35 (1995); Frank L. Schmidt, *What Do Data Really Mean? Research Findings, Meta-Analysis, and Cumulative Knowledge in Psychology*, 47 AM. PSYCHOLOGIST 1173, 1175–76 (1992).

13 Ezra Hauer, *The Harm Done by Tests of Significance*, 36 ACCIDENT ANALYSIS & PREVENTION 495 (2004).

14 STEPHEN JAY GOULD, THE PANDA'S THUMB: MORE REFLECTIONS IN NATURAL HISTORY 243 (1980).

law has a material, lasting effect on the incidence of the social behaviors it targets, but if law has no such effect, the concept must be reformulated or abandoned.[15]

4. Empirical research on the causes of law will yield a larger number of practical benefits than empirical research on the effects of law. If law on socially central activities has no more than a minimal and/or temporary influence on the incidence of the activities, the content of law and patterns of social behavior in a modern society are generally in harmony with each other because the patterns and the macro-level factors that produce them determine the law, not because the law determines the patterns. Research on the consequences of law for the incidence of social activities accordingly shifts attention to, and increases the importance of, research on the macro-level sources of concepts and doctrines of law.

What benefits could be derived from studying the societal conditions and macro-level forces that shape law? Let me mention one—a reduction in social conflict. Research on the societal origins of the content of law is based on the premise that new law on socially important activities in a structurally complex, democratically governed nation arises from fundamental shifts in the fabric of society. If the premise is correct, this law cannot be permanently blocked or reversed through the political process even though the law upends tradition, and attempts to thwart such law or restore tradition-endorsed law will prove futile in the long run. For example, there has been opposition in the United States to court rulings that eliminate or curtail government-imposed restrictions on access to abortion. The most prominent of these rulings, of course, is the 1973 decision of the U.S. Supreme Court in the case of Roe v. Wade.[16] In concluding that a constitutional right to privacy bars government from severely limiting the circumstances in which the pregnancies of adult women can be terminated prior to fetus viability, the Court in *Roe* provoked an intense reaction that has included acts of violence.[17] Extreme reactions to new law can be expected to decrease, however, with advances in research on the macro-level conditions that drive law: As the premise that is the foundation of this research garners empirical support, it will come to be generally acknowledged, and new law on socially significant activities will be understood to result from changes in the character of social life that neither political action nor conflict can alter.

---

15 I elaborate on points #2 and #3 in THE PLACE OF LAW, *supra* note 7, at 198–204.

16 410 U.S. 113 (1973).

17 THE PLACE OF LAW, *supra* note 7, at 250 n.188.

In wrapping up, I want to thank those who were of help as I wrote *Explaining Law*. A book is neither a simple undertaking nor the outcome of efforts by just its author. Not surprisingly, preparation of a book depends heavily on the resources of a library—in my case, the library of the Widener University School of Law in Delaware. The director of the library, Michael Slinger, was ever-conscientious and always accommodating. His professionalism and dedication are mirrored in the library staff, which promptly dealt with my numerous requests for materials. Three members of the staff merit mention—Maggie Adams, Enza Klotzbucher, and Janet Lindenmuth. Their efforts were complemented by the diligence of my secretary, Debbie Dantinne. In addition, the School of Law supported my scholarship with teaching packages that allowed me to work on the manuscript during semesters. Obviously, none of the foregoing is responsible in any way for mistakes in the book.

I end my list of persons who warrant acknowledgment by drawing on ancient Greece, where the poet Simonides of Ceos observed that of all of the assets a man might have for his journey on earth, "the best is a good wife."[18] Although these words were penned more than two thousand years ago, I have personally found them to be true today. As I drafted this preface, my wife Linda and I marked our fiftieth wedding anniversary, and *Explaining Law* could not have been written without her.

Wilmington, Delaware
December 2013

18 See Wikiquote, Wives, http://en.wikiquote.org/wiki/Wives.

List of Figures and Tables

Figures

Tables

PART 1

Macrosociology and Law

CHAPTER 1

A Macrosociological Approach to Concepts and Doctrines of Law

Abstract

Chapter 1 enumerates the key theoretical propositions of the macrosociological framework for concepts and doctrines of law that underlies the book. According to the framework, societal change in a structurally complex, democratically governed social system gradually produces the conditions that result in new doctrines of law designed to regulate society-important activities, but the doctrines do not appreciably alter the incidence of the activities. The framework suggests the hypothesis that the incidence of a society-important activity materially increases or decreases *before* a doctrine of law develops or is revised for the activity. The hypothesis is tested with data on crime and discrimination in the United States; on each of these subjects, a shift occurred in a doctrine of law during the last half of the twentieth century and time-series data on activity occurrence are available. The concept of social productivity, which views law as a mechanism to preserve and increase societal cohesion, is advanced to account for the link that was found between trends in the incidence of activities and substantive change in law on the activities.

1 Social Science and Law

Major advances in science can happen in a variety of ways—for example, they may occur in a continuous, incremental fashion, or they may be sudden, convulsive events[1]—but regardless of the manner in which they come about, the advances constitute responses to accumulations of knowledge. In terms of understanding the institution known as law, the strides that have been made by the social sciences during the last several decades are likely to produce two important advances in the foreseeable future—(i) the adoption of substantially different procedures for studying the many aspects of the institution, and (ii) the replacement of widely held assumptions about the institution. Together, these advances can be expected to produce fundamental alterations in

1 Xiang Chen et al., *Kuhn's Theory of Scientific Revolutions and Cognitive Psychology*, 11 PHIL. PSYCHOL. 5, 6, 23 (1998).

 | DOI 10.1163/9789004281219_002

approaches to law-related matters and in perceptions of law. Indeed, the magnitude of these alterations may come close to or reach that of another consequential change in the history of law in the United States—namely, the transformation of law schools during the late nineteenth century caused by the introduction of the case method for classroom instruction.[2]

a *The Study of Law*

Change (i) as well as change (ii) will be momentous, but both cannot be expected to take place at the same speed or during the same time period. Substantively, the changes are related in that their source is the social sciences, but they will probably unfold quite differently. Change (i) is likely to encounter relatively little overt resistance and occur smoothly, albeit gradually, over the next one to three decades. Change (ii), on the other hand, is likely to meet active opposition, and to the extent it does, the substitution of assumptions about law will be contentious if not disruptive. Furthermore, change (i)—the acceptance of different research procedures—has already commenced. In the United States and elsewhere, there is increased interest in examining law-related topics with empirical methods.[3] This shift will not abate, let alone cease, because it is being driven by, inter alia, extraordinary improvements in the social sciences, especially their data sets and the statistical techniques they have for data analyses.[4]

---

2 David D. Garner, Comment, *The Continuing Vitality of the Case Method in the Twenty-First Century*, 2000 BYU EDUC. & L.J. 307, 316–18.

3 *E.g.*, Shari Seidman Diamond & Pam Mueller, *Empirical Legal Scholarship in Law Reviews*, 6 ANN. REV. LAW & SOC. SCI. 581, 590–92 (2010); Theodore Eisenberg, *The Origins, Nature, and Promise of Empirical Legal Studies and a Response to Concerns*, 2011 U. ILL. L. REV. 1713, 1713–14, 1737; Gregory Shaffer & Tom Ginsburg, *The Empirical Turn in International Legal Scholarship*, 106 AM. J. INT'L L. 1, 7–8 (2012).

Even though law schools in the United States are starting to recognize the benefits of social science procedures for acquiring and analyzing data, they are doing so only after many years of being told that these procedures are relevant and important. For example, during the first half of the 1980s, U.S. law schools were explicitly warned against neglecting social science research methods; the warning appeared in an article published in the journal of the Association of American Law Schools. Derek C. Bok, *A Flawed System of Law Practice and Training*, 33 J. LEGAL EDUC. 570, 582 (1983) ("[w]e ignore the social sciences at our peril, for their techniques grow steadily more refined").

4 Shaffer & Ginsburg, *supra* note 3, at 8–9. Unfortunately, much of the empirical research that is presently being done in U.S. law schools is characterized by serious methodological problems. Lee Epstein & Gary King, *Empirical Research and the Goals of Legal Scholarship: The Rules of Inference*, 69 U. CHI. L. REV. 1, 6–7 (2002). The quality of this empirical research will continue to be hindered until law schools overcome their past neglect of the social sciences.

Compared to change (i), the substitution of new for existing assumptions about law—change (ii)—will almost certainly be protracted, and will probably not be completed until the last half of the twenty-first century. Change (i) will occur at a relatively rapid clip because it mainly involves the acquisition of new skills, but change (ii) will be slow because it compels a shift in key beliefs about a salient aspect of society, a type of shift that encounters resistance for psychological as well as social reasons.[5] The benefits to be provided by a skill are concrete and can motivate individuals to learn the skill, but the benefits of replacing a current worldview (or a major portion of it) may be uncertain. Moreover, individuals have a large personal investment in their present worldview, and may experience social disapproval for abandoning it.

Change (ii), in short, will not be hurried; indeed, it has yet to start. Nonetheless, the substitution of assumptions about the institution of law seems inescapable. The substitution will result from two lines of quantitative social science research. In combination, these lines—the first well-developed and the second presently developing—mount a broad challenge to the currently dominant view regarding the place of law in society. Scholars based in U.S. law schools have to date resisted the findings of the two lines of research, but they cannot indefinitely continue to do so, and the view of the societal role of law that is accepted today will in time be replaced. Even conventional beliefs eventually succumb when contradicted by a body of credible evidence. Until mistaken beliefs substantially diminish in prevalence, however, they can seriously hinder progress in understanding the phenomena to which they apply.[6]

What are these two lines of research? Before each is discussed, several characteristics that are common to the two lines should be noted. In particular, both lines have focused on doctrines of law that seek to regulate, i.e., on law that mandates or prohibits certain types of conduct. Furthermore, most of the studies in both lines dealt with law that sought to regulate social activities that are deeply embedded in society, e.g., abortion, crime, and divorce. In addition, both lines of research have focused mainly on nations that are structurally

5 Elliot Aronson, *Back to the Future: Retrospective Review of Leon Festinger's—A Theory of Cognitive Dissonance*, 110 AM J. PSYCHOL. 127, 134 (1997) (book review). *See* Łukasz Afeltowicz, *The Cognitive Closure of Science*, 2012 POLISH SOCIOL. REV. 497.

6 This problem is likely to exist in all intellectual disciplines, including the humanities. It certainly exists, and has long existed, in disciplines that make use of the methods and data of science. Fully a century ago, Albert Einstein observed that, because their "worldly origin" is overlooked, established ideas can "make the road of scientific progress often impassable for long times." Albert Einstein, *Ernst Mach*, 17 PHYSIKALISCHE ZEITSCHRIFT 101, 102 (1916), *reprinted in* 6 THE COLLECTED PAPERS OF ALBERT EINSTEIN: THE BERLIN YEARS: WRITINGS, 1914–1917, at 141, 142 (Alfred Engel trans., 1997).

complex and democratically governed. The discussion that follows, therefore, is drawn from studies of regulatory law that primarily targeted society-important forms of social behavior in modern nations.

Keeping in mind what is common to the two lines of research, let us turn to what differentiates them, namely, their subject matter. The first line consists of quantitative studies that are concerned with the societal *impact* of regulatory law. To be exact, the studies in the first line attempt to answer the following question: To what extent did a doctrine of law that was designed to regulate an activity achieve the goal that was set for it and do so without unwanted consequences? As will be pointed out later in Part 1-b, a body of well-designed quantitative research has found that doctrines of law in a socially complex democracy have no more than small and/or temporary effects on the society-central activities they are adopted to regulate.[7] Of equal importance, this line of research has occasionally unearthed "side effects" to law that is intended to regulate. Doctrines of law can thus have consequences that are unanticipated, unwelcome, and/or socially harmful[8] while having little impact on the activities for which the doctrines were crafted.

The second line of research is formed by quantitative studies of the societal *causes* of regulatory law, i.e., of the influence that the sociological, economic, and demographic characteristics of jurisdictions (nations and states) have on the concepts and doctrines of law in the jurisdictions. Because it began much later, the second line contains appreciably fewer studies than the first line; by my count, the second line of research currently includes approximately thirty studies (listed in Appendix A to the present chapter). Perhaps not surprisingly, the principal methodological and statistical issues in the second line differ from those in the first line[9] even though both lines have focused mainly on modern societies. Each line of research, consequently, is a separate area of specialization.

---

7 Text accompanying *infra* note 26; *infra* note 27 and accompanying text.

8 *E.g.*, Jerry Anthony, *State Growth Management and Housing Prices*, 87 Soc. Sci. Q. 122 (2006); Thomas B. Marvell & Carlisle E. Moody, *The Lethal Effects of Three-Strikes Laws*, 30 J. Legal Stud. 89 (2001). A study that illustrates this point in a non-Western nation is by Hongbin Li et al., *Estimating the Effect of the One-Child Policy on the Sex Ratio Imbalance in China: Identification Based on the Difference-in-Differences*, 48 Demography 1535 (2011).

9 *Compare* Chester L. Britt et al., *A Reassessment of the D.C. Gun Law: Some Cautionary Notes on the Use of Interrupted Time Series Designs for Policy Impact Assessment*, 30 Law & Soc'y Rev. 361 (1996) (discussing key methodological issues in the first line of research) *with* Larry D. Barnett, The Place of Law: The Role and Limits of Law in Society 458–69 (2011) (discussing important methodological issues in the second line of research) [hereinafter The Place of Law].

b A Macrosociological Framework for Law

Because the second line of research is largely unknown, it merits amplification. The cornerstone of this line of research is the assumption that concepts and doctrines of regulatory law for important social activities in a jurisdiction do not arise fortuitously but, instead, have their origin in macro-level characteristics of the jurisdiction. The assumption, in turn, underlies a set of propositions that provide a macrosociological framework for understanding concepts and doctrines of law in a society that is structurally complex and democratically governed. Theory in the sociology of law has been criticized for failing to make clear society–law connections and to delineate quantitatively testable propositions regarding these connections.[10] While the proposed framework will not by itself rectify either problem, it can guide empirical studies. In doing so, the framework will, I hope, aid in building useful theory on the ties that exist between a society and its law. In addition, the framework will ideally encourage an explicit focus on law in general sociological theory, which has not often considered law even though it guided the development of the framework.[11] I must stress, however, that the framework does not encompass all activities in a modern society and the law on them. Instead, the framework is concerned only with *social* activities—i.e., behavior by individuals that involves interaction with other individuals—that are significant to the society. As a result, the framework I propose for law does not apply to, inter alia, (i) requirements imposed by law on the physical equipment and processes that are used in producing economic outputs (goods and services), (ii) law-specified restrictions on the components of and ingredients in these outputs, and (iii) law-mandated mechanisms such as tax rates and deadlines that allow government to operate.

Before laying out the propositions of my framework, some observations are in order regarding the nature of the social activities to which the framework applies. I label these activities "significant," "important," or "central" to a society, or at the "core" of a society. The foregoing words are intended to be synonyms, and they thus have a single, common referent, namely, patterns of human interaction through which a society maintains its present overall state and/or direction. Significance, of course, is a matter of degree and hence can vary, but across societies of a given type, this degree is assumed to be roughly the same for a particular pattern. Within societies, however, the significance of a social pattern can change over time. Indeed, a change in the degree to which

---

10 William M. Evan, Social Structure and Law: Theoretical and Empirical Perspectives 231 (1990).

11 The Place of Law, *supra* note 9, at 19–21; *infra* note 143 & text accompanying note 144.

a pattern is significant may mark a shift in historical eras in a society. After a new era begins, some behavioral patterns that had previously been significant may no longer be so, while other behavioral patterns may have moved in the opposite direction, i.e., from insignificance to significance.

In science, theory seeks to capture causes and effects, and in pursuing this objective, it unavoidably uses abstract concepts so that multifaceted, complicated phenomena, and the relationships between the phenomena, are described in a relatively simple fashion. For researchers, however, the abstractness of theory-pertinent concepts can create difficulties. If a theory or a theory-grounded framework is to be tested, one or more empirical (especially quantitative) measures of each of the variables captured by its concepts must be developed, but the operationalization of a variable may not be simple or quick because credible measures of the variable may be few and elusive. When such a situation is encountered, a painstaking effort will be necessary to devise a suitable yardstick for the variable. Thus, an acceptable empirical measure of the significance to society of social activity may not be found or formulated without a search of multiple sources. Measures of the variable may exist in, for example, responses to questions asked in sample surveys, expressions of social views in documents such as legislative histories and court opinions, and agency-compiled data on the prevalence of certain behaviors. The search will be made harder if it uncovers potential measures that yield, or seem to yield, inconsistent conclusions as to the societal centrality of an activity. When this happens, of course, researchers will be forced to reconcile the measures or choose between them. Even after a measure is in place, moreover, the concept of the societal significance of activities cannot be used until a final matter is resolved. Specifically, a criterion for classifying an activity as significant or not significant will have to be adopted. At what threshold does an activity become significant? The question may not be easily answered.

Let me now turn to the propositions of my framework. The initial proposition is a specific statement of the general theme of the sociology of law—viz., that law is embedded in, and must be examined as a component of, a society. The proposition is:

> Proposition 1: Society-level conditions determine the concepts and doctrines of law that are used to regulate society-central activities in a jurisdiction having a complex structure and a democratic government.

Proposition #1 posits that large-scale societal factors such as the level of knowledge are responsible for the key social activities that are lawful in a modern nation and for those that are unlawful. Six additional propositions flow from or are corollaries of this proposition, and being complementary, the seven propositions in combination form a mutually reinforcing set. All of the propositions are believed to characterize law in socially complex, democratically governed jurisdictions, but the propositions may be inapplicable in jurisdictions that have different characteristics. Like proposition #1, therefore, the additional propositions are limited to nations that are "developed" socially and economically.

> Proposition 2: New concepts and doctrines of law on activities that are central to a society result from change in society-level properties and the macro-level forces that generate these properties.[12]

An example of proposition #2 is the liberalization of law on induced abortion in the United States. That liberalization was probably due in large part to the long-term growth of knowledge, which growth increased rationality and promoted individualism.[13]

---

12 In some respects, my framework is similar to the thesis of Eugen Ehrlich, an early theorist in the sociology of law. EUGEN EHRLICH, FUNDAMENTAL PRINCIPLES OF THE SOCIOLOGY OF LAW (Walter L. Moll trans., 1936); Neil O. Littlefield, *Eugen Ehrlich's Fundamental Principles of the Sociology of Law*, 19 MAINE L. REV. 1 (1967). Notably, Professor Ehrlich developed the first internally consistent conceptualization of the sociology of law. Klaus A. Ziegert, *On Eugen Ehrlich, Fundamental Principles of the Sociology of Law*, *in* CLASSIC WRITINGS IN LAW AND SOCIETY 123, 124 (A. Javier Treviño ed., 2d ed. rev. & expanded 2011). Propositions #1 and #2 of my framework, however, diverge from the Ehrlich thesis in fundamental ways. Specifically, Professor Ehrlich believed that in all types of societies, doctrines of law and their concepts arise from the ordering of interpersonal relationships in society and evolve in response to changes in this ordering. EHRLICH, *supra*, at 35–41, 119–20, 346, 396; Littlefield, *supra*, at 3–5, 8–11, 21–22. According to his thesis, moreover, doctrines and concepts of law are not confined to statutes, court opinions, and administrative-agency rules; they also are present in the prevailing patterns of interpersonal relationships. EHRLICH, *supra*, at 34–38; Littlefield, *supra*, at 4. My framework, on the other hand, is limited to (i) societies of just one type, viz., societies with a democratic government and a complex structure, and (ii) concepts and doctrines that are expressed in writing in statutes, court opinions, and/or agency rules, i.e., that have been formalized by government. In my framework, furthermore, the sources of the content of law include not only the structure of a society, which structure covers patterns of interpersonal relationships in the society, but also the large-scale forces that act over time to shape the structure. In the view of Professor Ehrlich, finally, some concepts and doctrines of law materially affect the incidence of social behaviors. EHRLICH, *supra*, at 41–42, 192–93, 195–97, 202–03; Littlefield, *supra*, at 17. This position is rejected by my framework, at least for society-important social behaviors. See *infra* proposition #6.

13 Part 3-b of *infra* Chapter 2 in the present book.

Proposition #2 distinguishes between the properties of a society (e.g., female–male equality in schooling and employment) and the macro-level forces (e.g., the growth of knowledge) that are responsible for these properties. The distinction is also in propositions #3 and #4, which I present together because they have an important implication for the study of law that I will discuss *infra.*

> Proposition 3: The properties of society that shape the concepts and doctrines of law typically change slowly, and the macro-level forces that determine the properties typically develop gradually.
> Proposition 4: Macro-level forces and their resulting societal properties do not immediately alter concepts and doctrines of law on activities that are at the hub of a society.

Proposition #4 stresses that the content of law on society-important activities does not as a normal matter respond instantaneously to its societal context. Why does the lag occur? One of the chief reasons is likely to be the existence of thresholds. Specifically, a macro-level force must probably have reached a certain level before it is able to produce a societal property, and a societal property must probably be present in a certain amount before it can trigger a new concept or doctrine of law.[14] Another important reason for the lag is that, if the proposed framework is correct, intervening variables operate between macro-level forces and the content of law. Given intervening variables, macro-level forces do not have a direct impact on law; rather, the forces create one or more properties of society that are the antecedents of the content of law. Moreover, the intervening variables, like the macro-level forces that precede them, are unlikely to be the same for all concepts and doctrines of law. If so, the length of the time lag between the forces and law can be expected to differ with (i) the particular forces that lie behind regulatory law on an activity, (ii) the specific intervening variables at work and their configuration,[15] and (iii) the centrality to society of the activity that law seeks to regulate.

---

14 THE PLACE OF LAW, *supra* note 9, at 263–64, 376 n. 36, 465–66.

15 Intervening variables may not operate concurrently but seriatim. For instance, the long-term expansion of knowledge is believed to alter sex roles, and the alteration of sex roles in turn can be expected to result in groups that work politically to replace existing law pertinent to sex as an attribute. *Id.* at 267–69, 307–09. In this illustration, the state of sex roles and the makeup of the political process are intervening variables. All else being equal, intervening variables that function sequentially will increase the time between change in the initial societal force (here, the growth of knowledge) and the impact of that change on the content of law. Furthermore, as this time interval lengthens, a weaker relationship between the initial societal force and the content of law is likely to be reported by statistical measures such as regression coefficients.

Proposition #4, however, should not be considered by itself. In conjunction with proposition #3, proposition #4 has a significant implication for the study as well as the practice of law. To be precise, the two propositions in combination raise the possibility that concepts and doctrines of law can be predicted. Indeed, propositions #3 and #4 together suggest that new concepts and doctrines of law on key activities in a society are predictable long before the concepts and doctrines are adopted. Although the societal factors that determine the content of law are not sufficiently understood to permit generally correct predictions to be made today, the factors are in principle capable of being identified by research. Once those factors have been pinpointed, prediction will require comprehensive, accurate time-series data on each macro-level factor. If the stock of knowledge in a society influences the content of law, for example, the long-term expansion of knowledge can be quantified (albeit imperfectly) using the annual number of patents issued for inventions.[16]

> Proposition 5: To the extent they target core societal activities, new doctrines of law—even those that are inconsistent with traditional social values—cannot be indefinitely prevented or reversed by political confrontations and conflict when the doctrines result from and are in line with societal conditions.

Illustrations of proposition #5 are likely to include law that authorizes same-sex marriage and law that relaxes the grounds for terminating an unwanted pregnancy.[17] According to the proposition, any law to which it applies will be thwarted just temporarily in a developed nation by political demonstrations and acts of violence; once adopted, moreover, such law will not be permanently suppressed either through the efforts of politically oriented groups or through politically motivated attacks on property or individuals.[18] What is the basis for proposition #5? The answer lies in the probable role of law in society—specifically, in the contribution of law to social cohesiveness. Law on society-central activities, to be exact, combats erosion in societal cohesiveness. In carrying out this function, law acts by providing symbols, by dealing with negative reputations on the part of important segments of society, and by

---

16 *Id.* at 264–67.

17 Proposition #5 applies to same-sex marriage and induced abortion if and to the extent these activities stem from change in the structure of society.

18 Proposition #5, if widely accepted, can reduce social strife. THE PLACE OF LAW, *supra* note 9, at 232.

maintaining or enhancing trust.[19] Of the foregoing three agents, symbols have received the most attention and are evidently thought by scholars to be the chief source of the social cement that law produces.[20] Reputation and trust, however, should not be discounted as additional agents of law that affect cohesiveness.

The agents that law uses to benefit society, however, do not tell us either the reason(s) that law supplies a benefit or the reason(s) that law supplies the specific benefit it does. If law assists society, in other words, we need to understand both why it does so and why the assistance happens to be in the form of social cohesion. Each question is distinct, and both questions are important. The answer to the first question—the reason(s) that law aids society—is found, I believe, in a fundamental attribute of every society. Specifically, a society is a *system* of components, i.e., of institutions.[21] As a system, a society depends on its institutions even though it is more than a mere aggregate of them, and hence in the long run each institution, including law, must make a positive contribution to the societal system. The process of doing so involves the interstices between institutions and between an institution and the society in which the institution is embedded. The interstices are not empty, and each institution is neither sealed off from others nor from the society as a whole. Law thus does not operate in isolation and does not independently determine its content; instead, law has close ties to the system, and its concepts and doctrines on society-central activities are molded by the system. Additionally, a system tends to change over

---

19 *Id.* at 51, 121–22, 127.

20 Thurman Arnold, for example, thought that law as a phenomenon, while impossible to define, "is primarily a great reservoir of emotionally important social symbols." THURMAN ARNOLD, THE SYMBOLS OF GOVERNMENT 34, 36 (1935). In his view, the law of a society produces symbols by embodying the ideals that represent "the good life" in the society. *Id.* at 44–45, 54. In particular, Arnold contended that law, through its presence in a "mystical haze…where all our dreams of justice in an unjust world come true," makes possible the existence, as well as the continuation, of government, and nurtures the status quo. *Id.* at 34–35, 44. Indeed, Arnold considered law to be the foremost societal institution promoting stability in social life. *Id.* at 35.

21 An "institution" of a society is defined in the instant book as a set of distinct and socially acknowledged positions, and the socially approved and expected behaviors attached to each position, that the society employs to carry out a broad type of societally important activity. In sociological terminology, the positions are labeled "statuses" and the behaviors are labeled "roles." Howard B. Kaplan, *The Concept of Institution: A Review, Evaluation, and Suggested Research Procedure*, 39 SOC. FORCES 176, 179 (1960).

time, and the type of societal system that is the subject of the instant book is especially prone to do so. Under proposition #2, the nature of such change affects the content of law.[22]

We are accordingly brought to the second question—why law promotes social cohesion in particular. The answer, which should not be surprising, is that a system, to exist and persist, must possess a minimum degree of internal order.[23] Sociologically, this order rests on social cohesiveness, and hence law, as a system participant and supporter, will preserve and, when necessary, build cohesiveness.[24]

---

22 As one U.S. state appellate court wrote, a "society is not static; it is fluid.... Therefore, the law, both statutory and common law, must keep pace." Ferreira v. Barham, 40 Cal. Rptr. 739, 744 (Cal. Ct. App. 1964).

23 KENNETH D. BAILEY, SOCIOLOGY AND THE NEW SYSTEMS THEORY: TOWARD A THEORETICAL SYNTHESIS 44 (1994) (defining a system as "a bounded set of interrelated components that has an entropy value below the maximum" and defining entropy as "degree of disorder").

24 Some theory treats the institution of law as a system. RICHARD NOBLES & DAVID SCHIFF, A SOCIOLOGY OF JURISPRUDENCE 211, 216 (2006) [hereinafter NOBLES & SCHIFF 2006]; RICHARD NOBLES & DAVID SCHIFF, OBSERVING LAW THROUGH SYSTEMS THEORY 1 (2013) [hereinafter NOBLES & SCHIFF 2013]. At least three noteworthy differences exist between this theory (i.e., law-as-system theory) and the framework I am proposing. First, my framework considers law to be a subsystem within a larger system, viz., within a society, and contends that the societal system eclipses its subsystems, i.e., its institutions. Law-as-system theory, while recognizing interplay between the institution of law and other institutions, does not give precedence either to the societal system over an institution or to one institution over another. NOBLES & SCHIFF 2006, *supra*, at 9–10, 19, 45–47, 101, 112, 213–14; NOBLES & SCHIFF 2013, *supra*, at 16–17, 22–23. The second difference is that my framework explicitly directs attention to the macro-level forces that broadly alter a society and, in turn, change the content of its law. *Supra* propositions #2, #3, and #4 and their accompanying text. Law-as-system theory does not look at, or at least does not emphasize, these forces. *See, e.g.*, NOBLES & SCHIFF 2006, *supra*, at 215 n. 8 (suggesting that social stratification may affect the institution of law but not mentioning large-scale forces that may modify the manner in which a society is stratified); NOBLES & SCHIFF 2013, *supra*, at 120 (attributing the emergence of modern society and the institution of law to the differentiation of societal functions, but not naming society-level forces that may have been responsible for functional differentiation).

The third difference entails a set of points that surround the question of the societal role of the institution of law. According to my framework, law is a mechanism that supports and increases societal cohesiveness, while according to law-as-system theory, law acts in a society as a mechanism for communication. In pointing to social cohesion, however, my framework is limited to societies that are structurally complex and democratically governed. See the text accompanying *supra* notes 19 & 20 and proposition #1 in the text *supra*; THE PLACE OF LAW, *supra* note 9, at 2–3. Structural complexity in my

The institution of law, in short, cannot avoid being socially productive.[25]

The preceding five propositions are extended by two others. Both of the latter propositions, though based on findings from the first line of research, are consistent with the premise of the second line. Both supplement the initial five propositions. The seven propositions are thus a set, and in combination they underscore the critical point that doctrines of law on society-central activities in a structurally complex, democratically governed social system are embedded in, and cannot be separated from, that system.

> Proposition 6: A doctrine of law that prescribes or proscribes a key social activity does not have an appreciable, permanent effect on the incidence (frequency or rate) of the activity.[26]

---

framework, moreover, encompasses social, demographic, and economic divisions as well as specialization of operations (functions). On the other hand, law-as-system theory, in focusing on social structure, is concerned with only specialization of operations. To be exact, law-as-system theory believes that a modern society is characterized by institutions that are distinguished by what each communicates, and it considers law to be one of the institutions of a society that has subdivided the content of its communications. NOBLES & SCHIFF 2013, *supra*, at 9–10, 92, 120–22. In terms of whether law alters behavior, my framework maintains that prescriptions and proscriptions of law addressing societally important social activities in a modern society have effects on the incidence of the activities that are at most small in magnitude or, if large, short in duration. Proposition #6 in the text *infra*. Law-as-system theory takes a not-dissimilar position, although it suggests that, while no institution is able to control occurrences in a modern society, "the rule of law" facilitates the development of democracy in the governance of such a society, even one with a monarch or dictator. NOBLES & SCHIFF 2013, *supra*, at 183, 207–09, 214. Law-as-system theory is thus both narrower and broader than my framework. It is narrower in focusing on just one type of partitioning in a society (viz., partitioning by functions), and broader in evidently being intended to cover a larger range of societies (viz., societies that are not, as well as societies that are, democratically governed).

25 The concept of social productivity is developed in THE PLACE OF LAW, *supra* note 9, at ch. 2.

26 Proposition #6, however, is not applicable to a situation in which a doctrine of law neither endorses a certain type of activity nor labels it unlawful (and hence punishable by government). As to such an activity, law is simply silent. After a doctrine of law is adopted that furnishes the activity with a legal form, the activity may be frequent. An example of such an activity and form is found, respectively, in marital breakdown and divorce. The number of divorces granted in a jurisdiction will be zero before the jurisdiction has legislation that allows divorce, and the number may be large afterward. However, if law is a macrosociological phenomenon, the incidence of marital breakdown will not be markedly and permanently affected by whether law authorizes divorce. A doctrine of law that does not acknowledge and give a legal status to a certain type of activity—here, withdrawal by spouses from their marriage relationship—will not appreciably reduce the

Proposition #6, of course, contradicts common beliefs about law, but it is based on a substantial body of credible empirical evidence.[27] For some types of activity (e.g., marital breakdown and divorce), a doctrine of law may have no effect on activity incidence because the doctrine is adopted or reformulated after the incidence of the activity it is designed to regulate has substantially changed in the direction that is accepted or favored by the doctrine.[28] For other types of activity (e.g., crime), a new doctrine of law follows change in activity incidence in order to reassure the public that relevant social values remain important. For both types of activity, doctrines of law do not alter materially activity incidence because the activities, even when harmful to social life, stem from macro-level conditions that operate apart from the institution of law. In a macrosociological framework, law accommodates and embodies shifts in the needs and values of society, but it does not anticipate or shape them.

The last proposition to be enumerated in this chapter follows logically from the conjunction of propositions #1, #2, and #6:

> Proposition 7: Individuals, including individuals who are prominent political figures, have no long-term, substantial impact either on the content of law concerned with society-central activities or on the incidence of the activities.

As a set, the foregoing seven propositions are key elements of a macrosociological framework for law in a society that is complex structurally and governed democratically. Although they pose a direct challenge to the paradigm that today dominates the study of law, the propositions merit consideration

---

long-term incidence of the activity when the activity results from societal conditions in a structurally complex, democratically governed jurisdiction. However, when a government in a modern society withholds the imprimatur of its law from such an activity, alternative social arrangements and practices (e.g., cohabitation of individuals who are not married to each other) can be expected to emerge. In a society that requires but lacks a certain legal doctrine, these alternatives can distort social life.

27 The sources of the evidence are listed in Appendix B to the present chapter. My framework is distinguished from other sociological approaches to law by, inter alia, proposition #6. See *supra* notes 12 & 24 and *infra* note 143.

28 An early study of whether state statutes authorizing no-fault divorce affected marital-dissolution rates suggests the thesis that law does not materially alter the incidence of a society-central activity because the law on the activity develops or changes in response to a trend that has already taken hold in the occurrence of the activity. Gerald C. Wright, Jr. & Dorothy M. Stetson, *The Impact of No-Fault Divorce Law Reform on Divorce in American States*, 40 J. MARRIAGE & FAM. 575, 577, 580 (1978).

because they are supported by a body of credible evidence. The currently accepted paradigm—which includes the popular concept of "the rule of law"[29]—contends inter alia that (i) the doctrines of law used by a society largely control the behaviors that occur in the society and (ii) the content of the doctrines[30] depends on the particular individuals who hold key positions in government bodies (i.e., legislatures, courts, and administrative agencies) and/or in organizations that are involved in politics. When used to explain the history of a society, the paradigm suggests that behavioral patterns change when individuals in influential government positions are replaced[31] by other individuals who have different preferences as to these patterns and who rewrite or reinterpret the law applicable to the patterns.[32]

The instant chapter, however, contends that concepts and doctrines of law are, and must be understood as, creations of the society in which they are found. If this contention is correct, law does not determine behavior in a society that has a complex structure and democratic government even though law is a salient feature of that society. Law in such a society, rather, is a component of a system, and the concepts and doctrines of law bearing on society-central activities are molded by the needs and values of the system. In a macrosociological framework, therefore, law is regarded as an institution within a society, i.e., a pattern of interpersonal activity that is deemed important by the society and that contributes to the operation of the society.[33] As an aspect of this institution, concepts and doctrines of law contribute to maintaining social order not by shaping behavior, as is commonly assumed, but by supplying symbols, protecting (or restoring) the reputation of salient entities, and preserving (or strengthening) the twin dimensions of trust and perceived fairness.[34] If law is a macrosociological phenomenon, in short, law serves rather than reigns, at least insofar as it is pertinent to the core activities of a modern society.

But does the above macrosociological framework correctly portray law? The question cannot be answered definitively at the moment. While the framework is promising, it is in need of further empirical testing, and like any general

29 The Place of Law, *supra* note 9, at 198–204.

30 The content of a doctrine may be found in the wording of a statute, constitution, and/or agency rule. It can also be in an authorized interpretation of the foregoing by, inter alia, a court.

31 The replacement may occur directly or indirectly through elections, or it may occur through retirements, deaths, and resignations.

32 The presently dominant paradigm is an ideal construct, and not all of its elements may be accepted by every proponent.

33 The Place of Law, *supra* note 9, at 43–44, 152, 200, 394.

34 *Id.* at 203–04.

approach, it must be tested piecemeal. Thus, the instant chapter deals with just a single hypothesis suggested by several of the propositions in the framework, namely, propositions #2, #3, #4, and #6. According to these propositions, macro-level forces over time lead to change in the social structure of complex, democratically governed societies; the change in social structure results in the conditions that eventually are responsible for the adoption of new doctrines of law designed to regulate society-important activities; but the doctrines do not materially and permanently alter the incidence, i.e., frequency and/or rate, of the activities. The propositions, if accurate, imply that (i) the incidence of a society-important activity increases or decreases *before* a doctrine of law develops or is revised for the activity; and that (ii) the post-law trend in the incidence of the activity continues the pre-law trend (with perhaps a temporary law-produced deviation) as long as the societal conditions responsible for the pre-law trend persist into the post-law period. Under this line of reasoning, new law targeting a society-important activity can be expected to emerge after the incidence of the activity has appreciably risen or fallen. The foregoing hypothesis thus derives from a theoretical framework that views shifts in regulatory law as part of the broad changes in society-level properties that occur during the course of history in a modern nation.

The hypothesis is not without some empirical support. In particular, the adoption of statutes permitting no-fault divorce in the United States was preceded by substantial growth in the likelihood of divorce.[35] However, additional evidence is necessary to evaluate the hypothesis. Part 2 *infra* is devoted to that evidence.

c A Note of Caution

To assess the hypothesis as applied to a particular activity, data are required on the incidence (i.e., numerical frequency and/or rate) of the activity at each time point comprising a specifiable historical era.[36] With data on incidence, change over time in activity occurrence can be quantitatively captured by (i) the *absolute differences* in incidence between contiguous time points and/or (ii) the *percent differences* in incidence between contiguous time points. Dimension (i), of course, is the amount of movement in activity incidence, while dimension (ii) is the pace, i.e., the speed, of movement in activity incidence. Unfortunately, macrosociological theory on law supplies no guidelines on which dimension is necessary to assess the hypothesis, or whether both dimensions are essential. The choice thus unavoidably depends on the personal judgment of the investigator.

---

35 *Id.* at 10–14.

36 *Id.* at 464, 468.

A point that should not be overlooked in this regard is that dimensions (i) and (ii) may yield different conclusions regarding the change that has taken place in the occurrence of an activity. To illustrate, assume that change from one time point to the next involves increments of the same size. In such a situation, change will be constant in absolute terms but will decline over time in proportional terms—i.e., will be the same in amount but will become progressively less in pace. The illustration underscores the importance of building a macrosociological theory that guides the choice between dimension (i) and dimension (ii).

In short, the data analyses in Part 2 are exploratory, and the conclusions drawn from them cannot be treated as definitive. The conclusions are made even more tentative by aspects of the research design. One of these aspects is that the evidence in Part 2 is based on just a small number of activities that were targeted by law, and the law that was chosen is drawn from a single historical period in just one nation, namely, the United States. Even if the conclusions suggested by the evidence are correct for all society-central activities in this period and nation, they may be incorrect in another era in that nation. Similarly, the conclusions may be wrong when applied to activities—whether the same as or different than those studied in Part 2—that take place in a nation having a markedly dissimilar social structure and/or culture. The hypothesis tested in Part 2 assumes that everything else is equal, and until a large volume of credible research is available, readers should be wary of assuming that all changes in law take only one path. Even a macro-level force whose impact is spread over concepts and doctrines of law on numerous activities may not produce its impact in a single way and in every societal context.

2 Law-Targeted Activities

Part 2 will examine a number of activities in the United States that attracted considerable public attention during the last half of the twentieth century. The activities were chosen because each met all of the following three criteria: (i) state and/or federal law applicable to the activity underwent a notable, identifiable change at some point in the period; (ii) the change in law was intended and/or expected to affect the incidence (frequency and/or rate) of the activity; and (iii) quantitative data on the incidence of the activity were available from a credible source for a time interval that began appreciably before and ended appreciably after the law changed. These criteria, of course, are essential for testing the hypothesis that new law on a society-central activity is preceded by change in the incidence of the activity. However, criterion (iii) severely limited the activities that could be examined in Part 2, because accurate data on the incidence of many society-significant activities (e.g., unlawfully performed abortions) are not available for all or most time points in a long period. Criterion (iii), in short, necessitated the use of a non-probability sample of activities.[37] Since the activities covered in Part 2 were not selected randomly from the universe of all society-central activities on which there was a major shift in applicable regulatory law, the conclusions reached about the activities that were studied cannot, with a known degree of confidence, be generalized to other activities.

a *Crime*

A society must believe that a particular type of behavior damages social life before its law will designate the behavior as criminal. Given this necessary condition for law on crime, a person believed to have committed a crime is punished by government pursuant to authorizing law.[38] A chief goal of government in punishing crime, of course, is to deter criminal behavior by the perpetrator and others,[39] but some sociological theory contends that, in a viable society, crime is built into the character of social life and therefore cannot be

37 RONALD CZAJA & JOHNNY BLAIR, DESIGNING SURVEYS: A GUIDE TO DECISIONS AND PROCEDURES 127–28 (2d ed. 2005). The type of sample employed in Part 2 can be labeled a "purposive" sample. *Id.* at 127.

38 Government is solely responsible for imposing punishment for criminal conduct because at least two conditions are necessary for social order. The first condition is widespread perceptions in a jurisdiction that social justice exists. Government is more likely than private parties to promote and maintain the belief that participants in a society are treated fairly inasmuch as government constitutes a single source of punishment for crime in a jurisdiction and hence is capable of applying the same or an equivalent penalty across multiple instances of a particular form of criminal behavior. If penalties for criminal conduct were meted out by victims and/or their allies (i.e., by private parties), inconsistencies in the penalties, and hence perceptions of injustice, would be common. The second necessary condition for social order that accounts for government monopolization of punishment is the prevention of retaliation by victims and/or their allies against those thought to have perpetrated the crimes. The prevention of such retaliation avoids feuds that can be long-lasting and/or violent. LARRY D. BARNETT, LEGAL CONSTRUCT, SOCIAL CONCEPT: A MACROSOCIOLOGICAL PERSPECTIVE ON LAW 31 (1993).

39 John M. Darley, *On the Unlikely Prospect of Reducing Crime Rates by Increasing the Severity of Prison Sentences*, 13 J.L. & POL'Y 189, 191 (2005). Congress has set deterrence as an important objective of punishment for crime in the United States. 18 U.S.C. § 3553(a)–(a)(2) (2006). The thesis of deterrence that is found in law is consistent with, and undoubtedly results from, the beliefs of Americans, most of whom think that penalties deter crime. THE PLACE OF LAW, *supra* note 9, at 126, 148 n. 208.

eliminated even though its incidence may be reduced.[40] In light of this theory, crime and the principal means employed to minimize it are deemed to be society-central activities and appropriate topics for Part 2. In particular, Part 2 considers the antecedents of law on two methods that have been used in the United States to control crime—(i) capital punishment and (ii) penalties for "three-strikes."

i Capital Punishment

The last half of the twentieth century witnessed noteworthy changes in the frequency of executions and in constitutional law on the death penalty, a societal mechanism that is employed as retribution against perpetrators of specified crimes, especially homicide, and as a deterrent to the commission of such crimes by others.[41] In 1972, the Supreme Court of the United States, applying

---

40 ÉMILE DURKHEIM, THE RULES OF SOCIOLOGICAL METHOD 66–68 (George E.G. Catlin ed., Sarah A. Solovay & John H. Mueller trans., Free Press 8th ed. 1938); KAI T. ERIKSON, WAYWARD PURITANS: A STUDY IN THE SOCIOLOGY OF DEVIANCE 12–14, 19–27 (1966). Durkheim believed that crime was "normal" and even labeled it "a factor in public health, an integral part of all healthy societies." DURKHEIM, *supra*, at 67. In his view, crime and its punishment can benefit society by, inter alia, increasing social cohesion. James Hawdon et al., *Crime as a Source of Solidarity: A Research Note Testing Durkheim's Assertion*, 31 DEVIANT BEHAV. 679, 680, 698–99 (2010). Similarly, Erikson thought that, in limited amounts, crime contributed to maintaining societal stability, because it fixed the boundaries of social life; by doing so, crime allowed non-deviant individuals and groups to identify with the society. ERIKSON, *supra*, at 13. According to both Durkheim and Erikson, crime accompanied social differentiation. ERIKSON, *supra*, at 19; Gregory C. Leavitt, *General Evolution and Durkheim's Hypothesis of Crime Frequency: A Cross-Cultural Test*, 33 SOCIOL. Q. 241, 243–44 (1992).

41 These purposes were noted by the U.S. Supreme Court in Ennund v. Florida, 458 U.S. 782, 798 (1982) (quoting from the three-justice opinion announcing the judgment of the Court in Gregg v. Georgia, 428 U.S. 153, 183 (1976)).

Capital-punishment statutes do not appreciably reduce the incidence of homicide, i.e., are of minimal importance in deterring murder. THE PLACE OF LAW, *supra* note 9, at 439 n. 66; Craig J. Albert, *Challenging Deterrence: New Insights on Capital Punishment Derived from Panel Data*, 60 U. PITT. L. REV. 321, 363, 365 (1999); Tomislav V. Kovandzic et al., *Does the Death Penalty Save Lives? New Evidence from State Panel Data, 1977 to 2006*, 8 CRIMINOLOGY & PUB. POL'Y 803, 837 (2009). *See* Aaron Chalfin et al., *What Do Panel Studies Tell Us About a Deterrent Effect of Capital Punishment? A Critique of the Literature*, 29 J. QUANTITATIVE CRIMINOLOGY 5, 8, 41 (2013) (reviewing research that uses panel data on U.S. states and counties to investigate whether the death penalty affects homicide rates and concluding that the research fails to provide persuasive evidence of deterrence). In the macrosociological framework that I have proposed, capital-punishment statutes are thus believed to serve mainly as symbols of dominant social values. THE PLACE OF

LAW, *supra* note 9, at 401–02. To the extent symbols endorse prevailing social values, they facilitate the operation of a society and are sociologically important. *Id.* at 59–61.

A study of the use of the death penalty in Texas, where three or four out of every ten executions in the country have taken place in recent decades, found that executions lowered the number of murders in the state during the twelve months after the executions, and it described the homicide-curbing impact of executions during the period covered (1994–2005) as "substantial." Kenneth C. Land et al., *The Short-Term Effects of Executions on Homicides: Deterrence, Displacement, or Both?*, 47 CRIMINOLOGY 1009, 1018, 1038 (2009) [hereinafter Land et al. 2009]. Specifically, the study estimated that, for each execution, there were either 0.5 or 2.5 fewer murders in the twelve months following the execution. *Id.* at 1030–31, 1038. However, murders that executions prevent at one point in time may not be permanently averted; rather, they may merely be pushed back in time and happen later. *Id.* The possibility of such a delay is evidently not considered in the higher estimate (i.e., a reduction of 2.5 murders per execution) but is taken into account in the lower estimate (i.e., a reduction of 0.5 murders per execution). *Id.* at 1030–31. The higher estimate, therefore, may overstate the decrease in homicides attributed to executions.

Assuming that the lower estimate in the study by Land et al. is correct, the use of the death penalty in Texas during the 1994–2005 period was responsible for reducing the yearly number of homicides in the state by less than one percent. The latter figure was calculated from a numerator and denominator that were obtained from data in *id.* at 1023 tbl. 1 panel b:

Numerator: 1.97 executions per month × 12 months × 0.5 = 11.82 fewer homicides per year due to executions.

Denominator: (118.97 homicides per month × 12 months) = 1427.64 homicides per year + 11.82 homicides avoided by executions = 1439.46 homicides per year, the total of homicides that did occur and of homicides that would have occurred without any executions.

Percent decrease in number of homicides attributable to executions: 11.82/1439.46 = 0.0082 × 100 = 0.82%.

In a subsequent article, Land et al. describe the results of their initial study as evidence that executions have a "modest," but brief, homicide-decreasing effect. Kenneth C. Land et al., *The Differential Short-Term Impacts of Executions on Felony and Non-Felony Homicides*, 11 CRIMINOLOGY & PUB. POL'Y 541, 556 (2012) [hereinafter Land et al. 2012]. In an analysis of monthly data on Texas for the period 1994 through 2007, they differentiated the impact of executions on the number of felony homicides in the state from the impact of executions on the number of non-felony homicides in the state. *Id.* at 545. During the study period, non-felony homicides in Texas were much more frequent than felony homicides. *Id.* at 548 tbl. 1. A homicide was classified as a "felony homicide" when a human being was killed during the commission of a separate felony, e.g., a robbery; a "non-felony homicide" was any other homicide, i.e., any homicide other than a felony homicide, that was deemed not to be justifiable and not to be negligent. Justifiable and negligent homicides were omitted from the study. *Id.* at 546. The data analyses, which included an assessment of the extent to which executions delayed homicides, revealed

the ban on cruel and unusual punishment in the Eighth Amendment to the U.S. Constitution,[42] vacated a series of death sentences on the grounds that, because specific criteria to guide the sentencing decision were absent, the sentences could have been imposed arbitrarily.[43] Capital-punishment statutes, to satisfy the Eighth Amendment, must contain explicit criteria ensuring their application in a manner that is "evenhanded, rational, and consistent."[44]

In terms of constitutional law on the death penalty, the year 1972 marks a clear break with the past. Before 1972, no statute that authorized capital punishment for crime had been invalidated by a federal court or a state court in the United States,[45] although from 1964 to 1969 such statutes had been repealed by the legislatures of six states.[46] The constitutional standard that appeared in

---

that an execution in Texas did not affect the net number of felony homicides, but lowered the net number of non-felony homicides by 0.9 during the twelve months after the execution. *Id.* at 556–57. Land et al. describe the prevention of 0.9 non-felony murders over twelve months as an effect whose magnitude is "slight." *Id.* at 557. The calculation procedure used above for the initial study (Land et al. 2009), when followed for and limited to non-felony homicides covered by the subsequent study (Land et al. 2012), indicated that an execution in Texas depressed the number of non-felony homicides in the state during the twelve months after the execution by 21.49/1208.41 = 0.0178 × 100 = 1.78%. Data from *id.* at 548 tbl. 1.

A study assessing the impact that the law of a jurisdiction, or the enforcement of the law of the jurisdiction, has on a targeted activity is in danger of reaching an erroneous conclusion unless it includes another jurisdiction as a control, i.e., a jurisdiction that lacks such law or enforcement but that is similar in other relevant respects. Britt et al., *supra* note 9, at 365–66. Both studies by Land et al. were confined to Texas; neither study employed a control jurisdiction and compared Texas to it. Land et al. 2009, *supra*, at 1017, 1033–34; Land et al. 2012, *supra*, at 542, 557 n. 13.

42 "Excessive bail shall not be required, nor excessive fines imposed, nor cruel and unusual punishments inflicted." U.S. CONST. amend. VIII.

43 Furman v. Georgia, 408 U.S. 238 (1972); Albert, *supra* note 41, at 341 & n. 117. Furman v. Georgia was the first decision of the U.S. Supreme Court that struck down death penalty statutes; the ruling of the Court and opinions of the justices in *Furman* were announced on June 29, 1972. *Furman*, 408 U.S. at 238. However, four months earlier—on February 18, 1972—the Supreme Court of California had concluded that a California capital-punishment statute was unacceptable under the state constitution. People v. Anderson, 493 P.2d 880 (Cal. 1972).

44 Jurek v. Texas, 428 U.S. 262, 276 (1976) (Stewart, Powell & Stevens, J.J., concurring in judgment).

45 William J. Brennan, Jr., *Constitutional Adjudication and the Death Penalty: A View from the Court*, 100 HARV. L. REV. 313, 314 (1986).

46 WILLIAM J. BOWERS, LEGAL HOMICIDE: DEATH AS PUNISHMENT IN AMERICA, 1864–1982, at 9 (1984).

1972 for capital-punishment statutes, however, was a barrier to death sentences for only four years. In 1976, the U.S. Supreme Court concluded that the standard was satisfied by the death-penalty statutes of several states that since 1972 had revised their statutes[47] in response to substantial public support for executing persons convicted of murder.[48]

The number of executions in the United States is shown in Figure 1.1 for each year from 1946 through 2002.[49] The data are limited to executions of prisoners that were carried out under civil (as distinguished from military) authority. The year 1946 was chosen as the starting point for the data because that year marks the beginning of the period that followed World War II. The U.S. social system may have been markedly affected by the war and the economic depression that preceded it, especially since these events extended over a full decade-and-a-half.[50] Executions under civil authority that occurred during and before World War II, therefore, may not be comparable sociologically to executions in the era after.[51]

---

47 Gregg v. Georgia, 428 U.S. 153 (1976); Rupert V. Barry, Note, *Furman to Gregg: The Judicial and Legislative History*, 22 HOWARD L.J. 53, 86–91, 95–103, 108–09 (1979). The judgment of the Court and opinions of the justices in Gregg v. Georgia were announced on July 2, 1976. *Gregg*, 428 U.S. at 153.

48 Pew Res. Ctr., Continued Majority Support for Death Penalty 1 (2012) (on file with author), *available at* http://www.people-press.org/files/legacy-pdf/1-6-12%20Death%20penalty%20release.pdf (last visited April 26, 2015).

49 The data for Figure 1.1 are from M. Watt Espy & John Ortiz Smykla, Executions in the United States, 1608–2002: The ESPY File, Inter-university Consortium for Political and Social Research, Univ. of Michigan (Study No. 8451) (4th ed. 2004). A description of the Espy-Smykla study is available at http://www.icpsr.umich.edu/icpsrweb/ICPSR/studies/8451?author[0]=Espy%2C+M.+Watt&paging.startRow=1. The last year for which the Espy-Smykla study estimates the yearly number of executions is 2002. Data for subsequent years are published by the U.S. Department of Justice. TRACY L. SNELL, BUREAU OF JUSTICE STATISTICS, CAPITAL PUNISHMENT, 2010—STATISTICAL TABLES 13 table 9 (2011), http://bjs.ojp.usdoj.gov/content/pub/pdf/cp10st.pdf. However, the estimated number of executions is not identical in every year covered by both the Espy-Smykla study and the U.S. Department of Justice. To avoid an apparent inconsistency between the two sources in their definitions of concepts and/or their measurement procedures, the data for Figure 1.1 are drawn from a single source, viz., the Espy-Smykla study. The final year in the Figure is thus 2002.

50 Many of the social effects of the economic depression and World War II are likely to have been subtle and hence may not be detectible even with current social science measurement techniques.

51 The period being examined has a theoretically meaningful starting point (1946), but not a theoretically meaningful ending point (2002). Unfortunately, no year after 1976 is obvious as a theoretically defensible point at which to terminate the time series.

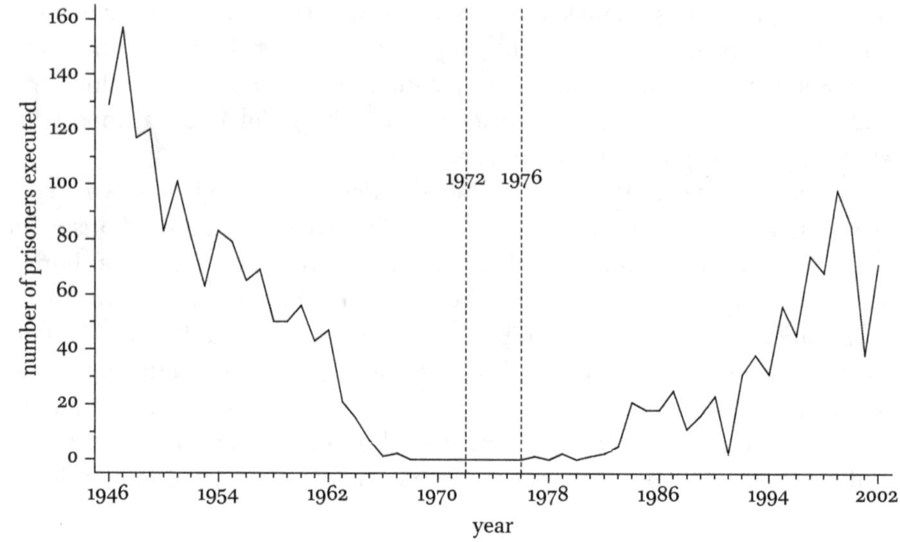

FIGURE 1.1 *Number of prisoners executed in the United States: executions under civil authority by year*
SOURCE: SEE FN. 49 IN THIS CHAPTER.

As Figure 1.1 reveals, there were no executions in the United States for several years prior to 1972—specifically, from 1968 through 1971. Before 1968, moreover, a secular decline in the number of executions is observable.[52] Accordingly, the U.S. Supreme Court, in its decisions in 1972 on capital-punishment statutes, was presumably reacting to and/or embodying societal change that had brought the death penalty into disfavor. Notably, the percentage of adults in the United States who expressed support for the death penalty fell, and the percentage who expressed opposition to the death penalty rose, from the early 1950s to the middle of the 1960s.[53] However, the decisions of the Court in 1972 were followed by increases in the prevalence of attitudes favorable to the death penalty,[54] suggesting the possibility that these decisions contributed to a reawakening of public support for the death penalty[55]—i.e., altered the societal conditions determining the use of the death penalty—and led, in turn, to

52 The peak from which the decline occurred was in 1947, when 157 executions took place.

53 Pew Res. Ctr., *supra* note 48, at 1.

54 *Id.*

55 In response to the decisions of the Court in 1972, thirty-four states adopted revised legislation authorizing the death penalty. BRYAN VILA & CYNTHIA MORRIS (EDS.), CAPITAL PUNISHMENT IN THE UNITED STATES: A DOCUMENTARY HISTORY 148 (1997).

the enactment of the capital-punishment statutes that were approved by the Court in 1976. Pursuant to the new statutes, executions recommenced.

ii "Three-Strikes" Penalties

During the 1990s, a number of states adopted law that mandated a lengthy prison sentence (e.g., a minimum of twenty-five years) for a person who is convicted of a felony and who has been convicted of a felony on at least one previous occasion when the current and earlier convictions entailed specified types of conduct.[56] This "three-strikes" law[57] differed from habitual-offender statutes, which many states already possessed, in terms of whether trial-court judges were allowed discretion in imposing the law-prescribed enhanced sentence for the current conviction. Habitual-offender statutes permitted such discretion; "three-strikes" law did not.[58] However, in a jurisdiction that has "three-strikes" law, discretion may exist during the period prior to trial, because prosecutors may not be required to charge a defendant under the "three-strikes" law.[59]

Nineteen states adopted "three-strikes" law as defined above. The following are the states with "three-strikes" law and the implementation year of the law in each state:[60] Arkansas (1995), California (1994), Colorado (1994), Delaware (1994), Georgia (1995), Illinois (1994), Maryland (1994), Montana (1997), New Jersey (1995), New Mexico (1994), North Carolina (1994), Pennsylvania (1995), South Carolina (1996), Tennessee (1994), Texas (1996), Virginia (1994), Washington (1993), West Virginia (1994), Wisconsin (1994). "Three-strikes" law in the nineteen states thus appeared during the five-year period from 1993 through 1997. However, while the nineteen states acted at essentially the same

56 Franklin E. Zimring, *Populism, Democratic Government, and the Decline of Expert Authority: Some Reflections on "Three Strikes" in California*, 28 PAC. L.J. 243, 244–49 (1996); Franklin E. Zimring & David T. Johnson, *Public Opinion and the Governance of Punishment in Democratic Political Systems*, 605 ANNALS 266, 277 (2006).

57 A uniform definition of "three-strikes" law does not exist. *See* Michael Vitiello, *Three Strikes: Can We Return to Rationality?*, 87 J. CRIM. L. & CRIMINOLOGY 395, 400–01 (1997) (noting that "multiple offender" statutes, which have been popularly labeled "three-strikes" law, are not identical in content across all jurisdictions). Consequently, not all sources are likely to assign to "three-strikes" law the attributes that are listed in the first sentence of the instant paragraph in the text.

58 Zimring & Johnson, *supra* note 56, at 277.

59 "Three-strikes" law in general expanded the discretion of prosecutors while curtailing the discretion of judges. *Id.* at 277.

60 The list of states and implementation years is based on information in Vitiello, *supra* note 57, at 402–09, 418 & n. 125, 422 n. 152, 463–80. The lengthy prison sentence mandated by "three-strikes" law is imposed in some states for a second felony conviction. *Id.* at 463–80.

point in time, one state—California—stands out, because of every 100 sentences imposed on convicted felons who have been prosecuted under "three-strikes" law in the United States, more than ninety of the sentences are estimated to have emanated from courts in California.[61] The prominence of the California "three-strikes" law is likely to stem from the purpose of that law. According to one scholarly assessment, the California "three-strikes" law is notable because it aspired to have far-reaching effects;[62] simply put, the law aimed to launch "the biggest penal experiment of any kind in modern American history."[63]

Having the most notable "three-strikes" law in the country, California is the only state whose crime trends are included in Figure 1.2 *infra*. The Figure, which was constructed from data published by the California Department of Justice, presents the yearly number of known violent crimes in California, and the yearly number of known property crimes in California, for every 100,000 people in the state.[64] The rates in the Figure begin in 1952 and end in 2010, with a vertical line marking the year in which California adopted its "three-strikes" law, viz., 1994.[65] Although rates starting in 1946 may have been preferable,[66] rates of violent crime and property crime in California are unavailable for years prior to 1952.

What specific crimes constitute violent offenses, and what specific crimes are property offenses? The category of violent offenses covers the four crimes of homicide, forcible rape, robbery, and aggravated assault. The category of property offenses, on the other hand, involves just two crimes—burglary and motor-vehicle theft. Notably, Figure 1.2 omits larceny-theft and arson from property offenses. The omission was necessary because yearly rates of larceny-theft and of arson are not available for the entire 1952–2010 period.[67] If the data

---

61 Franklin E. Zimring et al., Punishment and Democracy: Three Strikes and You're Out in California 20 (2001).

62 *Id.* at ix.

63 *Id.* at 22.

64 The data in Figure 1.2 were obtained or computed from: Leonard A. Marowitz, California Dep't of Justice, *Why Did the Crime Rate Decrease Through 1999? (And Why Might It Decrease or Increase in 2000 and Beyond?): A Literature Review and Critical Analysis* 35 table A2, CJSC Research Series, <http://ag.ca.gov/cjsc/publications/misc/why/rpt.pdf?> (last visited April 26, 2015); Criminal Justice Statistics Ctr., California Dep't of Justice, Crime in California 2010 6 table 1, <http://ag.ca.gov/cjsc/publications/candd/cd10/preface.pdf?> (last visited April 26, 2015).

65 People v. Romero, 917 P.2d 628, 630–31 (Calif. 1996). The law began to be applied in the year it was adopted, i.e., in 1994. *Id.*

66 Text preceding *supra* note 50.

67 The data on larceny-theft that exist for California are for calendar years 1983 and later, and are for incidents that involve property worth more than $400. Data on arson in California

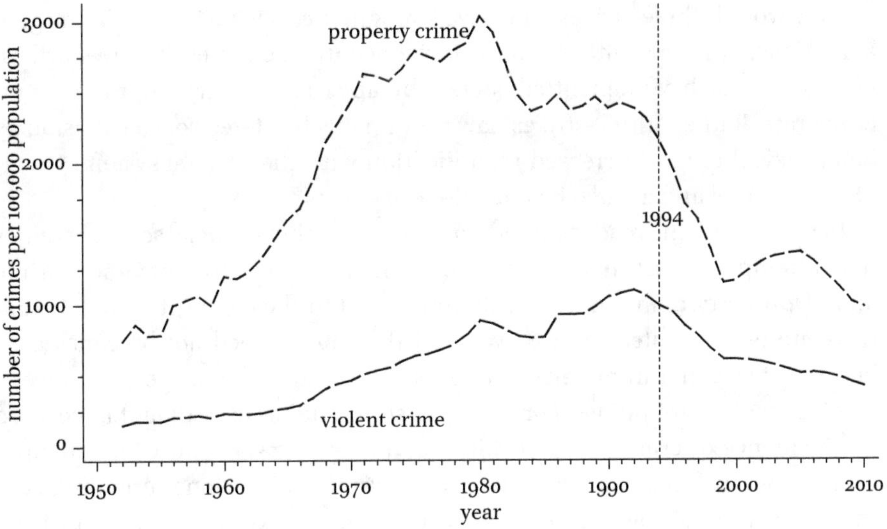

FIGURE 1.2 *Crime rates in California, by year*
SOURCE: SEE FN. 64 IN THIS CHAPTER.

that are available on larceny-theft and on arson had been included, the property-offense rates in Figure 1.2 would not have been comparable across time.

What course did crime rates take before California adopted "three-strikes" law in 1994? Figure 1.2 shows that the incidence of property crime had fallen markedly from the peak it reached more than a decade earlier,[68] but that a steady, substantial rise over the course of four decades had occurred in the incidence of violent crime. Thus, while the law was not a reaction to mounting property crime, it was evidently a response to rising violent crime. In particular, "three-strikes" law in California was probably an attempt to counter a threat to societal functioning, an hypothesis that is supported by some sociological research. Although the topic has not been investigated in depth, there is empirical evidence that violent crime erodes social cohesiveness.[69]

---

start with calendar year 1980. CRIMINAL JUSTICE STATISTICS CTR., *supra* note 64, at 6 table 1, 63.

68 The property-offense rate reached its high in 1980.

69 Terry E. Duncan et al., *A Multilevel Contextual Model of Neighborhood Collective Efficacy*, 32 AM. J. COMMUNITY PSYCHOL. 245, 248, 250 (2003). However, findings on the sociological consequences of violent crime depend on how data are analyzed. R. Marie Garcia et al., *Impacts of Violent Crime and Neighborhood Structure on Trusting Your Neighbors*, 24 JUST. Q. 679, 699 (2007).

How would "three-strikes" law have strengthened social life? Given the general inefficacy of law with regard to society-central activities,[70] "three-strikes" law would not have benefitted society by appreciably lowering the violent-crime rate. Rather, "three-strikes" law presumably bolstered social cohesion by being a symbol that increased identification with the societal system. Law is often a symbol and as such has sociological effects.[71]

In this regard, the reader should note that a number of social science studies have attempted to estimate the degree to which the incidence of violent crime and of property crime in California responded to the "three-strikes" law that the state implemented in 1994. Many of the studies need not be considered because they suffer from defects in research design that damage the utility or credibility of their findings. For example, some studies used data that covered the incidence of crime in California over a relatively short post-implementation period; such data do not permit an assessment of the long-term impact of the "three-strikes" law on crime.[72] Other studies, though having data for a lengthy post-implementation period, lacked a suitable control group.[73] The

---

70 Text accompanying *supra* note 26; *supra* note 27 and accompanying text.

71 Jeffers v. Lewis, 38 F.3d 411, 427 (9th Cir. 1994) (en banc) (Noonan, Pregerson, and Norris, J.J., dissenting) (observing that a considerable portion of law is symbolic and that law as a symbol has a significant societal impact).

72 Joanna M. Shepherd, *Fear of the First Strike: The Full Deterrent Effect of California's Two- and Three-Strikes Legislation*, 31 J. LEGAL STUD. 159, 165, 182 (2002) (using county-level data on the monthly incidence of crime in California during the thirty-three months after implementation of "three-strikes" law); Lisa Stolzenberg & Stewart J. D'Alessio, *"Three Strikes and You're Out": The Impact of California's New Mandatory Sentencing Law on Serious Crime Rates*, 43 CRIME & DELINQ. 457, 460–61 (1997) (using city-level data on the monthly incidence of crime in California during the twenty-two months after implementation of "three-strikes" law).

73 An appropriate control group is essential in a study that attempts to assess the impact of law; the absence of a suitable control group substantially raises the risk that the study will yield erroneous conclusions. Britt et al., *supra* note 9. In studying the impact of law, the control group must be a jurisdiction that (i) is similar in relevant attributes to the jurisdiction whose law is under evaluation but that (ii) did not have the same type of law during the period covered by the study. *Id.* at 365–66. For assessing the impact of "three-strikes" law in a state, a suitable control group must thus be a state that did not implement such law during the pertinent time period but that is otherwise comparable. Studies of the impact of the California "three-strikes" law will not have an appropriate control group if the data they employ are confined to California. Studies that rely on data for just California include: Juan R. Ramirez & William D. Crano, *Deterrence and Incapacitation: An Interrupted Time-Series Analysis of California's Three-Strikes Law*, 33 J. APPLIED SOC. PSYCHOL. 110 (2003) (using data on the monthly state-level incidence of crime in

foregoing limitations are not insignificant. They undermine the usefulness of, or the confidence that can be placed in, the conclusions of the studies, and as a result, I set aside the studies.

Turning to methodologically sounder quantitative studies, there is scant reason to believe that "three-strikes" law in California had a material, general, and long-term impact on crime rates in the state. If the law had a crime-curbing effect that was unequivocal and large, the studies would have unearthed it and their findings would be uniform. Instead, the findings of the studies have been inconsistent,[74] suggesting that any post-implementation reductions in

---

California for fifty-eight months after implementation of "three-strikes" law); Shepherd, *supra* note 72; Stolzenberg & D'Alessio, *supra* note 72; John L. Worrall, *The Effect of Three-Strikes Legislation on Serious Crime in California*, 32 J. CRIM. JUST. 283 (2004) (using data on the yearly state-level incidence of crime in California for six years after implementation of "three-strikes" law). In the Ramirez-Crano study *supra*, one statistical procedure yielded results indicating that the California "three-strikes" law substantially curbed rates of "instrumental" crime (robbery, burglary, and motor-vehicle theft) but had no impact on rates of violent crime (homicide, aggravated assault, and rape); another statistical procedure in the Ramirez-Crano study yielded results indicating that the law appreciably decreased rates of both types of crime. Ramirez & Crano, *supra*, at 130, 136, 139. However, the lack of a suitable control group casts doubt on any conclusion drawn from the studies cited above, including the Ramirez-Crano study.

74 Elsa Y. Chen, *Impacts of "Three Strikes and You're Out" on Crime Trends in California and Throughout the United States*, 24 J. CONTEMPORARY CRIM. JUST. 345, 348, 357–58, 364 (2008) (using pooled time-series, state-level yearly crime-incidence data on seven types of major crime in each state in the United States for eleven or twelve years after implementation of a "three-strikes" state law; finding that the California "three-strikes" law decreased rates of robbery and motor-vehicle theft in California but did not affect rates of murder, rape, aggravated assault, burglary, and larceny in the state; finding that the impact of the California "three-strikes" law on the rates of all crime types, including robbery and motor-vehicle theft, did not increase with the passage of time; and describing the crime-curbing effect of less-stringent "three-strikes" law in the United States as "slight" for robbery, burlary, larceny-theft, and motor-vehicle theft and the effect added by the California "three-strikes" law as "small or nonexistent for nearly every category of crime"); Tomislav V. Kovandzic et al., *"Striking Out" as Crime Reduction Policy: The Impact of "Three Strikes" Laws on Crime Rates in U.S. Cities*, 21 JUST. Q. 207, 209, 214, 219, 233–34 (2004) (using pooled time-series, city-level yearly crime-incidence data for a minimum of four, and a maximum of seven, post-implementation years for 188 U.S. cities having a population of 100,000 or more; finding that in California cities, the state "three-strikes" law decreased, by at least 10.0%, rates of robbery and motor-vehicle theft, but increased by 14.7% the rate of rape; and finding that, among the 188 U.S. cities as a whole, state "three-strikes" law had no consistent effect on the city-level rate of any crime except homicide, whose rate was raised by the "three-strikes" law in eight states and lowered by the "three-

crime that are estimated by the data analyses reported by the studies arise from the design of the research,[75] are randomly occurring statistical results, and/or are attributable to one or more unrelated, concurrent societal changes.[76] For instance, implementation of the law was found by one study to be associated with a substantial increase in rape,[77] but the increase cannot be tied to the law by theory. Indeed, the increase is contrary to theory. One strong relationship that contradicts theory damages the credibility of other, theoretically acceptable relationships that were estimated from the data.

A final point needs to be mentioned with regard to the California "three-strikes" law. Specifically, even if social science research had proven that the law was responsible for a large, permanent decrease in major types of crime, the

---

strikes" law in one state). *See generally* Ngozi Obeta Anadi, The Impact of Three Strikes Laws on Crime Rates in the United States: A Panel Data Analysis 42–46 table 1, 54–55, 58–59, 70–73, 88 (2011) (unpublished Ph.D. dissertation, Southern University and A&M College) (on file with author) (using pooled time-series, state-level yearly data on rates of crime in each state in the United States for thirteen to sixteen years after implementation of "three-strikes" law; finding that "three-strikes" law had no statistically significant effect on state rates of all crime, on state rates of violent crime, or on state rates of property crime; but reporting positive, albeit statistically non-significant, regression coefficients for the impact of "three-strikes" law on state rates of all crime, of violent crime, and of property crime); Thomas B. Marvell & Carlisle E. Moody, *The Lethal Effects of Three-Strikes Laws*, 30 J. LEGAL STUD. 89, 93–94, 104–06 (2001) (using pooled time-series, state-level yearly crime-incidence data on each U.S. state for a minimum of three years and a maximum of five years after implementation of the state "three-strikes" law; and finding that such law had no impact on the state-level rate of any crime other than homicide, the occurrence of which was increased by the law).

75 The studies in *supra* note 74 involved analyses of pooled time-series crime-incidence data on jurisdictions in the United States. The essence of these analyses was a comparison of (i) the state of California, or cities within California, to (ii) jurisdictions of the same level that did not have or were not subject to "three-strikes" law. At least one of the comparison states/cities was presumably suitable as a control site. *Supra* note 73. In the pooled time-series data of the studies in *supra* note 74, however, many of the comparison states/cities are likely to have differed in important ways from their California counterparts and hence were unsuitable control sites. The use of unsuitable control sites in pooled time-series data will stem from (i) error in the measurement of included independent variables that are held constant and/or (ii) the omission of independent variables that influenced both whether such law was adopted and the crime rate. Unfortunately, the presence of inappropriate comparison sites in the pooled time-series crime-incidence data of the studies in *supra* note 74 has unknown consequences for the accuracy of estimates of the degree to which crime incidence is affected by the California "three-strikes" law and other law.

76 Kovandzic et al., *supra* note 74, at 232.

77 *Id.* at 233 table 4.

law has evidently reduced the frequency of plea bargains and added to the number of jury trials in cases involving alleged criminal conduct, thereby burdening the courts. In addition, the law has appreciably enlarged the number of prisoners[78] and, in turn, raised California government expenditures on prisons.[79] Even assuming that the California "three-strikes" law materially lowered the incidence of major forms of crime, its full and continued application is thus unlikely to be sustainable. Of course, to the extent the law starts to be less vigorously applied, any crime-curbing benefit it provided will end, and the law will not produce a continuing decrease in crime.

b *Discrimination*

A word typically has more than one meaning, and because "discrimination" is such a word, it needs to be defined for the instant chapter. As I will use it, the word "discrimination" refers to a society-prevalent classification scheme that has three characteristics: (i) the classification scheme differentiates individuals on the basis of a demographic variable, e.g., race or religious faith; (ii) the classification scheme is associated with a preference for all persons who on that variable have a certain trait, e.g., who are Caucasian or who belong to a Christian religion; and (iii) the classification scheme carries an inflexible disapproval of all persons who on that variable possess other traits, e.g., who are not Caucasian or who are not members of a Christian religion. Discrimination, in short, is a socially invidious grouping of humans by humans.

In a society, however, not every sorting of humans constitutes discrimination. Differentiation on a particular demographic variable comes to be labeled discrimination when the operation of society is impaired by the differentiation. Accordingly, discrimination involving a given demographic variable is not inherent in the society but is, instead, a function of societal properties,[80] and the differentiation of a group on a specific demographic variable can be regarded by a society as not discriminatory at one point in its history but discriminatory at another. Because differentiation and discrimination cannot be

---

78 State of California Legislative Analyst's Office, A Primer: Three Strikes—The Impact After More Than a Decade figure 3 (Oct. 2005), http://www.lao.ca.gov/2005/3_Strikes/3_strikes_102005.htm (last visited April 26, 2015).

79 State of California Legislative Analyst's Office, The Impact of the "Three Strikes and You're Out" Law on California's Justice System (Feb. 1996), http://www.lao.ca.gov/handouts/pre_1999/h0022096_3_strikes_impact.html (last visited April 26, 2015); Mac Taylor, State of California Legislative Analyst's Office, Reducing Prison Overcrowding in California 4 (Aug. 2011), http://www.lao.ca.gov/reports/2011/crim/overcrowding_080511.pdf (last visited April 26, 2015).

80 The Place of Law, *supra* note 9, at 342–43.

divorced from their societal context, they are sociological phenomena and important topics for a macrosociological treatment of law.

Change in major doctrines of law is an indicator of societal shifts, and one of the notable sociological developments in the United States during the last half of the twentieth century was the emergence of law that applied the label of discrimination to the differentiation of individuals on certain demographic variables. The emergence of this law produced an historical era,[81] and some of the demographic variables covered by the law permit a test of the hypothesis that is being examined in the instant chapter. I turn now to that law and certain of the demographic traits on which it focused. Specifically, I examine three demographic variables and the law on them—chronological age, the status of children based on the marital classification of their biological parents when the children were born, and biological sex. In Part 2 of Chapter 7, I consider an additional demographic attribute—race—and a federal statute pertinent to it.

i Age

On December 15, 1967, Congress adopted legislation[82]—the Age Discrimination in Employment Act ("ADEA" or "Act")[83]—that prohibited covered employers, employment agencies, and labor unions from discriminating on the basis of age against individuals who are in the age range 40 through 64.[84] The Act went into force six months later.[85] Subsequently, amendments to the Act removed an upper age limit for all but a few categories of employees.[86] Although the

81 For a summary of the statutes approved by Congress that were concerned with discrimination in the context of employment, see *id.* at 268–70.

82 Pub. L. No. 90–202, 81 Stat. 602 (1967) (codified at 29 U.S.C. § 621 et seq. (2006)). Before 1967, some states had approved legislation banning age discrimination in employment. David Neumark & Wendy A. Stock, *Age Discrimination Laws and Labor Market Efficiency*, 107 J. POL. ECON. 1081, 1090–99 table 1 (1999).

83 An overview of the provisions and history of the ADEA is found in HAROLD S. LEWIS, JR. & ELIZABETH J. NORMAN, EMPLOYMENT DISCRIMINATION LAW AND PRACTICE § 6.1 (2d ed. 2004).

84 Pub. L. No. 90–202, § 12, 81 Stat. 607 (1967). An employer was covered by the Act if it operated in an industry that affected commerce and if, after June 1968, it had a minimum of twenty-five employees on every working day during twenty or more calendar weeks in the current calendar year or in the preceding calendar year. Pub. L. No. 90–202, § 11(b), 81 Stat. 602, 605 (1967) (codified at 29 U.S.C. § 630 (2006)).

85 Pub. L. No. 90–202, § 15, 81 Stat. 602, 607 (1967).

86 Pub. L. No. 95–256, §§ 3(a), 3(b), 92 Stat. 189, 189, 190 (1978); Pub. L. No. 99–592, §§ 2(c), 3, 7(a), 100 Stat. 3342, 3342, 3344 (1986); Pub. L. No. 104–208, Div. A. § 119, 110 Stat. 3009, 3009–23 (1996).

statute and its amendments manifested the conclusion of Congress that there was widespread age discrimination directed at persons age 40 or over who held or wanted to hold positions in the economy that paid monetary compensation,[87] the extent of age discrimination against older labor force participants seems not to have been frequent in the United States when Congress acted, i.e., in 1967. According to data from this period, approximately 7 percent of all men age 45 and older in a national sample believed that they had experienced age discrimination in the context of employment.[88] If so, no more than one in fourteen men within the age range covered by the ADEA had suffered work-related age discrimination.

Figure 1.3 shows the yearly civilian labor force participation rate of White men and of White women in the United States in each of two age ranges—45–54 and 55–64—during the period 1954 through 2010.[89] In the top graph and in the bottom graph, a vertical line marks 1967, the year in which the ADEA was approved. Certain aspects of the Figure merit explanation. First, the Figure is limited to Whites because data on non-Whites at age 45–54 and at age 55–64 are unavailable for years prior to 1972. Pre-1972 data, of course, are essential to testing the hypothesis of the instant chapter, i.e., to ascertaining whether congressional approval of the ADEA was preceded by a downward trend in the civilian labor force participation rates of persons who were covered by the Act. Second, the Figure uses the rate of labor force participation, which is based on the concept of "labor force" and is a broad measure that captures the extent to which a population is attracted to paid economic activity. In the United States,

87 In the Act, Congress stated that "arbitrary age limits" in employment were "common" in the United States, described unemployment as "high among older workers…and their employment problems grave," and implied that these problems were due to age discrimination. Pub. L. No. 90–202, § 2(a), 81 Stat. 602, 602 (1967) (codified at 29 U.S.C. § 621 (2006)).

88 Richard W. Johnson & David Neumark, *Age Discrimination, Job Separations, and Employment Status of Older Workers*, 32 J. HUM. RESOURCES 779, 782–83, 787–89 (1997). Respondents were asked in 1971 whether they had suffered age discrimination "at work" in the preceding five years, i.e., at any time from 1966 to 1971. *Id.* at 783. Answers, if complete and correct, would have included incidents of age discrimination before, and not just after, enactment of the ADEA.

89 The data used in Figure 1.3 were obtained from the interactive data-retrieval service of the Bureau of Labor Statistics, U.S. Dep't of Labor, Labor Force Statistics from the Current Population Survey, http://www.bls.gov/cps/lfcharacteristics.htm#laborforce (under "Labor Force" category and "Database: Retrieve historical data series" subcategory, follow "More options" hyperlink to http://data.bls.gov/pdq/querytool.jsp?survey=ln) (last visited April 26, 2015). The Bureau of Labor Statistics does not publish age-specific rates of labor force participation for years prior to 1954.

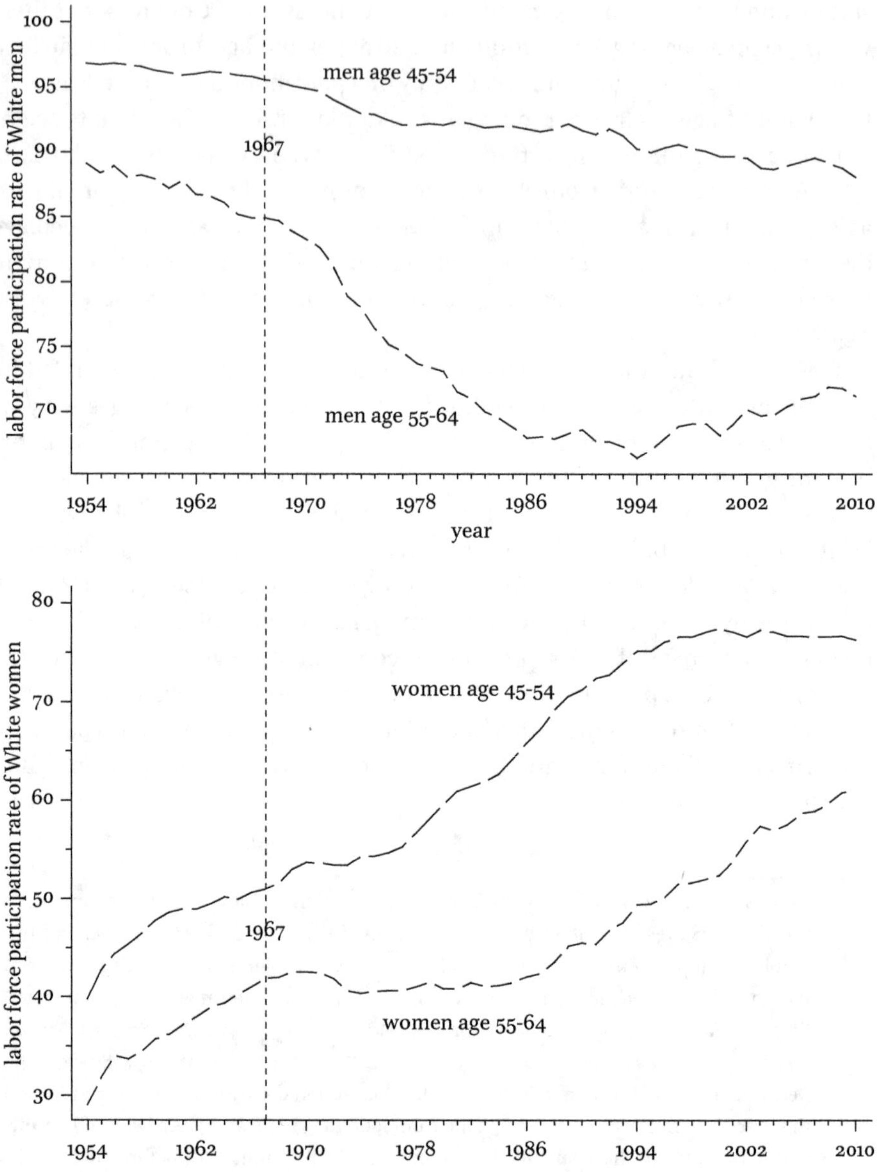

FIGURE 1.3 *Civilian labor force participation rate: United States, by year*
SOURCE: SEE FN. 89 IN THIS CHAPTER.

two types of persons who are at least 16 years old comprise the labor force: (i) persons who are currently employed, and (ii) persons who are not employed but have sought employment during the previous four weeks and are presently available for employment.[90] Unemployed persons who are not attempting to find employment, however, are outside the labor force. The rate of labor force participation for a given time period is the percentage of the civilian noninstitutionalized population that was in the labor force in this period.[91]

Figure 1.3 indicates that adoption of the ADEA was triggered by the labor market situation of men, not women. Specifically, in the years prior to the Act that are covered in the Figure, the labor force participation rate among White men, although much higher than among White women, was noticeably declining, especially at age 55–64. By contrast, the rate among White women during the pre-Act period, while appreciably lower than the rate among White men, was briskly rising at both age 45–54 and age 55–64. Since men comprised most of the labor force at this point in history,[92] their deteriorating position in the economy would logically have been the paramount concern that prompted Congress to approve the ADEA.[93]

---

90 U.S. CENSUS BUREAU, STATISTICAL ABSTRACT OF THE UNITED STATES: 2012, at 374 (131st ed. 2011), *available at* http://www.census.gov/prod/2011pubs/12statab/labor.pdf (last visited April 26, 2015).

91 The labor force participation rate is an imperfect gauge of the extent to which a population prefers paid economic activity. By way of example, the labor force participation rate fails to account for persons who want to be employed but who, after unsuccessful attempts to find employment, have stopped searching for jobs. In a study of age discrimination, however, the labor force participation rate is more defensible than the employment rate, i.e., the percentage of the labor force that is employed. The quarterly employment rate of each of the four age-sex groups of Whites in Figure 1.3 is provided by the Bureau of Labor Statistics, *supra* note 89, for calendar years 1954 onward. Although employment rates could have been used in Figure 1.3, they were not, because they exclude unemployed persons who are actively pursuing employment. The labor force participation rate includes this segment of the unemployed and, hence, more fully measures the pressure on Congress to write and approve the ADEA.

92 In 1965, for example, White men were 65.6%, and White women were 34.4%, of all Whites age 16 years and older in the labor force. Computed from U.S. CENSUS BUREAU, STATISTICAL ABSTRACT OF THE UNITED STATES: 1970, at 213 table 316 (91st ed. 1970), *available at* http://www2.census.gov/prod2/statcomp/documents/1970-01.pdf (last visited April 26, 2015).

93 Congress believed that the ADEA was necessary because unemployment among persons who were middle age and older was "growing." Pub. L. No. 90–202, § 2(a)(3), 81 Stat. 602, 602 (1967) (codified at 29 U.S.C. § 621(a)(3) (2006)). The Figure indicates that, in these age ranges, the job market was becoming inhospitable only to men and that women were not encountering major age-based impediments to employment.

Did the ADEA fulfill its goal? Congress wanted the Act to raise employment among persons age 40 and older by eliminating unfounded negative stereotypes regarding these persons.[94] However, quantitative social science research on whether the Act did so has not yielded consistent conclusions. Two studies of White males have reported that the ADEA and comparable state legislation was helpful to older men in employment-related matters,[95] but a recent study, also of White males, concluded that this (federal and state) law has had detrimental effects on a range of such matters for men who were older than 50.[96] Law forbidding age discrimination in employment was found by the last study to have reduced, for example, the hiring of men over age 50 and the number of weeks they worked in a year. Although none of the three studies is ideal methodologically, the last study is superior in research design to its predecessors.[97] Certainly, its conclusions are consistent with the post-1967 trends seen in the top graph of Figure 1.3.

The annual labor force participation rates of White men in the two age groups included in Figure 1.3 have an additional dimension that warrants mention. That dimension involves the changes in the rates from year-to-year, and it can be measured in terms of the absolute size of the changes or in terms of their speed. To capture the latter (i.e., speed), I computed the *percent* (not percentage-point) change, from one year to the next, in the labor force participation rate among White men age 45–54 and among White men age 55–64. Both the standard deviation and mean of the percent change were then calculated for each age group in each of two five-year periods—1963 through 1967, the pre-Act period, and 1968 through 1972, the post-Act period. The calculation was limited to men because of the evidence above that the ADEA was primarily concerned with the conditions that men faced in the job market.[98]

A statistical measure that is useful for comparing the volatility of a variable in each of two (or more) time periods is the ratio, for each period, of the standard deviation of the variable to the mean of the variable. The measure is known as the coefficient of variation, and because coefficients of variation standardize the standard deviation of each period on the mean of the period,

94 Pub. L. No. 90–202, § 2(b), 81 Stat. 602, 602 (1967) (codified at 29 U.S.C. § 621(b) (2006)); Gen. Dynamics Land Systems, Inc. v. Cline, 540 U.S. 581, 591–93 (2004).

95 David Neumark, *The Age Discrimination in Employment Act and the Challenge of Population Aging*, 31 RES. AGING 41, 54–55 (2009) (summarizing two studies).

96 Joanna Lahey, *State Age Protection Laws and the Age Discrimination in Employment Act*, 51 J.L. & ECON. 433, 450–53 (2008).

97 *Id.* at 438–39.

98 *Supra* notes 92–93 and accompanying text.

the coefficients measure the *relative* volatility of each of the periods. For White men in each age group, the coefficients of variation were as follows for the percent changes in the civilian labor force participation rate in 1963–1967 and for the percent changes in the civilian labor force participation rate in 1968–1972:

Age group	1963–1967	1968–1972
45–54	2.05	0.68
55–64	0.99	0.63

The coefficients of variation reveal that the volatility of the speed with which change occurred in the labor force participation rate was noticeably larger in the years leading up to the ADEA than in the years immediately after its adoption and implementation. Among White men 55–64 years old, for instance, the pre-Act coefficient (0.99) exceeded the post-Act coefficient (0.63) by a factor of 1.57. The difference in volatility between the two periods is potentially important to a macrosociological framework for law, and its implications for the framework will be discussed *infra* in Part 3.

ii Birth Status

Until the last half of the twentieth century, law in Western societies generally disfavored nonmarital childbearing and disadvantaged both children born out-of-wedlock and their parents.[99] In the United States, the movement of law towards equality of treatment of nonmarital children and marital children—i.e., equality of treatment on the basis of birth status—is captured in a series of decisions, rendered on constitutional grounds, by the United States Supreme Court.[100] The shift began in 1968[101] when the Court decided two cases,[102] and in 1988 the Court unequivocally endorsed an elevated standard under the equal protection guarantee for determining whether government action is

99 Richard F. Storrow, *"The Phantom Children of the Republic": International Surrogacy and the New Illegitimacy*, 20 AM. U.J. GENDER SOC. POL'Y & L. 561, 568–87 (2012).

100 JOHN E. NOWAK & RONALD D. ROTUNDA, CONSTITUTIONAL LAW 955–72 (8th ed. 2010).

101 Melissa Murray, *What's So New About the New Illegitimacy?*, 20 AM. U.J. GENDER SOC. POL'Y & L. 387, 393 (2012).

102 Levy v. Louisiana, 391 U.S. 68 (1968); Glona v. Am. Guarantee & Liability Ins. Co., 391 U.S. 73 (1968). The decisions in *Levy* and *Glona* were announced on May 20, 1968.

constitutional when it classifies a birth on the basis of the marital status of the biological parents of the child.[103] The years 1968 and 1988, accordingly, delimit the period of the shift in U.S. law on births out-of-wedlock, and they will be used in the data analyses *infra*. Although law has not been found to exercise a large influence on childbearing,[104] the shift in U.S. constitutional law on birth status is sociologically important as a symbol.

The discipline of demography provides two measures that the instant chapter will employ to assess change in the extent of childbearing outside of marriage in the United States. One measure—the "nonmarital birth ratio"[105]—is the percentage of all live births in a given year that are to unmarried women. The other measure is the number of live births in a given year to unmarried women of all ages and is calculated per 1,000 unmarried women who are 15 to 44 years old in the middle of that year. The technical name for the second measure is the "general nonmarital fertility rate,"[106] but the measure is also known as the "nonmarital birth rate."[107] In the instant chapter, I will employ the latter label, i.e., "nonmarital birth rate," because it is less cumbersome than the alternative. The words "illegitimacy" and "legitimacy," because of their moral connotations,[108] will not be employed with reference to childbearing in spite of their continued appearance in scholarship.

Each of the two measures described above supplies useful information about the prevalence of births in- versus out-of-wedlock, and the information provided by one supplements the information provided by the other. The nonmarital birth *ratio* answers the following question: Among the births that took place in

---

103 Clark v. Jeter, 486 U.S. 456, 461, 465 (1988) (stating that the test for the constitutionality of a government classification that involves birth status is whether the classification is "substantially related to an important governmental objective," and referring to the test as "heightened scrutiny"). The decision in *Clark* was announced on June 6, 1988.

104 Anne H. Gauthier, *The Impact of Family Policies on Fertility in Industrialized Countries: A Review of the Literature*, 26 POPULATION RES. & POL'Y REV. 323, 342 (2007); Ann E. Horvath-Rose et al., *Capping Kids: The Family Cap and Nonmarital Childbearing*, 27 POPULATION RES. & POL'Y REV. 119, 134 (2008).

105 Sharon Estee, *Natality: Measures Based on Vital Statistics*, *in* THE METHODS AND MATERIALS OF DEMOGRAPHY 371, 386 (Jacob S. Siegel & David A. Swanson eds., 2d ed. 2004).

106 *Id.* at 385.

107 NAT'L CTR. FOR HEALTH STATISTICS, U.S. DEP'T OF HEALTH & HUMAN SERVICES, REPORT TO CONGRESS ON OUT-OF-WEDLOCK CHILDBEARING 6, DHHS Pub. No. (PHS) 95–1257 (1995) (on file with author), *available at* http://www.cdc.gov/nchs/data/misc/wedlock.pdf (last visited April 26, 2015) [hereinafter REPORT TO CONGRESS].

108 Erica N. Beck, Casenote, *State ex rel. Wilson v. Wilson: Determining the Proper Payor of Child Support in the Context of Dual Paternity*, 51 LOY. L. REV. 203, 208 (2005).

a particular year, how prevalent were out-of-wedlock births? The nonmarital birth *rate* answers a very different question: Among unmarried women of childbearing age in a particular year, how prevalent were births? Thus, while the nonmarital birth rate portrays the extent to which childrearing-associated problems will be experienced by unmarried women, the nonmarital birth ratio portrays the extent to which childrearing-associated problems arising for a society from all births will involve problems that are unique to out-of-wedlock births:

> The nonmarital birth ratio is useful for understanding the proportion of all children who begin life with unmarried parents, and the extent to which children born in a given year may be affected by any disadvantage—economic, social, emotional or health—associated with being born outside of marriage.[109]

Figure 1.4 presents the course of each measure over time. The top graph in the Figure shows the nonmarital birth ratio during the period from 1946 through 2003,[110] and the bottom graph shows the nonmarital birth rate among women 15–44 years old during the period from 1950 through 2007.[111] The Figure covers all calendar years after World War II for which data are available. Both the nonmarital birth ratio and the nonmarital birth rate are for White live births in the

---

109 Report to Congress, *supra* note 107, at 6.

110 The nonmarital birth ratios were obtained from Centers for Disease Control and Prevention, Nat'l Ctr. for Health Stat., Vital Statistics of the United States, 2003, vol. 17: Natality, Table 1–17. Number and Percent of Births to Unmarried Women, by Race and Hispanic Origin: United States, 1940–2003 (no date) (on file with author), http://www.cdc.gov/nchs/products/vsus/vsus_1980_2003.htm (last visited April 26, 2015). Data exist for every year from 1946 through 2003. The race designated for a birth was the race of the mother for the years 1980 to 2003 and was the race of the child for the years 1946 through 1979. As a result, the data for 1980 and later years are not completely comparable to the data for 1979 and earlier years.

111 The nonmarital birth rates were obtained from the following sources: Stephanie J. Ventura & Christine A. Bachrach, Centers for Disease Control, *Nonmarital Childbearing in the United States, 1940–99*, Nat'l Vital Statistics Rep., vol. 48, no. 16 (rev.) (2000), at 25 table 3 (data to year 1990) (on file with author); Joyce A. Martin et al., *Births: Final Data for 2007*, Nat'l Vital Statistics Rep., vol. 58, no. 24 (2010), at 47–48 table 19 (data for 1991 and later years). The nonmarital birth rate is available for 1950 and for every year starting in 1955, but it is not available for 1951, 1952, 1953, and 1954. In the data for the period that starts in 1980, the race designated for a birth was the race of the mother; in the data for the period that ends in 1979, the race designated for a birth was the race of the child. The data used for the former period, therefore, are not fully comparable to the data used for the latter period.

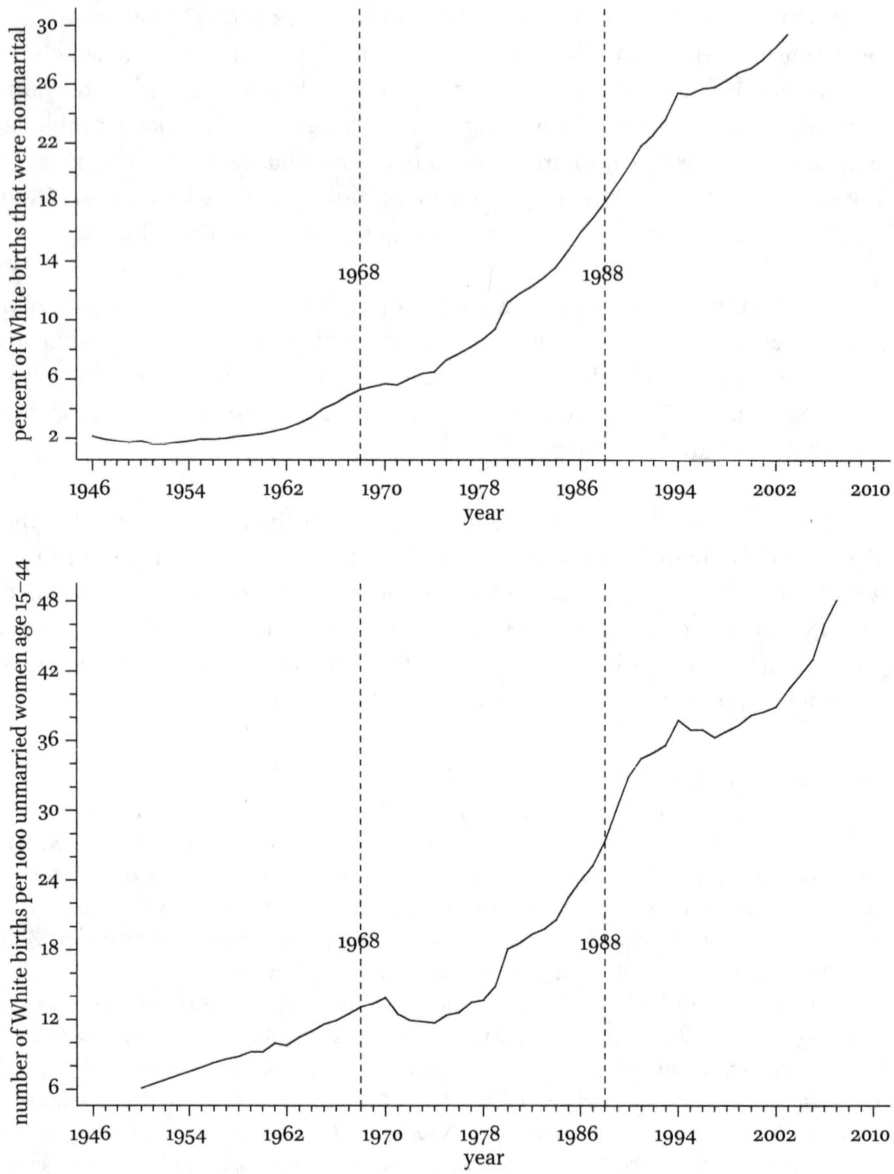

FIGURE 1.4 *Nonmarital childbearing: United States, by year*
SOURCE (TOP GRAPH): SEE FN. 110 IN THIS CHAPTER.
SOURCE (BOTTOM GRAPH): SEE FN. 111 IN THIS CHAPTER.

United States.[112] The graphs do not include data on Black births, because for Blacks the nonmarital birth ratio and the nonmarital birth rate are not reported prior to 1969. Blacks and Whites may have experienced different trends in one or both measures before 1968, the year in which constitutional law on birth status began to change, and if so, the divergence by race would distort the trend lines for both races combined. To avoid the possibility of such a distortion, Figure 1.4 is confined to White births.

As seen in the top graph, the nonmarital birth ratio increased rapidly prior to 1968. From a low of 1.6 percent in 1951 and in 1952, births outside of marriage rose to 4.9% of all White births in 1967. In 1968, when change began in doctrines of constitutional law on birth status, nonmarital births were 5.3% of all White births, and in 1987, the last full year before change in the doctrines ended, 16.9% of all White births took place out-of-wedlock. The nonmarital birth ratio thus tripled during the fifteen-year period before change occurred in the doctrines, and tripled again over the nineteen-year period from the start of the change through the final year in which the ratio could have set the stage for the last step in the change.[113] The growth in the ratio during each period seems sufficient to engender pressure to alter law on birth status. Moreover, when the mean annual growth in each of these periods is considered, the amount of the increase in the nonmarital birth ratio was somewhat larger in the earlier period than in the later period,[114] which may indicate that the initiation of change in law on birth status demanded a greater increment in pressure than did continuation of the change.

Turning to the bottom graph, we see that the direction of the nonmarital birth rate deviated for several years from the direction of the nonmarital birth ratio. Until 1970, both measures rose steadily, but while the ratio continued its generally upward course, the rate decreased from 1970 to 1974 before resuming its climb.[115] The decrease is notable for its timing—by happening after the

---

112 The criteria for classifying the race of a birth and for determining whether the birth was live are explained in CENTERS FOR DISEASE CONTROL AND PREVENTION, NAT'L CTR. FOR HEALTH STAT., TECHNICAL APPENDIX FROM VITAL STATISTICS OF THE UNITED STATES, 2003 (2005), at 7–8, 14–16 (on file with author), http://www.cdc.gov/nchs/data/TechApp03_1-09.pdf (last visited April 26, 2015).

113 Text accompanying *supra* notes 101–103.

114 During the fifteen years from 1952 through 1967, the nonmarital birth rate increased by a factor of 3.063; during the nineteen years from 1968 through 1987, it grew by a factor of 3.189. The yearly mean of the factor gain in the nonmarital birth rate, therefore, was 0.204 in the 1952–1967 period (3.063/15 = 0.204) and 0.168 in the 1968–1987 period (3.189/19 = 0.168).

115 The bottom graph shows a sizeable increment in the nonmarital birth rate for White births from 1979 to 1980. A portion of that increment may be due to the use, starting in

onset of the shift in law on bearing a child out-of-wedlock, the decrease may have undercut the ability of the nonmarital birth rate to generate pressure for the final step of the shift, viz., the explicit recognition of a higher constitutional standard for whether a government classification grounded on birth status is acceptable under the equal-protection guarantee. Logically, uninterrupted gains in the rate might be expected to precede the final step. On the other hand, after 1974 and through the last year prior to the final step, the increases in the rate are striking in magnitude. Indeed, the rate more than doubled between 1974 and 1987 (from 11.7 to 25.3 births per 1000 unmarried women of childbearing age).[116] These increases could well have contributed to the social pressure that was required for the express endorsement of the higher constitutional standard.

iii Sex

During the last half of the twentieth century, the ideal of sex-role egalitarianism was salient in the United States and was manifested in law. Yet that ideal, while prominent, was not extended to all aspects of social life. Without objection from parents or government, for instance, babies born in the United States are generally assigned sex-linked first names, and the popularity of these names remained virtually constant throughout the twentieth century.[117] Because the biological attribute of sex is immutable, it unavoidably permeates society in spite of the ideal that females and males should be equal socially, and thus certain sex-based differentiations are accepted.

In the context of education, the ideal of male–female social equality sharply limits sex-based distinctions, and the ideal has been incorporated into law in an attempt to minimize the occurrence of such distinctions in higher education. The embodiment of the ideal in law applicable to universities and colleges is evidenced by two decisions of the U.S. Supreme Court that were grounded on the equal protection guarantee of the Constitution.[118] It is also

---

1980, of the race of the mother rather than, as in earlier years, the race of the child in classifying a birth as White. Ventura & Bachrach, *supra* note 111.

116 The first year of the individual-year data on nonmarital birth rates is 1955. *Supra* note 111. Between 1955 and 1967, the rate rose from 7.9 to 12.5, i.e., by a factor of 1.582 or 0.132 annually. Between 1974 and 1987, the rate increased by a factor of 2.162 or 0.166 annually. The nonmarital birth rate thus grew by a slightly larger amount in the later period than in the earlier period.

117 Stanley Lieberson et al., *The Instability of Androgynous Names: The Symbolic Maintenance of Gender Boundaries*, 105 AM. J. SOCIOL. 1249, 1260–61, 1285 (2000).

118 Mississippi Univ. for Women v. Hogan, 458 U.S. 718 (1982); United States v. Virginia, 518 U.S. 515 (1996).

evidenced by legislation, which was enacted by Congress fully a decade before the first of these decisions, to combat discrimination against women in education programs and facilities,[119] including colleges and universities. The legislation, commonly labeled Title IX, was adopted in 1972[120] and targeted sex discrimination in inter alia "institutions of…professional education, and graduate higher education," that were beneficiaries of economic support from the federal government.[121] While Title IX is widely thought to have markedly curtailed sex discrimination in the programs it covered,[122] a rigorous quantitative social science study has not been done on whether Title IX reduced discrimination against women in academic programs. Notably, with regard to medical schools, a national pattern of discrimination did not exist against female applicants from the middle of the twentieth century onward;[123] if a pattern of sex discrimination was absent in the admissions process of medical schools well before Title IX, it could not, of course, have been eliminated by Title IX. Unfortunately, claims that Title IX has made a major contribution to female–male equality in education appear to stem from the deeply entrenched, uncritically accepted belief that law necessarily has a large, enduring effect on the social behaviors it targets. As pointed out *supra* in Part 1-b, however, credible empirical evidence for this belief is lacking for regulatory law on social patterns generally,[124] and while there seems to be no plausible evidence on the extent to which Title IX accomplished its expressed objective for academic programs,[125] Title IX is unlikely to have larger effects than law on social activities as a whole.

---

119 McCormick v. Sch. Dist., 370 F.3d 275, 286 & n.11 (2d Cir. 2004).

120 Title IX was included in the Education Amendments of 1972, Pub. L. No. 92–318, 86 Stat. 235, 373, 381 (1972).

121 20 U.S.C. § 1681(a)–(a)(1) (2006). Title IX also applied to "institutions of vocational education…and to public institutions of undergraduate higher education" that were recipients of economic assistance from the federal government. *Id.*

122 Julie A. Davies & Lisa M. Bohon, *Re-imagining Public Enforcement of Title IX*, 2000 BYU EDUC. & L.J. 25, 26 ("[b]y most accounts Title IX has been extraordinarily successful" in achieving its goal). A resolution adopted by the United States Senate in 2007 contended that "title IX has been instrumental in fostering 35 years of progress toward equality between men and women in educational institutions and the workplace." S. Res. 242, 110th Cong. (June 20, 2007), https://www.congress.gov/bill/110th-congress/senate-resolution/242/text (last visited April 26, 2015).

123 Stephen Cole, *Sex Discrimination and Admission to Medical School, 1929–1984*, 92 AM. J. SOCIOL. 549 (1986).

124 Text accompanying *supra* note 26; *supra* note 27 and accompanying text.

125 Scholarship on Title IX has been mainly concerned with athletic programs, not academic

Turning to the hypothesis of the instant chapter, I will limit my discussion to the Title IX ban on sex discrimination in "graduate higher education." Did Title IX emerge after there had been considerable movement toward male–female equality in post-baccalaureate programs in U.S. universities?[126] Data on law schools can provide some evidence pertinent to the question. Figure 1.5 is concerned with the prevalence of women among first-year students who were enrolled at law schools that had been approved by the American Bar Association during each academic year from 1947–1948 through 2009–2010. However, without data on the sex composition of the yearly pools of applicants for admission to law schools, Figure 1.5 cannot provide direct evidence on whether, and the extent to which, U.S. law schools, in admitting students, were discriminating against women before and after Title IX.[127] Figure 1.5 shows only the sex composition of applicants who were admitted and matriculated.

The top graph presents the yearly percentage of all first-year students who were women,[128] while the bottom graph presents the percent change from one academic year to the next in the percentage of first-year students who were women.[129] The vertical line in each graph is at academic year 1972–1973.[130] Title IX became law during the last half of June 1972,[131] and as a result, the sex

programs. Public interest in Title IX has also focused largely on application of the statute to athletic programs. C. Peter Goplerud III, *Title IX: Part Three Could Be The Key*, 14 MARQ. SPORTS L. REV. 123, 126–27 (2003). However, enforcement measures may not have been especially effective in bringing the athletic programs of colleges and universities into compliance with the requirements of Title IX. Sarah L. Stafford, *Progress Toward Title IX Compliance: The Effect of Formal and Informal Enforcement Mechanisms*, 85 SOC. SCI. Q. 1469, 1485 (2004) (using data on Division I universities).

126 In terms of access to U.S. medical schools, the question has an affirmative answer. *See* Cole, *supra* note 123, at 556–57 (reporting that the percentage of women among all applicants to medical schools doubled between (i) the academic years in the period 1949–1953 and (ii) academic year 1971–1972).

127 Cole, *supra* note 123, at 553–58.

128 The percentages in the top graph are from American Bar Ass'n, Sect. on Legal Education, First Year and Total J.D. Enrollment by Gender, http://www.americanbar.org/groups/legal_education/resources/statistics/statistics-archives.html (under "Longitudinal Charts," follow "First Year & Total Enrollment by Gender" hyperlink) (last visited April 26, 2015).

129 The data in the bottom graph are *percent* changes, not changes in percentage points, and were computed from the percentages used for the top graph.

130 The horizontal axis uses academic years, not calendar years, but to conserve space, its labels are the calendar years in which academic years started. Thus, 1972 on the horizontal axis represents the 1972–1973 academic year, which began in 1972.

131 Pub. L. No. 92–318, 86 Stat. 235, 381 (1972); Richard Nixon, Statement on Signing the Education Amendments of 1972, June 23, 1972, http://www.presidency.ucsb.edu/ws/index.php?pid=3473#axzz1tkcDxPnr (last visited April 26, 2015).

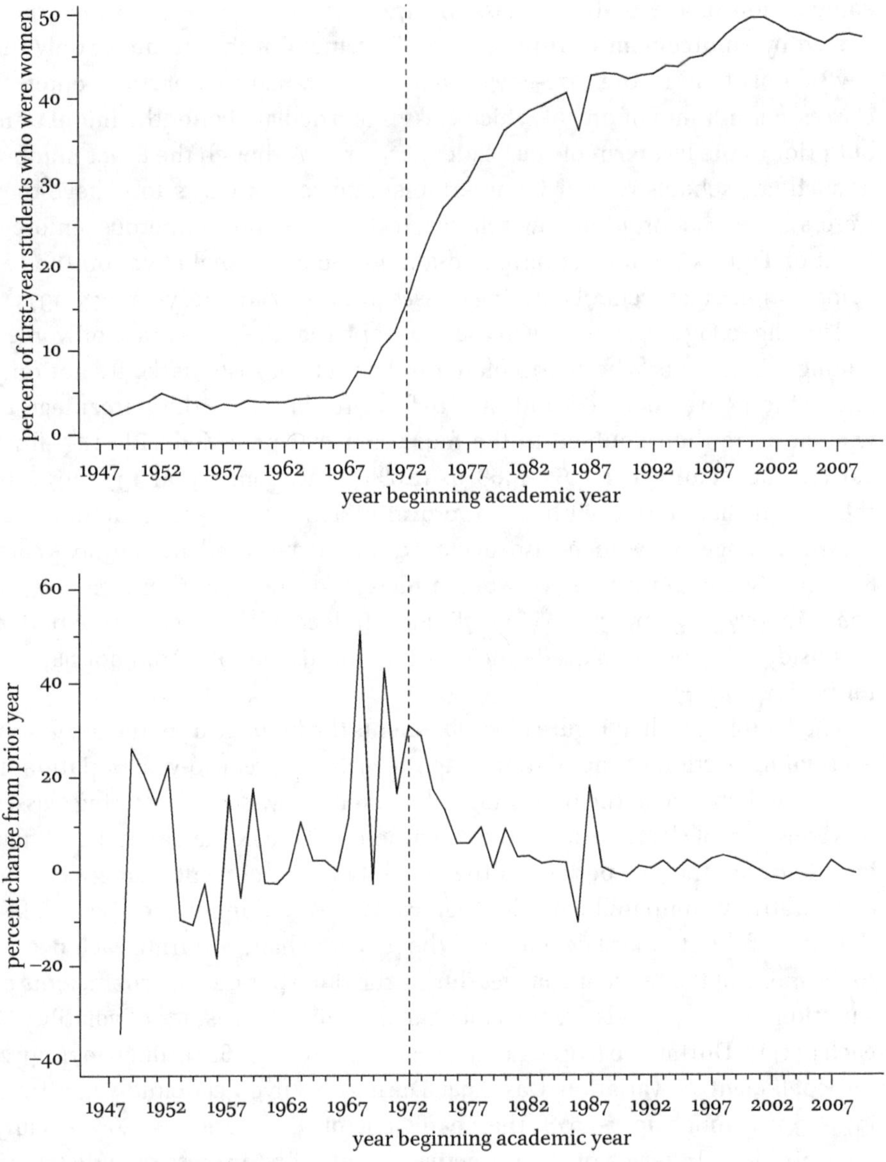

FIGURE 1.5 *Women in first-year class at U.S. law schools: A.B.A.-approved law schools, academic years 1947–48 to 2009–10*
SOURCE (TOP GRAPH): SEE FN. 128 IN THIS CHAPTER.
SOURCE (BOTTOM GRAPH): SEE FN. 129 IN THIS CHAPTER.

composition of the first-year class in 1972–1973 could have been materially altered by enforcement or threatened enforcement of the statute at only the law schools that, in the 1972–1973 academic year, had two or more entering classes, a minimum of one of which classes matriculated after the initial term but prior to the last term of the academic year.[132] Although the exact number of such law schools cannot be ascertained, no reason exists to believe they were a large fraction of all law schools. If they were not numerous, enforcement of Title IX would not have had a noticeable national effect on the sex composition of law school entering classes prior to academic year 1973–1974.

Turning to Figure 1.5, we see in the top graph that the percentage of women among all students who matriculated in law school rose markedly not only after Title IX was enacted, but also before. To illustrate, the percentage of women more than doubled in the four years that preceded Title IX—from 4.9% in academic year 1967–1968 to 12.0% in academic year 1971–1972. In the period that started with the approval of Title IX in 1972, a doubling of the percentage of women also occurred, but it required five or six years. Specifically, the percentage of women increased from 15.7% in 1972–1973 to 30.1% in 1977–1978 and 32.9% in 1978–1979. Indeed, if the post-statute period is considered to begin in academic year 1973–1974, a doubling did not happen for twelve years.[133]

The bottom graph in Figure 1.5 supplements the findings from the top graph. A visual inspection of the bottom graph reveals that year-to-year variation in the percent change in the percentage of women in law-school entering classes was considerably larger prior to the enactment of Title IX than after. The difference between the two periods in the volatility of the percent changes can be quantitatively compared with the coefficient of variation for each period, i.e., the ratio of the standard deviation of the percent changes during each period to the mean of the percent changes during the same period. The coefficients of variation for two periods are thus mean-standardized measures of volatility in each period. During the five academic years from 1967–1968 through 1971–1972, the coefficient of variation was 0.94. During the five academic years from 1973–1974 through 1977–1978, the coefficient of variation was 0.66—nearly one-third less. In terms of the attractiveness of a first-professional degree in law, the pace of social change in the United States evidently fluctuated more in

132 Anticipation of the adoption and enforcement of the statute, of course, may have had an effect on the sex composition of the 1972–1973 entering class.

133 The percentage of women in the first-year class increased from 20.2% in academic year 1973–1974 to 40.5% in academic year 1985–1986.

the five-year period leading up to the enactment of Title IX than in the five-year period that began when Title IX became applicable to law schools.[134]

What conclusions can be drawn from the graphs in Figure 1.5? Let me suggest two. First, the Figure indicates that when discrimination against a sex-identified group is thought to be practiced by post-baccalaureate schools conferring professional degrees, the advent of law designed to suppress such discrimination is preceded by intensifying pressure in society for the law. This reasoning, of course, is implicit in the hypothesis of the instant study and in the macrosociological framework outlined in the chapter, but it does not add to the framework. On the other hand, the second conclusion, if supported by further research, has the potential to extend and improve the framework. In particular, Figure 1.5 indicates that variability in the speed of change in a societal pattern is considerably greater during the period before law becomes consistent with the new or emerging pattern than during the period after the law is in place. Notably, the same finding appeared in Part 2-b-i *supra* with respect to the Age Discrimination in Employment Act.

3 Analysis

The data in Part 2 indicate that, in the United States during the era that began in the middle of the twentieth century, new doctrines of regulatory law on important social activities developed after the incidence of the activities underwent change. However, Part 2 covered only a handful of social activities and the law applicable to them, and whether the activity-to-law sequence occurs generally will not be known until substantially more empirical research has been done. In particular, future research should ascertain whether the sequence characterizes all society-important activities in the United States during the post-World War II period; whether it characterizes society-important activities in other historical eras in the United States; whether it characterizes society-important activities in structurally complex, democratically governed societies that are located outside the United States; and whether it characterizes society-important activities in jurisdictions that are dissimilar to the United States in social structure and governance. Nonetheless, Part 2 provides

134 For the percentages of women in entering law-school classes—the subject of the top graph—the coefficient of variation was 0.33 in the period from 1967–1968 to 1971–1972, and 0.15 in the period from 1973–1974 to 1977–1978. The percentages, consequently, were roughly twice as changeable before Title IX was adopted than they were after Title IX was in force.

some confidence in the conclusion that doctrines of regulatory law trail conditions in the societal system in which the doctrines exist. The findings, in short, are consistent with, although they do not conclusively prove, the hypothesis pursued in the instant chapter.

Future research on the hypothesis, however, will need to consider not only different activities, eras, and types of societies. It must also take into account that the purpose of law can vary with the type of activity sought to be regulated. Indeed, three purposes are identifiable from the law that was covered in Part 2. First, a doctrine of law can be adopted (i) to lessen or remove law-imposed penalties for an activity or (ii) to endorse an activity. The former (penalty reduction) is illustrated by the emergence of constitutional law on out-of-wedlock childbearing, which was the subject of Figure 1.4;[135] the latter (activity endorsement) is illustrated by the approval of legislation applicable to the enrollment of women in law schools, which was the subject of Figure 1.5. Second, a new doctrine of law on an activity can be an attempt to reverse a secular trend in the incidence of the activity. Examples (from Figure 1.2 and Figure 1.3, respectively) include law that enhances penalties for persons who have been repeatedly convicted of felonies and law that imposes penalties on economic-sector entities that, when making employment-related decisions, discriminate on the basis of age. Third, a new doctrine of law on an activity can be adopted to impose standards on government decisions regarding the activity. An illustration is constitutional law on capital punishment, which was the concern of Figure 1.1.

Of course, differences in the goals of law cannot be simply noted and forgotten when they are uncovered in the course of testing a macrosociological framework for law. Instead, the different goals must be incorporated into the framework, and each goal must be explained by the framework. This task will not be simple, as I hope the following discussion will make clear.

History demonstrates that many doctrines of law that are designed to minimize or eliminate a certain activity do not last, and the hypothesis of the instant chapter leads to the expectation that, ceteris paribus, some of these doctrines will be supplanted or supplemented by new ones after a substantial increase has occurred in the incidence of the activity. But under what condi-

135 Statutes permitting "no-fault" divorce arose after a secular increase had taken place in the probability of divorce. THE PLACE OF LAW, *supra* note 9, at 10–14. The statutes, which harmonized law with the trend in activity incidence, attempted to reduce, if not eliminate, law-created penalties in the then-existing marital-dissolution process. James Herbie DiFonzo, *Customized Marriage*, 75 IND. L.J. 875, 887–88 (2000); *In re* Marriage of Morrison, 573 P.2d 41, 49–50 (Cal. 1978); Lynn D. Wardle, *No-Fault Divorce and the Divorce Conundrum*, 1991 B.Y.U.L. REV. 79, 92–93.

tions will the regulatory law that arises create or augment penalties for the activity, and under what conditions will the new law lessen or eliminate current penalties? To use concrete examples, why did the state of California adopt law that harshly penalized persons who repeat felonies?[136] Why, by contrast, did the United State Supreme Court bar the application of criminal sanctions to medically qualified personnel who intentionally terminate the first-trimester pregnancies of adult women?[137] The answer to each of the preceding questions probably depends on the magnitude of the threat posed by the activity to the operation of society and, if so, requires that concepts and doctrines of law be regarded as macrosociological phenomena.

Viewed in this light, law-imposed penalties for an activity are likely to be added when the activity disrupts social life and society will benefit from a lower incidence of the activity; conversely, law-imposed penalties for an activity are likely to be removed or reduced when the activity facilitates social life and must be accommodated. Whether an activity undermines or promotes social life, in turn, will depend on the particular needs of society, and societal needs do not remain the same over time. Law, accordingly, intensified or expanded the penalties for repeated convictions of felonies after crimes of violence became more frequent, because violent crime directly damages social life.[138] In the case of law on abortion, however, the opposite happened—law permitting pregnancies to be surgically ended was substituted for law that attempted to restrict severely the surgical termination of pregnancies. Not coincidentally, the substitution occurred only after the social status of women (measured mainly by their college-attendance and -graduation rates) had risen[139] and when the risk of death faced by women from induced illegal abortions was minimal.[140] Since the incidence of abortion was not materially

136 *Supra* text accompanying notes 56, 61–63.

137 Roe v. Wade, 410 U.S. 113 (1973); Connecticut v. Menillo, 423 U.S. 9 (1975). The decision in *Roe* was announced by the Court on January 22, 1973. 410 U.S. at 113. In the United States, the abortion rate—the number of induced abortions per 1,000 women 15–44 years old—rose steadily from 1973 until 1980. Rachel K. Jones et al., *Abortion in the United States: Incidence and Access to Services, 2005*, 40 PERSP. SEXUAL & REPROD. HEALTH 6, 9 table 1 (2008). However, the emergence of law that eased the grounds for inducing an abortion did not have a large, enduring effect on the incidence of abortion. THE PLACE OF LAW, *supra* note 9, at 440–41 n. 67. Consequently, the rise in the abortion rate from 1973 to 1980 was evidently a continuation of increases in the rate that had started well before 1973, i.e., before *Roe*.

138 *Supra* text accompanying note 69.

139 Figure 2.2 and its accompanying text in *infra* Chapter 2.

140 THE PLACE OF LAW, *supra* note 9, at 16–19.

affected by law,[141] the shift in law on abortion can be explained by change in society: In the social order that existed, access to induced abortion had already become easy, and the abortion procedure had already become safe. The content of law thus caught up with societal needs and circumstances.[142]

That the goal of new law will depend on the type of activity targeted and the societal context of the activity is not the sole matter that is raised for a macrosociological framework by the data in Part 2. Other matters are also presented and must be addressed. Two such matters can be expressed as questions:

1. Why do doctrines of regulatory law on society-central activities follow movement in the incidence of the activities?
2. Why is the pace of change in the incidence of such activities more volatile before than after the development of new doctrines of regulatory law on the activities?

Question #1, of course, is critical. The hypothesis that was tested in Part 2 describes a way in which society works, but it does not explain why society operates in this way. An explanation is necessary, however, and a macrosociological framework for law will be incomplete if it does not account for the sequence in the hypothesis, i.e., the sequence from activity incidence to law content. The framework must supply a comprehensive understanding of the concepts and doctrines of law that a society uses.

The explanation I propose begins with the problem-solving responsibility that the institution of law has been assigned. At least in modern nations, law has been given the task of remedying social problems,[143] and this assign-

---

141 *Id.* at 440–41 n.67.

142 The concept of societal need as it is used in my macrosociological framework is explained in Part 3 of *infra* Chapter 2.

143 Theorists generally in the sociology of law, including those whose analyses are grounded on the sociological theory of structural-functionalism, have taken the position that law mitigates or cures social ills, although they have not ranked such an effect as the principal contribution that law makes to social life. A. Javier Treviño, The Sociology of Law: Classical and Contemporary Perspectives 440 (2008); Dragan Milovanovic, An Introduction to the Sociology of Law 10, 164–67 (3d ed. 2003). The macrosociological framework for law that I outlined in Part 1-b of the present chapter rests to a large extent on the theory of structural-functionalism. See Part 3, especially Part 3-a, of *infra* Chapter 2. However, according to the research evidence that is the basis of proposition #6 in my framework, law does not have an appreciable and sustained impact on the incidence of socially important behaviors deemed by a modern

ment implicitly recognizes that a problem must occur before law is adopted or revised to deal with the problem. However, the view that law mends problems does not, by itself, lead to an exploration of the societal character of law. Rather, the view of law-as-antidote focuses attention on just the surface of the sequence from activity incidence to law content and does not prompt an inquiry into the ties that fasten law to its society. It is, in a word, superficial.

The explanation for the activity-to-law sequence, I believe, lies in the nature of social life. In macrosociological theory, an institution of a society is a component of a system, i.e., a society, and the system can be effective and efficient only to the extent that, inter alia, it is internally cohesive.[144] To build this cohesion, an institution provides symbols that bond individuals and groups to their society; protects or improves the reputation of important entities in the society; and/or preserves or promotes trust in others in the society.[145] An institution that does not fulfill this mission, i.e., a socially unproductive institution, will fail to contribute to the operation of the society that houses it. Unless and until such an institution changes so that it fosters social cohesion, the institution will wither in prestige and influence.

Macrosociological theory thus contends that the societal utility of an institution depends on whether, and the degree to which, the institution augments social cohesiveness. Law as an institution in the United States has evidently been

---

society to be problematic. In this respect, therefore, my framework deviates from structural-functionalism and stands apart from most other theory in the sociology of law. The exception is recent systems theory. The latter contends that law is ineffective as a tool for directly changing a society but believes that law is able to do so indirectly, viz., by altering other institutions that then guide themselves. NOBLES & SCHIFF 2013, *supra* note 24, at 78, 207–09, 214–16. My framework, too, recognizes indirect effects of law. For example, the institution of law in a modern society, according to my framework, preserves and augments social cohesion, and thereby has a substantial, diffused impact on the society. However, in terms of core societal activities, my framework views law as a reactive institution. My framework also differs from recent systems theory in several other notable ways, as explained in *infra* note 24.

144 *See* BAILEY, *supra* note 23, at 44 (defining a system to include a less-than-maximum level of disorder). *See also* David Lockwood, *Social Integration and System Integration, in* EXPLORATIONS IN SOCIAL CHANGE 244, 245–46, 249 n. 6 (George K. Zollschan & Walter Hirsch eds., 1964) (suggesting that a society is a system and that social integration and system integration in a society are inextricably related).

145 THE PLACE OF LAW, *supra* note 9, at 51, 121–22, 127.

a socially productive member of society[146] through its concepts and doctrines.[147] By temporally following and keeping in line with trends in the incidence of key societal activities, the concepts and doctrines of law adjust to the needs and values of society, and thus reassure participants in the society that law endorses their social patterns and values. Even though law has no more than a negligible impact on the frequency with which a socially significant activity occurs,[148] such reassurance strengthens the ties of the participants to their society.[149]

Let me turn now to question #2. The question stems from the findings in Part 2-b-i and in Part 2-b-iii that the pace of change in the incidence of at least some societal activities is more volatile before than after the arrival of new law applicable to the activities, at least when the new law is in the form of federal legislation that is designed to curb discrimination grounded on demographic attributes. Notably, the societal patterns in Part 2-b-i and in Part 2-b-iii were, in their prevalence, moving in opposite directions at the time that Congress approved the doctrines of law on which the instant chapter focused. Specifically, the civilian labor force participation rates of older men were falling prior to the enactment of the Age Discrimination in Employment Act, while the representation of women in entering law-school classes was rising before the adoption of Title IX. Accordingly, a pre- and post-law differential in volatility in the pace of change in activity incidence does not seem to depend upon the direction of the trend in the incidence of an activity.

Why is volatility in the speed of social change elevated before, and depressed after, the advent of new law targeting discrimination? The explanation presumably lies in the nature of societal change, and in particular it may

146 A quantitative indicator of the societal helpfulness of the institution of law in the United States is the secular increase that occurred after the middle of the twentieth century in the number of first-professional (LL.B. or J.D.) degrees earned each year. During the five decades that began with the 1960s, for instance, the yearly number of first-professional degrees in law more than quadrupled. Thomas D. Snyder & Sally A. Dillow, Nat'l Ctr. for Educ. Stat., U.S. Dep't of Educ., Digest of Education Statistics, 2011, at 438 table 294 (2012), http://nces.ed.gov/pubsearch/pubsinfo.asp?pubid=2012001 (last visited April 26, 2015).

147 Doctrines of law may not be equal in the degree to which they must be socially productive. This differential may account for variation in the amount by which the incidence of an activity rises or declines before new law on the activity emerges. An activity as to which law must be more socially productive may require less movement in activity incidence before new law develops. The degree of social productivity necessary for a doctrine of law will presumably vary directly with the societal centrality of the activity covered by the doctrine.

148 Text accompanying *supra* note 26; *supra* note 27 and accompanying text.

149 *See* ARNOLD, *supra* note 20, at 34 (observing that the function of law is "not so much to guide society, as to comfort it").

involve the concept of social tension. New law on a society-central activity can logically be expected to emerge in the context of social tension, because without some minimum degree of tension,[150] a society will not be under pressure to alter its concepts and doctrines of law.[151] Once new law is adopted, the level of social tension would, of course, subside.

In this regard, a final observation is warranted. The instant chapter ascertained relative levels of volatility in the pace of social change—and indirectly ascertained relative levels of social tension—with coefficients of variation. However, if measures of social tension can help to predict the evolution of law, their variety should be expanded and their precision should be increased. Because research on law using the tools of sociology will be only as fruitful as the number and quality of the tools that are available, an array of quantitative measures to gauge social tension can improve our understanding of the societal reasons for change in concepts and doctrines of law.

Appendix A

The second line of research includes the studies listed below. Studies on the list focus primarily (rather than incidentally) on societal factors that shape the content of law and, in doing so, analyze quantitative data with a multivariate statistical procedure.

- Chapters 2, 3, 4, and 5 in the present book; chapters 6, 7, and 8 in THE PLACE OF LAW, *supra* note 9.
- Sebastian Braun & Michael Kvasnicka, *Men, Women, and the Ballot: Gender Imbalances and Suffrage Extensions in the United States*, 50 EXPLORATIONS ECON. HIST. 405 (2013).
- William J. Collins, *The Political Economy of Race, 1940–1964: The Adoption of State-Level Fair Employment Legislation* (Nat'l Bureau of Econ. Research, Historical Paper No. 128, 2000).
- Karen Smith Conway & Michael R. Butler, *State Abortion Legislation as a Public Good—Before and After Roe v. Wade*, 30 ECON. INQUIRY 609 (1992).

150 Although social tension must presumably reach a threshold before new concepts and doctrines of law arise, the threshold may be just a necessary condition for change in law.

151 A social movement that is successful—that leads to new law on the targeted societal activity—is thus likely to be one that is associated with a higher degree of volatility in the pace of societal change, and to be accompanied by a higher level of social tension, than a social movement that is unsuccessful.

- John B. Dorris, *Antidiscrimination Laws in Local Government: A Public Policy Analysis of Municipal Lesbian and Gay Public Employment Protection*, in GAYS AND LESBIANS IN THE DEMOCRATIC PROCESS 39 (Ellen D.B. Riggle & Barry L. Tadlock eds. 1999).
- David John Frank & Elizabeth H. McEneaney, *The Individualization of Society and the Liberalization of State Policies on Same-Sex Sexual Relations, 1984–1995*, 77 SOC. FORCES 911 (1999).
- Rick Geddes & Dean Lueck, *The Gains from Self-Ownership and the Expansion of Women's Rights*, 92 AM. ECON. REV. 1079 (2002).
- Yehonatan Givati & Ugo Troiano, *Law, Economics, and Culture: Theory of Mandated Benefits and Evidence from Maternity Leave Policies*, 55 J.L. & ECON. 339 (2012).
- Donald P. Haider-Markel & Kenneth J. Meier, *The Politics of Gay and Lesbian Rights: Expanding the Scope of the Conflict*, 58 J. POL. 332 (1996).
- David Jacobs & Jason T. Carmichael, *The Political Sociology of the Death Penalty: A Pooled Time-Series Analysis*, 67 AM. SOCIOL. REV. 109 (2002).
- David Jacobs & Marc Dixon, *The Politics of Labor-Management Relations: Detecting the Conditions that Affect Changes in Right-to-Work Laws*, 53 SOC. PROBS. 118 (2006).
- Brian C. Janssen & David Jacobs, Explaining the Severity of Rape Law: Stratification and Threat Theory Analysis of State Rape Laws (unpublished paper presented at meeting of the American Sociological Ass'n, Aug. 14–17, 2004) (available in EbscoHost).
- Valerie Jenness & Ryken Grattet, *The Criminalization of Hate: A Comparison of Structural and Polity Influences on the Passage of "Bias-Crime" Legislation in the United States*, 39 SOCIOL. PERSP. 129 (1996).
- Marieka Klawitter & Brian Hammer, *Spatial and Temporal Diffusion of Local Antidiscrimination Policies for Sexual Orientation*, in GAYS AND LESBIANS IN THE DEMOCRATIC PROCESS 22 (Ellen D.B. Riggle & Barry L. Tadlock eds. 1999).
- Jeongho (John) Lee & Younghoon Choi, *What Determinants Influence the Implementation of Growth Management Policy in Colorado?*, 16 INT'L REV. PUB. ADMIN. 135 (2011).
- Matthew D. Mathias, *The Sacralization of the Individual: Human Rights and the Abolition of the Death Penalty*, 118 AM. J. SOCIOL. 1246 (2013).
- Marc S. Mentzer, *A Quantitative Approach to National Culture and Employment Law*, 19 EMPLOYEE RESPONSIBILITIES & RIGHTS J. 263 (2007).
- Christopher Z. Mooney & Mei-Hsien Lee, *Legislating Morality in the American States: The Case of Pre-Roe Abortion Regulation Reform*, 39 AM. J. POL. SCI. 599 (1995).
- Sharon Kay Parsons, Abortion Policy in the Fifty States: A Comparative Analysis (1991) (unpublished Ph.D. dissertation, Florida Atlantic University).
- Vijayan K. Pillai & Guang-zhen Wang, *Social Structural Model of Women's Reproductive Rights: A Cross-National Study of Developing Countries*, 24 CANADIAN J. SOCIOL. 255 (1999).

- Christopher P. Scheitle & Bryanna B. Hahn, *From the Pews to Policy: Specifying Evangelical Protestantism's Influence on States' Sexual Orientation Policies*, 89 SOC. FORCES 913 (2011).
- Margie Skeer et al., *Town-Level Characteristics and Smoking Policy Adoption in Massachusetts: Are Local Restaurant Smoking Regulations Fostering Disparities in Health Protection?*, 94 AM. J. PUB. HEALTH 286 (2004).
- Sarah A. Soule, *Going to the Chapel? Same-Sex Marriage Bans in the United States, 1973–2000*, 51 SOC. PROBS. 453 (2004).
- Katherine Trent & Anthony W. Hoskin, *Structural Determinants of the Abortion Rate: A Cross-societal Analysis*, 46 SOC. BIOLOGY 62 (1999).
- Kenneth D. Wald et al., *The Politics of Gay Rights in American Communities: Explaining Antidiscrimination Ordinances and Policies*, 40 AM. J. POL. SCI. 1152 (1996).

Appendix B

The evidence for proposition #6 in the instant chapter is from social science studies that are summarized and cited in LARRY D. BARNETT, THE PLACE OF LAW: THE ROLE AND LIMITS OF LAW IN SOCIETY 29 n. 47, 61, 87 n. 126, 118–19, 126, 142–44 nn. 160–163 & 165, 148 n. 209, 376 n. 26, 402, 439–41 nn. 66–67 (2011). Further supporting evidence is in Part 2 of the instant chapter (see notes 41, 74, and 96 and accompanying text). Findings consistent with proposition #6 have also been reported by the following recently published studies: Bruno Federico et al., *Impact of the 2005 Smoke-Free Policy in Italy on Prevalence, Cessation and Intensity of Smoking in the Overall Population and by Educational Group*, 107 ADDICTION 1677 (2012); Richard A. Grucza et al., *Long-Term Effects of Laws Governing Youth Access to Tobacco*, 103 AM. J. PUB. HEALTH 1493, 1496–97 (2013); Sam Harper et al., *Do Medical Marijuana Laws Increase Marijuana Use? Replication Study and Extension*, 22 ANNALS EPIDEMIOLOGY 207, 211–12 (2012); Sarah D. Lynne-Landsman et al., *Effects of State Medical Marijuana Laws on Adolescent Marijuana Use*, 103 AM. J. PUB. HEALTH 1500, 1504–05 (2013); Sandra McPhedran & Gary Mauser, *Lethal Firearm-Related Violence Against Canadian Women: Did Tightening Gun Laws Have an Impact on Women's Health and Safety?*, 28 VIOLENCE & VICTIMS 875, 879–80 (2013); Reino Sirén & Jukka Savolainen, *No Evidence of Specific Deterrence under Penal Moderation: Imprisonment and Recidivism in Finland*, 14 J. SCANDINAVIAN STUD. CRIMINOLOGY & CRIME PREVENTION 80, 94–95 (2013); Victor Stango & Jonathan Zinman, *Fuzzy Math, Disclosure Regulation, and Market Outcomes: Evidence from Truth-in-Lending Reform*, 24 REV. FIN. STUD. 506, 523 tbl. 2, 527, 529–30 (2011). In addition, the manner in which the institution of law is organized in a jurisdiction—in accordance with common law or in accordance with civil law—may not materially affect the rate of economic growth in the jurisdiction. Daniel M. Klerman et al., *Legal Origin or*

Colonial History?, 3 J. LEGAL ANALYSIS 379 (2011), *available at* http://jla.oxfordjournals.org/content/3/2.toc (last visited April 26, 2015).

The findings of social science research on the federal Voting Rights Act of 1965 are also compatible with proposition #6. At the time of its enactment, the Act was principally focused on Blacks in the South. S. REP. NO. 94–295, pt. A, at 12, 13 (1975), *as reprinted in* 1975 U.S.C.C.A.N. 774, 778, 779; Laughlin McDonald, *The Quiet Revolution in Minority Voting Rights*, 42 VAND. L. REV. 1249, 1250 (1989). Notably, in states in the South, the percentage of Blacks who were registered to vote had appreciably increased prior to the Act. NAT'L RESEARCH COUNCIL, A COMMON DESTINY: BLACKS AND AMERICAN SOCIETY 233 tbl. 5–7 (Gerald David Jaynes & Robin M. Williams, Jr. eds., 1989). A study of the effect of the Act, therefore, must ascertain the degree to which post-Act movements in the percentage departed from the pre-Act trend. The best study completed to date concluded that, for a while, the Act quickened the pace of the increase in voter registration among Blacks. James E. Alt, *The Impact of the Voting Rights Act on Black and White Voter Registration in the South*, *in* QUIET REVOLUTION IN THE SOUTH: THE IMPACT OF THE VOTING RIGHTS ACT, 1965–1990, at 351 (Chandler Davidson & Bernard Grofman eds., 1994). Specifically, in counties in the South where a majority of the population was Black and the Act was enforced, the gains made by Blacks in voter registration were found to have occurred approximately ten years earlier than they would have happened without the Act and its enforcement. *Id.* at 353. However, had the Act not been adopted, the gains that it produced in voter registration among Blacks in the South would generally have taken place eventually; the Act compressed into a relatively short period the increases that would have been spread over a longer period. *Id.* at 353, 371, 458 n. 73. Moreover, according to the study, whether the Act had a permanent impact on voter registration among Blacks was uncertain; an enduring impact evidently did not occur throughout the South. *Id.* at 368–69.

Two recent studies, using data from national sample surveys of the United States population, have examined whether the minimum age set by state statutes for access to alcoholic beverages affected the consumption of such beverages once this age was reached. Robert Kaestner & Benjamin Yarnoff, *Long-Term Effects of Minimum Legal Drinking Age Laws on Adult Alcohol Use and Driving Fatalities*, 54 J.L. & Econ. 365 (2011); Andrew D. Plunk et al., *The Persistent Effects of Minimum Legal Drinking Age Laws on Drinking Patterns Later in Life*, 37 ALCOHOLISM: CLINICAL & EXPERIMENTAL RES. 463 (2013). Notably, both studies needed to determine the statutory minimum age that the survey respondents encountered when they were 18–20 years old, but the determination was likely to have been incorrect for no less than one out of seven respondents. Kaestner & Yarnoff, *supra*, at 371, 373–74; Plunk et al., *supra*, at 464, 465. Because the studies employed data that contained not-inconsiderable measurement error, some of their findings may be wrong. The first study concluded that, when the state of residence allowed consumption of alcoholic beverages at age 18–20 rather than at age 21, consumption was substantially higher among adult males, though not among adult females. Kaestner & Yarnoff, *supra*, at 385, 386. According to the data analyses, however, state-law differences in the statutory minimum age for drinking (age 18 versus age 21) did not have a uniform impact across measures of the frequency and amount of alcohol consumed by adult males. Of the four measures that were employed, two of the measures for men were unaffected by the proportion of years from age 18 through age 20 that the respondents lived in states where alcoholic beverages could be lawfully consumed at that age, the independent variable that the investigators considered "key." Kaestner & Yarnoff, *supra*, at 370, 371, 376 tbl. 1 (results for "full sample"), 379 tbl. 3 (results for "full sample"). While the study reported that on the other two measures this variable was associated with elevated alcohol consumption by adult males, Kaestner & Yarnoff, *supra*, at 377 tbl. 2 (results for "full sample"), 380 tbl. 4 (results for "full sample"), no theory seems able to account for the inconsistency in results between the four measures. Therefore, the findings of greater alcohol use by men on the two measures, if not due to measurement error, may represent random responses on the part of adult males to minimum-age alcohol-access statutes. Each of the foregoing possibilities—error and chance—is enhanced by findings in the second study. According to the latter, minimum-age alcohol-access statutes had no impact on multiple aspects of alcohol consumption among adult females or on most aspects of alcohol consumption among adult males. Plunk et al., *supra*, at 466–67. For adult males, state statutes that permitted alcohol access prior to age 21 were reported to have had a material effect on the incidence of immoderate ("binge") drinking and the incidence of moderate drinking, but the effects were in opposite directions—the statutes increased the odds of high-frequency immoderate drinking, but they decreased the odds of both low- and high-frequency moderate drinking. Plunk et al., *supra*, at 467 tbl. 3, tbl. 4. Because such a difference in the direction of effects is implausible as well as inexplicable, the effects found for men may be statistical artifacts.

A prominent deficiency in the above studies of minimum-age alcohol-access state statutes is the absence of a measure of social views and concerns relevant to the consumption of alcoholic beverages, especially consumption by persons not yet 21 years old. Consequently, neither of the studies was able to ascertain whether states were dissimilar in their social sentiments regarding such consumption and whether these dissimilarities led to both (i) differences in the minimum age set by the states for alcohol access and (ii) differences in the extent and amount of use of alcoholic beverages after that age. If state variation in social sentiments is the direct antecedent of (i) as well as of (ii), the level of consumption of alcoholic beverages in a state is attributable to the social persuasions that bear on such consumption, and the law-designated lowest age for access to alcoholic beverages is a correlate, not a cause, of the degree to which alcoholic beverages are consumed. Both studies thus needed to include data for each state on dominant social sentiments pertinent to drinking and ascertain the effect of the sentiments on drinking behavior as well as on the minimum age that law allowed for alcohol access.

Research has not found that the incidence of employment discrimination against Blacks in the United States was widely and unequivocally reduced by federal legislation that prohibited such discrimination. Studies of this impact are reviewed in Part 2-c of *infra* Chapter 7.

Proposition #6, despite the evidence supporting it, is subject to three qualifications. First, proposition #6, which describes the effect of law in nations that have a complex structure and democratic government, may not be descriptive of the effect of law in nations that lack such a structure and government. Thus, in nations that are developing economically and technologically, regulation by law may have a material, enduring impact on the incidence of many society-central behaviors. *E.g.*, Minzee Kim et al., *When Do Laws Matter? National Minimum-Age-of-Marriage Laws, Child Rights, and Adolescent Fertility, 1989–2007*, 47 LAW & SOC'Y REV. 589 (2013). A second qualification, and a corollary of the first, involves history: Proposition #6 may not apply to a particular nation in one era but may apply to that nation in another era, because the nation has undergone a change in its type of social structure and type of government. LARRY D. BARNETT, THE PLACE OF LAW: THE ROLE AND LIMITS OF LAW IN SOCIETY 467–68 (2011). The third qualification deals with law that leads to the availability of resources allowing or facilitating the achievement of socially favored goals (e.g., childbearing and physical health) in nations that are structurally complex and democratically governed. Such law may have a substantial, lasting effect on the incidence of behaviors relevant to the goals. Angela Luci-Greulich & Olivier Thévenon, *The Impact of Family Policies on Fertility Trends in Developed Countries*, 29 EUR. J. POPULATION 387 (2013); Kenneth E. Warner et al., *Impact of Tobacco Control on Adult per Capita Cigarette Consumption in the United States*, 104 AM. J. PUB. HEALTH 83 (2014); LARRY D. BARNETT, LEGAL CONSTRUCT, SOCIAL CONCEPT: A MACROSOCIOLOGICAL PERSPECTIVE ON LAW 165 (1993).

SECTION A

United States

CHAPTER 2

Law on Abortion

Abstract

Sixteen of the forty-eight states in the continental United States liberalized their law on therapeutic abortion during the period from 1967 to 1972, i.e., before the U.S. Supreme Court ruling in Roe v. Wade. As a test of the macrosociological framework that was proposed in Chapter 1, state-level data were obtained from Census Bureau reports on the 1960 decennial census and analyzed with logistic regression. The odds that, prior to *Roe*, a state in the coterminous United States removed from its law provisions thought to hinder access to abortion rose with the prevalence of women who had completed four or more years of college and, to a lesser degree, with the rate at which women participated in the labor force. The odds, however, fell with greater cultural heterogeneity. In addition, the odds were affected by culture as measured by geographic region: Relative to states in the Northeast, states in the North Central region had lower odds, and states in the West had higher odds, of easing their law on access to therapeutic abortion. Urbanization and the income of women in a state had no bearing on the odds. Based on these findings, the liberalization of U.S. law on abortion during the late 1960s and early 1970s is hypothesized to have resulted mainly from the long-term growth of knowledge and the influence of that growth on the role of women in society.

1 Introduction

Therapeutic abortion—medical intervention to end a pregnancy that is believed to endanger the physical and/or psychological health of the pregnant woman—is an emotionally charged topic in the United States and is likely to remain so for the foreseeable future. As a justice of the U.S. Supreme Court observed at the start of the twenty-first century, "[t]he issue of abortion is one of the most contentious and controversial in contemporary American society,"[1] and historians who are interested in social issues that became prominent

1 Stenberg v. Carhart, 530 U.S. 914, 947 (2000) (O'Connor, J., concurring). Since the mid-1970s, between four and five of every ten adults in the United States have had polar views on abortion, i.e., have believed that abortion should be "legal under any circumstances" or have

 | DOI 10.1163/9789004281219_003

in the United States during the twentieth century will inescapably be attracted by abortion and the shift that occurred during the 1960s and 1970s in the grounds permitted by law for a medically induced termination of a pregnancy. This shift was substantial, took place in a remarkably short period of time, and has involved significant political agitation. As a result, the transformation of U.S. law on therapeutic abortion is important to the macrosociological framework that was described in Chapter 1. Was this transformation due to change in society-level properties and forces? If the proposed framework is correct, the answer is affirmative, but the link between societal conditions and law must be established empirically. It cannot be left to conjecture.

The most conspicuous break in U.S. law on abortion took place in January 1973 when the Supreme Court of the United States announced its decision in Roe v. Wade and ruled that government does not have unlimited authority under the federal Constitution to select the conditions under which adult women can lawfully terminate pregnancies prior to fetus viability.[2] Under the rationale of *Roe*, which the Court views as "a watershed decision,"[3] law and government policy cannot construct grounds for a therapeutic abortion that are major impediments for adult women who want to terminate pregnancies. *Roe*, however, did not initiate major reform in abortion law in the United States—a point that is frequently overlooked. On the contrary, *Roe* was decided only after numerous states had relaxed their law-permitted reasons for a physician-induced abortion. The shift in state law occurred during the six-year period that preceded *Roe*, i.e., from 1967 through 1972, and during this time, fully one third of the states in the continental United States acted. The states that liberalized their law on abortion before 1973 were Arkansas, California, Colorado, Delaware, Florida, Georgia, Kansas, Maryland, New Mexico, New York, North Carolina, Oregon, South Carolina, Vermont, Virginia, and Washington.[4] As altered, the law of the foregoing states did not necessarily

believed that abortion should be "illegal in all circumstances." In almost every year, the former belief has been more common than the latter. Gallup, Inc., Abortion, http://www.gallup.com/poll/1576/Abortion.aspx (last visited April 28, 2015).

2 Roe v. Wade, 410 U.S. 113 (1973). Under *Roe*, government can prohibit abortion of a pregnancy only after the fetus is viable, i.e., "has the capability of meaningful life outside the mother's womb," but even at this stage of a pregnancy, an abortion must be allowed when it "is necessary, in appropriate medical judgment, for the preservation of the life or health of the mother." *Id.* at 163, 164–65.

3 Planned Parenthood of Southeastern Pennsylvania v. Casey, 505 U.S. 833, 867 (1992).

4 Additional information on the change in law that occurred in these states is available in LARRY D. BARNETT, THE PLACE OF LAW: THE ROLE AND LIMITS OF LAW IN SOCIETY 325 n.91 (2011) (© 2011 by Transaction Publishers) [hereinafter THE PLACE OF LAW].

permit therapeutic abortion as readily as *Roe*, but the change that occurred in state law on abortion during 1967–1972 is nonetheless notable for its break with the past and for its prevalence. An indicator of this prevalence is that approximately two-fifths of the U.S. population in 1972 resided in the sixteen states that had liberalized their law on abortion by the end of that year.[5] *Roe*, in short, had forerunners at the state level and was part of a change in law that was already underway.

a Societal Causes of the Demand for Therapeutic Abortion

The likelihood that pregnancies will be aborted in a society can be traced to (i) the economic, psychological, and social costs that childrearing imposes on women[6] and (ii) the nature of the role of women.[7] A medically induced abortion of a pregnancy can be anticipated as childrearing becomes more costly to women and fits less comfortably within their accepted societal role. Three variables in particular have been thought to affect the extent to which women incur costs from childrearing and the degree to which childrearing is incompatible with the female role. The variables are labor force participation by women, formal schooling and educational attainment among women, and the marital status of women. If these variables are related to the probability that pregnancies will be aborted, the course of each variable over time can indicate, ceteris paribus, a strengthening or weakening of a societal need for law that explicitly authorizes, or that at least implicitly tolerates, therapeutic abortion. The three variables, therefore, are potentially helpful in a sociological analysis of law on abortion.

Quantitative social science research conducted to date is insufficient to permit unequivocal conclusions regarding the attributes of women that predict whether pregnancies will be aborted in the United States. According to the evidence that is presently available, however, the marital status and schooling of women are important predictive variables, but the employment of women may not be.[8] In terms of the first two variables, the likelihood of abortion has been found to increase with the formal schooling of women and to be higher

5 Computed from U.S. BUREAU OF THE CENSUS, STATISTICAL ABSTRACT OF THE UNITED STATES: 1974, at 12 tbl. 11 (95th ed. 1974), *available at* http://www.census.gov/prod/www/statistical_abstract.html (last visited April 28, 2015).

6 Lawrence B. Finer et al., *Reasons U.S. Women Have Abortions: Quantitative and Qualitative Perspectives*, 37 PERSP. ON SEXUAL AND REPROD. HEALTH 110, 117 (2005).

7 For a discussion of the costs of children in the context of the role and fertility of women, see Steven L. Nock, *The Symbolic Meaning of Childbearing*, 8 J. FAM. ISSUES 373 (1987).

8 THE PLACE OF LAW, *supra* note 4, at 272–79.

among women who are unmarried than among women who are married.[9] In terms of the third variable, a relationship between female employment and the probability that a pregnancy will be aborted has not been empirically proven to exist, but such a relationship has not been disproven either. Hence, female employment should not be excluded when considering jurisdiction-level variables that may shape law on physician-induced abortion, especially since an impact of female employment on the societal demand for abortion is plausible.[10] Furthermore, the evidence regarding whether female employment is related to abortion likelihood has been derived from data on individual women.[11] State rates of female employment may have a major impact on state frequencies of therapeutic abortion and on state law pertinent to therapeutic abortion even though employment among individual women does not clearly affect the probability that women will opt to abort their pregnancies. A relationship between particular variables measured at the level of jurisdictions, in short, may not match the relationship between the same variables for the individuals in the jurisdictions.[12]

b *Measures of a Societal Need for Therapeutic Abortion*

Let me now examine the course of the three variables in the United States during the twentieth century. I focus on the period after World War II, because before that point, consecutive-year measures of the variables do not exist. The data that I present are confined to the United States and to women in age ranges in which abortion is most common.[13] Figure 2.1 presents the data for each variable from the last half of the 1940s until 1990. In particular, the figure shows the percentage of women in the age range twenty to twenty-four who

---

9 *Id.* at 278.

10 *Supra* notes 6 & 7 and their accompanying text.

11 THE PLACE OF LAW, *supra* note 4, at 278–79.

12 W.S. Robinson, *Ecological Correlations and the Behavior of Individuals*, 15 AM. SOCIOL. REV. 351 (1950).

13 Among females age eighteen and over in the United States from 1976 to 1979, females who were younger than age twenty-five are estimated to have had the highest abortion rate, i.e., the largest number of abortions per 1000 females of the same age, and to have accounted for slightly more than half of all abortions. STANLEY K. HENSHAW & JENNIFER VAN VORT, ABORTION FACTBOOK: READINGS, TRENDS, AND STATE AND LOCAL DATA TO 1988, at 172 tbl. 1 (1992). For years prior to 1976, abortion rates and distributions of abortions by the age of women having abortions have not been estimated for women who were eighteen or nineteen years old, but if such estimates were available for years prior to 1973, they would presumably be comparable to the estimates for 1976–1979.

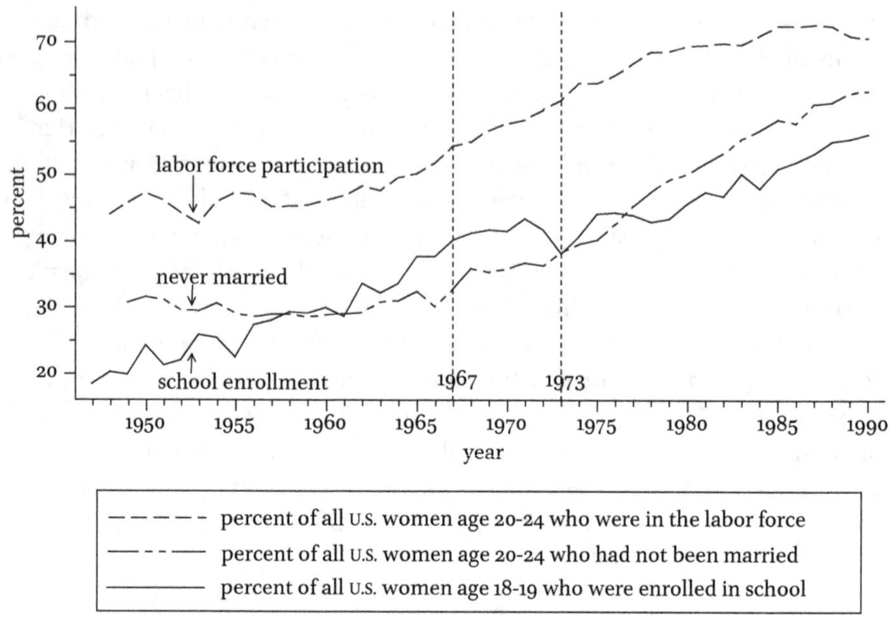

FIGURE 2.1 *Measures of social change among women: United States*
SOURCE: SEE FN. 15 IN THIS CHAPTER.

participated in the labor force[14] and the percentage of women who had not married by age twenty to twenty-four. The figure also shows the incidence of school enrollment among women who were eighteen or nineteen years old.[15]

14 Women as well as men are considered to be in the labor force (i) when they are currently working as well as (ii) when they are not currently working but are available for, and within the last four weeks have sought, a job. HANDBOOK OF U.S. LABOR STATISTICS 4, 5 (Eva E. Jacobs ed., 8th ed. 2005). Given their commitment to finding employment, women in the labor force who are presently unemployed can be expected to deal with unwanted pregnancies in a manner not unlike women who are employed.

15 Figure 2.1 was constructed with data from the following sources:

- Labor force participation: U.S. Bureau of Labor Statistics, Current Population Survey, http://data.bls.gov/pdq/querytool.jsp?survey=ln (last visited April 28, 2015). Figure 2.1 uses seasonally adjusted rates of labor force participation among civilian women during the fourth quarter of each covered year.
- Marital status: Except for 1990, age-specific data on the marital status of the population are from U.S. BUREAU OF THE CENSUS, STATISTICAL ABSTRACT OF THE UNITED STATES (71st ed. through the 111th ed.), *available at* http://www.census.gov/prod/www/statistical_abstract.html (last visited April 28, 2015). For 1990, the data on marital status are from U.S. BUREAU OF THE CENSUS, MARITAL STATUS AND LIVING ARRANGEMENTS: MARCH 1990, CURRENT POPULATION REPORTS, Series P-20, No. 450 (May 1991), at Table 1.

In examining Figure 2.1, readers should keep in mind that the data in it are illustrative; they do not exhaust all of the data that are pertinent.[16]

To mark the years when law on therapeutic abortion in the United States underwent its main shift, Figure 2.1 has a vertical line for 1967 (when revisions of state law on abortion began) and a vertical line for 1973 (when the U.S. Supreme Court decided Roe v. Wade). These reference lines are intended to aid the reader in ascertaining whether a particular variable is a plausible causal agent in the shift. A variable can be such an agent *only* if it increased prior to 1967. Otherwise stated, the level and/or extent of a variable must have become greater *before* the shift occurred in abortion law in order for the variable to have produced and/or intensified a societal need for lawful therapeutic abortion.

Figure 2.1 reveals distinct patterns. Both the rate of labor force participation and the rate of school enrollment among women underwent secular increases before the period (1967–1972) when many states altered their law on therapeutic abortion. Accordingly, the pre-1967 movement of each rate is consistent with the possibility that it fostered a societal need for law that accepted therapeutic abortion. Indeed, the rates were moving precisely as they ought to have moved if female involvement in the labor force and in schooling were promoting a society-level need for a change in and a liberalization of law on abortion. On the other hand, the share of twenty to twenty-four year-old women who had never been married remained in essence stationary before 1967, and

- School enrollment: Age-specific rates of school enrollment are in U.S. Census Bureau, Table A-2: Percentage of the Population 3 Years Old and Over Enrolled in School, by Age, Sex, Race, and Hispanic Origin: October 1947 to 2011, http://www.census.gov/hhes/school/data/cps/historical/index.html (last visited April 28, 2015). The rates are for women in the civilian non-institutionalized population and are based on data from the Current Population Survey. The Survey covers "any type of public, parochial, or other private school in the regular school system. Such schools include nursery schools, kindergartens, elementary schools, high schools, colleges, universities, and professional schools. Attendance may be on either a full-time, or part-time basis and during the day or night. Regular schooling is that which may advance a person toward an elementary or high school diploma, a college, university, or professional school degree." U.S. Bureau of the Census, Current Population Survey Data on School Enrollment, http://www.census.gov/hhes/school/data/cps/index.html (last visited April 28, 2015).

16 Additional data on labor force participation, marital status, and school enrollment among women of childbearing age during this period are in THE PLACE OF LAW, *supra* note 4, at 280–83. The data in Figure 2.1 continue until 1990 in order to furnish a long-term perspective on trends.

although the share expanded generally after 1967, its failure to do so in a clear manner until the shift in abortion law had started undermines the hypothesis that the variable was responsible for, or was a contributor to, the shift. While currently unmarried women are more likely than currently married women to abort a pregnancy,[17] resistance on the part of women to entering marriage had not been spreading in the United States before the shift began and thus could not have been an important determinant of the shift.

2 A Study of the Effect of State-Level Variables on State Abortion Law

Why was law in the United States altered between 1967 and 1973 to remove restrictions that were viewed as barring or severely hindering access to therapeutic abortion? If law is a macrosociological phenomenon, the properties of society generate the concepts and doctrines that dominate law on society-important activities at any particular point in history, and change in these properties leads to the replacement of existing concepts and doctrines of law in a democracy. With regard to the 1967–1973 transformation of U.S. law on the availability to adult women of physician-induced abortion, influential societal properties may be those that altered the role of women and the burdens that childrearing imposed on women. Because prevalence and length of schooling, extent of labor force participation, and distribution of marital status among women are in principle capable of bringing about these alterations, the course of each of these variables over time was examined in Figure 2.1. Relative stability prior to 1967 in the share of never-married women among all young women eliminated marital status as a possible explanation of the transformation of

17 THE PLACE OF LAW, *supra* note 4, at 278. During the period 1973 to 1979, the yearly number of abortions per 1000 unmarried women of childbearing age exceeded the yearly number of abortions per 1000 married women of childbearing age by a ratio that ranged from 3.5 to 4.2. Calculated from the estimates of abortion rates in HENSHAW & VAN VORT, *supra* note 13, at 176. During the same period, 71% to 79% of all abortions in a year were estimated to have been performed on unmarried women. *Id.* Because the percentage did not fluctuate markedly during the years that immediately followed the U.S. Supreme Court ruling in Roe v. Wade, unmarried women before *Roe* are likely to have accounted for a similar percentage, i.e., for about three out of four abortions. Women were classified by Henshaw and Van Vort as "unmarried" if they had never been married or if they were currently single due to divorce or the death of their spouse. Married women who were separated from their spouse were also classified as "unmarried." *Id.* at 177.

U.S. law on abortion.[18] However, the remaining two variables bearing on sex roles and childrearing burdens—viz., educational attainment and labor force participation—were found to hold promise as explanatory factors.[19] The study reported below employs quantitative data on the two variables as well as others, and analyzes the data with a multivariate statistical test, in an attempt to identify societal factors that were responsible for the changes that states made in their law on abortion during the late 1960s and early 1970s.

a *Design of the Study*

The study that I report below involved applying the statistical technique of regression to state-level data on a set of "independent" variables, i.e., factors that theory suggests as potential causes of the phenomenon being investigated. This phenomenon—i.e., the dependent variable—in the instant study was whether states eased their law-imposed restrictions on abortion in the years 1967 to 1972. Each state was assigned the number 0 or the number 1. The number 0 was assigned to states that did *not* liberalize their law on therapeutic abortion during 1967–1972; the number 1 was assigned to states that *did* liberalize their law on therapeutic abortion during 1967–1972.[20] Because the dependent variable was measured as a dummy, i.e., in binary form with the digits 0 and 1, the data were analyzed with maximum-likelihood logistic regression, not least-squares regression.[21] The mnemonic label for the dependent variable was ABORTLAW.

In an attempt to account for differences between states on the dependent variable, six independent variables were included in the regression model. Three of the six independent variables—cultural heterogeneity, culture, and urbanization—had empirical indicators that were not sex-specific. The remaining independent variables—education, income, and labor force participation—were measured among just women. All of the six were considered to be explanatory variables, i.e., possible explanations of state differences on the dependent

18 A further reason for not including marital status as an independent variable in the instant study is that marital status may often have been recorded incorrectly in the census that provided the data for the study. THE PLACE OF LAW, *supra* note 4, at 295–96.

19 These conclusions are supported by additional data on the course over time of the three variables. See *id.* at 280–83.

20 The following states were coded 1 on ABORTLAW: Arkansas, California, Colorado, Delaware, Florida, Georgia, Kansas, Maryland, New Mexico, New York, North Carolina, Oregon, South Carolina, Vermont, Virginia, and Washington. The coding is based on information in the sources cited in *id.* at 325 n.91.

21 FRED C. PAMPEL, LOGISTIC REGRESSION: A PRIMER 1–10 (Paper No. 132, Sage University Paper Series on Quantitative Applications in the Social Sciences, 2000).

variable; none of the six was introduced as a control variable.[22] The data for all of the independent variables are from the census of the U.S. population conducted in 1960 and were determined as of the enumeration date for that census, viz., April 1, 1960.[23] The age ranges that I used for state populations were necessarily selected from the age ranges for which the census reported data. All of the forty-eight states in the continental United States were included in the study.[24]

I discuss the independent variables in alphabetical order and thus begin with the two culture-pertinent variables. Given the nature of these variables, the concept of culture requires a brief explanation. To social scientists, what is culture? Perhaps not surprisingly, definitions vary. However, culture can be discerned in the contact that human beings have with social and physical environments. In dealing with their environments, the members of a human group perceive the environments, but the perceptions, and the responses that ensue

---

22 The regression model in the instant study differs from previous regression models that I have used to explain, with jurisdiction-level factors, the modification by the sixteen states of their law on abortion before Roe v. Wade was decided by the U.S. Supreme Court. The present model includes, inter alia, the independent variables of cultural heterogeneity, culture, and urbanization; these three variables were not in the earlier models. The present model, furthermore, lacks an independent variable for marital status, which the prior models contained. THE PLACE OF LAW, *supra* note 4, at 284–86, 290; Larry D. Barnett, *The Roots of Law*, 15 AM. U.J. GENDER, SOC. POL'Y & L. 613, 654, 656–57, 660 (2007) [hereinafter *The Roots of Law*]. Marital status was not an independent variable in the model used in the present study for the reason given in the last paragraph of *supra* Part 1-b. See also *supra* note 18.

23 U.S. BUREAU OF THE CENSUS, U.S. DEP'T OF COMMERCE, CENSUS OF POPULATION: 1960. VOL. I, CHARACTERISTICS OF THE POPULATION, at xiii (1963), *available at* http://www.census.gov/prod/www/decennial.html [hereinafter CHARACTERISTICS OF THE POPULATION: 1960] (last visited April 28, 2015).

24 Alaska and Hawaii were omitted from the data because, being geographically outside the continental United States, their law may be influenced by macro-level forces that are not present in, and do not affect law in, the coterminous United States. To the extent that the law-molding forces at work in Alaska and Hawaii are dissimilar to those in other states, the inclusion of Alaska and Hawaii could have affected the findings of the instant study. In addition, Alaska as well as Hawaii had achieved statehood in 1959, i.e., just one year prior to the 1960 census. Proclamation No. 3269, 24 Fed. Reg. 81 (1959) (Alaska); Proclamation No. 3309, 24 Fed. Reg. 6868 (1959) (Hawaii). The effect of non-state status until 1959 on the characteristics of the population of Alaska and Hawaii in 1960 is unknown. Alaska and Hawaii were also excluded from my prior studies of factors that might account for the 1967–1972 change in state law on abortion. THE PLACE OF LAW, *supra* note 4, at 284–98, 330 n.134; *The Roots of Law, supra* note 22, at 651–66 & 652 n.130.

from the perceptions, are not determined solely by the inherent attributes of the environments. Rather, perceptions of an environment are partially a function of a set of premises that the group possesses regarding that environment. These premises comprise the culture of the group, and being deeply embedded in the group, they frequently if not usually operate at a subconscious level. In essence, the premises work in the background, and through their continuous and mechanical application by the members of the group, they help to organize the worlds of the group and shape the reality of its members.[25]

Because culture influences the comprehension and characterization of a phenomenon, it necessarily influences social life. The nature of social life, in turn, is logically a factor not only in whether law is formulated for an activity but in the content of any law that is formulated. Investigators, accordingly, should not ignore culture when searching for possible determinants of the prescriptions and proscriptions of law. Although it is a subtle force shaping the views and actions of the members of a society, culture is likely to have a powerful influence on a society and its components, including its institution of law.[26] Recognizing this, the present study had two culture-related independent variables in the regression model for the 1967–1972 shift in state law on abortion.

The heterogeneity of culture within states was one of the two independent variables that sought to capture an aspect of culture. The indicator of cultural heterogeneity was the percentage of the population of each state in 1960 that had been born in a country other than the United States.[27] The variable was given the mnemonic label FOREIGNPOP. Ceteris paribus, substantial cultural heterogeneity would seem to be a source of ferment in a society and hence a contributor to change in the content of law in the society. In the instant research, therefore, greater cultural diversity in a state was expected to raise the odds that during 1967–1972 the state relaxed its law-allowed grounds for a therapeutic abortion.

In addition to within-state cultural heterogeneity, the regression model ascertained whether between-state cultural differences were related to the pre-1973 revision by states of their law on abortion. The culture of a state was measured by the geographic region of the United States in which the state was

---

25 Richard Handler, *Afterword: Mysteries of Culture*, 106 AM. ANTHROPOLOGIST (New Series) 488, 489 (2004).

26 THE PLACE OF LAW, *supra* note 4, at 218–19, 243 n.133.

27 Campbell Gibson & Kay Jung, U.S. Census Bureau, *Historical Census Statistics on the Foreign-Born Population of the United States: 1850–2000*, at Table 14 (Working Paper 81, 2006) (on file with author), http://www.census.gov/population/www/documentation/twps0081/twps0081.html (last visited April 28, 2015).

located. Region is a variable in which American sociology has long been interested,[28] and regional differences in culture are embedded in, and a continuing feature of, the United States.[29] The instant study followed the four-region classification scheme that was used by the U.S. Census Bureau in 1960[30]—North Central, Northeast, South, or West[31]—and every state in the coterminous United States was coded with a dummy variable for its region. The dummy variables for North Central, Northeast, South, and West were given the mnemonic labels NOCENTRAL, NOEAST, SOUTH, and WEST, respectively. In the data analysis, the reference region was the Northeast, and its dummy variable was accordingly omitted in estimating the regression coefficients and odds ratios for the independent variables.[32]

The next independent variable is education. I operationalized the variable using women who were in the age range twenty-five to twenty-nine in 1960. Education was measured with the percentage in each state of all women in this

---

28 Alvin L. Bertrand, *Regional Sociology as a Special Discipline*, 31 SOC. FORCES 132 (1952); Samuel E. Wallace, *Regional Sociology: The South*, 1 SOCIOL. SPECTRUM 429 (1981).

29 Joel Lieske, *Regional Subcultures of the United States*, 55 J. POL. 888, 907 Figure 2 (1993); Joel Lieske, The Changing Regional Subcultures of the American States and the Utility of a New Cultural Measure 10, 58 Figure 2 (original version, in pdf, of an article by the same title in 63 POL. RES. Q. 538 (2010)) (no date) (on file with author) [hereinafter Lieske (original version)]; J. Scott Carter & Casey A. Borch, *Assessing the Effects of Urbanism and Regionalism on Gender-Role Attitudes, 1974–1998*, 75 SOCIOL. INQUIRY 548, 554–55, 558 (2005). Regional differences in culture underwent little change between 1980 and 2000. Lieske (original version), *supra*, at 15, 17; Carter & Borch, *supra* at 558. Furthermore, residents of the United States today are cognizant of the region in which they reside. Wendy Griswold & Nathan Wright, *Cowbirds, Locals, and the Dynamic Endurance of Regionalism*, 109 AM. J. SOCIOL. 1411 (2004).

30 U.S. BUREAU OF THE CENSUS, STATISTICAL ABSTRACT OF THE UNITED STATES: 1960, at xii (81st ed. 1960).

31 The states in each region were:

North Central:	Illinois, Indiana, Iowa, Kansas, Michigan, Minnesota, Missouri, Ohio, Nebraska, North Dakota, South Dakota, Wisconsin.
Northeast:	Connecticut, Maine, Massachusetts, New Hampshire, New Jersey, New York, Pennsylvania, Rhode Island, Vermont.
South:	Alabama, Arkansas, Delaware, Florida, Georgia, Kentucky, Louisiana, Maryland, Mississippi, North Carolina, Oklahoma, South Carolina, Tennessee, Texas, Virginia, West Virginia.
West:	Arizona, California, Colorado, Idaho, Montana, Nevada, New Mexico, Oregon, Utah, Washington, Wyoming.

32 MELISSA A. HARDY, REGRESSION WITH DUMMY VARIABLES 7–12, 26–28 (Paper No. 93, Sage University Paper Series on Quantitative Applications in the Social Sciences, 1993).

age range who had completed at least four years of college as of 1960.[33] The variable was thus given the mnemonic label COLL2529. Readers should note that the indicator of the variable was the number of years of college that had been finished rather than possession of a degree.[34] The age range twenty-five to twenty-nine was used rather than the age range twenty to twenty-four, because in 1960, current college enrollment was less common among women twenty-five to twenty-nine years old than among women twenty to twenty-four years old.[35] Consequently, the majority of women who eventually completed four years of college at this time did so before they were twenty-five to twenty-nine years old. Very few finished a fourth year of college after that.[36]

The regression equation included the income of women as an independent variable, because as women receive more income, they presumably have added resources to end unwanted pregnancies as well as a stronger motivation to do so. The motivation to abort a pregnancy can be expected to intensify as income rises among women, because childrearing consumes income and will interfere with other pursuits that a higher income makes possible.[37] A societal system, to avoid long-lasting harm to itself, must acknowledge an important problem that is widespread among its members and make allowance for the solution(s) they seek to the problem. As a result, gains in the income of women will facilitate

33 The data for COLL2529 were derived from Tables 37 and 103 in the state reports for the 1960 census. CHARACTERISTICS OF THE POPULATION: 1960, *supra* note 23.

34 Age-specific data on the percentage of women who hold college degrees are not provided by the state reports for the 1960 census. *Infra* note 87.

35 In the continental United States in 1960, less than 2% of all women in the age range twenty-five to twenty-nine were enrolled in college. Not surprisingly, the percentages were considerably higher among women who were younger. To illustrate, 15% of twenty year-old women, 11% of twenty-one year-old women, and 5% of twenty-two year-old women were enrolled in college in 1960. U.S. BUREAU OF THE CENSUS, U.S. DEP'T OF COMMERCE, U.S. CENSUS OF POPULATION: 1960. VOL. I, CHARACTERISTICS OF THE POPULATION. PART 1, UNITED STATES SUMMARY, at 1–374 tbl. 167 (1964), *available at* http://www.census.gov/prod/www/decennial.html (last visited April 28, 2015) [hereinafter UNITED STATES SUMMARY: 1960]. The preceding percentages include white women as well as nonwhite women.

36 Of all women who were thirty to thirty-four years old in 1960, only 1% were enrolled in college in that year. *Id.*

37 *See generally* Marshall H. Medoff, *Constituencies, Ideology, and the Demand for Abortion Legislation*, 60 PUB. CHOICE 185, 186 (1989). The likelihood that a pregnancy will be aborted becomes greater as the family income of women increases. Joanne M. Badagliacco, Who Has Abortions: Determinants of Abortion Choice among American Women 64, 165 (1987) (unpublished Ph.D. dissertation, Columbia University) (on file with Widener University School of Law Delaware Campus Library).

acceptance of an activity (in this case, abortion) that is necessary if women are to deal with a problem (unwanted pregnancy) that they often confront.

Was pregnancy problematic for numerous women at the time that states started to change their law on therapeutic abortion? The answer is evidently affirmative. During the first half of the 1960s, a considerable fraction of all pregnancies were unwanted by pregnant women in the United States.[38] A likely reason for the size of the fraction is that childbirth and childrearing were curtailing employment among women in the United States at this time[39]

---

38 I approximated the fraction—i.e., the proportion of pregnancies that were unwanted by pregnant women—using (i) estimates of the number of medically induced abortions and (ii) data on the number of live births. Because therapeutic abortions result from and hence represent unwanted pregnancies, the numerator for the fraction consisted of credible estimates of the number of therapeutic abortions that were being performed annually in the United States around 1960. The estimates are between 200,000 and 1,000,000 each year. Mary Steichen Calderone, *Illegal Abortion as a Public Health Problem*, 50 AM. J. PUB. HEALTH 948, 950 (1960). The denominator, which was a measure of total pregnancies, was the sum, for a given year, of the estimated number of medically induced abortions and the number of registered live births. During the first half of the 1960s, live births in the United States were in the range of 4.0 million to 4.3 million annually. U.S. PUBLIC HEALTH SERVICE, VITAL STATISTICS OF THE UNITED STATES: 1964. VOL. I—NATALITY 1–4 tbl. 1–2 (1966), *available at* http://www.cdc.gov/nchs/products/vsus/vsus_1939_1964.htm (last visited April 28, 2015). The foregoing data suggest that, in 1960–1964, between 4% and 20% of all pregnancies in a year were unwanted by the women who were pregnant. The calculation omits pregnancies that miscarried on the assumption that the rate at which miscarriages occur does not differ between unwanted pregnancies and wanted pregnancies. The omission of pregnancies that ended in miscarriage, therefore, would have equally affected the numerator and the denominator.

The fraction estimated above (4% to 20%) understates the incidence of unwanted pregnancy, because many unwanted pregnancies are excluded from its numerator and included in its denominator. These pregnancies, even though unwanted, were not aborted but, instead, were carried to term. Indeed, one-fifth of the children born during 1960–1965 to married, husband-present women in the United States were not wanted by their mother and/or by their father, i.e., were not the result of pregnancies that were merely mistimed. Larry Bumpass & Charles F. Westoff, *The Perfect Contraceptive Population*, 169 SCI. 1177, 1178 tbl. 1, 1179 (1970). This finding, which is based on data gathered during the four months from October 1965 through January 1966, is from a survey of a nationwide sample that was designed to be representative of white and black married women who were no older than 55 years of age and who were residing with their spouse. Norman B. Ryder & Charles F. Westoff, *Use of Oral Contraception in the United States, 1965*, 153 SCI. 1199, 1199 (1966).

39 Diane H. Felmlee, *A Dynamic Analysis of Women's Employment Exits*, 21 DEMOGRAPHY 171, 180–81 (1984); GUS HAGGSTROM ET AL., CHANGES IN THE LIFESTYLES OF NEW PARENTS 146 (1984).

and hence were impeding women in their achievement of both career and financial goals. Additionally, well before the reform of state abortion law began in the 1960s, the extent to which occupations were segregated by sex was declining,[40] a trend that prior to the reform is likely to have appreciably reduced the difference in status between female and male sex roles. Because of lessened inequality in sex roles, women would have had more social latitude by the 1960s to terminate pregnancies and, with increases in their financial means, would be more able to do so. Women's income, therefore, cannot be discounted as a substantial macro-level determinant of whether states liberalized their law on abortion during 1967–1972.

To measure income for the instant study, I used the median number of dollars of income that was received in 1959 by women twenty-five to thirty-four years old who had any income in 1959.[41] Reflecting the measure, the mnemonic label for the variable was INCOME2534. The U.S. Census Bureau, when reporting income by state, merged the two five-year age groups encompassed by the twenty-five to thirty-four age range, thereby preventing the use of data for just one of the five-year age groups. While state data on the income of women were published for women who were twenty to twenty-four years old, the percentage of women who were in school in 1960 was materially higher at age twenty to twenty-four than at age twenty-five to thirty-four.[42] Because the ability to earn income is hindered by school attendance, income at age twenty to

---

40 Kim A. Weeden, *Revisiting Occupational Sex Segregation in the United States, 1910–1990: Results from a Log-Linear Approach*, 35 DEMOGRAPHY 475, 480 index A (1998).

41 The data for this variable were derived from Table 134 in the state reports for the 1960 census. CHARACTERISTICS OF THE POPULATION: 1960, *supra* note 23. Not all money that was received by individuals was deemed to be income. For instance, money received by individuals was not regarded as income if, inter alia, it constituted a tax refund, a bank-deposit withdrawal, a gift, a loan, a lump-sum inheritance or insurance-policy benefit, or the proceeds of a sale of property. UNITED STATES SUMMARY: 1960, *supra* note 35, at LXXIX.

Paid employment was not necessarily the sole source of income for individuals, but ninety-seven out of every 100 females age fourteen and over in the United States in 1960 reported earned income in 1959. UNITED STATES SUMMARY: 1960, *supra* note 35, at 1–232 tbl. 98. Employment, therefore, can be assumed to have supplied most of the income that women twenty-five to thirty-four years old received in 1959.

42 Nationwide in the United States, 19% of all women who were twenty years old, 14% of all women who were twenty-one years old, and 7% of all women who were twenty-two years old were enrolled in school in 1960. By contrast, among women twenty-five to twenty-nine years old and among women thirty to thirty-four years old, only 3% and 2%, respectively, were enrolled in school. Women of all races are included in the percentages. UNITED STATES SUMMARY: 1960, *supra* note 35, at 1–369 tbl. 165.

twenty-four is less likely than income at age twenty-five to thirty-four to be a force in the pre-1973 change in state law on abortion.

Although age twenty-five to thirty-four encompasses many women who were older than the women who supplied the data I used for the other sex-specific independent variables (education and labor force participation) in the regression model, the income of women twenty-five to thirty-four years old in 1960 is pertinent to the instant study because women at this age are able to bear children.[43] For women who were twenty-five to thirty-four years old, unwanted pregnancy was not a remote possibility,[44] therefore, and law on abortion was unlikely to have been an academic issue. In addition, change in a social system is usually slow, allowing a cohort to formulate an estimate of what it will experience in the future. The cohort that is twenty-five to thirty-four years old will thus normally provide a younger cohort with a rough but correct prediction of the income that the latter will have when it moves into the age range twenty-five to thirty-four. Because income at age twenty-five to thirty-four can be significant to women who are younger, it is logically a barometer of both the actual and the expected financial circumstances of adult women during much of the human lifespan for bearing children.

I turn now to labor force participation. In exploring whether involvement by women in the job market was a factor in the revision of state law to increase access to abortion during 1967–1972, the study used the rate of labor force participation among women in each state who were twenty-five to twenty-nine years old.[45] Given the nature of the variable and its indicator, the mnemonic label for the variable was LABOR2529. The measure of labor force participation was limited to the age range twenty-five to twenty-nine for two reasons: First, the same age range was used for education. When a single age group provides the data for two independent variables that are affected by age, correlates of age do not differ (or do not differ as much) between the variables, and any such correlate is less likely to distort the relationship of one or both of the

---

43 In 1960, women in the age range twenty-five to thirty-four were responsible for approximately two-fifths (41.8%) of all live births in the United States. Calculated from NAT'L CENTER FOR HEALTH STATISTICS, U.S. DEP'T OF HEALTH, EDUCATION & WELFARE, VITAL STATISTICS OF THE UNITED STATES: 1960. VOL. I, NATALITY, at 2–59 tbl. 2–16 (1964), *available at* http://www.cdc.gov/nchs/products/vsus/vsus_1939_1964.htm (last visited April 28, 2015). In the same year, live births in the United States numbered 197 per 1000 women age twenty-five to twenty-nine and 113 per 1000 women age thirty to thirty-four. *Id.* at 1–19 tbl. 1-E.

44 *Supra* note 38.

45 The data for this variable were derived from Table 115 in the state reports for the 1960 census. CHARACTERISTICS OF THE POPULATION: 1960, *supra* note 23.

independent variables to the dependent variable. Second, after Roe v. Wade, women twenty-five to twenty-nine years old were the source of about one-fifth of all medically induced abortions each year, and because this fraction fluctuated minimally during the decade-and-a-half that followed *Roe*,[46] it is likely to be a continuation of the fraction that existed for many years before *Roe*, including the period on which the instant study is focused. Although adult women who were twenty to twenty-four years old accounted for a much larger percentage of all therapeutic abortions after *Roe* than did women twenty-five to twenty-nine years old,[47] the former (younger) group has a higher rate of school enrollment.[48] If school enrollment expanded the share of medically induced pregnancy terminations that are attributable to women age twenty to twenty-four, the instant study had fewer uncontrolled factors that are pertinent to abortion because its data on labor force participation were confined to women in the age range twenty-five to twenty-nine.

The inclusion of the last independent variable—urbanization—was prompted by sociological theory, which contends that, ceteris paribus, the character of social life differs between geographic areas that are markedly dissimilar in population density. According to the theory, societal heterogeneity and change are generated, or at least facilitated, by a large population, while they are hindered or minimized by a small population.[49] The social experience, in short, is a function of population concentration.[50] If the societal context of the institution of law is responsible for the society-important concepts and doctrines of the institution, as the framework in Chapter 1 posits, the degree of urbanization in a jurisdiction has the potential to affect the content

---

46 HENSHAW & VAN VORT, *supra* note 13, at 172–73 tbl. 1.

47 *Id.*

48 THE PLACE OF LAW, *supra* note 4, at 281 Fig. 6.4. See *supra* note 42 for exact percentages of females in the age range twenty to twenty-nine who were enrolled in school in 1960.

49 THE PLACE OF LAW, *supra* note 4, at 201, 344–45, 376 nn.35–36.

50 *E.g.*, J. Scott Carter & Casey A. Borch, *Assessing the Effects of Urbanism and Regionalism on Gender-Role Attitudes, 1974–1998*, 75 SOCIOL. INQUIRY 548, 558 (2005) (finding that, in the 1970s and 1980s but not in the 1990s, traditional definitions of sex roles were more common in areas of low population concentration than in areas of high population concentration); Patricia L. McCall & Paul Nieuwbeerta, *Structural Covariates of Homicide Rates: A European City Cross-National Comparative Analysis*, 11 HOMICIDE STUD. 167, 175, 179 (2007) (finding that homicide rates are higher in cities that are more urban than in cities that are less urban); Thomas C. Wilson, *Urbanism and Unconventionality: The Case of Sexual Behavior*, 76 SOC. SCI. Q. 346 (1995) (finding that tolerance of unconventional sexual activity is more prevalent in areas having numerous inhabitants than in areas having relatively few inhabitants).

of law in the jurisdiction as well as shifts in this content. Logic, accordingly, dictates that urbanization be in the regression model of the instant study.

Urbanization was measured by the percentage of the population of each state in 1960 that was in an "urbanized area" having at least 500,000 inhabitants,[51] and was given the mnemonic label URBAN. As defined in the decennial census of 1960, an "urbanized area" included both (i) a minimum of one city that had 50,000 or more residents in 1960 and (ii) the territory that bordered each such city.[52] The components of an urbanized area were thus a "central city, or cities, and the remainder of the area, or the urban fringe."[53] In the United States as a whole, urbanized areas having a half-million or more residents were the home of 37.5% of the total population in 1960.[54]

I conclude the instant Part of Chapter 2 with a short summary of the independent variables in the regression model of the study. Because the above discussion of these variables has been detailed, an overview is likely to be helpful. The independent variables of the regression model are thus listed below (left-hand column) along with a sketch of their empirical indicators (right-hand column).

Cultural heterogeneity	Cultural heterogeneity was measured by the percentage of the population in each state in 1960 that had been born in a country other than the United States. Mnemonic label: FOREIGNPOP.
Culture	Culture was measured by geographic region. Each state was coded in terms of the region—North Central, Northeast, South, or West—in which it was located.[55] The mnemonic labels of the regions were, respectively, NOCENTRAL, NOEAST, SOUTH, and WEST.

51 The data were obtained from Table 2 in the state reports on the 1970 census. U.S. BUREAU OF THE CENSUS, CENSUS OF POPULATION: 1970. VOL. I: CHARACTERISTICS OF THE POPULATION Table 2, *available at* http://www.census.gov/prod/www/decennial.html. Table 2 in the state reports on the 1970 census includes data on urbanized areas in 1960; the state reports on the 1970 census were used because the data on urbanized areas in 1960 are missing from, or difficult to read in, some of the state reports on the 1960 census that are accessible through the Internet as PDF documents. CHARACTERISTICS OF THE POPULATION: 1960, *supra* note 23.

52 UNITED STATES SUMMARY: 1960, *supra* note 35, at xxvi.

53 *Id.* at xxvi.

54 *See id.* at 1–11 tbl. 5 (reporting that 28.9% of the U.S. population in 1960 was in urbanized areas with 1,000,000 or more residents and that 8.6% of the U.S. population in 1960 was in urbanized areas with 500,000 to 1,000,000 residents).

55 The states that comprised each region are named in *supra* note 31.

- A state was assigned the number 1 on NOCENTRAL if it was in the North Central region and was assigned the number 0 if it was not.
- A state was assigned the number 1 on NOEAST if it was in the Northeast and was assigned the number 0 if it was not.
- A state was assigned the number 1 on SOUTH if it was in the South and was assigned the number 0 if it was not.
- A state was assigned the number 1 on WEST if it was in the West and was assigned the number 0 if it was not.

Education	Education was measured by the percentage of twenty-five to twenty-nine year-old women in each state who had finished four or more years of college. Age and years of college completed were as of 1960. Mnemonic label: COLL2529.
Income	Income was measured by the median number of U.S. dollars of income received in 1959 by women in each state who had any income in that year and who were twenty-five to thirty-four years old in 1960. Mnemonic label: INCOME2534.
Labor force participation	Labor force participation was measured by the percentage of twenty-five to twenty-nine year-old women in each state who were in the labor force. Age and labor force participation were as of 1960. Mnemonic label: LABOR2529.
Urbanization	Urbanization was measured by the percentage of the population in each state in 1960 that resided in an urbanized area having at least 500,000 inhabitants in 1960. Mnemonic label: URBAN.

b *Findings*

For the forty-eight states in the continental United States, Table 2.1 reports the mean and standard deviation of the empirical indicator of each independent variable in the regression model that was measured with a ratio scale.[56] Table 2.1 does not report a mean and standard deviation for the empirical

56 Quantitative social science research measures variables with four types of scales. The scales, listed from simplest to most precise, are named nominal, ordinal, interval, and

TABLE 2.1 *Means and standard deviations of independent variables measured with a ratio scale*

Indicator of variable	Mean	Standard deviation
FOREIGNPOP	4.1	3.3
COLL2529	7.2	1.7
INCOME2534	1641.9	357.0
LABOR2529	33.6	4.7
URBAN	22.0	23.9

indicator of one independent variable (culture) or for the empirical indicator of the dependent variable (change by a state in its law on abortion). Because these variables were measured with nominal scales, their indicators have no interpretable mean or standard deviation.

The odds ratios of the independent variables were computed with the LOGISTIC command in Stata Release 12.1.[57] All such computations included the intercept. Through its NOCONSTANT option, Stata version 12 allows odds ratios to be calculated without an intercept,[58] but no guidelines have thus far

ratio, and their properties are cumulative. In brief, a nominal scale is measurement using two or more categories that cannot be ranked because the phenomenon measured varies in type rather than in amount. Geographic region, the empirical indicator of culture in the present study, is an example of a nominal scale. The other scales use measurement units (categories) that are ranked because the phenomena measured by these scales vary in amount. An ordinal scale is measurement in which the difference in amount between the (ranked) measurement units of the scale is not the same across all adjacent units. Such a scale distinguishes only more of the phenomenon from less of it. An interval scale is measurement in which the difference in amount between adjacent measurement units of the scale remains constant, but no measurement unit exists for absolute zero, i.e., for none of the variable. A ratio scale is measurement of a phenomenon using the properties of an interval scale and a measurement unit for absolute zero. A ratio scale can thus be applied to cases that have none of the phenomenon. In the instant study, all of the independent variables except culture were measured with ratio scales. A fuller explanation of each type of scale is in Anwer Khurshid & Hardeo Sahai, *Scales of Measurements: An Introduction and a Selected Bibliography*, 27 QUALITY & QUANTITY 303 (1993).

57 STATACORP., STATA BASE REFERENCE MANUAL: RELEASE 12 (2011), at 932–42.

58 *Id.*, at 503, 932, 970. Prior to Release 12, the NOCONSTANT option was available for the LOGIT command but not for the LOGISTIC command. 2 STATACORP., STATA BASE REFERENCE MANUAL: RELEASE 10, at 179 (2007); STATACORP., STATA USER'S GUIDE: RELEASE 12, at 14 (2011).

been formulated in the sociology of law as to the circumstances in which an intercept should be omitted when assessing relationships between jurisdiction characteristics and the content of law. I explain below why I did not drop the intercept when estimating the odds ratios of the independent variables in my study, but readers should be aware that two reasons counsel in favor of leaving the intercept out of data analyses that are concerned with society-level factors responsible for concepts and doctrines of law. First, the intercept seldom supplies helpful information in logistic regression.[59] Second, macrosociology seeks to understand concepts and doctrines of law by reference to attributes of societies, as illustrated by the framework that I proposed in Part 1-b of *supra* Chapter 1, but a society cannot develop and survive when it lacks one or more essential elements. The intercept must be viewed in this light. For logistic regression with a dependent variable that is measured as either 0 or 1, the intercept reveals the odds that cases (here, states) will be coded 1 on the dependent variable (here, ABORTLAW) when all of the independent variables in the regression model have a numerical value of zero. At least one independent variable in a study of macro-level determinants of law, however, is likely to involve a phenomenon that a society requires and to be measured with an absolute zero, i.e., with a ratio scale. To illustrate, an independent variable in the instant study that was measured with a ratio scale is labor force participation by women, a phenomenon that seems to be inherent in every modern society. For economic as well as social reasons, numerous adult females in structurally complex societal systems join the labor force, and a modern society without women in remunerated employment is not a realistic possibility. As a consequence, the numerical value of the intercept is of questionable meaning in the regression models of studies concerned with society-level forces and conditions that shape the content of law. In addition, the intercept, when calculated, is likely to affect the magnitude of the coefficients and odds ratios that are obtained for the independent variables in a regression model. The size of the impact that an independent variable is thought to have on the dependent variable can thus be contingent on whether the intercept was included or omitted when the coefficients and odds ratios were estimated.

Table 2.2 reports the results for three logistic-regression models that utilized data on the forty-eight states in the coterminous United States. Before I delve into the findings, however, let me mention several matters. First, Table 2.2 deals with the odds ratios, not the regression coefficients, derived from the data analysis. Readers should keep in mind that odds differ from probabilities and

59 David W. Hosmer & Stanley Lemeshow, Applied Logistic Regression 47 (2d ed. 2000).

that the former are based on and computed from the latter. A brief explanation of the difference may be helpful. A *probability* is a proportion and exists for the occurrence as well as for the nonoccurrence of an event. Because an event either will occur or will not occur, the sum of the probabilities of each is 1.0. The *odds* that an event will happen, on the other hand, is the quotient obtained from the division of one probability by another: the numerator in the division is the probability that the event will take place, and the denominator is the probability that the event will not take place. For instance, when the probability of an event happening is 0.60, the probability of its not happening is 0.40, and the odds of the event are 1.5 (often expressed as 1.5 to 1.0); i.e., the event is one-and-a-half times more likely to occur than not to occur. In logistic regression, the *odds ratio* for an independent variable discloses the change in the odds that the event will materialize when a case (state) moves up one category or one measurement unit on this variable or, if the variable is nominally scaled, moves from the chosen reference category to another category.[60]

The second preliminary matter concerns tests of statistical significance. Although levels of statistical significance for the odds ratios are shown in Table 2.2, just the odds ratios will be the basis for interpreting the results. When the cases supplying data to be analyzed constitute a defined universe rather than a randomly drawn sample from such a universe, as in the instant study,[61] tests of statistical significance ought not to be used.[62] Significance levels (two-tailed) are provided in Table 2.2, however, because some readers may wish to consider them.

Third, readers should not overlook that logistic regression (and regression generally) estimates the relationship to the dependent variable of each independent variable when every other independent variable in the regression model is held constant. The impact of an independent variable that is computed from regression, accordingly, is the impact of that independent variable on its own. Independent variables that are not in the regression model, of course, are not controlled. The results discussed below, in short, furnish an estimate, for the regression model being used, of the relationship of each independent variable by itself to whether states changed their abortion law during the 1967–1972 period.

---

60 A further explanation of the difference between probability and odds, and the nature of an odds ratio, is in THE PLACE OF LAW, *supra* note 4, at 424–25.

61 The universe for the present study was all states in the coterminous United States.

62 Jeff Gill, *Whose Variance Is It Anyway? Interpreting Empirical Models with State-Level Data*, 1 STATE POL. & POL'Y Q. 318, 319 (2001); EARL BABBIE, SURVEY RESEARCH METHODS 301–302 (2d ed. 1990).

Fourth, in perusing Table 2.2, readers should keep in mind that the magnitude of the relationship between an independent variable and the dependent variable depends on the degree to which the odds ratio for the independent variable deviates from 1.000. If the odds ratio for an independent variable is 1.000, the independent variable had no influence on the dependent variable. However, an odds ratio can be above or below 1.000, and as it diverges from 1.000, its independent variable has a larger impact. In the study that I report here, logistic regression estimated the change in the odds that a state liberalized its law on abortion during 1967–1972 due to (i) an increase of one unit of an independent variable that was measured with a ratio scale or (ii) a change of one category in an independent variable that was measured as a dummy, i.e., with a nominal scale using the digits 0 and 1. The odds that a state eased the restrictions its law placed on abortion were increased by an independent variable whose odds ratio was more than 1.000 and were decreased by an independent variable whose odds ratio was less than 1.000.

The final preliminary matter concerns the assessment of the degree to which all of the independent variables together (i.e., the regression model as a whole) fit the data. Table 2.2 reports both the coefficient of determination (pseudo-R^2) for each model and, in the bottom row, the percentage of predictions made by each model that were correct in terms of whether states liberalized their law on therapeutic abortion during the 1967–1972 period.[63] The former measure (pseudo-R^2), though frequently referenced in social science studies, is problematic when logistic regression is used,[64] and I therefore rely on the latter (percentages) as the chief criterion of model fit. The bottom row of Table 2.2 measures, for the model in the column, the accuracy rate of *all* state-by-state predictions that the model made, i.e., predictions by the model that, before *Roe*, state law on abortion had been relaxed as well as predictions by the model that, before *Roe*, state law on abortion had not been altered. The bottom row thus includes both predictions of states that would be coded 1 on ABORTLAW and predictions of states that would be coded 0 on ABORTLAW. Notably, the percentage was appreciably higher for model I when the odds ratios for the independent variables were estimated with an intercept than when they were estimated without an intercept (81.3% versus 66.7%). Because of the higher accuracy rate that model I achieved with the intercept, all of the

63 Use of these percentages is among the approaches to assessing model fit that are suggested by J. SCOTT LONG & JEREMY FREESE, REGRESSION MODELS FOR CATEGORICAL DEPENDENT VARIABLES USING STATA 104, 110–11 (2d ed. 2006). The percentages are generated in Stata with the ESTAT CLASSIFICATION command. *Id.* at 111.

64 JOSEPH M. HILBE, LOGISTIC REGRESSION MODELS 244 (2009).

estimations for the study included the intercept. A purely statistical criterion, therefore, was responsible for the decision regarding the intercept.[65]

The initial regression model that was applied to the data contained all of the independent variables and is labeled model I in Table 2.2. The interpretation of the odds ratios in Table 2.2 may be aided by converting each odds ratio into a percentage, a process that involves subtracting 1.000 from an odds ratio and multiplying the remainder by 100.[66] The findings of model I suggest that cultural heterogeneity, culture, education, and labor force participation had important relationships to whether a state liberalized its abortion law prior to Roe v. Wade. Specifically, the odds of liberalization declined by 34.1% with an

TABLE 2.2 *Regression models: odds ratios and prediction accuracy*

Indicator of independent variable	**Regression model**		
	I	II	III
FOREIGNPOP	0.659	0.473^{a}	0.671
NOCENTRAL	0.317	0.432	0.382
SOUTH	0.724	0.826	1.227
WEST	1.953	2.199	2.282
COLL2529	3.131^{b}	4.099^{b}	2.897^{b}
INCOME2534	0.999	0.999	—
LABOR2529	1.258	1.250	1.207
URBAN	1.011	0.964	—
INTERACT	—	1.008	—
INTERCEPT	1.2^{-06b}	4.2^{-07b}	1.2^{-06b}
N	48	48	48
Pseudo-R^2	0.338	0.375	0.331
Correct predictions	81.3%	81.3%	79.2%

Notes to Table 2.2: Levels of statistical significance for the odds ratios are designated by superscripts of the letters a, b, and c: ^{a} = 0.10 level; ^{b} = 0.05 level; ^{c} = 0.01 level.
For NOCENTRAL, SOUTH, and WEST, the reference was NOEAST.[67]

65 Although the decision was grounded on a statistical criterion, it should have been based on theory. Unfortunately, the decision could not be informed by theory, because macrosociological theory on concepts and doctrines of law has to date not explored the issue of whether the intercept should be present in regression analyses of data.

66 *See* LONG & FREESE, *supra* note 63, at 178, 180.

67 The states that comprised each region are listed in *supra* note 31.

increase of one percentage point in the percentage of the state population that had been born outside the United States; were lower by 68.3%, and higher by 95.3%, in states in the North Central region and West, respectively, than in states in the Northeast; jumped 213.1% with a gain of one percentage point in the percentage of women twenty-five to twenty-nine years old who had finished four or more years of college; and rose 25.8% with an increase of one percentage point in the labor force participation rate of women twenty-five to twenty-nine years old. On the other hand, women's income and urbanization did not evidently affect whether a state changed in its law on abortion before *Roe*. As explained earlier, each relationship to the dependent variable was separate from the relationship to the dependent variable of every other independent variable in the regression model, because the odds ratio for an independent variable in the model was estimated with all of the other independent variables held constant.

The odds ratios for model I, however, raise several questions that must be answered. The first is that the results of model I may suffer from excessive collinearity[68]—i.e., a strong correlation between the numerical values of a pair of independent variables in the model may be present and may have produced an unreliable odds ratio for at least one of the pair.[69] The Variance Inflation Factor ("VIF"),[70] however, yielded no evidence of excessive collinearity among the independent variables comprising model I. The largest VIF of any independent variable in the model was 6.49,[71] which is well within the range of VIF scores allowed for collinearity.[72] Not surprisingly, then, collinearity did not cause the

68 William D. Berry, *Understanding Regression Assumptions*, 92 QUANTITATIVE APPLICATIONS IN THE SOC. SCIENCES 1, 24–27 (1993).

69 DAVID A. BELSLEY ET AL., REGRESSION DIAGNOSTICS: IDENTIFYING INFLUENTIAL DATA AND SOURCES OF COLLINEARITY 115 (2004).

70 The Stata command COLLIN was used to estimate the VIF of each independent variable. UCLA Institute for Digital Res. & Educ., Logistic Regression Diagnostics, http://www.ats.ucla.edu/stat/stata/webbooks/logistic/chapter3/statalog3.htm (last visited April 28, 2015).

71 The VIF (6.49) was obtained for SOUTH. The next largest VIF was 5.52 and was obtained for FOREIGNPOP.

72 A VIF of 10.0 or higher is generally considered a signal that collinearity may be excessive. *E.g.*, DAMODAR N. GUJARATI & DAWN C. PORTER, BASIC ECONOMETRICS 340 (5th ed. 2009); Jeff Tayman et al., *Evaluating Population Forecast Accuracy: A Regression Approach Using County Data*, 30 POPULATION RES. & POL'Y REV. 235, 256 (2011); Tse-Chuan Yang et al., *Social Capital and Human Mortality: Explaining the Rural Paradox with County-Level Mortality Data*, 76 RURAL SOCIOL. 347, 363 (2011). However, a VIF of this magnitude (i.e., 10.0 or higher) is not conclusive evidence of excessive collinearity and does not necessarily require change in the regression model or data analysis. Robert M. O'Brien, *A Caution Regarding Rules of Thumb for Variance Inflation Factors*, 41 QUALITY & QUANTITY 673 (2007).

logistic regression program to drop any independent variable when computing the odds ratios for model I.

I next consider the question of interaction,[73] the possibility that the relationship of an independent variable to the dependent variable depends on another independent variable. For instance, in its relationship to the dependent variable, independent variable X_1 may differ in strength across categories or levels of independent variable X_2. The independent variables that I examine for potential interaction are those suggested by theory. Indeed, a search for interaction is undertaken only when theory provides reason to suspect that particular independent variables interact.[74] Of the independent variables in the instant regression model, theory directs attention to two—namely, cultural heterogeneity and urbanization. Sociological theory has attempted to account for the finding that an area with a large population has more nontraditional forms of social behavior than an area with a small population. In particular, such theory posits that (i) population growth in a geographic area enlarges the variety of subcultures in the area as well as magnifies the intensity of these subcultures; and (ii) contact between the members of the subcultures leads to change in the subcultures, which change affects the culture of the society as a whole.[75] By promoting shifts in culture, this theory suggests, highly urbanized areas are more often characterized by new social patterns than less urbanized areas. In the macrosociological framework that I have proposed, alterations in patterns of social behavior that are important to a structurally complex society will, ceteris paribus, cause pertinent concepts and doctrines of law to evolve in a democratically governed jurisdiction. Cultural heterogeneity and urbanization, accordingly, are expected to be factors driving change in state law on abortion during the 1967–1972 period, but in having such an effect, they may interact.

To investigate whether cultural heterogeneity and urbanization interacted, I multiplied the numerical values of FOREIGNPOP and the numerical values of URBAN to form a new variable.[76] The new variable (labeled INTERACT) was added as an independent variable in the data analysis to form model II, and as

---

73 JAMES JACCARD, INTERACTION EFFECTS IN LOGISTIC REGRESSION 12–13 (Paper No. 135, Sage University Paper Series on Quantitative Applications in the Social Sciences, 2001).

74 *Id.* at 12–13; F. David Schoorman et al., *The Role of Theory in Testing Hypothesized Interactions: An Example from the Research on Escalation of Commitment*, 21 J. APPLIED SOC. PSYCHOL. 1338, 1338, 1349, 1353 (1991).

75 Claude S. Fischer, *Toward a Subcultural Theory of Urbanism*, 80 AM. J. SOCIOL. 1319, 1324–30 (1975); Claude S. *Fischer, The Subcultural Theory of Urbanism: A Twentieth-Year Assessment*, 101 AM. J. SOCIOL. 543, 544–46 (1995).

76 JACCARD, *supra* note 73, at 14.

shown in Table 2.2, the odds ratio of INTERACT was 1.008.[77] Such an odds ratio does not support the conclusion that a relationship of notable magnitude existed between INTERACT and the dependent variable. Moreover, the measure of model fit—the accuracy of all predictions made by a model that were correct[78]—was no higher when INTERACT was included (model II) than when it was omitted (model I).[79] Because the variable created to test for interaction between the two independent variables exhibited no clear relationship to ABORTLAW and added nothing to the fit of the regression model, evidence of interaction between cultural heterogeneity and urbanization was absent.

Finally, consideration must be given to the possibility that, because of an outlier, the regression analysis yielded an incorrect odds ratio for at least one independent variable. In the instant study, an outlier is a state that the regression analysis calculated would not be in the category of the dependent variable (ABORTLAW) that the state was in. Simply put, the regression model was wrong in predicting the classification of the state on the dependent variable. Unfortunately, no procedure for identifying potentially influential outliers seems to be generally accepted by statisticians. The procedure that I chose involved calculating Cook's Statistic and visually inspecting a graph that plotted the numerical values obtained from the calculation.[80] The procedure, accordingly, had both a quantitative component and a qualitative component. Relatively large numerical values on Cook's Statistic were evident for six states, viz., Arkansas, Connecticut, Kansas, Nevada, New York, and Vermont. For each of these states, Cook's Statistic was at least 1.45, which exceeded the usual threshold revealing a possible influential outlier.[81] Therefore, I re-estimated the relationship to ABORTLAW of each of the independent variables in model I by

---

77 The level of statistical significance of the odds ratio for INTERACT was 0.151.

78 The coefficient of determination was slightly higher for model II than for model I, but as explained in the text accompanying *supra* note 64, the coefficient of determination is not regarded as conclusive in the instant study.

79 Such a comparison for ascertaining interaction is not dissimilar to the comparison that is made in studies in which tests of statistical significance are appropriate. JAMES JACCARD & ROBERT TURRISI, INTERACTION EFFECTS IN MULTIPLE REGRESSION 18 (Paper No. 72, Sage University Paper Series on Quantitative Applications in the Social Sciences, 2d ed. 2003) (suggesting that interaction is present when (i) the coefficient of determination for a model containing an interaction variable is larger than the coefficient of determination for an otherwise identical model that lacks the interaction variable and (ii) the difference between the two coefficients of determination is statistically significant).

80 LONG & FREESE, *supra* note 63, at 151.

81 An influential outlier usually has a Cook's Statistic of 1.00 or higher. HOSMER & LEMESHOW, *supra* note 59, at 173, 180.

dropping one of these states at a time, and forty-seven states were used to compute the odds ratios for the independent variables in model I.

None of the six states named above, when absent from the data, notably altered the odds ratios for any independent variable except culture. The indicators of culture, of course, were the geographic regions of the United States, and not surprisingly, the omission of a state from a region is likely to modify the odds ratio for the region. Consequently, no grounds exist to conclude that an influential outlier was responsible for the results that were obtained for model I with forty-eight states. In this regard, readers should keep in mind that the decision to designate a component of a system as an influential outlier has implications that must be carefully considered.[82] A component that is so designated must be set aside, i.e., taken out of the system, and the elimination from a system of one or more of its components may produce an incomplete system. Depending on the character of the component that is removed and the number of components removed, the remaining components may be a different system, or may not even be a system. A state, of course, is an individual jurisdiction within a larger, more-encompassing jurisdiction (viz., the United States), and hence is part of a system. Research on attributes of U.S. states that may affect the content of state law, therefore, should reluctantly treat a particular state as an influential outlier. Indeed, a presumption is warranted in such research that a state is not an influential outlier, and the presumption should be rebuttable only by strong evidence to the contrary.

Regression diagnostics for model I, in sum, failed to yield definitive evidence of excessive collinearity among independent variables, interaction between independent variables, or influential outliers among the observation units (states). However, while the foregoing regression diagnostics disclosed no problem with model I, that model requires further scrutiny. Quite possibly, some of the independent variables in model I—especially those whose indicators had an odds ratio close to 1.000—can be removed without appreciably reducing the degree to which there is a fit to the data. Can a simpler model be found that is as accurate, or almost as accurate, as model I in separating the sixteen states that eased their law on access to therapeutic abortion from the thirty-two states that did not? In science, simplicity is a virtue, and all else being equal, a simple explanatory model is preferable to a complex one.

In seeking a group of independent variables that are fewer in number but collectively similar to a larger group in explanatory power, sets of independent

82 THE PLACE OF LAW, *supra* note 4, at 468–69.

variables from model I were chosen and analyzed for their ability to predict accurately whether a state had liberalized its law on therapeutic abortion during 1967–1972. In this exercise, the independent variable URBAN was of special interest because it offered an opportunity to assess the theory of urbanism.[83] The findings of the analysis are reported in Table 2.3. The percentage of correct predictions was ascertained for predictions that law had been liberalized, for predictions that law had not been liberalized, and for both predictions combined. The bottom row of Table 2.3 shows the percentages for all of the independent variables that comprised model I.

What conclusion(s) can be drawn from Table 2.3? The smallest set of independent variables that approximated the accuracy rates of model I in Table 2.2 was the third-listed set in Table 2.3, i.e., the set composed of FOREIGNPOP, NOCENTRAL, SOUTH, WEST, COLL2529, and LABOR2529. Indeed, this set, which contains two fewer independent variables than model I, had just a small disadvantage in accuracy rates compared to model I. Specifically, the accuracy rate of the simple set was somewhat lower for predictions that law on therapeutic abortion had been liberalized, but it was essentially the same for predictions that law on therapeutic abortion had not been liberalized. Moreover, the slight disadvantage of the simple set relative to model I was due to a mistake that it made with regard to just one state when forecasting the category of the dependent variable in which each state would be found. The criterion of parsimony, therefore, recommends the simple set and makes it preferable to model I. Table 2.2 reports the odds ratios of the independent variables in the simple set and labels the set model III. Notably, model III omits URBAN.

c *Summary*

If the macrosociological framework that was proposed in Chapter 1 has utility, concepts and doctrines of law on society-important activities are tied closely to their societal context, at least when the society has a complex structure and a non-totalitarian government. To test how well this framework portrays law, Chapter 2 has sought to identify societal conditions in the United States that prompted one-third of the coterminous states during the late 1960s and early 1970s to liberalize provisions in their law that were believed to hinder access to therapeutic abortion. The analyses of data with logistic regression undertaken in Part 2-b *supra* produced the findings shown for the three models in Table 2.2, but model III, given its simplicity and explanatory power, will be the main basis for my summary of the findings. The estimated relationship to

83 See the text accompanying *supra* notes 49, 50, and 75.

TABLE 2.3 *Accuracy rates for predictions of whether states liberalized their law on therapeutic abortion: sets of independent variables in model 1*

Indicators of independent variables	Predictions of whether states liberalized their law on therapeutic abortion		
	Prediction: state liberalized its law (% accurate)	Prediction: state did not liberalize its law (% accurate)	Both predictions (% accurate)
FOREIGNPOP, NOCENTRAL, SOUTH, WEST	71.4%	73.2%	72.9%
FOREIGNPOP, NOCENTRAL, SOUTH, WEST, COLL2529	62.5%	81.3%	75.0%
FOREIGNPOP, NOCENTRAL, SOUTH, WEST, COLL2529, LABOR2529	68.8%	84.4%	79.2%
FOREIGNPOP, NOCENTRAL, SOUTH, WEST, COLL2529, INCOME2534	60.0%	78.8%	72.9%
FOREIGNPOP, NOCENTRAL, SOUTH, WEST, COLL2529, URBAN	60.0%	78.8%	72.9%
FOREIGNPOP, NOCENTRAL, SOUTH, WEST, COLL2529, LABOR2529, URBAN	68.8%	84.4%	79.2%
FOREIGNPOP, NOCENTRAL, SOUTH, WEST, COLL2529, INCOME2534, URBAN	62.5%	81.3%	75.0%
FOREIGNPOP, NOCENTRAL, SOUTH, WEST, COLL2529, INCOME2534, LABOR2529, URBAN	73.3%	84.8%	81.3%

ABORTLAW of each independent variable in model III, of course, is net of the influence of the other independent variables in the model.

Table 2.2 yields four important conclusions. The first concerns educational attainment among young women, a variable that, as it increased, raised the odds of a liberalization of state abortion law. The direction and magnitude of the relationship uncovered between COLL2529 and ABORTLAW in Table 2.2 is made more credible by social science studies of the characteristics of women that affect the likelihood they will abort a pregnancy,[84] by the pre-1967 trend in school enrollment among young women that is portrayed in Figure 2.1, and by the findings of prior studies in which I used the same dependent variable but accompanied COLL2529 with several independent variables that were quite different than those in model III.[85] In the instant study, according to model III, the odds that a state would ease its law-specified grounds for a therapeutic abortion before Roe v. Wade increased by approximately 190% with a one-point gain in the percentage of twenty-five to twenty-nine year-old women in the state who had completed a minimum of four years of college.[86]

Figure 2.2, which supplements Figure 2.1, sheds light on the historical context of schooling among young women in the United States. The figure consists of two graphs. The data in the top graph come from decennial censuses of the population, cover the period 1940 to 2000, and are for women who were twenty-five to twenty-nine years old at the time of each of the seven censuses during this period. The top graph shows the percentage of all women in the age range twenty-five to twenty-nine who were enumerated as having had (or who were assumed by the Census Bureau to have had) a bachelor's or higher degree in the year that is listed on the horizontal axis.[87] The bottom graph shows, for the

84 See the text accompanying *supra* note 9.

85 *The Roots of Law*, *supra* note 22, at 651–60; THE PLACE OF LAW, *supra* note 4, at 284–96.

86 This is a *percent* increase, not a percentage point increase. The range of COLL2529 was 7.28 percentage points; the low and high of the range were 3.95 and 11.23 percentage points, respectively. See Table 2.1 for the mean and standard deviation.

87 The data in the top graph are from U.S. CENSUS BUREAU, U.S. DEP'T OF COMMERCE, *A Half-Century of Learning: Historical Census Statistics on Educational Attainment in the United States, 1940 to 2000*, at Table 2 (2006), http://www.census.gov/hhes/socdemo/education/data/census/half-century/index.html (follow "Detailed Tables" hyperlink) (last visited April 28, 2015) [hereinafter *A Half-Century of Learning*]. In 1990 and 2000, the census asked whether a Bachelor's (or higher) degree had been received, but from 1940 to 1980, the census obtained information only on the last year or highest grade of school that had been completed. For the censuses of 1940 to 1980, *A Half-Century of Learning* deems college graduates to be persons who reported that they had finished at least four years of college. *Id.* at Introduction (follow "Introduction" hyperlink). The data in the top graph

percentages in the top graph, the *percent* change from one census year to the next. Specifically, the percent changes in the bottom graph were computed by applying the following formula to the census-year percentages in the top graph:

((census year 2 – census year 1)/census year 1) * 100

The numerical values represented in the bottom graph, accordingly, do not measure the amount of change (i.e., are not percentage-point changes) but instead measure the pace of change that took place between adjacent census years. Because the bottom graph presents change from one census to the following census, the time points on its horizontal axis refer to ten-year intercensal periods starting with 1940 to 1950 and finishing with 1990 to 2000.

The trend in the percentages found in the top graph of Figure 2.2 is similar to the trend that Figure 2.1 reveals for school enrollment among women who were eighteen or nineteen years old and is consistent with the pre-1967 trend in school enrollment rates among women who were twenty to twenty-four years old.[88] As is evident in Figure 2.2, the likelihood that women held a bachelor's (or higher) degree when they were age twenty-five to twenty-nine grew steadily during the period 1940–2000 (top graph), and the increase quickened between 1940 and 1970 (bottom graph). Available data indicate that the proportion of women who earned a bachelor's (or higher) degree at age twenty to twenty-four underwent a substantial rise in the 1950s and 1960s.[89] With the passage of time, these women became twenty-five to twenty-nine years old, and the percentage of women with a college degree thus rose at the latter age.[90] The 1960-to-1970 increase seen in the bottom graph of Figure 2.2 merits

---

begin with 1940, because before that time, the census questionnaire did not ask about years of schooling or grade completed or about receipt of a diploma/degree. Robert Kominski & Paul M. Siegel, *Measuring Education in the Current Population Survey*, Monthly Labor Rev., Sept. 1993, at 34, 34.

88 The Place of Law, *supra* note 4, at 281 Fig. 6.4, 329 n.128.

89 *Id.* at 281 Fig. 6.4, 329 n.128.

90 For individuals who possessed a bachelor's degree when they were twenty-five to twenty-nine years old, college matriculation generally occurred at age eighteen or nineteen. *See, e.g.*, United States Summary: 1960, *supra* note 35, at 1–378 tbl. 168; U.S. Bureau of the Census, U.S. Dep't of Commerce, Census of Population: 1970. Vol. 1, Characteristics of the Population. Part 1, United States Summary – Section 2, at 1–605 tbl. 197 (1973) *available at* http://www.census.gov/prod/www/decennial.html (last visited April 28, 2015). *Cf.* Dennis Ahlburg et al., *The Outlook for Higher Education: A Cohort Size Model of Enrollment of the College Age Population, 1948–2000*, 9 Rev. Pub. Data Use 211, 218 Fig. 1, 219 Fig. 2 (1981) (estimating, with cohort size, income

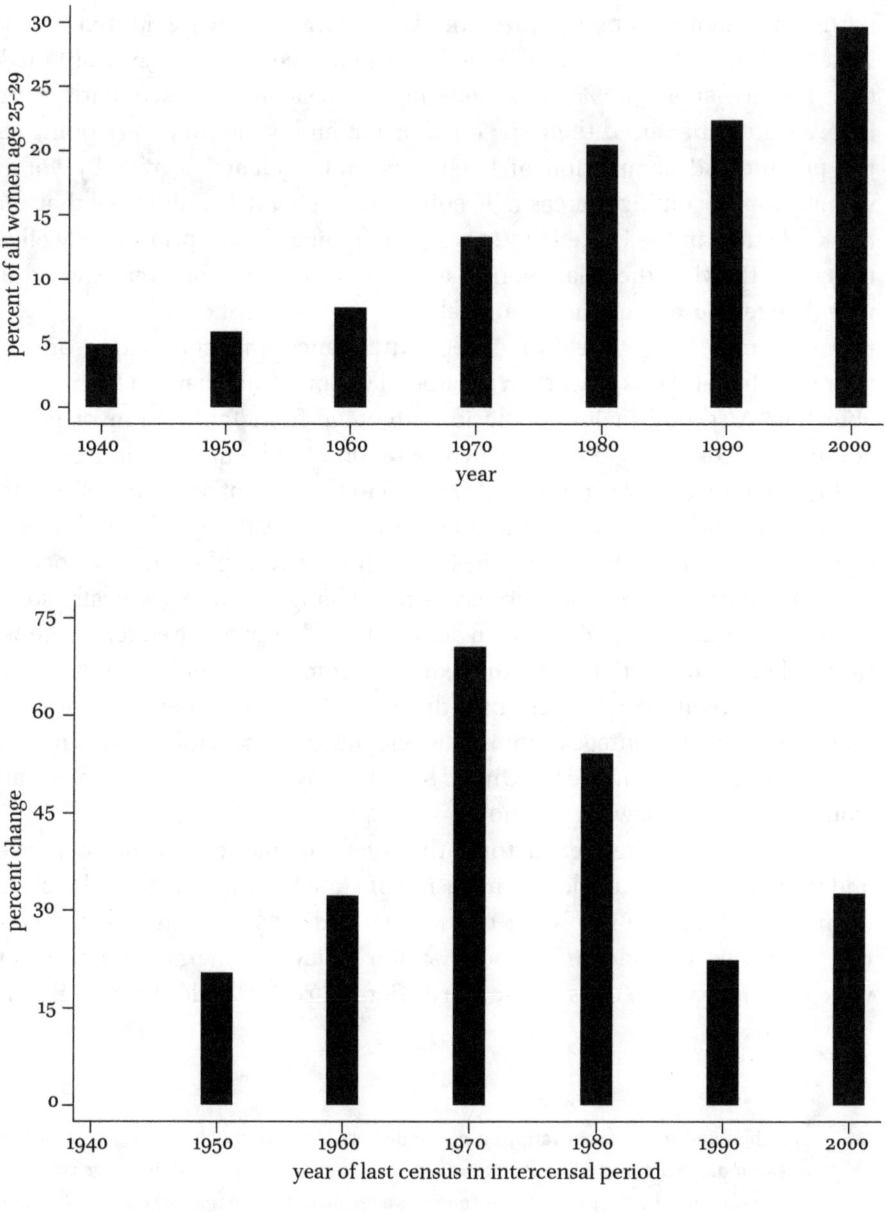

FIGURE 2.2 *College degrees among women age 25–29.*
Percent with bachelor's or higher degree, United States, 1940 to 2000 (top graph).
Change during intercensal period (bottom graph)
SOURCE (TOP GRAPH): SEE FN. 87 IN THIS CHAPTER.
SOURCE (BOTTOM GRAPH): SEE EXPLANATION IN TEXT AFTER FN. 87.

particular attention; at 70.5%, it is the single largest increase. Moreover, the increase during the intercensal period that preceded it (1950–1960), although only half as large (32.2%), was nonetheless sizeable.[91] Consequently, both before states liberalized their law on abortion and while they were doing so, the pursuit and completion of bachelor's and graduate degrees by young women was becoming increasingly common. Such a trend indicates that the role of women in the United States was undergoing change prior to, as well as concurrently with, the relaxation of abortion law restrictions that started in 1967. The temporal sequence is unlikely to be a product of chance.

Apart from rising levels of college attendance and completion among women, what else was at work in the liberalization of state law on therapeutic abortion? A second major conclusion emerging from Table 2.2 involves the culture-related factors, both of which were found to be important. Degree of cultural heterogeneity was inversely related to the odds of an easing of restrictions in state law on access to therapeutic abortion. Although the finding was contrary to what had been hypothesized[92] it may be explained by a societal condition that is likely to be a prerequisite to change in law. Specifically, some degree of shared social values on an activity is evidently required for an alteration of law on the activity, but the extent of commonly held social values is presumably reduced when cultural diversity rises. As model III shows, an increase of one percentage point in the percentage of state inhabitants in 1960 who had been born outside the United States cut by 32.9% the odds that a state would liberalize its law on abortion.

The other culture-related factor in the regression model was culture per se, and it, too, affected the odds of an easing of state law on abortion. The clearest impact of culture involves NOCENTRAL and WEST: Relative to states in the Northeast, the odds of a liberalization of law on therapeutic abortion were 61.8% lower in states in the North Central region and 128.2% higher in

---

of father, and military conscription controlled, substantially higher college-enrollment rates, among males as well as females, at age eighteen and nineteen than at age twenty to twenty-four during the period 1948–2000). As a result, change in the percentage of women who held a bachelor's degree at age twenty-five to twenty-nine manifested change in the role of females that had already occurred. Indeed, the change in sex roles may have happened many years before, and the social forces that were responsible for the change probably originated even earlier. THE PLACE OF LAW, *supra* note 4, at 226–28.

91 The increase was 54.1% during the 1970–1980 intercensal period. The percentages for all of the intercensal periods are in THE PLACE OF LAW, *supra* note 4, at 298 tbl. 6.4.

92 See text following *supra* note 27.

states in the West.[93] The particular cultural content that accounted for these differences, however, is not identifiable from the data that were used in the instant study.

A third conclusion to be drawn from Table 2.2 is that greater labor force participation by women twenty-five to twenty-nine years old contributed to the liberalization of state law on therapeutic abortion, although the effect was not large. The relatively small impact of labor force participation on the dependent variable is perhaps not surprising given that research has been unable to find a clear relationship between employment and the likelihood a woman will surgically terminate a pregnancy.[94] On the other hand, some research on women who have opted for an abortion[95] as well as theory[96] and the pre-1967 trend in labor force participation rates of young women (seen in Figure 2.1) provide grounds for believing that greater labor force participation by women of childbearing age was involved in the easing of state abortion law during the period from 1967 to 1972. As Table 2.3 shows, model fit was moderately improved by the labor force participation rate,[97] and as model III in Table 2.2 found, the odds that a state would liberalize its law on therapeutic abortion rose 20.7% with a gain of one percentage point in the labor force participation rate in 1960 of women who were twenty-five to twenty-nine years old. State differences in labor force participation among young women, in short, helped to distinguish states that relaxed their law-based restrictions on therapeutic abortion during 1967–1972 from states that did not, and while these differences did not have a major effect, they should not be ignored.

---

93 Model I and model III produced inconsistent effects for states located in the South. Specifically, the odds that a state would relax its law on abortion during 1967–1972 were reduced by SOUTH in model I but raised by SOUTH in model III. However, the odds ratio for SOUTH in model III is more plausible than the odds ratio for SOUTH in model I, because of the sixteen states that modified their law on abortion between 1967 and 1972, fully half were in the South. *Compare supra* note 20 *with supra* note 31.

94 *Supra* note 8 and its accompanying text.

95 Finer et al., *supra* note 6.

96 Nock, *supra* note 7.

97 In Table 2.3, compare the accuracy rates of the third set of independent variables (FOREIGNPOP, NOCENTRAL, SOUTH, WEST, COLL2529, LABOR2529) with the accuracy rates of the sets that omitted LABOR2529. In addition, a comparison of the third set with the fourth set of independent variables (FOREIGNPOP, NOCENTRAL, SOUTH, WEST, COLL2529, INCOME2534), and a comparison of the sixth set (FOREIGNPOP, NOCENTRAL, SOUTH, WEST, COLL2529, LABOR2529, URBAN) with the seventh set (FOREIGNPOP, NOCENTRAL, SOUTH, WEST, COLL2529, INCOME2534, URBAN), shows that accuracy rates were higher with labor force participation rate than with income.

Finally, Table 2.2 indicates that urbanization had no noteworthy impact on whether states eased their law on access to therapeutic abortion in the 1967–1972 period. Table 2.2 shows that the odds ratio for URBAN was very close to 1.000 (see model I), and Table 2.3 discloses that the fit of model III would not have been materially improved by adding URBAN.[98]

3 Macrosociological Theory and the Institution of Law

To advance, science blends theory and empirical research. Indeed, the blend is critical in scientific endeavors, because theory and research are mutually reinforcing—theory guides research and the findings of research inform theory. Improvements in science thus depend heavily on the degree to which the concepts of theory in a discipline mix with research in the discipline, especially its quantitative research.

The framework that I have proposed for the institution of law is grounded on a particular theory that has been and remains influential in macrosociology. The present chapter has used the concept of societal need in accounting for the content of law on abortion because I believe that the concept, which has been central to the theory from which the framework arises, is both a convenient and effective tool for understanding the shift in law on abortion during the late 1960s and early 1970s. In this regard, the reader should be aware that the needs on which I focus are those of the societal system rather than those of individuals. The two types of need may influence each other, and they may change concurrently in subject matter and intensity. However, the concept of societal need differs from the concept of individual need, and because each has a distinct referent, the two concepts must be kept separate. Abortion offers a useful example. A pregnancy that is unwanted may be aborted, and a pregnant woman who pursues this option is doing so because she believes that the pregnancy creates one or more difficulties for her.[99] Such difficulties, if intense, create *her* need for an abortion, but an individual-level need may not correspond to a society-level

98 In Table 2.3, compare the third set of independent variables (FOREIGNPOP, NOCENTRAL, SOUTH, WEST, COLL2529, LABOR2529) with the sixth set (FOREIGNPOP, NOCENTRAL, SOUTH, WEST, COLL2529, LABOR2529, URBAN).

99 In 1973, the U.S. Supreme Court ruled that, under the federal Constitution, law cannot allow a therapeutic abortion to be performed solely in cases where the life of the pregnant woman is jeopardized by the pregnancy. Indeed, under the ruling, law must permit a therapeutic abortion to be performed until the last trimester of pregnancy. Roe v. Wade, 410 U.S. 113, 164–65 (1973); *supra* note 2. In its rationale, the Court explicitly identified the difficulties that an unwanted pregnancy can pose for a pregnant woman:

need because the individuals who populate a societal system cannot be equated with the system. Indeed, sociology originated as a distinct discipline of science in order to recognize that a society has a structure and hence properties of its own, and that the activities of individuals in a society cannot be understood unless the structure and properties of the society are taken into account.[100]

According to the macrosociological thesis that I am advancing in the present book, a society is molded by large-scale forces, and the present chapter has posited that one or more of the forces operating in the United States during the twentieth century altered social life to produce a societal need for access to therapeutic abortion and doctrines of law supporting this access. The need was eventually met because (i) every social system in the long term works to maintain and, when necessary, build the commitment of its participants and (ii) every social system benefits from running efficiently and thus in the long term moves toward an optimal level of efficiency.[101] Both of these propensities of societies are likely to have been involved in the advent of U.S. law allowing therapeutic abortion in a broad range of circumstances.

Maternity, or additional offspring, may force upon the woman a distressful life and future. Psychological harm may be imminent. Mental and physical health may be taxed by child care. There is also the distress, for all concerned, associated with the unwanted child, and there is the problem of bringing a child into a family already unable, psychologically and otherwise, to care for it. In other cases, as in this one, the additional difficulties and continuing stigma of unwed motherhood may be involved.

410 U.S. at 153.

Because the Court was dealing with an extant societal situation, the preceding passage is an expression (qualitative indicator) of the societal need for new law on therapeutic abortion. For quantitative evidence that this need was prevalent in the United States in the 1960s and early 1970s, see *supra* note 38 and Jacqueline Darroch Forrest et al., *Abortion in the United States, 1976–1977*, 10 FAM. PLAN. PERSP. 271, 272 tbl. 1, 273 (1978) (estimating that among women who wanted to terminate a pregnancy in 1973, almost three out of five were unable to do so lawfully).

100 Bruce H. Mayhew, *Structuralism versus Individualism: Part 1, Shadowboxing in the Dark*, 59 SOC. FORCES 335, 338–39 (1980). The thesis that a society has attributes beyond those of individuals and shapes the lives of individuals was initially proposed by a Muslim philosopher, Ibn Khaldun, roughly half a millenium before the nineteenth-century writers who are usually considered to have founded sociology. Ali Arazeem Abdullahi & Bashir Salawu, *Ibn Khaldun: A Forgotten Sociologist?* 43 S. AFR. REV. SOCIOL. 24 (2012). Among the latter, Émile Durkheim was the first to offer an explanation of how a society can exist apart from its individual participants. R. Keith Sawyer, *Durkheim's Dilemma: Toward a Sociology of Emergence*, 20 SOCIOL. THEORY 227, 227, 233–34 (2002).

101 The foregoing sociological axioms are suggested by the processes of social integration and system integration. Axiom (i) corresponds to the process of social integration; axiom (ii) underlies the process of system integration. Although the processes of social integration and system integration are thought to be present in every society, each process is

As a matter of logic, therefore, the concept of societal need can be placed comfortably within a macrosociological framework for law. However, the concept is not without problems, as I discuss in *infra* Part 3-a, but if these problems can be overcome, an abstract concept such as societal need can aid theory in and contribute to the advance of macrosociology. In science, a concept is beneficial when it encompasses, and contributes to understanding, a wide range of phenomena. A useful concept, that is, permits numerous and seemingly disparate phenomena to be approached in ways that allow the prediction of events that have yet to be observed. Theory in a scientific discipline must have such concepts if it is to assist the discipline.

Does the concept of societal need help macrosociology to understand the institution of law? I believe that it does, at least if application of the concept comports with the meaning of the word "need" as an "[i]mperative call or demand for the presence, possession, etc., of something."[102] In the instant chapter, I have focused on law dealing with therapeutic abortion in the United States and the salient change that occurred in this law from 1967 to 1973. I attributed the change to, inter alia, the development of a society-level need for law authorizing therapeutic abortion on a wide variety of grounds. Let me now explain why I think the concept of societal need is helpful to formulating theory that can account for the 1967–1973 change in law, i.e., for the replacement of restrictive doctrines of law on abortion.

a *Functionalism Theory and the Concept of Societal Need*

Societal need is not a novel concept. In the sociological theory that is commonly labeled "structural functionalism," or more simply "functionalism," it has been a key concept.[103] Theory in sociology began with and was long dominated by functionalism, and although competing theories have emerged, sociological theory continues to be influenced by functionalism.[104] Functionalism with its concept of societal need has been, in a word, tenacious.[105]

---

presumably incomplete. Less-than-full integration leads to, or at least allows, change in the institutions of a society. The distinction between social integration and system integration was first made explicitly by David Lockwood, *Social Integration and System Integration*, *in* EXPLORATIONS IN SOCIAL CHANGE 244, 245–46, 249 n.6 (George K. Zollschan & Walter Hirsch eds., 1964).

102 10 OXFORD ENGLISH DICTIONARY 288 (2d ed. 1989) (definition 7.a of "need").

103 Jonathan H. Turner & Alexandra R. Maryanski, *"Is 'Neofunctionalism' Really Functional?"* 6 SOCIOL. THEORY 110, 117 (1988).

104 JONATHAN H. TURNER, THE STRUCTURE OF SOCIOLOGICAL THEORY 34, 37 n.31 (7th ed. 2003); JOHN SCOTT, SOCIOLOGICAL THEORY: CONTEMPORARY DEBATES 138–39 (1995).

105 Turner & Maryanski, *supra* note 103, at 118.

Functionalism, however, has not escaped criticism, and some of its adherents have removed the concept of societal need from their work on sociological theory or recommended doing so.[106] At least four of the criticisms[107] are pertinent to the macrosociological framework of the instant book.[108] They are:

1. The theory of functionalism is unable to account for change in society and its institutions, particularly change that is sharp.
2. The theory of functionalism with the concept of societal need is teleological.
3. Societal needs are indeterminate, rendering the theory of functionalism empirically untestable if it incorporates the concept of societal need.
4. The theory of functionalism is tautological insofar as it uses the concept of societal need.

As applied to my macrosociological framework for law, however, I do not view the criticisms as fatal even though the roots of the framework are in functionalism theory. The first criticism is simply inapplicable to my framework. Alterations in the concepts and doctrines of the institution of law are a central concern of the framework, and they are thought to arise from changes that have occurred in the nature of social life. The present chapter thus focused on the shift that occurred in U.S. law on abortion from the late 1960s to the early 1970s and sought to locate the societal conditions that accounted for the shift.

The other criticisms of functionalism also do not undermine a functionalism-based macrosociological framework for law that employs the concept of societal need. Quantitative data are available, or can be collected, to measure the society-level antecedent variables that are plausible causes of (i) the magnitude of a societal need for law on a specific activity and (ii) increases and decreases in this magnitude over time. Because such a need is well-defined, empirically measurable, and a logical precursor of law on the activity, a theory-based framework that employs the concept of societal need in this way is testable empirically, is not teleological, and does not give rise to tautological

106 *Id.* at 119.

107 The criticisms discussed in the text were derived from the following sources: MARK ABRAHAMSON, FUNCTIONALISM 37–49 (1978); JOHN REX, KEY PROBLEMS OF SOCIOLOGICAL THEORY 60–77 (1961); TURNER, *supra* note 104, at 23–37; Peter A. Munch, *The Concept of "Function" and Functional Analysis in Sociology*, 6 PHIL. SOC. SCI. 193 (1976); Turner & Maryanski, *supra* note 103, at 115–17.

108 These criticisms are discussed in more detail in THE PLACE OF LAW, *supra* note 4, at 302–307.

reasoning. Consequently, the second, third, and fourth criticisms of functionalism can be avoided—and in my framework, they are. Moreover, the concept of society need is not without an advantage: The concept has the potential to bring together multiple, seemingly disparate, phenomena under one roof. While only future work will determine whether this promise will be fulfilled, the difficulties with the concept in the past ought not be permitted to discredit uses of the concept in the future.

b *Social Forces and U.S. Law on Therapeutic Abortion*

Let me relate the discussion in *supra* Part 3-a to law on abortion. According to the findings in Part 2, the variable of schooling among young women is key to understanding the shift in law on therapeutic abortion in the United States during the late 1960s and early 1970s. The extent and length of formal education had increased among young women, evidently manifesting a change that had taken place in their role in society, and these alterations in the social fabric can logically be considered to have generated a societal need for law that was comparatively unrestrictive in terms of abortion. However, because a society is to a large degree integrated (even though not seamless), the gains that females experienced with regard to schooling almost certainly stemmed from powerful, albeit slow-acting, society-level forces. But were they?

A complete answer to the question must await the future and the advances in macrosociology that it will bring. However, I suggest that a critical force behind the change in the female sex role was expansion in the quantity and quality of knowledge possessed by society.[109] This expansion is likely to have been responsible for broad changes in social life, but because it happened gradually, it escaped attention.[110] Advances in knowledge thus cut a wide swath across the societal system even though their effects were subtle. However, that the effects were unrecognized should not be a reason to deny the existence of the force that produced them. In societies that are structurally complex and democratically governed, growth in the store of knowledge offers a credible explanation for the extension of the law-allowed circumstances in which therapeutic abortions can be performed. This growth presumptively increases

109 Knowledge is an elusive concept and difficult to define. As the word is employed here, "knowledge" covers both of the following: (i) that which is "useful in the knower's work, his decisions and actions"; (ii) that which "satisf[ies] intellectual curiosity" and is considered to be "scientific learning…; acquired, as a rule, in active concentration," though with the recognition that questions remain unanswered. 1 FRITZ MACHLUP, KNOWLEDGE AND KNOWLEDGE PRODUCTION 100, 108 (1980).

110 THE PLACE OF LAW, *supra* note 4, at 264–68, 308–10.

rationality and individualism: More knowledge brings more scrutiny of society-created restrictions and more choice among alternatives.[111] If the foregoing line of reasoning is correct, change in the role of women and in law pertinent to that role should have been expected.

A comment is in order with regard to population density (urbanization), because the variable was not found to be related to whether states eased their law on therapeutic abortion before *Roe*.[112] Given the plausibility and promise of the sociological theory of urbanism,[113] the failure to uncover a direct effect of urbanization was disappointing. Nonetheless, it is notable that the fraction of the U.S. population resident in highly populated areas increased continuously over the course of the twentieth century and that the fraction was large during the period before law on abortion underwent liberalization. Specifically, the share of the U.S. population in a metropolitan area doubled in the forty years from 1910 to 1950 (twenty-eight percent to fifty-six percent). Increases continued from 1950 to 1960 (fifty-six percent to sixty-three percent) and from 1960 to 1970 (sixty-three percent to sixty-nine percent).[114] Research indicates that, because college graduates disproportionately reside in urban areas,[115] nontraditional social values are more common in such areas.[116] Indeed, of all topics within the scope of civil liberties, a nontraditional role for women may receive the most support in an urban environment.[117] Consequently, the spread of metropolitan residence across the U.S. population, by promoting the concentration of college graduates, would have facilitated change in the sex role of women and, in turn, would have led to supporting doctrines of law. Indirectly, then, urbanization may have contributed to the advent of liberalized law on therapeutic abortion.

---

111 *Id.* at 267, 433, 453 n.223.

112 *Supra* note 98 and accompanying text.

113 The theory is described in the text accompanying *supra* notes 49, 50, & 75.

114 FRANK HOBBS & NICOLE STOOPS, U.S. CENSUS BUREAU, U.S. DEP'T OF COMMERCE, DEMOGRAPHIC TRENDS IN THE 20TH CENTURY: CENSUS 2000 SPECIAL REPORTS, at A-5 tbl. 3 (2002), *available at* www.census.gov/prod/2002pubs/censr-4.pdf. A "metropolitan" area contains "a large population nucleus, together with adjacent communities having a high degree of social and economic integration with that nucleus." *Id.* at B-4.

115 Laura M. Moore & Seth Ovadia, *Accounting for Spatial Variation in Tolerance: The Effects of Education and Religion*, 84 SOC. FORCES 2205, 2214 (2006).

116 Thomas C. Wilson, *Urbanism, Migration, and Tolerance: A Reassessment*, 56 AM. SOCIOL. REV. 117, 119–21 (1991).

117 Thomas C. Wilson, *Urbanism and Nontraditional Opinion: Another Look at the Data*, 73 SOC. SCI. Q. 610, 612 tbl. 1 (1992).

In summation, what was responsible for the modification of abortion law in the United States during the late 1960s and early 1970s? The question involves a puzzle all of whose pieces have yet to be located, but assembling the pieces that are available, I believe that the chief societal force was the growth of knowledge. That growth has long occurred in the United States,[118] and in reshaping the American social order during the twentieth century, it changed the core of society in a way or ways that prompted young women to attend school and complete college. An intervening variable in the alteration of the social system, or a corollary or consequence of this alteration, is likely to have been a widening of the range of non-childrearing activities that attract women and, in terms of childbearing, a rise in the burdens that children create relative to the benefits that children provide. The outcome was change in the societal role of women and the development of a societal need for access to therapeutic abortion. Of course, the findings that were reported in Table 2.2 require that the effects of educational attainment among women be considered in conjunction with the appreciable effects of the culture-related variables. Nonetheless, in bringing about the liberalization of law on abortion, the former (education) was probably a more important influence than the latter.[119]

C *Functionalism Theory and U.S. Law on Therapeutic Abortion*

When considered within sociological theory, the process I have posited can be explained by functionalism. According to functionalism, a society is a system

---

118 THE PLACE OF LAW, *supra* note 4, at 264–67.

119 The multiplicative nature of odds ratios precludes a simple comparison between an odds ratio above 1.000 and an odds ratio below 1.000. LONG & FREESE, *supra* note 63, at 179. In Table 2.2, the effect in model III of COLL2529 (odds ratio = 2.897) was roughly equivalent in size to the effect of NOCENTRAL (odds ratio = 0.382), but the magnitude of the effect of COLL2529 exceeded the magnitude of the effect of FOREIGNPOP (odds ratio = 0.671). Among the independent variables in model III with an odds ratio that was above 1.000, COLL2529 had the highest odds ratio.

To ascertain which of a number of independent variables had the largest effect on a dependent variable, the use of a regression coefficient that has been standardized on the standard deviation of its independent variable is questionable when the independent variable was measured as a dummy. PAMPEL, *supra* note 21, at 32–33. In the instant study, the empirical indicators of the independent variable of culture were measured with dummies, and standardized coefficients are thus not employed to determine whether the impact of culture on the dependent variable was greater than the impact of education. However, such standardized coefficients can be used to compare cultural heterogeneity with education, because both were measured with ratio scales. *Supra* note 56. The odds ratios derived from the standardized coefficients that were computed for model III in Table 2.2 indicate

and as such is more than the sum of the individual human beings in it. Being a system, a society shapes the social reality of its individual members by, inter alia, creating constraints and inducements that mold the behavior and values of the members. It follows logically, therefore, that with alterations in the character of society, existing constraints and inducements will be eliminated and new ones will be introduced.

The shift in U.S. law on abortion during the late 1960s and early 1970s was substantial and quick, but it was not isolated from other changes in the law of the country. Instead, the shift was part of a broad movement in U.S. law from the middle of the twentieth century onward towards embodying societal rationality and endorsing the primacy of the individual. Title VII of the federal Civil Rights Act of 1964 offers an illustration.[120] The statute prohibits employers, employment agencies, and labor organizations from discriminating in a variety of ways when the discrimination involves any one of five socio-demographic attributes, viz., "race, color, religion, sex, or national origin."[121] Under the statute, what matters in the workplace is the talent of the individual, not a characteristic of a human group to which the individual belongs.[122] The shift in abortion law, therefore, was a constituent of a broad historical era in law, and as such it is unlikely to have been a fortuitous event.

But what insights into the causes of the shift in abortion law can be derived from a functionalist analysis? A plausible hypothesis is that past and continuing growth in the stock of knowledge[123] altered the constraints and

---

that cultural heterogeneity had a much smaller effect on the dependent variable (ABORTLAW) than education. Specifically, while the odds that a state liberalized its law on abortion prior to Roe v. Wade were reduced 72.7% by an increase of one standard deviation in FOREIGNPOP, they were raised 527.3% by an increase of one standard deviation in COLL2529. Standardized coefficients and standardized odds ratios were computed using the LISTCOEF command in Stata. LONG & FREEZE, *supra* note 63, at 94–98, 464–65.

120 Pub. L. No. 88–352, §§ 701–716, 78 Stat. 241, 253–66 (1964) (codified as amended at 42 U.S.C. §§ 2000e to 2000e-17 (2006)).

121 42 U.S.C. § 2000e-2 (2006). The activities covered by Title VII are described more fully in Part 2-a of *infra* Chapter 7.

122 *E.g.*, City of Los Angeles v. Manhart, 435 U.S. 702, 707–708 (1978) (holding in breach of Title VII the policy of an employer that, because of the sex differential in mortality, required larger pension plan contributions from female employees than from male employees but that paid the same post-retirement monthly amount to women and to men who, at retirement, did not differ in age, seniority, and salary).

123 A measure of the growth of knowledge in the United States is in THE PLACE OF LAW, *supra* note 4, at 264–67.

inducements that affected women with respect to bearing and rearing children. In the social setting that ensued, women had a different role and underwent more formal schooling than in the past. Fertility-related social values are also likely to have changed, because childrearing duties in this social setting hampered women in their pursuit of both educational opportunities and alternatives to motherhood. The result was twofold—society needed to enlarge the availability of therapeutic abortion, and once this need developed, the institution of law had to eliminate prominent law-designated conditions that were thought to be major impediments to abortion.[124] During the late 1960s and early 1970s, in short, law in the United States responded to a societal situation pressing for ready access to therapeutic abortion and thereby acted as it could be expected to act.[125]

A final observation is warranted. As we saw in *supra* Part 1 of the instant chapter, the principal revision of law on therapeutic abortion in the United States began in 1967 at the state level mainly through legislation[126] and ended in 1973 at the national level through judicial action,[127] viz., the ruling of the U.S. Supreme Court in Roe v. Wade.[128] However, while the distinctions between state law and federal law and between legislatures and courts are regarded as fundamental by the institution of law in the United States, the distinctions probably add little to a macrosociological explanation of change in the content of law concerned with a society-central activity that matters to the country as a whole. In understanding the societal reasons for changes of this type, state law and federal law, and legislatures and the judiciary, are likely to be

124 Although the shift in law on therapeutic abortion during the 1967–1973 period was evidently a response to the expansion and lengthening of formal schooling among young women, the shift did not materially further schooling among white women and increased just minimally education among black women. Maya H. Klein, The Effects of Abortion Legislation on Women's Educational Attainment in the United States 83–84, 106, 109, 113–14 (1997) (unpublished Ph.D. dissertation, University of California, Berkeley) (on file with Widener University School of Law Delaware Campus library). Prior to the easing of law-based restrictions on therapeutic abortion, therefore, pregnancy generally seems not to have hindered women in reaching their educational goals, suggesting that law on abortion serves mainly as a symbol. THE PLACE OF LAW, *supra* note 4, at 402, 440–41 n.67.

125 *Supra* note 101 and accompanying text.

126 THE PLACE OF LAW, *supra* note 4, at 325 n.91.

127 "The genius of the common law has been its responsiveness to changing times, its ability to reflect developing moral and social values. Drawing upon the past, the law must serve—and traditionally has served—the needs of the present." United States v. Freeman, 357 F.2d 606, 624–25 (2d Cir. 1966).

128 410 U.S. 113 (1973).

inseparable and hence ought not to be viewed piecemeal. The recognition of their underlying sociological character, and hence the acknowledgement of their inextricable connection through a common denominator, facilitates the realization that the institution of law in the United States, in altering its treatment of abortion, was not acting on its own. Instead, law was manifesting a deep-seated shift in social life and conforming to a new social reality, as it was compelled to do if it was to remain a productive component of the societal system.

CHAPTER 3

"Three-Strikes" Law

Abstract

During the 1990s, nineteen states in the United States adopted law that mandated a lengthy prison sentence for a person who is convicted of a felony when that person has been convicted of a felony at least once before and the latest as well as the earlier convictions entailed specified types of conduct. Such law—popularly labeled "three-strikes" law—differed from habitual-offender legislation, which many states already possessed, in terms of whether trial-court judges were allowed discretion in imposing the law-designated and -augmented sentence for the latest conviction. Habitual-offender legislation permitted such discretion; "three-strikes" law did not. The instant chapter is based on the macrosociological framework of Chapter 1 and thus rests on the proposition that, in jurisdictions having a complex social structure and democratic government, concepts and doctrines of law on society-important activities are generated by society-level conditions and evolve in response to society-level changes. In such a framework, concepts and doctrines of law are the work of large-scale forces, not particular individuals. This framework was tested in the instant chapter by ascertaining the ability of a set of state-level conditions to predict which states had adopted, and which states had not adopted, "three-strikes" law. Applying logistic regression to data on the independent variables for 1960 and 1990, the odds that "three-strikes" law was present in a state were found to be unaffected by state rates of violent crime or state rates of property crime. However, the odds varied with three state attributes—culture (measured by geographic region), social disorder (measured by the percentage of all women age 30–34 who were unmarried due to divorce), and societal rationality (measured by the percentage of the population age 25+ that was college-educated). Specifically, the odds that "three-strikes" law had been adopted were elevated among states in the South and in the West, were lower among states in which social disorder was more widespread, and were higher among states having a greater degree of societal rationality.

1 Crime and Law in Society

In the United States, crime has been a major public concern since at least the middle of the twentieth century. A measure of this concern is found in the results of a series of national sample surveys in which U.S. adults have been

 | DOI 10.1163/9789004281219_004

asked whether they are "afraid to walk alone at night" in an area located near where they reside; from the 1960s onward, the belief that crime is a proximate threat has characterized approximately one-third to one-half of all adults.[1] Because a sizeable fraction of adults has perceived crime as a personal threat and the fraction has been relatively stable over time, the perception is likely to have had important consequences for social life and for the aspects of social life to which the resources of the nation are committed. Indicators of the reaction to the fear of crime include (i) the large size of the U.S. work force that is devoted to controlling crime and criminals[2] and (ii) the considerable number of studies that have been undertaken in an attempt to understand the causes and consequences of crime.[3] Not surprisingly, a vast body of U.S. law exists with regard to crime, the apprehension of its perpetrators, and the rights of persons who are suspected of being, or who have been charged with being, perpetrators of crime.[4]

As scholars who have studied law are aware, many if not most doctrines of law do not remain the same over time, and doctrines of law pertaining to crime are no exception. Indeed, law on crime underwent substantial change in the United States during the twentieth century.[5] An unequivocal shift in the content of law on a topic can, of course, be the basis of an historical era,[6]

1 Mark Warr, *Public Opinion on Crime and Punishment* 59 PUB. OPINION Q 296, 297, 304 (1995); Lydia Saad, Gallup, Inc., Nearly 4 in 10 Americans Still Fear Walking Alone at Night (Nov. 5, 2010) (on file with author), *available at* http://www.gallup.com/poll/144272/Nearly-Americans-Fear-Walking-Alone-Night.aspx (last visited May 1, 2015).

2 In 2007, the number of individuals employed in the criminal-justice sector in the United States was 2.45 million, having approximately doubled since 1982. TRACEY KYCKELHAHN, U.S. DEP'T OF JUSTICE, JUSTICE EXPENDITURES AND EMPLOYMENT, FY 1982–2007—STATISTICAL TABLES 7 tbls. 7 & 8 (2011) (on file with author), http://bjs.ojp.usdoj.gov/index.cfm?ty=pbdetail&iid=2192 (last visited May 1, 2015).

3 The quantity of this scholarship is reflected in *Criminal Justice Abstracts*, which covers crime-pertinent materials published in the United States and elsewhere, and contains bibliographic entries that presently number in excess of 475,000. EBSCO Publishing, Criminal Justice Abstracts™, http://www.ebscohost.com/academic/criminal-justice-abstracts (last visited May 1, 2015).

4 The online law library Lexis, for instance, has a web page exclusively for materials on the subject of "criminal law."

5 Alan C. Michaels, *"Rationales" of Criminal Law Then and Now: For a Judgmental Descriptivism*, 100 COLUM. L. REV. 54, 93 (2000).

6 An illustration of a law-delineated era in the United States is the enactment by Congress of statutes that are concerned with discrimination involving certain demographic attributes,

i.e., a period of time that is characterized by a distinct, relatively long-lasting set of beliefs and/or circumstances[7] that are manifested in salient doctrines of law. Indeed, the United States is currently in an identifiable era of law on crime. This era began in the middle of the 1980s and has emphasized the punishment of persons convicted of serious crimes, i.e., felonies.[8] The current era is based on the belief of the public that the key to reducing the incidence of crime is to punish convicted felons, not attempt to rehabilitate them through service programs, and the belief is manifested in the law of the era[9]—an era that will last until there is a fundamental change in public sentiments regarding crime. Indeed, the era may already be concluding.[10]

a *"Three-Strikes" Law*

The instant chapter will focus on one particular doctrine of law—widely known as "three-strikes" law—that emerged during the era the United States entered in the mid-1980s. Notably, the "three-strikes" doctrine was adopted by nineteen states in just five years, viz., from 1993 through 1997. Although "three-strikes" law has no generally accepted definition,[11] it will be regarded in the instant chapter as law that mandates a lengthy prison sentence for a person who is convicted of a felony when the person has been convicted of a felony at least once before and the latest as well as the earlier convictions entailed specified types of conduct.[12] "Three-strikes" law differs from habitual-offender legislation, which many states already possessed, in terms of whether judges of

---

e.g., race and sex. The statutes were adopted during the period from 1963 to 1990. LARRY D. BARNETT, THE PLACE OF LAW: THE ROLE AND LIMITS OF LAW IN SOCIETY 268–70 (2011) [hereinafter THE PLACE OF LAW].

7 5 OXFORD ENGLISH DICTIONARY 362 (2d ed. 1989) (def. 4.a. of the word "era").

8 Franklin E. Zimring, *Penal Policy and Penal Legislation in Recent American Experience*, 58 STAN. L. REV. 323, 331–34 (2005).

9 Kenneth E. Fernandez, Crime Policy in the New Millennium: The End of the "Tough on Crime" Era? [17] (unpublished paper presented at meeting of the State Politics and Policy Conference, June 3–4, 2011).

10 *Id.* at [19].

11 *See* Michael Vitiello, *Three Strikes: Can We Return to Rationality?* 87 J. CRIM. L. & CRIMINOLOGY 395, 400–401 (1997) (pointing out that "multiple offender" statutes, which have been popularly labeled "three-strikes" statutes, are not identical in content across all jurisdictions).

12 Franklin E. Zimring, *Populism, Democratic Government, and the Decline of Expert Authority: Some Reflections on "Three Strikes" in California*, 28 PAC. L.J. 243, 244–49 (1996); Franklin E. Zimring & David T. Johnson, *Public Opinion and the Governance of Punishment in Democratic Political Systems*, 605 ANNALS 266, 277 (2006).

trial courts are permitted discretion in imposing the law-designated, law-augmented sentence for the latest conviction. Habitual-offender legislation allows such discretion; "three-strikes" law does not.[13] However, discretion in dealing with suspected perpetrators of crime is not necessarily absent in a jurisdiction that has "three-strikes" law, because prosecutors may possess the authority to decide whether to charge a defendant under this law.[14]

Which states adopted "three-strikes" law as defined above? The states with "three-strikes" law, and (in parentheses) the year in which each state implemented its law, are as follows:[15] Arkansas (1995), California (1994), Colorado (1994), Delaware (1994), Georgia (1995), Illinois (1994), Maryland (1994), Montana (1997), New Jersey (1995), New Mexico (1994), North Carolina (1994), Pennsylvania (1995), South Carolina (1996), Tennessee (1994), Texas (1996), Virginia (1994), Washington (1993), West Virginia (1994), Wisconsin (1994). The states that accepted "three-strikes" law thus did so from 1993 to 1997.

b *Societal Pressure*

When a large number of states adopt a particular doctrine of law in a period that is remarkably brief in historical terms, their concurrent action is unlikely to be fortuitous in either content or timing. What accounts for the emergence of the "three-strikes" doctrine of law in certain states but not others during the mid-1990s? In the instant chapter, the movement to "three-strikes" law by numerous states at essentially the same time is considered to be a sociological phenomenon, and its explanation is thus sought with tools of sociology.[16]

---

13 Zimring & Johnson, *supra* note 12, at 277.

14 "Three-strikes" legislation in general expanded the discretion of prosecutors while curtailing the discretion of judges. *Id.* at 277.

15 The list of states and implementation years is based on information in Vitiello, *supra* note 11, at 402–409, 418 & n.125, 422 n.152, 463–80. The long prison sentence required by "three-strikes" law is imposed in some states for a second felony conviction. *Id.* at 463–80.

16 *See* Bruce H. Mayhew, *Structuralism Versus Individualism: Part 1, Shadowboxing in the Dark*, 59 SOC. FORCES 335, 338–39 (1980) (defining the discipline of sociology as the study of the structure of social life). Unfortunately, the boundary between sociology and psychology has become blurred in the United States. *Id.* at 337. In an attempt to give clarity to the framework I propose for law, I have labeled the framework "macrosociological," a word that hopefully directs attention to the structure of society. I use the word "structure" to refer to "the interrelation of parts as dominated by the general character of the whole." WEBSTER'S THIRD NEW INTERNATIONAL DICTIONARY 2267 (unabr. ed. 1993) (definition 5 of the noun "structure"). Macrosociology thus focuses on the components of a social system—i.e., on institutions as the elements of society—and on the effect of the

Macrosociological theory directs attention to the societal context of law, and if macrosociological theory is correct, the states that adopted "three-strikes" penalties were driven to do so by at least one society-level force. However, the pressure on society that the force(s) created may not have been confined to the states in which "three-strikes" law developed. Instead, the pressure may have operated across many states, and assuming this to have been the case, the states that adopted "three-strikes" law presumably acted as they did because they possessed attributes that sensitized them to the pressure—attributes that, in intensity or prevalence, differed from the attributes of states not accepting "three-strikes" law.

On logical grounds, increases in crime are a source of pressure on jurisdictions to "get tough on crime," because the increases have the potential to create or intensify an awareness of and sensitivity to crime. Of course, a potential may not be realized. In terms of the subject being investigated here, a social system may adjust to and accept elevated crime rates rather than attempt to reverse them through law.[17] If so, the factors must be identified that determine which course a social system follows. In the instant chapter, the primary focus is on the conditions under which a social system resists adapting to higher crime rates and, instead, tries to combat them by approving new law. To ascertain these conditions, however, the incidence of crime must be measured in a way that captures the degree to which social pressure is building in a society to

---

system on its elements. The key propositions comprising my proposed framework are catalogued in Part 1-b of *supra* Chapter 1.

17 Among counties of the United States, an inverse relationship has been found between (i) the prevalence of homicide and (ii) the likelihood and severity of punishment for homicide. Because the data on variable (i) were for an earlier point in time than the data on variable (ii), increases in the rate of homicide were followed by a reduction in the probability that persons charged with homicide would be convicted and by a lessening in the harshness of the sentences imposed on defendants who were convicted. Mark Cooney & Callie Harbin Burt, *Less Crime, More Punishment*, 114 AM. J. SOCIOL. 491, 496, 497, 520 (2008). The finding suggests that a society, as a social system, adapts to change in the occurrence of homicide rather than controls the incidence of homicide. *Id.* at 521. If crime incidence is inversely related to punishment likelihood and punishment severity for additional types of crime, societal adaptation may be common for all forms of deviant behavior or at least for those behaviors that law has designated as crime. However, if such adaptation is typical, an important sociological question arises with regard to "three-strikes" law. Specifically, the states that possess "three-strikes" law would not have adapted to higher rates of crime, while states that do not possess "three-strikes" law would have adapted. Assuming that this reasoning is correct, the findings in *infra* Part 2 will shed light on the conditions under which a social system does not adapt to crime but, instead, seeks to curtail it.

use government to control crime. A priori, a rate is more useful as a gauge of pressure than the absolute number of crimes.

A rate, of course, is computed not only with a numerator—the number of crimes occurring in a given period—but also with a denominator, and different denominators can be chosen. For crime rates in the United States as a whole, the denominator can be, inter alia, (i) the number of people in the total population, which includes U.S. citizens living outside the United States; (ii) the number of people in the resident population, which includes all persons located in the United States;[18] or (iii) the number of people in the age range that is responsible for the majority of criminal activity. The use of (iii) merits consideration because, when acts of crime are committed, their perpetrators are not distributed evenly across all stages of the life cycle. On the contrary, perpetrators are found disproportionately among teenagers and young-adults. Thus, most of the individuals who are arrested during a year are within the age range that begins at about age 15 and ends at about age 35.[19] Because the crime rate at a given time point is affected by the size of the main crime-committing age group, the crime rate in a jurisdiction will rise or fall, ceteris paribus, as shifts occur in the distribution of age in the population of the jurisdiction even though within each age group the percentage of individuals who engage in crime has been constant.[20]

Which denominator is the most suitable for the instant chapter? The measure of the crime rate must capture the societal sense of crime volume, and the measure that does so most accurately is likely to be that which uses denominator (ii).[21] Ideally, then, the instant chapter should relate the number of crimes to the number of inhabitants, but as explained *infra*, the crime rates employed in the chapter do not identify their denominator.

18 Residence in the United States is determined by criteria such as those employed in the latest (2010) decennial census. U.S. Census Bureau, Residence Rule and Residence Situations for the 2010 Census, http://www.census.gov/population/www/cen2010/resid_rules/resid_rules.html (last visited May 1, 2015).

19 Darrell Steffensmeier & Cathy Streifel, *Age, Gender, and Crime Across Three Historical Periods: 1935, 1960, and 1985*, 69 Soc. Forces 869, 875, 880, 881 Figure 1 (1991).

20 Gary LaFree, *Declining Violent Crime Rates in the 1990s: Predicting Crime Booms and Busts*, 25 Ann. Rev. Sociol. 145, 153 (1999).

21 Denominator (iii), when used to compute the crime rates for all time points in a period, removes the impact on the crime rates of shifts during the period in the distribution of age in the population. Denominator (iii) can thus supply evidence that is helpful when the goal is to *explain* changes in crime rates and the crime rates have been calculated with denominator (i) or denominator (ii).

Figure 3.1 shows, for each year from 1960 to 2010, the rates of property crime and of violent crime in the United States as a whole,[22] i.e., for all fifty states combined.[23] To mark the period during which "three-strikes" law developed, vertical lines are drawn in the Figure at 1993 and 1997. The top graph presents the number of property crimes[24] per 100,000 population, while the bottom graph presents the number of violent crimes[25] per 100,000 population. Although the source of the data (the U.S. Department of Justice) does not specify whether the denominator of the rates is the total population or the resident population or whether the denominator remained the same over time,[26] the total population and the resident population will yield very similar rates.[27]

"Three-strikes" law began in the United States, Figure 3.1 reveals, after the rate of property crime and the rate of violent crime reached post-1960 peaks.[28] However, while the pre-law peak in property crime forms a plateau lasting

---

22 All of the data in Figure 3.1 are from Bureau of Justice Statistics, U.S. Dep't of Justice, State-by-State and National Crime Estimates by Year(s), http://bjs.ojp.usdoj.gov/ucrdata/Search/Crime/State/StatebyState.cfm (last visited May 1, 2015).

23 Individual jurisdictions can and do deviate from the crime trend of the nation as a whole, i.e., of all states in combination. Thus, the crime trends of U.S. cities have an imperfect relationship to the crime trend of the nation. Nonetheless, crime trends in U.S. cities exhibit sufficient similarity to the national crime trend that the crime-rate experiences of localities are likely to be due in part to social and economic forces that operate nationwide. David McDowall & Colin Loftin, *Do US City Crime Rates Follow a National Trend? The Influence of Nationwide Conditions on Local Crime Patterns*, 25 J. QUANTITATIVE CRIMINOLOGY 307, 312, 318 Table 3, 318–19, 321 (2009) (study of cities that had at least 100,000 inhabitants for thirty or more years during the period from 1960 to 2004).

24 The category of property crime is composed of burglary, larceny-theft, and motor-vehicle theft.

25 The category of violent crime is composed of murder and nonnegligent manslaughter, forcible rape, robbery, and aggravated assault.

26 *E.g.*, U.S. DEP'T OF JUSTICE, CRIME IN THE UNITED STATES, 2007: METHODOLOGY 4 (2008) (on file with author).

27 The resident population comprised almost the entire total population throughout the 1960–1990 period. To be exact, the resident population of the United States was 99.6% of the total population in 1960, 99.5% in 1970, and 99.8% in 1980 and 1990. Computed from U.S. CENSUS BUREAU, STATISTICAL ABSTRACT OF THE UNITED STATES: 2006, at 8 Table 2 (125th ed. 2005), *available at* http://www.census.gov/prod/www/statistical_abstract.html (last visited May 1, 2015).

28 The rate of property crime reached a high of 5353.3 in 1980, fell to 4498.5 in 1984, and then rose to 5140.2 in 1991. The peak of the violent-crime rate was 758.2 in 1991. The rates of both crime types began a secular decline after 1991.

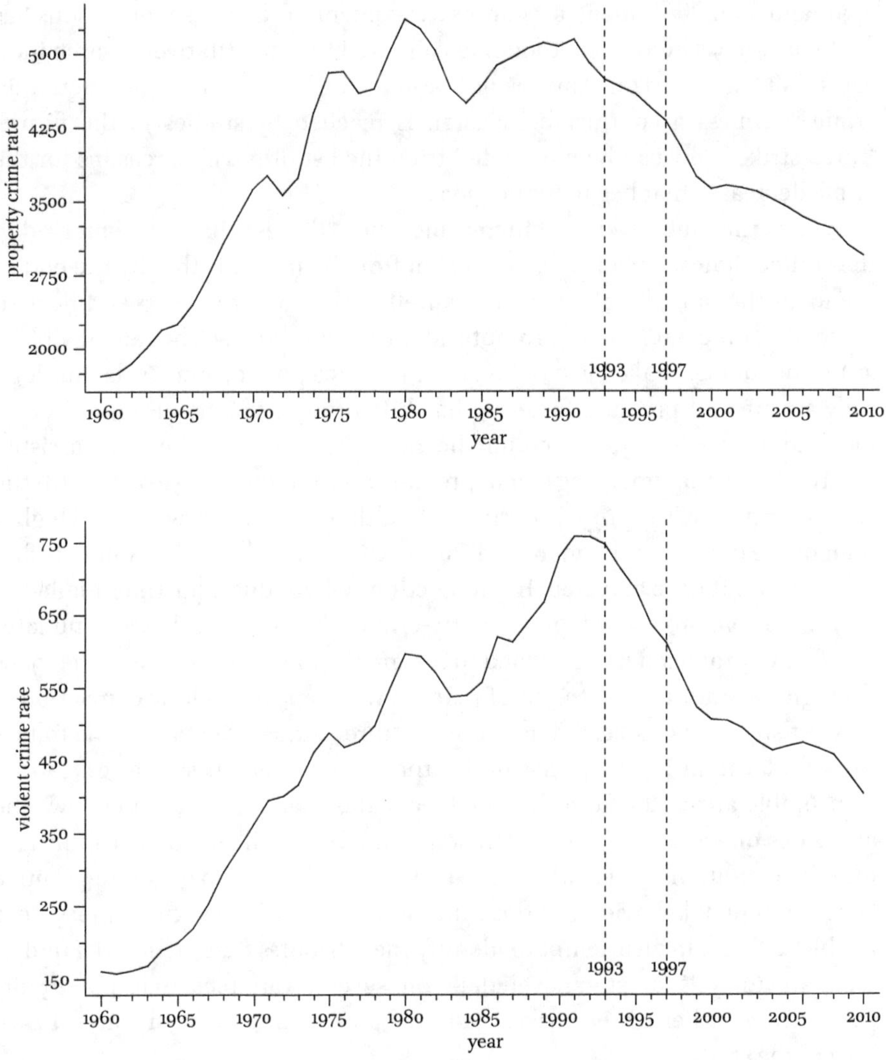

FIGURE 3.1 *Crime rates in the United States: number of crimes per 100,000 population—1960 to 2010*

SOURCE: SEE FN. 22 IN THIS CHAPTER.

approximately a decade-and-a-half, the peak in violent crime was short-lived, and the rates of both types of crime began to fall after 1991, i.e., prior to the advent of "three-strikes" law. Notably, the rate of property crime and the rate of violent crime continued to decline both during and after the period when states approved "three-strikes" law. Regrettably, social scientists to date have only speculated about the reasons that crime substantially decreased in the

1990s and later.[29] Although a rigorous assessment of the full set of reasons has yet to be done, a body of methodologically credible quantitative research indicates that "three-strikes" law has not produced a large, enduring reduction in crime.[30] Unless a contrary conclusion is reached by studies in the future, "three-strikes" law can be eliminated from the list of possible reasons for the crime decreases that began in the 1990s.

While crime rates were not increasing when "three-strikes" law emerged in the United States, a plausible conclusion from Figure 3.1 is that by the end of the 1980s the rate of violent crime, as well as the rate of property crime, had reached a sufficient level to promote adoption of such law. The rate of violent crime, of course, peaked just before the 1993–1997 period, and it was thus logically a source of pressure fostering harsh treatment of persons convicted of more than one felony. But could the rate of property crime have assisted in creating or augmenting such pressure? From the mid-1970s until the 1993–1997 period, the property-crime rate, although variable, was much higher than in the decade of the 1960s, a difference to which the social systems of all states may not have adjusted. In jurisdictions where this adjustment failed to occur, the *comparatively* high property-crime rate of the mid-1970s and later could have produced law designed to restore the lower crime rate of the 1960s through the punitive treatment of persons with repeated felony conviction.

Most states, of course, did not approve "three-strikes" law, and if the framework for law that I propose has utility, these states were dissimilar on certain measurable attributes from the nineteen states that embraced such law. The attributes on which the two sets of states differed are likely to furnish insight into the conditions under which societal pressure is able to generate punitive law for criminal behavior and the conditions under which societal pressure is unable to do so. In an attempt to identify the attributes that mattered, I undertook an analysis of state-level data on several variables that potentially explained whether "three-strikes" law was present or absent in states. I turn now to the study.

---

29 Possible reasons for the decrease are explored by, inter alia, Marc Ouimet, *Explaining the American and Canadian Crime "Drop" in the 1990s*, 44 CANADIAN J. CRIMINOLOGY 33 (2002) and by Sandeep Mishra & Martin Lalumière, *Is the Crime Drop of the 1990s in Canada and the USA Associated with a General Decline in Risky and Health-Related Behavior?* 68 SOC. SCI. & MED. 39 (2009).

30 The studies comprising this body of research are summarized and critiqued in Part 2-a-ii of *supra* Chapter 1.

2 A Study of State-Level Attributes and "Three-Strikes" Law

The study I undertook is within a relatively recent, slowly developing line of quantitative social science research. Succinctly described, research in this line is concerned with the societal conditions that are responsible for concepts and doctrines of law. The line is thus not concerned with the effects (expected or unexpected) of the content of law but with its causes,[31] a topic whose importance should not be underestimated. If the line of research fulfills its promise, the content of law at a given point in time and the evolution of law over time will be explained by factors that are deeply embedded in society rather than by specific individuals or groups. The findings of the studies in this line, accordingly, have the potential to force the abandonment of widely held assumptions about law and require the acceptance of a markedly different view of law—in particular, a macrosociological perspective that attributes concepts and doctrines of law on society-important activities to society-level characteristics, at least in jurisdictions having a complex social structure and a democratic government.

In choosing independent variables for the project at hand, some guidance was obtained from quantitative research on doctrines of law. Unfortunately, however, current knowledge regarding the macro-level determinants of the content of law arises from quantitative research that is not large in volume or free of major methodological limitations.[32] In pinpointing independent variables for the instant study, this research was thus supplemented by general macrosociological theory. All of the independent variables are discussed below.

a *Study Design*

The observation units (jurisdictions) in the present study were the forty-eight states in the continental United States, i.e., all U.S. states except Alaska and Hawaii.[33] The data employed by the study on its independent (explanatory and control) variables were compiled by, or were computed from data compiled by, agencies of the U.S. Government and are for two years, viz., 1960 and 1990.[34]

---

31 The studies in the line of research are listed in Appendix A to *supra* Chapter 1. The line evidently commenced in 1991. THE PLACE OF LAW, *supra* note 6, at 458, 469 n. 8.

32 THE PLACE OF LAW, *supra* note 6, at 458–69.

33 Alaska and Hawaii were excluded from the study in order to minimize uncontrolled factors that might have affected the dependent variable. *Id.* at 330 n. 134, 411.

34 The initial year in the study is 1960 because state-level data on all of the independent variables were not available for every state prior to 1960. A study of the macro-level determinants of law should use data that start at a point in time that is justified by history, and

For the explanatory variables that used interval or ratio scaling,[35] the source of the data was the decennial census conducted in each of these years. On the one explanatory variable that was measured as a dummy and hence nominally scaled, each state was assigned a category, which was the same in 1960 and 1990. Since the states that adopted "three-strikes" law did so in the mid-1990s,[36] the data on all of the independent variables were for points in time that preceded the law. The presence of a temporal lag between the time points for the independent variables and the time of occurrence of the dependent variable provides some assurance, though less-than-definitive evidence, that a relationship found between an independent variable and the dependent variable is causal.

A notable aspect of the study is that its data are for two years (1960 and 1990) and the years are separated by a lengthy time interval. By estimating the relationships of the independent variables to the dependent variable for each of these years, the study was able to supply some evidence on whether a relationship strengthened or weakened over time and whether a given independent variable was related to the dependent variable at one point in time but not at the other. Furthermore, for all but one of the independent variables that were measured with interval or ratio scales, the study was able to construct additional independent variables that measured the thirty-year change in amount or level of the original variables. The change over time that was captured by these variables may help to explain whether states developed "three-strikes" law. Accordingly, the data analyzed were not entirely cross-sectional, and a portion of the analysis in *infra* Part 2-b avoids the problems of causal inference that are created by purely cross-sectional data.

With regard to the specific variables in the study, the dependent variable was the presence or absence in each state of "three-strikes" law. The variable was measured by coding every state either 0 or 1, with the number 1 used to designate a state that had "three-strikes" law[37] and the number 0 used to designate a state that did not have "three-strikes" law. Because the dependent variable was measured as a dummy, the relationships of the independent variables

---

the time point should begin an identifiable historical era. THE PLACE OF LAW, *supra* note 6, at 464–65. Unfortunately, as the starting year for the data in instant study, 1960 is not an historically significant marker.

35 The four levels of scaling—nominal, ordinal, interval, and ratio—are explained in Anwer Khurshid & Hardeo Sahai, *Scales of Measurements: An Introduction and a Selected Bibliography*, 27 QUALITY & QUANTITY 303 (1993).

36 *Supra* note 15 and accompanying text.

37 The states with "three-strikes" law are listed in the text that accompanies *supra* note 15.

to it were estimated with maximum-likelihood logistic regression[38] using the LOGISTIC command in Stata version 12.1.[39]

Based on available macrosociological research and theory,[40] five independent variables—four explanatory variables and one control variable—were included when analyzing the data. The explanatory variables, listed alphabetically, were:

1. Culture
2. Social change
3. Social disorder
4. Societal rationality

---

38 When the dependent variable in a study is measured as a dummy, i.e., in binary form with the digits 0 and 1, least-squares regression is inappropriate, and logistic regression should be used. FRED C. PAMPEL, LOGISTIC REGRESSION: A PRIMER 1–10 (Paper No. 132, Sage University Paper Series on Quantitative Applications in the Social Sciences, 2000).

39 All of the estimates reported in Part 2-b of the instant chapter were produced without an intercept, i.e., with the NOCONSTANT option for LOGISTIC. STATACORP, STATA BASE REFERENCE MANUAL RELEASE 12 (2011), at 503, 932.

In regression analyses concerned with macro-level factors that may mold the content of law, the intercept may be omitted for the reasons given in the paragraph that accompanies note 59 in *supra* Chapter 2. When estimating the models in *infra* Part 2-b, model fit supplied no clear basis for including the intercept. Model fit was assessed using the percentage of states whose law was accurately predicted by each model. (As to this procedure, see note 63, and its accompanying paragraph, in Chapter 2.) The percentages revealed that the degree to which the models in Part 2-b of the instant chapter fit the data would not have been uniformly and substantially improved by the intercept. As shown in the bottom row of *infra* Table 3.3, all of whose models were estimated without the intercept, the key models had accuracy rates of 72.9% (model I), 72.9% (model III), and 68.8% (model IV) when predicting states that have and states that do not have "three-strikes" law. If the intercept had been included, these models would have had accuracy rates of 75.0% (model I), 75.0% (model III), and 77.1% (model IV). However, the presence of the intercept in model I and in model III allowed each of these models to predict correctly the law of just one additional state. While with the intercept model IV predicted correctly the law of four additional states, model IV was the sole model to benefit materially from the intercept. However, the accuracy rate of model IV without the intercept was lower than the accuracy rates of the other, i.e., intercept-absent, models in Table 3.3, and inclusion of the intercept did not raise the accuracy rate of model IV well above the rates of these other models. Model III in particular did not receive a large benefit from the intercept even though it is the most appealing. *Infra* Part 2-b.

40 *E.g.*, *supra* Chapter 1; THE PLACE OF LAW, *supra* note 6, at 200–201, 209, 267–68, 308–09, 342–43, 366, 372.

The fifth independent variable used in the data analysis—viz., crime rate—was introduced only as a control variable. All but one of the independent variables were measured with ratio scales. The exception was culture, which was captured by a set of dummies.

Why were these independent variables chosen, and what empirical referents were used for them? To include a particular independent variable, a study must have an explicit rationale for expecting it to be related to the dependent variable. Furthermore, every independent variable in the study must have a minimum of one quantitative indicator. These matters are covered next.

Culture as a societal property involves the commonality that exists among the members of a society in perceptions of and reactions to important phenomena. This commonality arises from reliance by the members of the society on collectively held concepts[41] and assumptions,[42] i.e., from reliance on a shared language and culture. Culture, like language, is essential to the existence of a society, because uniform perceptions and reactions make possible interaction, coordination, and cooperation among the members of the society. By shaping views of and responses to societal activities, culture is logically a potential determinant of the concepts and doctrines of law that develop.[43]

In the instant study, the indicator of the culture of a state was the geographic region of the United States in which the state was located. As a measure of differences in macro-level conditions, including the premises that underlie and form culture, the variable of region has long had a presence in American sociology.[44] The United States during the last half of the twentieth century was characterized by regional differences in culture,[45] and probably has been

41 Because a culture requires the presence of shared concepts, it is closely tied to the language of the society. Language may have an influence on the content of law, and the influence of language may be independent of the influence of culture. However, the two societal properties are difficult to separate in a quantitative study of societal factors that may account for concepts and doctrines of law. See Part 4 of *infra* Chapter 4.

42 See the paragraph that accompanies note 25 in *supra* Chapter 2.

43 THE PLACE OF LAW, *supra* note 6, at 218–19.

44 Alvin L. Bertrand, *Regional Sociology as a Special Discipline*, 31 SOC. FORCES 132 (1952); Samuel E. Wallace, *Regional Sociology: The South*, 1 SOCIOL. SPECTRUM 429 (1981).

45 Joel Lieske, *Regional Subcultures of the United States*, 55 J. POL. 888, 907 Figure 2 (1993); Joel Lieske, The Changing Regional Subcultures of the American States and the Utility of a New Cultural Measure 10, 58 Figure 2 (original version, in pdf, of an article by the same title in 63 POL. RES. Q. 538 (2010)) (no date) (on file with author) [hereinafter Lieske (original version)]; J. Scott Carter & Casey A. Borch, *Assessing the Effects of Urbanism and Regionalism on Gender-Role Attitudes, 1974–1998*, 75 SOCIOL. INQUIRY 548, 554–55, 558 (2005). Regional differences in culture underwent little change between 1980 and 2000.

throughout its history. Following the four-region classification scheme that has been used by the U.S. Census Bureau[46] since at least 1960,[47] every state was coded as in either the Midwest, Northeast, South, or West,[48] and four dummy variables were created, one for each region. When analyzing the data, the Midwest was chosen as the reference region,[49] and its dummy variable was accordingly omitted in each estimation.

As a societal property, *social change* logically has a bearing on the likelihood that a society will adopt novel law, including law on crime. By definition, social change involves alterations in existing social arrangements and/or adaptations to new social, economic, or demographic realities. The character of social change suggests that, to the extent the social moorings of a population shift—and especially when they decline in number and/or strength—the population will replace more of its existing doctrines of law.[50] Under this reasoning, the

---

Lieske (original version), *supra*, at 15, 17; Carter & Borch, *supra* at 558. Furthermore, residents of the United States today are cognizant of the region in which they reside. Wendy Griswold & Nathan Wright, *Cowbirds, Locals, and the Dynamic Endurance of Regionalism*, 109 AM. J. SOCIOL. 1411 (2004).

46 U.S. Census Bureau, Geographic Terms and Concepts – Census Divisions and Census Regions, https://www.census.gov/geo/reference/gtc/gtc_census_divreg.html (last visited May 1, 2015).

47 *Compare* U.S. BUREAU OF THE CENSUS, STATISTICAL ABSTRACT OF THE UNITED STATES: 1960, at xii (81st ed. 1960) *with* U.S. BUREAU OF THE CENSUS, STATISTICAL ABSTRACT OF THE UNITED STATES: 1994, at xii (114th ed. 1994). The region labeled "Midwest" in 1990 was labeled "North Central" in 1960, but contained the same states in both years. Indeed, no state was reclassified in terms of region during the period from 1960 to 1990.

48 The states in each region are:

Midwest:	Illinois, Indiana, Iowa, Kansas, Michigan, Minnesota, Missouri, Ohio, Nebraska, North Dakota, South Dakota, Wisconsin.
Northeast:	Connecticut, Maine, Massachusetts, New Hampshire, New Jersey, New York, Pennsylvania, Rhode Island, Vermont.
South:	Alabama, Arkansas, Delaware, Florida, Georgia, Kentucky, Louisiana, Maryland, Mississippi, North Carolina, Oklahoma, South Carolina, Tennessee, Texas, Virginia, West Virginia.
West:	Arizona, California, Colorado, Idaho, Montana, Nevada, New Mexico, Oregon, Utah, Washington, Wyoming.

49 MELISSA A. HARDY, REGRESSION WITH DUMMY VARIABLES 7–12, 26–28 (Paper No. 93, Sage University Paper Series on Quantitative Applications in the Social Sciences, 1993).

50 A society may seek to reduce the frequency of a certain activity and to this end adopt new law. "Three-strikes" law is an example. On the other hand, a society may develop new law not to curtail the frequency of a particular activity but to acknowledge and accommodate the activity. Constitutional law on access to and use of contraception and

jurisdictions with "three-strikes" law will disproportionately be those that are socially unsettled, ceteris paribus. As its quantitative indicator of the degree of social change in each state, the instant study used the percentage of the population age 5 and older whose residence at the time of the decennial census (i.e., in 1960 and in 1990) was not the same as five years earlier.[51] Higher levels of this percentage are assumed by the study to be a cause, or at least a correlate, of greater social change.

Social disorder is concerned with the degree to which there are disruptions in a society due to tensions in or failures of relationships between the members of the society. The members involved in problematic relationships may be individuals, of course, but they may also be organized groups and/or societal institutions.[52] As so defined, the concept of social disorder implicates social

---

abortion is an example. LARRY D. BARNETT, LEGAL CONSTRUCT, SOCIAL CONCEPT: A MACROSOCIOLOGICAL PERSPECTIVE ON LAW 128–30 (1993). Regrettably, macrosociological theory and empirical research cannot yet confidently predict which of the foregoing goals will be pursued when new law is formulated. Regardless of its goal, however, new law is likely to be preceded by elevated social change.

51 The percentages constituting this indicator were obtained or calculated from the state reports for the 1960 census and 1990 census:

1960 census: U.S. BUREAU OF THE CENSUS, CENSUS OF POPULATION: 1960. VOL. I. CHARACTERISTICS OF THE POPULATION Table 42 (1963), *available at* http://www.census.gov/prod/www/decennial.html.

1990 census: U.S. BUREAU OF THE CENSUS, 1990 CENSUS OF POPULATION: SOCIAL AND ECONOMIC CHARACTERISTICS Table 23 ([1993]), *available at* http://www.census.gov/prod/www/decennial.html.

The percentages are not given and cannot be determined for any age range other than 5 years and older.

In 1960, the residence of every person in each household was ascertained by questions that referred either to "this house (or apartment)" or to "this house," implicitly defining the word "house" to include an apartment (questions P12, P13). U.S. BUREAU OF THE CENSUS, CENSUS OF POPULATION: 1960. VOL. 1. CHARACTERISTICS OF THE POPULATION. PART 1: UNITED STATES SUMMARY XLVI, XLVII (1964), *available at* http://www.census.gov/prod/www/decennial.html. In 1990, the residence of every person in each household was ascertained by a question that referred to "this house or apartment" (question 14). U.S. BUREAU OF THE CENSUS, 1990 CENSUS OF POPULATION: SOCIAL AND ECONOMIC CHARACTERISTICS. UNITED STATES (1990 CP-2-1) app. E-5, E-14 ([1993]), *available at* http://www.census.gov/prod/www/decennial.html.

52 As the word is used in sociology, an "institution" is a pattern of interpersonal activity in a society that the society deems important and that in the long run benefits the operation of the society. THE PLACE OF LAW, *supra* note 6, at 43–44, 152, 200, 394.

integration as well as system integration.[53] The variable of social disorder, which others may label "social disorganization,"[54] is pertinent to the instant study, because to the extent that social life is troubled, i.e., is plagued by problems in relationships, a foundation logically exists for new law to develop. To elaborate, an increase in social disorder from a rise in the incidence of an activity may generate new law that (i) authorizes penalties (or enhanced penalties) in an attempt to reduce the incidence of the targeted activity or (ii) allows, if not approves, the activity. On the other hand, an increase in social disorder undoubtedly does not lead to new law in all circumstances. Perhaps by generating societal uncertainty regarding how to react, social disorder that has intensified in degree or expanded in prevalence may effectively paralyze a society, preventing a response by the institution of law. Unfortunately, the conditions that elicit new law of form (i) and form (ii) above, and the conditions that overwhelm a society and inhibit new law, have not yet been ascertained.[55] Thus, while state differences in degree and/or extent of social disorder are likely to be related to whether "three-strikes" law is present, the exact nature of the relationship cannot be predicted.

---

53 The distinction between the concepts of "social integration" and "system integration" was originally made by David Lockwood, *Social Integration and System Integration*, *in* EXPLORATIONS IN SOCIAL CHANGE 244, 245 (George K. Zollschan & Walter Hirsch eds., 1964). Both concepts are concerned with the degree to which relationships in a society are characterized by friction. "Social integration" concentrates on relationships between human individuals, between human groups, and between human individuals and human groups; "system integration" concentrates on relationships between institutions. The word "institution" is defined in *supra* note 52.

54 The term "social disorganization" has the disadvantage that its opposite is "social organization," a term whose referent in sociology may be identical to, or is at least very similar to, the referent of the term "social structure." Mayhew, *supra* note 16, at 388. The term "social organization" can be confusing because it has been used to refer both to the social structure of a society and to a specific group or entity in the society. When it approximates "social structure," however, "social organization" is comprised of the particular patterns and arrangements of the activities in a society, and it thus does not have exactly the same referent as "social order," the opposite of "social disorder."

Compared to the dimension of "social organization–disorganization," the dimension of "social order–disorder" more accurately depicts the explanatory variable I have in mind, namely, the incidence and extent of severe impairment or complete termination of relationships within a society. The dimension of "social order–disorder" includes relationships between individuals and relationships between groups. The groups may or may not be entities in a form that is recognized by law, e.g., a corporation or partnership.

55 When social disorder has intensified due to growth in the incidence of multiple activities, new law on the activities may be adopted that, for some of the activities, is of form (i) and

As its empirical indicator of social disorder in each state, the instant study employed a measure of marital status.[56] The measure was based on all women age 30–34 years in each state who were classified by the census as "divorced." Specifically, the study used the percentage of women 30–34 years old who had been but were no longer married and whose most recent marriage had ended in divorce.[57] As this percentage rises, ceteris paribus, marriage as a societal institution is presumably weaker, a situation that the study assumes is a component or at least a correlate of elevated social disorder. In computing the percentage for a state, the denominator was the total number of women 30–34 years old in the state, and the numerator was the number of unmarried women in this age range in the state who had been married, whose marriage (or last marriage in cases of more than one marriage) was terminated by divorce, and who had not remarried. The age range 30–34 was chosen because the marriage failures of its members would have happened in the not-distant past. As a result, the level of marriage failure and resistance to remarriage in this age range was thought likely to gauge accurately the fragility of marriage, and hence measure social disorder, at a temporal point close to when the census was conducted. The indicator was the same in 1960 and in 1990.

Several related points should be made regarding the indicator of social disorder. The most salient aspect of the indicator is that the data for it are confined to women. Because marriage is likely to have a greater impact on the social position of women than on the social position of men,[58] divorce can be

---

that, for other of the activities, is of form (ii). Particularly when multiple activities are the source of increased social disorder, however, a society may be unable to respond to, or may become resigned to, certain or many of the activities. These activities would then not be the subject of new law.

56 Among the explanatory variables in the instant study, social disorder is likely to have the largest number of dimensions, and more than one indicator of social disorder was desirable. Unfortunately, data could not be found for an additional suitable indicator.

57 The percentages were obtained from the state reports for the 1960 census and 1990 census:

1960 census:	U.S. BUREAU OF THE CENSUS, CENSUS OF POPULATION: 1960. VOL. I. CHARACTERISTICS OF THE POPULATION Table 105 (1963), *available at* http://www.census.gov/prod/www/decennial.html.
1990 census:	U.S. BUREAU OF THE CENSUS, 1990 CENSUS OF POPULATION: GENERAL POPULATION CHARACTERISTICS Table 37 ([1992]), *available at* http://www.census.gov/prod/www/decennial.html.

58 The practice in which a married person adopts the surname of her/his spouse is evidence of a sex differential in the degree to which social status is dependent on marriage if one

expected to disrupt the social status of women more than it disrupts the social status of men,[59] making the extent of divorce among presently unmarried women an appropriate gauge of social disorder. However, the indicator, though appropriate, is imperfect, because it captures only those women who, when the census was taken, were not married due to divorce. The indicator omits women whose last marriage ended in divorce but who had remarried and were still married; such women are classified as currently married. Furthermore, the divorces of the women covered by the indicator had occurred at unknown points in the past and had not necessarily happened in the year in which the census was conducted or even the year before. Of course, the divorces that terminated the marriages of these women are likely to have been relatively recent, because the data were for women in the age range 30–34. Nonetheless, the divorce rate (i.e., the number of divorces per 1000 population) in 1960 and in 1990 may have been preferable in order to measure the then-current level of social disorder. Unfortunately, the divorce rate was not an option for the study because the divorce rate for calendar year 1960 is not available for every state.[60]

The fourth explanatory factor in the instant study—*societal rationality*—involves the degree to which socially important phenomena are analyzed and critiqued in a society rather than routinely prejudged and accepted. As defined, societal rationality is closely related to the phenomenon of individualism and, indeed, may not be empirically separable from individualism. Societal rationality is presumed to be a function of the amount and utility of knowledge available to the society, and the attainment of a threshold in societal rationality has been posited as a major force behind two major shifts in U.S. law during the last half of the twentieth century—the expansion of the law-permitted grounds for inducing an abortion; and legislation enacted by Congress that prohibited employment discrimination based on specified demographic

sex engages in the practice much more often than the other sex. In the United States, marriage rarely leads a man to change his surname, but marriage commonly prompts a woman to replace her original surname with the surname of her husband or to use her original surname in conjunction with the surname of her husband. Indeed, just a minority of women, including women who have graduated from college, continue to rely on their original surname after they have married. Claudia Goldin & Maria Shim, *Making a Name: Women's Surnames at Marriage and Beyond*, 18 J. ECON. PERSP. 143, 143–44 (2004).

59 Shulamith Albeck & Dania Kaydar, *Divorced Mothers: Their Network of Friends Pre- and Post-Divorce*, 36 J. DIVORCE & REMARRIAGE 111, 114–15 (2002).

60 *See, e.g.*, U.S. BUREAU OF THE CENSUS, STATISTICAL ABSTRACT OF THE UNITED STATES: 1976, at 71 Table 103 (97th ed. 1976) (divorce rate in 1960 not reported for Arkansas, Kentucky, and Louisiana), *available at* http://www.census.gov/prod/www/statistical_abstract.html.

attributes such as biological sex and chronological age.[61] Being a likely mover of much law in the United States (as well as in sociologically similar nations), societal rationality is a candidate to be an independent variable in any study of the relationship between jurisdiction characteristics and law.

In the instant study, what relationship will be found between societal rationality and the likelihood that states will adopt "three-strikes" law? Logic, unfortunately, allows two opposing predictions. On the one hand, an inverse relationship can be expected because rationality produces flexibility and "three-strikes" law, as an approach to crime, is rigid. "Three-strikes" law, consequently, may be less likely in states where rationality is high and more likely in states where rationality is low. On the other hand, societal rationality may have a positive relationship to the likelihood of "three-strikes" law, i.e., states where societal rationality is comparatively high may be more likely to adopt "three-strikes" law. The latter (i.e., positive) relationship is made possible by the assumption, which is widespread in the United States,[62] that the incidence of a socially damaging behavioral form can be and is curtailed by punishment. A logical derivation from this assumption is that law is able to curb the incidence of specified activities by authorizing or increasing penalties for persons who engage in these activities. Under the assumption that punishment matters, "three-strikes" law with its inflexibly imposed, harsh penalties is rational, and states with higher levels of rationality can be expected to exhibit a greater inclination to adopt such law than states with lower levels of rationality.

To measure societal rationality, the instant study relied on the share of the adult population in each state that, at the time of the census, had reached a specified milestone in college-level schooling. The stock of knowledge that can be used by a society is manifested in the extent of college-level education among its young adults,[63] and the study assumed that, ceteris paribus, societal rationality increases with the prevalence of tertiary education. Unfortunately, the decennial census of 1960 and the decennial census of 1990 did not use the same categories in reporting data on college-level education, and as a consequence, the empirical indicators of societal rationality for these years could not be identical. To be exact, while the data for both the 1960 indicator and the 1990 indicator were confined to persons (female and male) who were age 25 or older when the census was conducted, the 1960 indicator was the percentage

61 The Place of Law, *supra* note 6, at 267–70, 307–10; Part 3-c in *supra* Chapter 2.

62 The Place of Law, *supra* note 6, at 126, 148 n. 208.

63 *Id.* at 308, 324 n. 85.

of this age group that had completed four or more years of college,[64] while the 1990 indicator was the percentage of this age group that had been awarded at least a Bachelor's degree.[65] The indicator in 1960, accordingly, is distinguishable from the indicator in 1990, and while the two indicators are related, the data that each yields for states may be characterized by not-insubstantial differences.[66]

---

64 The percentages were calculated from data in the state reports for the 1960 census. U.S. BUREAU OF THE CENSUS, CENSUS OF POPULATION: 1960. VOL. I. CHARACTERISTICS OF THE POPULATION Table 103 (1963), *available at* http://www.census.gov/prod/www/decennial.html. The college(s) attended may not have been located in the state of current residence.

65 The percentages were obtained from the state reports for the 1990 census. U.S. BUREAU OF THE CENSUS, 1990 CENSUS OF POPULATION: SOCIAL AND ECONOMIC CHARACTERISTICS (CP-2) Table 22 (1993), *available at* http://www.census.gov/prod/www/decennial.html. The college(s) that conferred the degree(s) may not have been in the state of current residence.

66 The 1960 census asked two questions pertinent to number of years of schooling completed by each household member. The first question was "What is the highest grade (or year) of regular school this person has ever attended?" and was accompanied by an option for number of years of college. The second question, which immediately followed the first, was "Did he finish the highest grade (or year) he attended?" U.S. BUREAU OF THE CENSUS, CENSUS OF POPULALTION: 1960. VOL. I: CHARACTERISTICS OF THE POPULATION. PART 1: UNITED STATES SUMMARY LI (1964) (underlining in original), *available at* http://www.census.gov/prod/www/decennial.html. According to the Bureau of the Census, a "yes" answer to the second question was evidence that "the person had successfully completed the entire grade or year indicated in response to the previous question on the highest grade ever attended." *Id.* However, the wording of the two questions in the 1960 census on number of years of schooling did not, for college-level schooling, ascertain whether a person attending college had been enrolled in sufficient courses to earn a Bachelor's degree in four years. Persons may thus have been reported as having completed four years of college, but in one or more of these years, they may have not accumulated an adequate number of academic credits to be able to receive a Bachelor's degree at the end of the fourth year. The frequency of such errors was probably enlarged by extensive reliance in 1960 on respondents to interpret and answer the questions on the census form. THE PLACE OF LAW, *supra* note 6, at 295, 332 n.155. Consequently, the percentage of persons who had four years of college in 1960 is undoubtedly higher than the percentage of persons who had been awarded a Bachelor's degree as of 1960. Regrettably, the difference between the former and latter percentages is not known. Because it may be appreciable (and may be larger in some states than in others), societal rationality was considered by the instant study to have distinct indicators in 1960 and in 1990. The 1960-to-1990 changes in the percentages comprising the indicators, accordingly, were not computed.

The final independent variable in the study was the *crime rate* in each state in the United States. Elevated levels of crime were assumed to be a source of pressure for "three-strikes" law,[67] but in the data analysis, crime rates were considered to be control variables in order to identify macrosociological factors that affected whether the pressure succeeded, i.e., led to "three-strikes" law. For 1960 and for 1990, the instant study used state rates of violent crime—i.e., the number of violent crimes per 100,000 population—as well as state rates of property crime—i.e., the number of property crimes per 100,000 population.[68] Violent crimes consist of murder, forcible rape, robbery, and aggravated assault; property crimes consist of burglary, larceny-theft, and motor-vehicle theft.

Table 3.1 summarizes the elements of the regression model in the instant study. In addition to listing all of the variables—the dependent variable as well as the independent (explanatory and control) variables—Table 3.1 gives the mnemonic label of each empirical indicator of every variable and succinctly describes the indicators. With one exception, an independent variable had the same indicator in 1960 as it had in 1990; the exception was societal rationality, whose indicators (as explained above[69]) were different in 1960 and 1990. For each independent variable other than culture, the mnemonic label for an indicator that employed 1960 data was assigned the suffix 60, and the mnemonic label for an indicator that employed 1990 data was assigned the suffix 90. Thus, data for 1960 were used in the case of DIFFRES60, DIVORCE60, VIOLCR60, and PROPCR60; data for 1990 were used in the case of DIFFRES90, DIVORCE90, VIOLCR90, and PROPCR90. With regard to culture, the suffixes were unnecessary, because no state was reclassified in terms of geographic region, i.e., the region to which a state was assigned in 1960 was the region to which it was assigned in 1990.[70] For three of the independent variables measured with ratio scales—social change, social disorder, and crime rate—the percent shifts from

67 *Supra* Part 1-b of the present chapter.

68 State rates of violent crime and of property crime in 1960 and 1990 were obtained using the table-building tool of the Federal Bureau of Investigation, U.S. Dep't of Justice, State and National Crime Estimates by Year(s), http://bjs.ojp.usdoj.gov/ucrdata/Search/Crime/State/StateCrime.cfm (follow "One year of data" hyperlink) (last visited May 1, 2015). This source, however, does not provide crime rates in 1960 for the state of New York. The rates of violent crime and of property crime in New York in 1960 were computed from data in U.S. BUREAU OF THE CENSUS, STATISTICAL ABSTRACT OF THE UNITED STATES: 1962, at 149 Table 190 (83d ed. 1962), *available at* http://www.census.gov/prod/www/statistical_abstract.html (last visited May 1, 2015).

69 *Supra* notes 64 & 65 and accompanying text.

70 *Supra* notes 46–48 and accompanying text.

TABLE 3.1 *Variables and empirical indicators of variables*

Variable	Mnemonic label of indicator	Description of indicator
Dependent variable		
Three-strikes law	TSLAW	A state was coded 1 on TSLAW if it had adopted "three-strikes" law and was coded 0 if it had not adopted "three-strikes" law.
Explanatory variables		
Culture		The culture of each state was measured by the geographic region (Midwest, Northeast, South, or West) in which the state was located.[71]
	MIDWEST	A state was coded 1 on MIDWEST if it was located in the Midwest and was coded 0 if it was not.
	NOEAST	A state was coded 1 on NOEAST if it was located in the Northeast and was coded 0 if it was not.
	SOUTH	A state was coded 1 on SOUTH if it was located in the South and was coded 0 if it was not.
	WEST	A state was coded 1 on WEST if it was located in the West and was coded 0 if it was not.
Social change	DIFFRES60 DIFFRES90	The percentage of the population age 5 and older in each state that had a different residence than five years earlier.
	DIFFRES6090	The percent change from 1960 to 1990 in the empirical indicator of social change.
Social disorder	DIVORCE60 DIVORCE90	The percentage of all women age 30–34 in each state who are not currently married but who were previously married and whose (latest) marriage was terminated by divorce.
	DIV6090	The percent change from 1960 to 1990 in the empirical indicator of social disorder.

71 The states that comprised each region are listed in *supra* note 48.

TABLE 3.1 *Variables and empirical indicators of variables* (cont.)

Variable	Mnemonic label of indicator	Description of indicator
Societal rationality	EDUC60	The percentage of all persons age 25 and older in each state who, as of 1960, had finished at least four years of college.
	EDUC90	The percentage of all persons age 25 and older in each state who, as of 1990, had been awarded a Bachelor's degree or higher degree.
Control variable		
Crime rate	VIOLCR60 VIOLCR90	Rate of violent crime: the number of violent crimes (murder, forcible rape, robbery, and aggravated assault) per 100,000 population in each state.
	VIOL6090	The percent change from 1960 to 1990 in the empirical indicator of the rate of violent crime.
	PROPCR60 PROPCR90	Rate of property crime: the number of property crimes (burglary, larceny-theft, and motor-vehicle theft) per 100,000 population in each state.
	PROP6090	The percent change from 1960 to 1990 in the empirical indicator of the rate of property crime.

1960 to 1990 were additional independent variables.[72] Change in societal rationality could not be included among the additional independent variables because of the difference that existed between 1960 and 1990 in the indicators of societal rationality.

72 The variables for change between 1960 and 1990 were measured in percents, not percentage points, and hence were calculated by subtracting the 1960 percentage or rate from the 1990 percentage or rate, dividing the result by the 1960 percentage or rate, and multiplying the outcome of the division by 100.

b *Data Analysis*

A brief consideration of two matters will be helpful before delving into the findings of the data analysis. The first matter involves tests of statistical significance. Particularly in research on the relationship between jurisdiction characteristics and the content of law, an important and unavoidable methodological issue is whether the tests should be used to make decisions on null hypotheses. Tests of statistical significance have an obvious appeal, because they offer an easily identifiable, objective criterion for these decisions. Not surprisingly, therefore, the tests have become widespread in sociological research.[73] Quantitative research that attempts to explain concepts and doctrines of law with jurisdiction-level independent variables, however, generally analyzes data from cases (jurisdictions) that comprise the entire universe of interest. Under these conditions, tests of statistical significance are at best unnecessary and at worst can yield erroneous conclusions.[74] Consequently, while levels of statistical significance are reported below for regression coefficients and odds ratios, they are supplied only because some readers may want them. In the instant study, statistical significance will not be the basis for concluding that a given independent variable is or is not related to the dependent variable.

The second matter to be explored is a set of issues that are potential problems in every study that analyzes quantitative data with multiple regression. Specifically, the interpretation of regression-produced findings will be problematic if interaction or high collinearity between independent variables is present or if any case included in the data is an influential outlier. Interaction between two independent variables occurs when the relationship of one of the independent variables to the dependent variable is affected by the other independent variable.[75] Collinearity between two independent variables is unacceptable when, on these variables, the numerical values of the cases are so strongly correlated that the data analysis yields unstable or erroneous estimates of the relationship to the dependent variable of one or both of the independent variables.[76]

---

73 Erin Leahey, *Alphas and Asterisks: The Development of Statistical Significance Testing Standards in Sociology*, 84 Soc. Forces 1, 4 Figure 1, 12 (2005).

74 Jeff Gill, *Whose Variance Is It Anyway? Interpreting Empirical Models with State-Level Data*, 1 State Pol. & Pol'y Q. 318, 319 (2001); Earl Babbie, Survey Research Methods 301–02 (2d ed. 1990).

75 James Jaccard, Interaction Effects in Logistic Regression 12–13 (Paper No. 135, Sage University Paper Series on Quantitative Applications in the Social Sciences, 2001).

76 Robert M. O'Brien, *A Caution Regarding Rules of Thumb for Variance Inflation Factors*, 41 Quality & Quantity 673, 673 (2007).

An influential outlier is a case (in the present study, a jurisdiction) whose numerical value on the dependent variable deviates to such a degree from the numerical value predicted for it by the regression model that the case distorts the relationship of one or more of the independent variables to the dependent variable[77] and retention of the case in the data cannot be justified by theory. A case that is deemed an influential outlier is thus regarded as an aberration.

Ties to theory, however, extend beyond the contribution that theory can make to the decision whether a given case is an influential outlier. Theory and the above three issues are intertwined in at least two additional ways.[78] First, theory guides the choice of independent and dependent variables to investigate; i.e., based on theory, certain potential relationships are selected for examination while others are ignored. As a result, the search for possible interaction, high collinearity, and influential outliers arises from the use of variables that theory has suggested. Second, the ability of theory to explain observations already made, and predict observations yet to be made, is affected by whether error exists in the conclusions drawn from quantitative data. Interaction, high collinearity, and influential outliers can produce erroneous conclusions. Of course, a conclusion that is incompatible with current theory may be thought to disprove that theory, and is likely to be viewed as doing so when the conclusion emanates from multiple studies, even though the conclusion is mistaken. In this event, current theory may be revised and replaced by theory that is less able to account for a phenomenon. When employing quantitative data, accordingly, investigators cannot ignore the potential presence of interaction, excessive collinearity, and influential outliers. If they do, their results can be incorrect and lead to flawed theory.

With regard to the instant study, let me begin by focusing on interaction. A probe of data for interaction should not be pursued indiscriminately; it should instead be driven by theory.[79] However, current macrosociological theory supplies a meager basis for expecting that any of the independent variables

---

77 J. Scott Long & Jeremy Freese, Regression Models for Categorical Dependent Variables Using Stata 151–52 (2d ed. 2006).

78 Theory has been defined as "a statement of what are held to be the general laws, principles, or causes of something known or observed." 17 Oxford English Dictionary 902 (2d ed. 1989) (def. 4.a. of "theory[1]").

79 Jaccard, *supra* note 75, at 12–13; F. David Schoorman et al., *The Role of Theory in Testing Hypothesized Interactions: An Example from the Research on Escalation of Commitment*, 21 J. Applied Soc. Psychol. 1338, 1338, 1349, 1353 (1991).

in the study interact. The situation may change, of course, as macrosociological theory improves. Nonetheless, even though sociologists generally have ignored culture as a phenomenon,[80] a suggestion of interaction between culture and societal rationality is present in the writings of certain theorists in macrosociology.[81] Because the possibility of interaction between these variables can be extracted from their works, it will be explored.

The data were also examined for excessive collinearity between independent variables and the potential presence of influential outliers. With regard to the former, Stata never found that its threshold for high collinearity[82] was reached, and it accordingly estimated an odds ratio for each independent variable. This, however, does not guarantee that collinearity had no major impact on the relationship of an independent variable to the dependent variable,[83] and the data were thus probed for collinearity. With regard to influential outliers, any set of quantitative data may contain cases whose numerical score on the dependent variable deviated so markedly from the score forecast by the regression model that the relationship of one or more independent variables to the dependent variable is seriously misestimated. A search for influential outliers in a dataset is necessary, therefore, even though an influential outlier

80 ROBERT WUTHNOW, MEANING AND MORAL ORDER: EXPLORATIONS IN CULTURAL ANALYSIS 2 (1987).

81 Some macrosociological theory, in dealing with culture, postulates that culture operates in tandem with, or is implanted in, the structural features of society. ROBERT K. MERTON, SOCIAL THEORY AND SOCIAL STRUCTURE 556 (enlarged ed., 1968); TALCOTT PARSONS: SOCIOLOGICAL THEORY AND MODERN SOCIETY 141–43 (1967). This theory also intimates that culture thereby helps to forge concepts and doctrines of law. MERTON, *supra*, at 187, 372–73 (asserting that culture, inter alia, "regulates and controls the acceptable modes of reaching out for" culturally supported goals and that the regulation and control of behavior is accomplished partly by law); PARSONS, *supra*, at 145 (contending that the values of culture, "through legal or informal norms," must affirm the ends sought by the operating units of a society). In addition, the level of rationality has been posited to vary with social structure. WUTHNOW, *supra* note 80, at 204. Although the foregoing does not directly suggest a culture-moderated impact of societal rationality on law, the data were probed for interaction between culture and rationality. The results are reported in *infra* note 102.

82 STATACORP, *supra* note 39, at 934, 975.

83 When collinearity materially affects the relationship of one or more independent variables to the dependent variable but statistical analysis software does not drop one of the independent variables because its threshold for high collinearity was not attained, some or all of the results produced by the software will be "clearly nonsense." DAVID W. HOSMER & STANLEY LEMESHOW, APPLIED LOGISTIC REGRESSION 140 (2d ed. 2000).

cannot be found solely with objective criteria.[84] My findings on both of these topics (collinearity and influential outliers) are reported below.

Turning to the data, the mean and standard deviation are shown in Table 3.2 for each indicator of an independent variable that was measured with an interval scale or a ratio scale. No mean or standard deviation is reported for the indicator of one independent variable (viz., culture) or for the indicator of the dependent variable, because these variables were measured with nominal scales. The statistics in Table 3.2 are for the forty-eight coterminous states.

Turning to Table 3.3, the data were analyzed with several regression models, and for each model, the table reports the odds ratios[85] estimated for the included independent variables along with the accuracy rate of the model

TABLE 3.2 *Means and standard deviations of independent variables measured with interval or ratio scales*

Indicator of variable	Mean	Standard deviation
DIFFRES90	46.46	5.63
DIVORCE90	12.56	2.54
EDUC90	19.62	3.77
VIOLCR90	539.56	287.56
PROPCR90	4639.70	1098.78
DIFFRES6090	−7.71	5.79
DIV6090	340.26	108.76
VIOL6090	518.54	320.85
PROP6090	227.21	102.59
DIFFRES60	50.45	6.32
DIVORCE60	3.01	0.95
EDUC60	7.41	1.62
VIOLCR60	108.14	73.81
PROPCR60	1565.86	647.65

84 *See* LONG & FREESE, *supra* note 77, at 151 (recommending visual plots of Cook's Statistic, a quantitative measure, to find cases that may be influential outliers, and leaving to the judgment of the investigator the decision whether a particular case is an influential outlier).

85 The concepts of probability, odds, and odds ratio are explained in PAMPEL, *supra* note 38, at 11–12.

in predicting whether states had or had not adopted "three-strikes" law. In reading Table 3.3, readers should keep in mind that:

- An independent variable is related to the dependent variable to the degree that its odds ratio deviates from 1.000.

TABLE 3.3 *Regression models: odds ratios and prediction accuracy*

Indicator of independent variable	Regression model				
	I	II	III	IV	V
NOEAST	0.190	0.333	0.146	1.287	1.369
SOUTH	21.539[b]	18.169[a]	24.916[c]	12.172[b]	11.953[a]
WEST	6.063	4.706	5.347	12.947[a]	4.198
DIFFRES90	1.071	1.061			
DIVORCE90	0.525[b]	0.552	0.582[c]		
EDUC90	1.215	1.349	1.290[b]		
VIOLCR90	1.002	1.001			
PROPCR90	1.000	1.000			
DIFFRES6090		1.016			1.105
DIV6090		0.998			0.993
VIOL6090		0.997			0.998
PROP6090		1.003			0.998
DIFFRES60				0.918	1.062
DIVORCE60				0.746	0.370
EDUC60				1.411	1.718
VIOLCR60				1.013[b]	1.011
PROPCR60				0.999	0.998
N	48	48	48	48	48
Correct predictions	72.9%	77.1%	72.9%	68.8%	72.9%

Notes to Table 3.3: Levels of statistical significance for the odds ratios are designated by superscripts of the letters a, b, and c: [a] = 0.10 level; [b] = 0.05 level; [c] = 0.01 level.

For NOEAST, SOUTH, and WEST, the reference was MIDWEST.[86]

86 The states that comprised each region are listed in *supra* note 48.

- When a state gains one unit or moves one category on a given independent variable, the odds that the state has "three-strikes" law (i) increase to the degree that the odds ratio for the independent variable is above 1.000 and (ii) decrease to the degree that the odds ratio for the independent variable is below 1.000.
- The odds ratio for a given independent variable in a set of independent variables estimates the influence of that independent variable on the dependent variable when all of the other independent variables are held constant. The influence of a given independent variable on the dependent variable, accordingly, is separate and apart from the influence of the other independent variables on the dependent variable.
- Instead of a coefficient of determination (pseudo-R^2), which is not estimated when the intercept is omitted from logistic regression,[87] the table reports the accuracy with which a regression model predicted that "three-strikes" law had been adopted or had not been adopted by each of the states in the data analyzed by the model. The bottom row in the table shows, for each model, correct predictions as a percentage of all predictions that the model made for the states[88] and provides a measure of the degree to which the model fit the data.

An overview of the five models in Table 3.3 may be helpful. As shown in the row that is labeled N, all models used data on forty-eight states.[89] The independent variables in models I and IV were culture, social change, social disorder, societal rationality, and rates of crime (violent and property); the independent variables in model I were measured as of 1990 and in model IV as of 1960. Model II expanded model I, and model V expanded model IV, by adding as independent variables the speed of the shift between 1960 and 1990 in social change, social disorder, and rates of crime.[90]

87 As explained in *supra* note 39, the results reported in part 2-b were obtained from regression analyses without an intercept.

88 Prediction accuracy was computed with the ESTAT CLASSIFICATION postestimation command for LOGISTIC and its default cutoff. STATACORP, *supra* note 39, at 946, 957–58.

89 *Supra* note 33 and accompanying text.

90 Models II and V were unable to include the 1960-to-1990 percent difference in societal rationality because, as explained in the text accompanying *supra* notes 64 and 65, the indicator of societal rationality in 1960 was not the same as the indicator of societal rationality in 1990.

Let me begin with models I and II. A comparison of the results from the two models reveals that the speed-of-shift independent variables raised correct predictions by roughly four percentage points. Given its base, however, a gain in accuracy of this magnitude is not large, and the speed-of-shift independent variables have odds ratios that are very close to 1.000, indicating that their relationships to TSLAW were weak or nonexistent. Because model II is less parsimonious than model I, which correctly predicted the presence or absence of "three-strikes" law in 72.9% of the forty-eight states, model II will be set aside in favor of model I. Among the model I independent variables—all of which are measured as of 1990—three stand out as possible factors affecting TSLAW. They are culture, social disorder, and societal rationality; notably, neither the rate of violent crime nor the rate of property crime are among the possible factors. With regard to culture, Table 3.3 shows the odds that, relative to the Midwest, "three-strikes" law was present in the states of a region: With Midwest states as the reference, the odds of such law were approximately four-fifths lower in the Northeast, twenty-one times higher in the South, and six times higher in the West. With regard to social disorder and societal rationality, Table 3.3 reveals that a one-unit increase in DIVORCE90 changed the odds of "three-strikes" law by a factor of 0.525, i.e., cut the odds of such law nearly in half, and that a one-unit increase in EDUC90 raised the odds of "three-strikes" law by a factor of 1.215, i.e., by 21.5%. The relationships of the foregoing to the dependent variable were also examined with standardized regression coefficients. Specifically, the coefficient of each independent variable was standardized on the variance of that independent variable, and was also standardized on both the variance of that independent variable and the variance of the dependent variable.[91] Although the resulting standardized coefficients are of limited usefulness,[92] they indicated that SOUTH and DIVORCE90 had the

91 Standardization was done with the LISTCOEF command. LONG & FREESE, *supra* note 77, at 177–80, 464–65.

92 A standardized coefficient is problematic in logistic regression when the coefficient has been standardized on the variance of a variable that was measured in binary form, e.g., as a dummy. The variance of such a variable is unclear. JOSEPH M. HILBE, LOGISTIC REGRESSION MODELS 100–101 (2009); PAMPEL, *supra* note 38, at 32–33. Consequently, a standardized coefficient cannot be easily interpreted when: (i) the coefficient is for an independent variable that has been measured as a dummy and has been standardized on its own variance; or (ii) the coefficient is for an independent variable that, although measured with an interval scale or a ratio scale, has been standardized on the variance of the dependent variable and the dependent variable was measured as a dummy. In the instant study, region as well as TSLAW were dummy variables.

strongest relationships to TSLAW and that their relationships to TSLAW were roughly equal in magnitude. The standardized coefficients for NOEAST, WEST, and EDUC90, which were about the same size, were noticeably smaller than those for SOUTH and DIVORCE90.

Model I was tested further by exploring whether collinearity between independent variables might be distorting relationships to the dependent variable. Two tests allayed concern regarding collinearity. In the first, the Variance Inflation Factor ("VIF") of every independent variable was calculated[93] and was found to be well below the threshold at which excessive collinearity is typically considered a possibility.[94] Second, a correlation matrix for the indicators of the independent variables that were measured with interval or ratio scales indicated that one indicator—PROPCR90—was closely correlated with the indicators of two other independent variables.[95] Accordingly, the odds ratios for the independent variables were re-estimated without PROPCR90 in the regression equation. The odds ratios for the remaining independent variables were very similar to the odds ratios that were obtained when PROPCR90 was included, and the percentage of model-generated predictions that were correct was unchanged. In short, there is no reason to believe that high collinearity skewed the results that Table 3.3 shows for model I.

In addition to a search of the data for high collinearity, the data were probed for possible influential outliers that affected the results obtained with model I. Following the initial estimation of model I, Cook's Statistic was computed,[96] and model I was reestimated with forty-seven states. In reestimating model I,

93 The Stata command COLLIN was used to estimate the VIF of each independent variable. UCLA Institute for Digital Res. & Educ., Logistic Regression Diagnostics, http://www.ats.ucla.edu/stat/stata/webbooks/logistic/chapter3/statalog3.htm (last visited May 1, 2015).

94 In model I, the largest VIF score was 3.59. A VIF of 10.0 or higher is commonly thought to indicate the possibility that collinearity has distorted the results obtained from regression. *E.g.*, DAMODAR N. GUJARATI & DAWN C. PORTER, BASIC ECONOMETRICS 340 (5th ed. 2009); Jeff Tayman et al., *Evaluating Population Forecast Accuracy: A Regression Approach Using County Data*, 30 POPULATION RES. & POL'Y REV. 235, 256 (2011); Tse-Chuan Yang et al., *Social Capital and Human Mortality: Explaining the Rural Paradox with County-Level Mortality Data*, 76 RURAL SOCIOL. 347, 363 (2011). However, a VIF of 10.0 or higher is not definitive evidence of excessive collinearity and does not necessarily demand change in the regression model and/or in the data analysis. Robert M. O'Brien, *A Caution Regarding Rules of Thumb for Variance Inflation Factors*, 41 QUALITY & QUANTITY 673 (2007).

95 The coefficient for the correlation of PROPCR90 and DIFFRES90 was +0.566; the coefficient for the correlation of PROPCR90 and VIOLCR90 was +0.689. PROPCR90 had the largest VIF score (3.59).

96 LONG & FREESE, *supra* note 77, at 151.

each of the eight states that had a Cook's Statistic of 0.70 or higher was omitted one at a time.[97] No odds ratio for an independent variable (other than region) was markedly altered by a reestimation of model I.[98] In terms of the non-region independent variables, differences found between the odds ratios produced by the original estimation (for forty-eight states) and the odds ratios produced by the reestimations (for forty-seven states) were judged insufficient to overcome the caution that should attend the decision to classify a jurisdiction as an influential outlier, and hence to remove it from the data, in a study of the macro-level determinants of law.[99]

In sum, neither high collinearity nor influential outliers seem to have been present in the data, and as a consequence, the results reported in Table 3.3 for model I—the odds ratios and the prediction accuracy rate—need not be revised. The odds ratios in Table 3.3 indicate that model I includes independent variables that exercised a substantial influence on whether states adopted "three-strikes" law, and given the rate at which model I accurately predicted whether states had "three-strikes" law, it provides a good fit to the data. At the same time, however, not all of the model I independent variables had a strong relationship to the dependent variable, suggesting the possibility that a simpler model can be developed that is not-dissimilar to model I in the degree to which it fit the data.

To investigate this possibility, the data were analyzed with a regression model that omitted two of the model I independent variables, viz., social change and crime rates. The model thus included three independent variables—culture, social disorder, and societal rationality—and was labeled model III. Table 3.3 reports the results obtained for model III. Notably, model I and model III were identical in the percentages of their predictions that were correct, and comparable odds ratios were obtained for the indicators of the independent variables that were included in both models. Because in their fit to the data the two models did not differ materially—indeed, because they did

97 Cook's Statistic for a case must usually exceed 1.00 for the case to be an influential outlier, but a Cook's Statistic below 1.00 may identify a case that is an influential outlier for a particular model when this Cook's Statistic, even though less than 1.00, is noticeably higher than the Cook's Statistic obtained for other cases. HOSMER & LEMESHOW, *supra* note 83, at 173, 180. In the instant study, a plot of Cook's Statistic for model I revealed that Cook's Statistic for this model was infrequent at or above 0.70. Every state whose Cook's Statistic was at least 0.70 was thus considered to be a potential influential outlier.

98 Because every state is part of a region, the odds ratio for a particular region can be expected to change when a state in that region is left out.

99 THE PLACE OF LAW, *supra* note 6, at 468–69.

not differ at all—the criterion of parsimony dictates that model III be preferred over model I.[100]

Before models IV and V are discussed, the fit of model III merits further exploration. The explanatory variables in model III may not predict the presence of "three-strikes" law with the same degree of accuracy that they predict the absence of "three-strikes" law. In this regard, readers should note that Table 3.3 reports only the overall accuracy rate, i.e., the accuracy rate for *both* predictions that such law has been adopted *and* predictions that such law has not been adopted. A further important point is that all of the model III explanatory variables need not be considered together. Sets of explanatory variables can be differentiated, and every set can be assessed for its accuracy in making each type of prediction. Additional analysis of prediction accuracy, therefore, may yield worthwhile insights. The results of that analysis are reported in Table 3.4.

A number of points emerge from Table 3.4. One is that the explanatory variables in model III were consistently more accurate in predicting that "three-strikes" law was absent than in predicting that it was present. In addition, prediction accuracy was not much lower for region and social disorder together than for region, social disorder, and societal rationality in combination. When the indicator of societal rationality (EDUC90) was removed from model III, however, the odds ratios for some indicators of region differed markedly from those found for models I and III. Specifically, with EDUC90 removed, the relationship of NOEAST to TSLAW (odds ratio = 2.244) reversed direction and became positive, while the relationship of WEST to TSLAW (odds ratio = 11.748) perceptibly strengthened. Moreover, without EDUC90 in the regression equation, the relationship of DIVORCE90 to TSLAW (odds ratio = 0.821) may have weakened.[101] The shift in the direction of the relationship between NOEAST and TSLAW in

100 Two standardized regression coefficients were estimated for each independent variable in model III. Specifically, for a given independent variable, one coefficient was standardized on the variance of that independent variable; the other coefficient was standardized on the variance of both that independent variable and the variance of the dependent variable. The standardized coefficients for SOUTH and DIVORCE90 were similar in size, as were the standardized coefficients for NOEAST and WEST; the standardized coefficients in the former set were larger than the standardized coefficients in the latter set. EDUC90 had standardized coefficients whose magnitudes were between the former and latter sets of coefficients.

Information on the standardization procedure is in *supra* note 91 and the source cited in that note; an explanation of the limitations of standardized coefficients is in *supra* note 92.

101 The relationships between the independent variables in model III and TSLAW were evidently not affected by collinearity. Every independent variable in model III had a VIF

TABLE 3.4 *Accuracy rates for predictions of "three-strikes" law in states: independent variables in model III*

Indicators of independent variables	Predictions of "three-strikes" law		
	Prediction: law present (% accurate)	Prediction: law absent (% accurate)	Both predictions (% accurate)
NOEAST, SOUTH, WEST	42.9%	65.0%	52.1%
DIVORCE90	0.00%	60.4%	60.4%
EDUC90	0.00%	60.4%	60.4%
NOEAST, SOUTH, WEST, DIVORCE90	64.7%	74.2%	70.8%
NOEAST, SOUTH, WEST, EDUC90	58.8%	71.0%	66.7%
DIVORCE90, EDUC90	50.0%	62.5%	60.4%
NOEAST, SOUTH, WEST, DIVORCE90, EDUC90	68.8%	75.0%	72.9%

the absence of EDUC90 suggested that culture and societal rationality might be interacting, but the data yielded no clear evidence of such interaction.[102]

---

score below 2.00; the mean VIF score for all of the independent variables in model III was 1.59. The VIF score as a criterion for identifying problematic collinearity is discussed in *supra* note 94.

102 Possible interaction between culture and societal rationality was investigated using three interaction variables. The interaction variables were created by multiplying (i) the numerical values of the dummy variables representing each of the geographic regions other than MIDWEST and (ii) a mean-centered transformation of the variable EDUC90. An interaction variable is typically formed by multiplication of the numerical values of its component variables. JACCARD, *supra* note 75, at 14. When investigating possible interaction, mean-centering is recommended for a variable that is measured without an absolute zero. JAMES JACCARD & ROBERT TURRISI, INTERACTION EFFECTS IN MULTIPLE REGRESSION 24–25 (Paper No. 72, Sage University Paper Series on Quantitative Applications in the Social Sciences, 2d ed. 2003). Mean-centering was used here on the assumption that EDUC90 will not be zero in a state (or, for that matter, in any modern society) and that an absolute zero for EDUC90 was thus nonsensical in terms of theory.

The three interaction variables were included in a single no-intercept regression equation along with the independent variables in model III (NOEAST, SOUTH, WEST,

In sum, the accuracy rates in Table 3.4 are evidence of the degree to which model III fit the data.[103] The rates in the table indicate that the three independent variables comprising the model—viz., culture, social disorder, and societal rationality—provided a fit that was exceptionally good. Although this fit was due mainly to culture and social disorder, the absence of societal rationality caused a modest reduction in the accuracy rate of predictions that "three-strikes" law was present. In addition, as discussed in the preceding paragraph, the omission of societal rationality from the regression equation yielded an unexpected and unexplained result for culture. Among the first three models, therefore, model III is to be preferred.

Finally, let us turn to models IV and V. These models, being based on data for the independent variables in 1960,[104] offer an opportunity to explore whether societal structures, in affecting the adoption of "three-strikes" law, shifted over time in ways that were generally uniform across states. To the extent that the

---

DIVORCE90, and EDUC90). However, application of the equation to the data revealed that the VIF score for EDUC90 was 16.4, which indicated that collinearity was excessive. *Supra* note 94. On the other hand, the degree of collinearity was acceptable for the three equations having just one interaction variable. Specifically, when each interaction variable was included one at a time in a regression equation with NOEAST, SOUTH, WEST, DIVORCE90, and EDUC90, the highest VIF score for EDUC90 was 2.99, and this was the highest VIF score of any of the independent variables, including the interaction variables.

For the three equations that contained a single interaction variable, the accuracy rate of all predictions was 75.0% in the case of two equations and 72.9% in the case of one equation. ("All predictions" include *both* predictions of the states expected to possess "three-strikes" law *and* predictions of the states expected not to possess "three-strikes" law.) As seen in the column for model III in Table 3.3 and in the last column of Table 3.4, the accuracy rate of all predictions made by model III, which lacked an interaction variable, was 72.9%. Consequently, the accuracy rate of 75.0% achieved for all predictions by the two equations somewhat exceeded the accuracy rate for all predictions achieved by model III. However, the two equations had a higher accuracy rate (75.0%) because, in predicting the states that would have "three-strikes" law *or* in predicting the states that would not have "three-strikes" law, they correctly predicted only one state more than did model III. An interaction variable thus added little to the fit exhibited by model III, and as discussed in *supra* note 81, theory furnishes at best a weak foundation for believing that culture and societal rationality interact in shaping law. Because such interaction lacks a substantial basis in theory, the marginally better fit of the two regression equations containing an interaction variable was regarded as insufficient to warrant the conclusion that interaction occurred between culture and societal rationality.

103 LONG & FREESE, *supra* note 77, at 104, 110–11. Model III was estimated without an intercept. Its accuracy rate when estimated with an intercept is reported in *supra* note 39.

104 *Supra* note 34.

shifts were not nationally uniform, the relationships between the independent variables and the dependent variable that existed in 1990 may not be the same in direction (i.e., coefficient sign) as the relationships that existed in 1960. To the extent the shifts were uniform across states, the direction of the relationships will be the same in 1990 and in 1960. Of course, since the advent of "three-strikes" law was in the mid-1990s,[105] the independent variables measured as of 1960 can be expected to have weaker relationships to the dependent variable than the independent variables measured as of 1990.

Returning to Table 3.3, we find that in models IV and V the odds ratios for the independent variables other than region are generally not dissimilar to the odds ratios for the comparable independent variables in models I and II. With regard to region, the most notable difference between 1960 and 1990 involves states in the Northeast. Specifically, the odds that states in the Northeast would adopt "three-strikes" law were, relative to states in the Midwest, much lower when the independent variables were measured as of 1990, but states in the Northeast had higher odds of subsequently approving "three-strikes" law than states in the Midwest when the independent variables were measured as of 1960. The reversal of the direction of the NOEAST–TSLAW relationship from 1960 to 1990 is curious and merits exploration in future research.

3 Discussion

What conclusions can be drawn from the data analysis in Part 2-b? An answer to the question must recognize that quantitative research concerned with the impact of jurisdiction attributes on the content of law is in its infancy, suffers from insufficient data (especially time-series data) on potentially important independent variables, and faces unresolved methodological issues.[106] The conclusions that can be drawn from studies of the relationship between jurisdiction characteristics and law are unavoidably tentative, therefore, and are most appropriately expressed in general, not precise, terms. Nonetheless, I believe that four noteworthy findings emerge from Part 2-b. Specifically, the odds that "three-strikes" law was present in a state were:

1. Unrelated to the rate of violent crime and the rate of property crime in the state.

105 The year in which "three-strikes" law was adopted by states that did so is given in the text accompanying *supra* note 15.

106 THE PLACE OF LAW, *supra* note 6, at 458–69.

2. Lower in states in which social disorder was relatively widespread than in states in which social disorder was less prevalent.
3. Higher among states in the South and states in the West than among states in other regions.
4. Greater in states with a comparatively high level of societal rationality than in states with a lower level of societal rationality.

The first finding—the absence of a relationship between the incidence of major forms of crime and whether "three-strikes" law had been adopted—was unexpected. Ceteris paribus, elevated crime rates in a social system seem likely on logical grounds to press the system to devise new law designed to combat crime. Does finding #1 require that the foregoing hypothesis be abandoned? The answer, of course, is that no plausible hypothesis is disproven by a single study. The hypothesis that rates of crime are important in shaping law on crime should be discarded only if the hypothesis is contradicted by further research. In this research, the dependent variable should be law that attempts to reduce crime not only through "three-strikes" penalties but through other approaches as well, and when "three-strikes" law is the dependent variable, the independent variables should differ from or supplement those in *supra* Part 2. In this regard, a promising independent variable is the public salience of crime. Rates of crime may affect the odds that "three-strikes" and other types of law will be adopted when, and only when, the public is aware of crime, an awareness that may be triggered by a particular set of societal conditions and involve sociological phenomena such as social movements and collective behavior.[107] Crime rates by themselves may thus not explain the advent of "three-strikes" law or other law on crime; the explanation may lie instead in the combination of crime rates with the extent to which the public perceives crime, the nature of its view of crime, and/or the intensity of its concern with crime.

This brings me to finding #2. With the other independent variables (including crime rates) held constant, the prevalence of social disorder in a state was inversely related to the odds that "three-strikes" law was present in the state. The indicator of social disorder, of course, was the prevalence of divorced, currently unmarried women among all women in the state who were 30–34 years old, but social disorder can have—and ideally should have—more than

107 *See* Catherine L. Carpenter, *Legislative Epidemics: A Cautionary Tale of Criminal Laws that Have Swept the Country*, 58 Buffalo L. Rev. 1, 12–13, 35–40 (2010) (relating crime-focused legislation such as "three-strikes" law to its social context, including public awareness of crime).

one indicator.[108] Because in other sociological research, an indicator of social disorder has been the incidence of crime,[109] sociology furnishes a basis for expecting that the relationship to whether "three-strikes" law is present in a jurisdiction will be the same for crime rates in the jurisdiction as it is for the extent of divorced, currently unmarried women in the population of the jurisdiction. Why did the instant study find that the relationships were dissimilar? The answer may be that there are different types of social disorder and that, while the rate of crime captures one type, the prevalence of divorce without remarriage captures another type. Unfortunately, each type of social disorder has yet to be conceptualized and defined, but if different types of social disorder exist, the reason for lower odds of "three-strikes" law in a state where divorced, currently unmarried women are a relatively large percentage of the population may be that the state had adjusted to social disorder of a particular type. Furthermore, adaptation to this type of social disorder may explain not only whether "three-strikes" law is adopted but also how law on homicide is applied: The impact of homicide rates on the outcomes of homicide prosecutions[110] suggests that a society makes adjustments to this type of social disorder and, in doing so, harmonizes the application, if not the written content, of its law on crime with the level of social disorder.

Turning to finding #3, why do states in the South and states in the West have elevated odds of adopting "three-strikes" law? Not coincidentally, the relative size of state prison populations—the number of prison inmates in a state per 100,000 residents—has been found to be higher in the South and in the West than in other geographic regions of the United States.[111] If region is a useful indicator of culture, as the instant study contends, at least one important aspect of culture is the same or similar in the South and

108 *Supra* note 56.

109 John O.G. Billy et al., *Contextual Effects on the Sexual Behavior of Adolescent Women*, 56 J. MARRIAGE & FAM. 387, 389 (1994).

110 Cooney & Burt, *supra* note 17.

111 *See* David Jacobs & Jason T. Carmichael, *The Politics of Punishment across Time and Space: A Pooled Time-Series Analysis of Imprisonment Rates*, 80 SOC. FORCES 61, 77 Table 4 (model 3) (2001) (showing, for state imprisonment rates, a positive regression coefficient for states in the South relative to states in the West, and negative regression coefficients for states in the Northeast and states in the Midwest relative to states in the West). In the study by Jacobs and Carmichael, none of the regression coefficients for region were statistically significant. *Id.* at 77 Table 4 (model 3). However, the appropriateness of statistical significance as a criterion for making decisions on null hypotheses is questionable when, as in the Jacobs-Carmichael study, data are not obtained by a probability sampling procedure. *Id.* at 70.

West, but different in the Midwest and Northeast.[112] Regrettably, plausible clues to the nature of this aspect are unavailable in social science research published to date.

Let me consider the last finding—that the inclination of states to adopt "three-strikes" law is greater in states with more societal rationality than in states with less. Although this relationship could be anticipated,[113] it is noteworthy because it calls attention to an important point that should not be overlooked in studies of the macrosociological determinants of concepts and doctrines of law. Specifically, both empirical studies and theory on these determinants must focus on the quantity and quality of knowledge accessible to a society. As a society is permeated by a larger and improved body of knowledge, it is likely to undergo gradual but broad changes, one of which is an increase in societal rationality. That increase, in turn, probably helps to mold law on a variety of topics, including crime. If so, when seeking to account for the emergence of a law-defined historical era such as the current era of law on crime,[114] scholarship will be incomplete if it fails to explore, as a possible driving force, the expansion of knowledge that preceded the onset of the era.

---

112 An alternative exists to the foregoing hypothesis. Specifically, there may be a variable that was not in the instant study, that is not cultural, but that has a sizeable impact on whether "three-strikes" law is adopted by states. If this variable differentiates regions—and especially if it differentiates states in the South and West from states in the Midwest and Northeast—it may fully account for regional differences in the presence of "three-strikes" law.

113 See the text accompanying *supra* note 62.

114 See text accompanying *supra* notes 8–10.

SECTION B

Europe

CHAPTER 4

Law on Divorce in Western Europe

Abstract

A popular assumption in the United States is that doctrines and concepts of law are attributable to particular individuals, but if the assumption is correct, the content of law would differ randomly across jurisdictions and across time. The instant book advances an alternative thesis—that law on society-significant activities is due to society-level conditions. The thesis was tested by applying logistic regression to time-spaced cross-sectional data on seventeen Western European nations in order to ascertain whether country-level characteristics affected the odds that a nation had law authorizing unilateral no-fault divorce, i.e., termination of a marriage when just one spouse believed the marriage was unworkable. Independent variables included between-nation differences in language and culture, which differences were measured by whether a nation was Scandinavian. Notably, law in all of the Scandinavian countries (Denmark, Norway, and Sweden) permitted unilateral no-fault divorce. Among the fourteen nations outside Scandinavia, law on divorce was found to have been influenced by three independent variables—educational attainment (measured by the gross enrollment ratio for tertiary schooling); urbanization (measured by the percentage of the population residing in urban agglomerations); and wealth (measured by gross domestic product per person). Specifically, the odds that law would permit unilateral no-fault divorce in a non-Scandinavian nation increased with tertiary schooling but decreased with urbanization and with wealth. Given that quantitative studies support generally the thesis that the concepts and doctrines of law are macrosociological phenomena, the chapter concludes with a discussion of the neglect of the thesis by scholarship originating in law schools in the United States.

1 A Macrosociological Framework for Law

Western societies share a broad social philosophy,[1] a component of which seems to include the premise that effective solutions can be devised for aspects

1 As evidenced by the frequent use of phrases such as "Western thought," the social philosophy of Americans and Western Europeans seems to be similar in fundamental respects.

 | DOI 10.1163/9789004281219_005

of a society that undermine its operation. The premise may be due to the belief that the growth of knowledge is beneficial if not necessary—a belief whose tangible consequences are evidenced in the general commitment of the populations of Western nations to science in general.[2] However, the premise that solutions exist to societal problems is less relevant to the instant chapter than another premise with which it is aligned—viz., the premise that current problems can be markedly reduced, and future problems can be largely prevented, by law.[3] In the view of the body politic, law furnishes a tool that is capable of dealing with threats to the fabric of society. As the widespread acceptance of the concept of "the rule of law" illustrates,[4] law is thought to be critical for repairing and avoiding damage to the social order.[5]

See Francis J. Mootz III, *Is the Rule of Law Possible in a Postmodern World?* 68 WASH. L. REV. 249, 252 (1993) (noting that the concept of the rule of law is found in the origin of "modern Western thought in ancient Greece" and "implicates much of the Western tradition of legal and political philosophy"); Jason Morgan-Foster, *Third Generation Rights: What Islamic Law Can Teach the International Human Rights Movement*, 8 YALE HUM. RTS. & DEV. L.J. 67, 75–76, 78–79 (2005) (describing the concept of a duty of individuals to their community as possessing "strong historical roots in Western political thought" and suggesting that this concept of duty prevailed until it was displaced in Western nations by the concept of individualism); Makau Mutua, *Savages, Victims, and Saviors: The Metaphor of Human Rights*, 42 HARV. INT'L L.J. 201, 201 n. 2, 213–14 (2001) (observing that, in the United States and Western Europe, societies are seen as changing in a single direction that is driven by, inter alia, advances in knowledge from scientific research).

2 NATIONAL SCIENCE BOARD, SCIENCE AND ENGINEERING INDICATORS 2010 7–28 to 7–29 (2010), *available at* http://www.nsf.gov/statistics/seind10/pdfstart.htm; *id.* at Appendix table 7–18, http://www.nsf.gov/statistics/seind10/appendix.htm#c7 (last visited May 3, 2015).

3 The premise has occasionally been recognized explicitly by courts in the United States. 680 Fifth Ave. Assoc. v. Mut. Benefit Life Ins. Co. in Rehabilitation, 156 B.R. 726, 734 (Bankr. Ct. S.D. N.Y. 1993) ("When Congress or any other legislative body creates a statute, it acts to remedy a problem confronting society."); Felder v. Butler, 438 A.2d 494, 499 (Md. 1981) ("Of course, the common law is not static. Its life and heart is its dynamism—its ability to keep pace with the world while constantly searching for just and fair solutions to pressing societal problems...").

4 The popularity of the concept is illustrated by the action of the member-states of the United Nations approving a resolution that "reaffirm[s] our commitment to the rule of law and its fundamental importance for political dialogue and cooperation among all States and for the further development of the three main pillars upon which the United Nations is built: international peace and security, human rights[,] and development." G.A. Res. 67/1, U.N. Doc. A/RES/67/1 (Nov. 30, 2012). *See* Jeff Breinholt, *Resolved, or Is It? The First Amendment and Giving Money to Terrorists*, 57 AM. U.L. REV. 1273, 1273 (2008) (characterizing the concept of the rule of law as "embrace[d] so passionately that we seek to instill it in developing countries").

5 LARRY D. BARNETT, THE PLACE OF LAW: THE ROLE AND LIMITS OF LAW IN SOCIETY 198 (2011) [hereinafter THE PLACE OF LAW].

But does law in fact offer effective solutions to activities that weaken a society? An assumption is hazardous if taken on faith, not because the assumption may form an incorrect foundation for academic discussions in journals and books but because an erroneous assumption about a type of problem will lead to efforts that are ineffective in solving problems of this type. Indeed, a mistaken assumption about a particular problem may result in action that intensifies the problem and/or creates a new problem.[6] For very practical reasons, then, the assumption that law solves problems facing a society warrants examination. An evaluation of the assumption is especially appropriate at this point in time because a body of credible empirical evidence that conflicts with the assumption has accumulated in the social sciences.[7] Of course, the assumption that law cures (or helps to cure) social ills is not irrational inasmuch as individuals and groups generally behave in line with the prescriptions and proscriptions of law. On purely logical grounds, therefore, change in a form of social behavior can be expected to follow the introduction of a new doctrine of law applicable to that behavioral form. However, the general correspondence between law and behavior does not prove that law determines behavior. Indeed, currently available social science evidence supports the belief that causality in general runs in the opposite direction—*from* patterns of social behavior *to* the content of law.

This view is embodied in the concept known in United States law as the "police power." The concept, which has long been prominent in U.S. jurisprudence, is regarded as the source of authority for government action to mitigate damage and perceived harm to the integrity of the societal system. *See* Lawton v. Steele, 152 U.S. 133, 136 (1894) (opining that "everything essential to the public safety, health, and morals" is within the scope of the police power). *See also* Noble State Bank v. Haskell, 219 U.S. 104, 111 (1910) ("It may be said in a general way that the police power extends to all the great public needs. It may be put forth in aid of what is sanctioned by usage, or held by the prevailing morality or strong and preponderant opinion to be greatly and immediately necessary to the public welfare.").

6 Given the study of law on divorce in Western Europe that is the subject of Parts 3 and 4 *infra*, a pertinent illustration is the increase in violence evidently caused in the United States by the advent of law authorizing divorce upon the petition of just one spouse when that spouse is required only to allege that the marriage is damaged beyond repair and is not required to prove that the damage was caused by the other spouse. Such law has been found responsible for an appreciable number of murders of husbands by their wives (but not of murders of wives by their husbands) in states that favor husbands in the division of marital property. Thomas S. Dee, *Until Death Do You Part: The Effects of Unilateral Divorce on Spousal Homicides*, 41 ECON. INQUIRY 163, 181 (2003).

7 THE PLACE OF LAW, *supra* note 5, at 118 & nn. 160–63, 119 & n. 165, 199 & nn. 20–21, 402 & nn. 66–67; Appendix B in *supra* Chapter 1.

a *The Framework in Brief*[8]

Succinctly expressed, the present chapter is grounded on the thesis that, in a democratically governed, structurally complex jurisdiction (e.g., nation), the institution of law contributes in the long run to the social cohesion that a societal system requires to operate effectively. Law serves this function with regard to society-important activities, however, not by responding to the wishes and preferences of particular personalities; if law was no more than a mechanism for pleasing specific individuals, its concepts and doctrines would develop and change randomly. Instead, law protects the social system by satisfying the macro-level demands of the system and, in doing so, is a mechanism for the continuation of the system. The concepts and doctrines of law, then, result from social, economic, and demographic conditions,[9] and when these conditions vary between jurisdictions and/or change within a jurisdiction, the concepts and doctrines of law differ across space and/or time. Unfortunately, the preceding macrosociological thesis, though far from new,[10] has not been the subject of extensive quantitative research.

b *A Case Study*

A timely illustration of the proposed framework is the adoption by the island nation of Malta of legislation authorizing divorce. The legislation, which was passed in July 2011 following a referendum that was approved by a majority of Maltese voters two months earlier, was in force as of October 2011.[11] When Malta revamped its law in 2011, it was the sole nation in Europe that did not dissolve marriages by divorce,[12] but if the macrosociological thesis that informs

---

8 The framework is developed more fully in Part 1-b of *supra* Chapter 1.

9 Technology is one such condition, but disagreement is possible over its classification, i.e., the category of conditions to which it should be assigned. In my view, technology can be subsumed under social conditions and/or under economic conditions.

10 EUGEN EHRLICH, FUNDAMENTAL PRINCIPLES OF THE SOCIOLOGY OF LAW 392–93 (Walter L. Moll trans., Harvard Univ. Press, 1936) (originally published in 1913 under the title GRUNDLEGUNG DER SOZIOLOGIE DES RECHTS).

11 *Malta: Divorce Finally Allowed After Referendum Win*, GUARDIAN (U.K), July 26, 2011, 2011 WLNR 14734195.

12 *Id.* Although Malta did not terminate marriages by divorce before 2011, it recognized divorces granted by another jurisdiction and recognized annulments of marriages. A marriage could be annulled in Malta by a tribunal of the Roman Catholic Church if the marriage had been formalized in conformity with Canon Law. LAWS OF MALTA Ecclesiastical Courts (Constitution and Jurisdiction) Law Chap. 1 § 3 (1828), Marriage Act Chap. 255 §§ 19A, 20, 23(1), 33 (1975), *available at* http://www.justiceservices.gov.mt/LOM.aspx?pageid=24;

the instant chapter is correct, the chief factor prompting Malta to abandon its position was not pressure to conform to the law of other European Union ("E.U.") countries.[13] Rather than deciding to "fall into line" with E.U.. countries generally, Malta accepted law permitting divorce mainly because it was being pushed by society-level forces *within* Malta.

If the macrosociological perspective proposed in Part 1-a *supra* accurately depicts the institution of law, new concepts and doctrines develop in the law of a society after change has taken place in the needs[14] and values of the society. Consequently, what law says—e.g., in statutes—is attributable in the long run to the character of the social system in which the institution of law operates, and the referendum in Malta, together with the ensuing legislation, was preceded by distinct, empirically measurable changes in Maltese society that created a need for law permitting divorce as well as a set of social values consistent with this need.

What change(s) occurred in Malta that can plausibly be regarded as having generated a need for, and social values favoring,[15] law that allows divorce? For a change to qualify, its direction must indicate that marriage as a societal form was weakening in Malta during the period that preceded the referendum and legislation on divorce.[16] The demographic indicators of two such changes are shown in Figure 4.1.[17] In both the top and bottom graphs of the figure, the measures begin with the year 1960 and end with the year 2011.

Ruth Farrugia, *International Marriage and Divorce Regulation and Recognition in Malta*, 29 FAM. L.Q. 627, 627, 631–32 (1995).

13 Malta joined the European Union in May 2004. European Union, http://europa.eu/about-eu/eu-history/2000-2009/index_en.htm (last visited May 3, 2015).

14 The concept of societal need is explained in Part 3 of *supra* Chapter 2.

15 During the last half of the 1990s, social values in Malta became more supportive of divorce for a married person who "no longer loves" his/her spouse or whose spouse has an "incompatible personality." Anthony M. Abela, *Who Wants Divorce?: Marriage Values and Divorce in Malta and Western Europe*, 11 INT'L REV. SOCIOL. 75, 80 (2001).

16 Unfortunately, data have not been published on the percentage of the members of different birth cohorts in Malta that had not married by specified ages. A secular increase in this percentage over successive birth cohorts before the referendum and legislation on divorce would be evidence of a decrease in Malta in the societal importance of marriage.

17 The data in Part 1-b cover all residents of Malta. The data, accordingly, are not limited to citizens of Malta who were at least eighteen years old; i.e., the data are not limited to the persons who were eligible to vote on referenda in Malta and who were eligible to vote on candidates for the parliament of Malta. MALTA CONST. art. 57 (1964); LAWS OF MALTA Referenda Act Chap. 237 § 11 (1973), *available at* http://www.justiceservices.gov.mt/LOM.aspx?pageid=24.

The top graph in Figure 4.1 focuses on the total fertility rate ("TFR") in Malta.[18] By way of explanation, the TFR is the mean number of births per female that can be expected during the lifetime of a cohort of females who attain age 15 in a given year ("year X"). The expectation is grounded on the assumption that the fertility rates prevailing in year X at every age from 15 through 49 will remain constant until the cohort reaches age 50. The TFR thus calculates, for a particular year (year X), the average number of children that would be borne by a female in a cohort of females who have their fifteenth birthday in year X and who, as they grow older, experience through age 49 each age-specific birth rate that existed in year X.

It is important to recognize that the TFR does not calculate the actual mean number of children produced by a cohort of women during the lifetime of the cohort, because age-specific fertility rates do not stay the same from year to year.[19] Nonetheless, the TFR is a useful sociological indicator because, as age-specific rates of childbearing vary over time, the TFR does, too. By quickly revealing change in the direction of average childbearing, the TFR can indicate whether marriage is becoming less central or more central to a society given that the social values of Western societies have traditionally favored the birth of children within marriage rather than outside it.[20] Specifically, an appreciable fall in the TFR is evidence of a decline in the importance of marriage in a society.

As the top graph in Figure 4.1 reveals, the TFR in Malta underwent an appreciable decline between 1996 and 2004, at which point it stabilized. To be exact, the TFR dropped by roughly one-third (2.01 to 1.37) between 1996 and 2004.

The discussion in Part 1-b assumes that the data used depict citizens of Malta who are age eighteen or older.

18 Data on the TFR in Malta have been published by the National Statistics Office of Malta for every fifth year from 1960 to 1980 and for every year from 1980 onward. National Statistics Office Malta, Statistical Table Options: Crude Death Rate, Crude Birth Rate & Total Fertility Rate (data for 1980 to 2011), http://nso.gov.mt/en/Pages/NSO-Home.aspx (under "Services," follow "StatDB" hyperlink and expand seriatim "National Statistics Office" tree and "Demography" tree) (last visited May 3, 2015); NATIONAL STATISTICS OFFICE MALTA, CHILDREN 2010 21 table 2.8 (2010), http://nso.gov.mt/en/Pages/NSO-Home.aspx (select "Publications" and "View by Date") (data for 1960, 1965, 1970, and 1975) (last visited May 3, 2015).

19 "The TFR represents the average number of children a woman *would* have were she to fast-forward through all her childbearing years in a single year, under all the age-specific fertility rates for that year." Wikipedia, *Total Fertility Rate*, http://en.wikipedia.org/wiki/Total_fertility_rate (last visited May 3, 2015).

20 Henri Leridon, *Extra-Marital Cohabitation and Fertility*, 44 POPULATION STUD. 469 (1990).

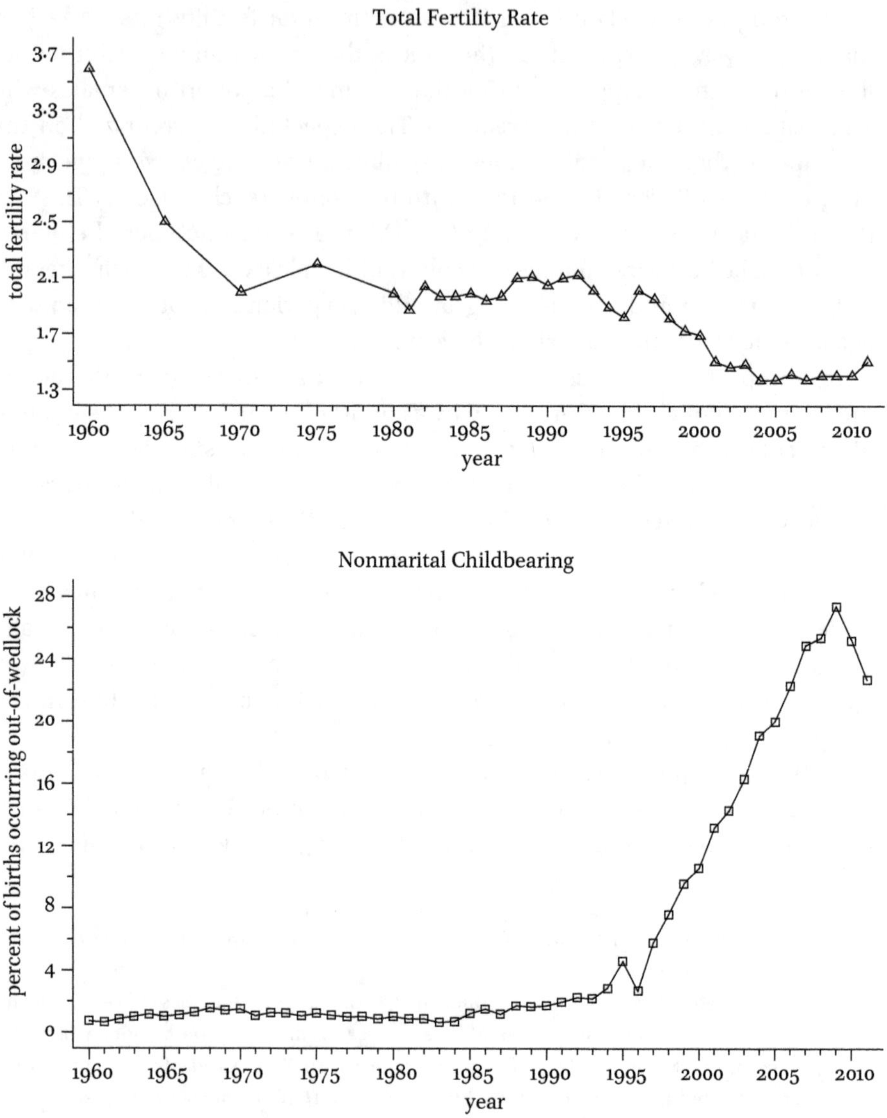

FIGURE 4.1 *Measures of fertility: Malta.*
Total fertility rate (top graph).
Nonmarital childbearing (bottom graph)
SOURCE (TOP GRAPH): SEE FN. 18 IN THIS CHAPTER.
SOURCE (BOTTOM GRAPH): SEE FN. 21 IN THIS CHAPTER.

However, the slide of the TFR is relevant to a macrosociological framework for law not simply because of its magnitude. Rather, it is relevant because of both its magnitude and its timing—the TFR moved to a markedly lower level during the period that preceded the referendum and legislation on divorce. Since one of the traditional functions of marriage has been the production of children, the downward movement of the TFR indicates that, in the decade-and-a-half before the law of Malta was rewritten to permit divorce, the societal importance of marriage had decidedly waned in that nation.

Let us now turn to a related topic—the marital status of the women in Malta who gave birth to children. The TFR, in measuring overall fertility, does not separate childbearing among married women from childbearing among unmarried women, but the distinction is pertinent to whether the societal significance of marriage is rising or falling. The bottom graph in Figure 4.1 reports the percentage of all live births in Malta whose mothers were unmarried when their births occurred.[21] A substantial increase in this percentage, ceteris paribus, is evidence that a conventional function of marriage has declined and that marriage has thus become less central to the social system.

The bottom graph in the figure discloses that, starting in the mid-1990s, childbearing outside marriage markedly increased as a share of all childbearing in Malta, and the rise continued for more than a decade. At the end of the period covered in the figure, unmarried women accounted for approximately one out four births in Malta. Because the rise happened during the period leading up to the adoption by Malta of law permitting divorce, it supports the thesis that the acceptance of law allowing divorce can be traced to a reduction in the societal importance of marriage.

However, our inquiry into nonmarital childbearing in Malta is not ended by the data in Figure 4.1. A major change in the prevalence of out-of-wedlock childbearing raises a question about the demographic components of the change. These components are not just a demographic matter, because they are directly pertinent to dimensions of social life. A shift in the prevalence of

21 The percentage is reported for every year from 1960 onward by the European Commission (Eurostat), http://ec.europa.eu/eurostat/data/database (expand the "Data Navigation Tree," choosing seriatim "Database by themes," "Population and social conditions," "Demography and migration," "Fertility"; then choose "Data explorer" for "Fertility indicators") (last visited May 3, 2015) (data for 1960 to 2011). The bottom graph in Figure 4.1 was constructed using the percentages reported by the European Commission, because the National Statistics Office of Malta does not publish, for women of all ages, the yearly percentage of births in Malta that occur out of wedlock.

nonmarital childbearing may stem from change in childbearing outside marriage, from change in childbearing within marriage, or from both. The secular increase experienced by Malta in the extent of out-of-wedlock births since the mid-1990s, consequently, may have included the following components:

1. Among *unmarried* women, (a) the percentage giving birth may have grown and/or (b) the percentage giving birth may have been constant while the average number of children borne by unmarried women rose.
2. Among *married* women, (a) the percentage remaining childless may have become larger and/or (b) the percentage remaining childless may have been constant while the average number of children borne by married women fell.

Unfortunately, the data that are presently available do not allow an unequivocal conclusion as to which of the above four components—1(a), 1(b), 2(a), and/or 2(b)—contributed to the secular increase that Malta experienced since the mid-1990s in the share of all births occurring outside of marriage.

Identification of the contributing components would be helpful, of course, in determining the ability of a macrosociological framework to furnish an understanding of the institution of law, because three of the four possible components seem particularly likely to be indicators of the degree to which marriage serves important functions for a society. The three components are 1(a), 1(b), and 2(a). Marriage has presumably become less significant in a society that has experienced a sustained increase in the percentage of unmarried women who bear a child, in the total number of children who are borne by unmarried women, and/or in the percentage of married women who, during their lifetimes, do not bear any children.

Although the changed prevalence of out-of-wedlock childbearing cannot be definitively traced to one or more specific demographic sources, a clue to these sources is offered by the mean age at first marriage among women in Malta. Between 1980 and 2002, that age was essentially stable, but between 2002 and 2011, it noticeably increased—to be exact, from 25.4 years to 28.7 years.[22]

---

22 Data on the mean age at first marriage that include contiguous individual years begin in 2000; prior to 2000, data are available for just 1980, 1990, and 1995. The data were obtained from the following sources: United Nations Economic Commission for Europe, UNECE Statistical Database, http://w3.unece.org/pxweb (follow "Fertility, families and households" hyperlink under "Population and Gender" and "Mean age at first marriage by sex" hyperlink) (data for 1980, 1990, 1995, and 2000) (last visited May 3, 2015); NATIONAL STATISTICS OFFICE MALTA, MALTA IN FIGURES: 2004 (2004), at 9 table 12 (data for 2001 and 2002);

The mean age at which women in Malta married for the first time thus jumped by more than three years in only a decade. A rapid shift of this magnitude suggests that the trend observed in Malta in the prevalence of nonmarital births was at least partially due to a decline in childbearing within marriage. A higher first-marriage age among women shortens the time that women have within marriage before they reach menopause, and ceteris paribus, it also reduces the biological ability of women to conceive and carry a pregnancy to term within marriage.[23] The rising mean age at first marriage among women in Malta, therefore, is likely to have reduced the average number of births occurring to married women, and based on data on women in the United States[24]—which probably are similar to data on Western Europe[25]—this reduction would have involved, at least in part, more childlessness among married women. Further, an increase in childlessness would be unlikely to result entirely from a rise in involuntary childlessness; based on findings from the United States, it would probably have involved an expansion of voluntary childlessness as well, i.e., larger percentages of women who chose not to have any children.[26] If this line

---

National Statistics Office Malta, Malta in Figures: 2007 (2007), at 6 table 11 (data for 2003, 2004, and 2005); National Statistics Office Malta, Malta in Figures: 2010 (2010), at 9 table 12 (data for 2006); National Statistics Office Malta, Malta in Figures: 2011 (2011), at 9 table 13 (data for 2007); National Statistics Office Malta, Malta in Figures: 2012 (2012), at 9 table 12 (data for 2008, 2009, 2010, and 2011). All of the cited publications from the National Statistics Office of Malta are available at http://nso.gov.mt/en/Pages/NSO-Home.aspx (select "Publications" and "View by Date") (last visited May 3, 2015).

23 Donald T. Rowland, *Historical Trends in Childlessness*, 28 J. Fam. Issues 1311, 1328–29 (2007).

24 G.F. de Jong & R.R. Sell, *Changes in Childlessness in the United States: A Demographic Path Analysis*, 31 Population Stud. 129, 138–39, 140 (1977); G.F. de Jong & R.R. Sell, *Changes in Childlessness for All Women in the United States: A Reply to Spencer*, 32 Population Stud. 196, 197 (1978).

25 See the paragraph that follows *infra* note 35.

26 In the United States, increases occurred from 1988 to 2002 both in the percentage of ever-married women who were childless, whether involuntarily or voluntarily, and in the percentage of ever-married women who were childless voluntarily. The increases were found even when the age distribution of ever-married women was standardized across time. However, involuntary childlessness among ever-married evidently began to rise before voluntary childlessness. Laurie Chancey, Voluntary Childlessness in the United States: Recent Trends by Cohort and Period 18, 19 table 1, 20 figure 1 (May 2006) (unpublished M.A. thesis, Louisiana State University) (on file with author).

of reasoning is correct, the rise that occurred from 2002 to 2011 in the age of entry into first marriage by women in Malta is an indicator of a decline in a key societal function of marriage, viz., childbearing. Malta adopted law to allow divorce, in short, because its social system was benefiting less from marriage than it had in the past.

2 Societal Benefits of Marriage

Divorce presupposes marriage, of course, and if a societal need for divorce accounts for law allowing divorce—as my macrosociological framework for law contends—the factors creating that need must be identified. Where, however, should the search for these factors begin? The benefits that a society receives from the institution of marriage constitute a logical starting point, because a substantial reduction in, let alone the elimination of, one or more of the benefits of marriage would presumably be a necessary, if not a sufficient, condition for law in the society to allow divorce. To the degree that any of the benefits a society receives from marriage diminish or disappear, in other words, the society can be expected to have less of a commitment to law that bars, or limits the grounds for, divorce.

Why did marriage become, and why has marriage remained, a prominent feature in Western nations? In Europe and the United States, the prevalence of marriage has made it a societal institution,[27] and although marriage at the present time may not be as central to Western societies as it was in the past (or may be in the future), marriage in Western nations has been common.[28] Indeed, marriage has been thought to lie at the core of the social system, as the Congress of the United States illustrated during the 1990s when it labeled marriage "an essential institution of a successful society."[29] Consequently, major advantages have presumably accrued to society from marriage, and the

27 The macrosociological concept of an institution is explained by Howard B. Kaplan, *The Concept of Institution: A Review, Evaluation, and Suggested Research Procedure*, 39 SOC. FORCES 176, 179 (1960). As a macrosociological phenomenon, an institution is not a particular entity (e.g., public facility) but, rather, a widespread, socially approved pattern of interpersonal behavior. THE PLACE OF LAW, *supra* note 5, at 394.

28 U.N., DEP'T OF ECON. & SOC. AFFAIRS, POPULATION DIV., WORLD MARRIAGE DATA 2012 (2013), http://www.un.org/esa/population/publications/WMD2012/MainFrame.html (last visited May 3, 2015).

29 Personal Responsibility and Work Opportunity Reconciliation Act of 1996, Pub. L. No. 104–193, § 101(2), 110 Stat. 2105, 2110 (1996).

identification of the advantages can be expected to furnish insights into the factors that affect the likelihood of divorce. The likelihood of divorce, in turn, is an immediate antecedent of the likelihood that law will authorize divorce and, when divorce is allowed, of the stringency of the law-designated grounds for divorce.[30]

Unfortunately, all of the benefits that Western societies have derived from the institution of marriage cannot be listed with a high degree of certainty, because such certainty requires studies done with an experimental or quasi-experimental design. Nonetheless, the following three societal benefits of marriage are suggested by the published literature in the social sciences:[31]

1. Marriage has furnished an environment favorable for bearing and raising children.
2. Marriage has provided psychological and financial support to both spouses as well as to their children.
3. Marriage has increased social cohesion within communities by promoting ties to the community.

On the assumption that the preceding have been the key advantages that a society has garnered from the institution of marriage, I will attempt to ascertain what has happened to each advantage over time. For Western societies in recent decades, have the above-listed advantages continued unabated, or have they ebbed? The answer to the question would ideally be based on time-series data that directly measure each benefit. However, direct measures are unavailable, requiring that one or more suitable indicators of each benefit be found. Acceptable indicators could be located, however, only for the first two benefits, and hence the discussion is confined to them.

The two graphs in Figure 4.2 supply data pertinent to whether change has taken place in the societal advantage from bearing and rearing children within marriage (benefit #1). The data in each graph cover the period from 1950 to 1995. The year 1950 was selected as the starting point for the graphs in order to

30 Before states in the United States adopted legislation permitting "no fault" divorce—i.e., divorce without evidence that at least one spouse who is seeking to dissolve his/her marriage is under applicable law responsible for the breakdown of the marital relationship—a substantial increase occurred in the rate at which marriages ended in divorce. THE PLACE OF LAW, *supra* note 5, at 10–16.

31 *Id.* at 346–47. The listed benefits are not unrelated; indeed, one benefit may reinforce another.

minimize the sociological effects of World War II—a major event in Western history. The year 1995 ends the period for the reason that the study undertaken in Part 3 *infra* uses no data after 1995.[32]

The top graph in the Figure presents two time series showing the percentages of all births during this period that were to unmarried women; one of the two time series is for the United States while the other is for fifteen European countries combined.[33] European countries are represented only in the top graph, because data for them on the two measures in the bottom graph could not be found. The top graph is important, nonetheless, because it permits a determination whether, in terms of the percentages of total births that took place outside marriage, Western Europe and the United States have experienced the same trends. If in the top graph the trends for Western Europe and the United States are generally similar during the period when data are available for both, we can assume that, in the bottom graph, the trend in the marital birth rate and the trend in the nonmarital birth rate in Western Europe throughout the entire 1950–1995 period were not dissimilar to the trends in the United States.

For the United States, the graphs in Figure 4.2 use data from 1950 to 1995 on three indicators—(i) the percentage of total births in the United States that were to unmarried women of all ages (top graph), (ii) the number of births in the United States per 1,000 unmarried women who were 15–44 years old (bottom graph), and (iii) the number of births in the United States per 1,000 married women who were 15–44 years old (bottom graph).[34] Each graph in Figure 4.2, therefore, supplies a different type of information for the United States during the 1950–1995 period. Specifically, the upper graph provides a measure of the distribution of births annually *between* the two marital statuses and reports the

---

32 See *infra* Part 3-b-ii.

33 The fifteen countries are Austria, Belgium, Cyprus, Finland, France, Germany, Greece, Ireland, Italy, Luxembourg, Malta, Netherlands, Portugal, Slovenia, and Spain. News Release, Eurostat Press Office, Construction Output Down by 0.6% in the Euro Area [2] n. 2 (Aug. 20, 2008) (on file with author), http://www.elpais.com/elpaismedia/ultimahora/media/200808/20/espana/20080820elpepunac_1_Pes_PDF.pdf. For convenience, I will label these countries "Western Europe" in the text.

34 The data on the United States that were used in Figure 4.2 are from CARMEN SOLOMON-FEARS, CONGRESSIONAL RESEARCH SERV., NONMARITAL CHILDBEARING: TRENDS, REASONS, AND PUBLIC POLICY INTERVENTIONS 56–57 table A-1 (2008), *available at* http://www.fas.org/sgp/crs/misc/RL34756.pdf (last visited May 3, 2015). Except for (iii), the time series in Figure 4.2 include data for every year in the 1950–1995 period. As to (iii), data on birth rates among married women are available for every fifth year from 1950 to 1960 (i.e., for 1950, 1955, and 1960); from 1960 through 1995, yearly birth rates are reported for married women. All data reported for the 1950–1995 period are included in the Figure.

extent to which childbearing took place outside of marriage. The lower graph shows the incidence of childbearing *within* each marital status, i.e., the lower graph reports the birth rate among women who were not married and the birth rate among women who were married. In addition, the upper graph includes the yearly percentage of births for which unmarried women were responsible not just in the United States but also in the fifteen nations of Europe. The data for the European countries, however, were available for a shorter time span, namely, 1961 to 1995, than the data for the United States.[35]

Perhaps the initial observation that should be made when considering Figure 4.2 involves the top graph. In particular, the representation of nonmarital births within all childbearing, while virtually identical in the United States and Western Europe at the start of the 1960s, diverged thereafter, and by the last half of the 1960s, the U.S.-to-Europe ratio of the percentage of total births occurring outside of marriage reached the general vicinity of two-to-one—a level that continued for the rest of the period covered by the graph. The ratio remained relatively stable because the percentage rose in each area from the second half of the 1960s onward, and by the 1980s, the pace of the rise did not materially differ between the United States and Western Europe. Consequently, while the *magnitude* of fertility measures is dissimilar in the United States and Western Europe, *trends* in these measures seem to be very similar in the two geographic areas, although the trends may develop somewhat later in Western Europe than in the United States.

What else can be gleaned from the graphs in Figure 4.2? During the last half of the twentieth century, as the top graph makes clear, childbearing outside of marriage became a considerably larger component of total childbearing. The preceding change is seen in the bottom graph to have had two demographic sources in the United States—a marked decrease in the birth rate of married women and an appreciable increase in the birth rate of unmarried women.[36]

---

35 The data for Europe that were used in Figure 4.2 are from Eurostat, European Comm'n, Fertility Indicators (2011), http://ec.europa.eu/eurostat/data/database (expand the "Data Navigation Tree," choosing seriatim "Database by themes," "Population and social conditions," "Demography and migration," "Fertility"; then choose "Data explorer" for "Fertility indicators") (last visited May 3, 2015).

36 With the exception of women born during 1910–1919 and 1940–1949—the cohorts of women who reached their twentieth birthday during, respectively, the 1930s and the 1960s—the number of births per 1,000 unmarried women in the United States increased from earlier birth cohorts to more recent birth cohorts. Robert D. Plotnick, *Seven Decades of Nonmarital Childbearing in the United States* 34 table 3 (Univ. of Washington Ctr. for Studies in Demography & Ecology, Working Paper 04–09, [2004]), *available at* http://csde.washington.edu/downloads/04-09.pdf (last visited May 3, 2015).

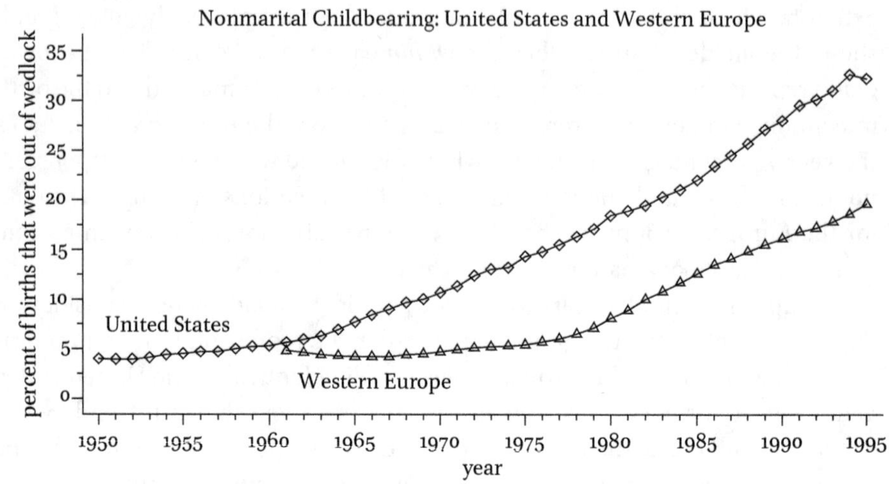

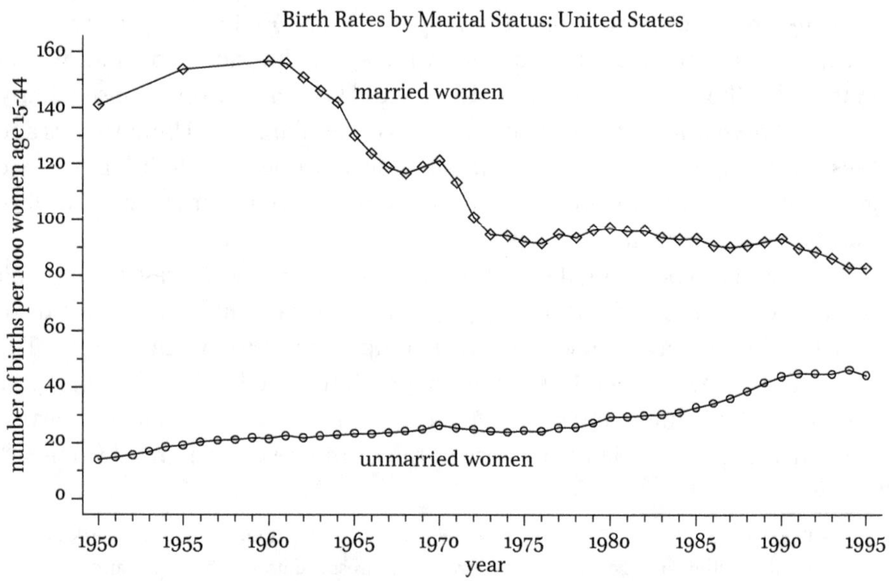

FIGURE 4.2 *Measures of fertility.*
Nonmarital childbearing: United States and Western Europe (*top graph*).
Birth rates by marital status: United States (*bottom graph*)
SOURCE: SEE FN. 34 AND 35 IN THIS CHAPTER.

The preceding changes reduced the ratio of the birth rate of married women to the birth rate of unmarried women by approximately three-fourths during the period covered by the Figure. As a result, while the marital birth rate was more than seven times the nonmarital birth rate in 1960, it was less than twice the nonmarital birth rate in 1995:

Year	Ratio
1960	7.3
1965	5.6
1970	4.6
1975	3.8
1980	3.3
1985	2.8
1990	2.1
1995	1.9

If essentially the same trends occurred in Western Europe—which I assume to be the case—marriage in Western nations generally became much less common as the environment into which children were born during the last half of the twentieth century. Consequently, unless the women who bore children out of wedlock married relatively soon afterwards,[37] an appreciably smaller fraction of children would have been raised by a pair of adults who were married to each other. In short, for the United States—and presumably for Western Europe also—the first-enumerated benefit of marriage evidently eroded to a material degree in the decades after 1950.

A decline also seems to have occurred in the second benefit of the institution of marriage—the psychological and financial support that marriage furnishes the marital partners and their children. Two indicators of this change are (i) the percentage of all households that are family households containing a married couple[38] and (ii) the percentage of all persons younger than age 18 who reside

37 At least during the 1980s, research has found, most women in the United States had married by their fortieth birthday, but marriage was considerably less likely among women who had borne a child out of wedlock than among women who had not. Neil G. Bennett et al., *The Influence of Nonmarital Childbearing on the Formation of First Marriages* 4–6, 19–20, Figure 2 (Nat'l Bureau of Econ. Research, Working Paper No. 4564, 1993).

38 The U.S. Census Bureau, which furnished the data used *infra* for the indicators, defines a household as "all individuals (related family members and all unrelated individuals) whose usual place of residence at the time of the interview is the sample unit." U.S. CENSUS BUREAU, CURRENT POPULATION SURVEY DESIGN AND METHODOLOGY 5–1 (Technical Paper 66, 2006), *available at* http://www.census.gov/prod/2006pubs/tp-66.pdf. A family is considered to be "a group of two or more individuals residing together who are related by birth, marriage, or adoption; all such individuals are considered members of one family. Families are further classified either as married-couple families or as families maintained by women or men without spouses present." *Id.* at 5–1 to 5–2.

TABLE 4.1 *Household composition and living arrangements of children: United States, 1950 to 1995*

Year	Percentage of total households that were married-couple family households	Percentage of all persons under age 18 who lived with two parents[39]
1950	78.2	—
1955	75.7	—
1960	74.3	87.7
1965	72.6	—
1970	70.5	85.2
1975	66.0	80.3
1980	60.8	76.7
1985	58.0	73.9
1990	56.0	72.5
1995	54.4	68.7

with two parents. In the United States, as Table 4.1 reveals, both percentages fell during the last half of the twentieth century.[40] Because of these declines, progressively fewer adults and children in the United States were exposed to, and would have received the benefits of, the environment that marriage creates. Not-dissimilar changes presumably occurred in Western Europe, too.

3 Law on Divorce in Europe

I now consider law on divorce in seventeen nations in Western Europe and report a study that constitutes a quantitative social science approach to comparative law—admittedly an atypical approach in current law school

39 — = data not available.

40 The percentage of total households in each year that were married-couple family households was calculated from U.S. Census Bureau, Families and Living Arrangements, Table HH–1: Households, by Type: 1940 to Present (2010), http://www.census.gov/hhes/families/data/households.html (last visited May 3, 2015).

The percentage of persons below age 18 who lived with two parents in each year was calculated from U.S. Census Bureau, Families and Living Arrangements, Table CH–1: Living Arrangements of Children Under 18 Years Old: 1960 to Present (2010), http://www.census.gov/hhes/families/data/children.html (last visited May 3, 2015).

scholarship on law in general and comparative law in particular since such scholarship has tested hypotheses with evidence derived from reading, and subjectively (i.e., qualitatively) interpreting, documents on the law of a few countries.[41] In general terms, the study that is the subject of Part 3 examines the relationship between demographic, economic, and sociological characteristics of jurisdictions, on the one hand, and doctrines of law on divorce in these jurisdictions, on the other. The study is within a line of quantitative social science research that is recent[42] and still in its infancy. Not surprisingly, therefore, the study is inconsistent with the conventional approach used by scholars who are based in law schools.[43] However, as explained in Part 3-a below, the knowledge that this line of investigation can provide regarding the institution of law is potentially of considerable practical utility.

a *Law on Divorce as a Macrosociological Phenomenon*

As the data in Part 2 *supra* demonstrate, the institution of marriage was in the process of weakening—a process that began in the late 1960s and extended through the 1980s—when states in the United States enacted legislation authorizing "no-fault divorce," i.e., divorce without evidence that one spouse to a marriage had created a fault-based ground for divorce.[44] The hypothesis that the societal importance of marriage was declining at this time receives support, however, not only from the data in Part 2 but also from data on the probability that a marriage would end in divorce. That probability had started to rise—indeed, had risen substantially—before law on no-fault divorce was approved in the United States.[45] This evidence, in combination with the

---

41 Holger Spamann, *Large-Sample, Quantitative Research Designs for Comparative Law?* 57 AM. J. COMP. L. 797, 798 n. 4, 802, 804–805 (2009).

42 The first study to be devoted to the topic of this line of research was a Ph.D. dissertation that was completed in 1991. THE PLACE OF LAW, *supra* note 5, at 458, 469–70 n. 8.

43 *See* Douglas W. Vick, *Interdisciplinarity and the Discipline of Law*, 31 J.L. & SOC'Y 163, 178–79 (2004) (observing that scholarship in law has traditionally confined itself to documents emanating from within the institution of law and that such scholarship views the institution of law as "a sealed system").

44 THE PLACE OF LAW, *supra* note 5, at 27 n. 32, 28 n. 37. The nations of Western Europe generally liberalized their law on divorce during roughly the same time period. *Id.* at 9. Prior to this liberalization, Western Europe presumably experienced a trend in the incidence of divorce that was comparable to the trend in The Netherlands. The divorce rate in the Netherlands was rising when, in 1971, that nation adopted legislation authorizing no-fault divorce. Frans van Poppel & Joop de Beer, *Measuring the Effect of Changing Legislation on the Frequency of Divorce: The Netherlands, 1830–1990*, 30 DEMOGRAPHY 425, 430, 431 figure 1 (1993).

45 THE PLACE OF LAW, *supra* note 5, at 10–14.

findings of well-designed studies done on the effect of law on divorce rates (see below), leads to a key macrosociological proposition regarding the manner in which the institution of law operates in modern societies.

What can be concluded from quantitative social science research into the effect of law on divorce? Succinctly summarized, the research strongly suggests that law[46] accepting one form of divorce (e.g., divorce based on evidence of spousal fault) but not another (e.g., divorce without evidence of spousal fault) has no long-term, permanent impact on the probability of divorce.[47] As a result, law on the subject of divorce must be assumed not to shape social life but to be shaped by it. Rather than controlling the social system, law instead incorporates societal needs and recognizes the character of social life.

Although the response of law to its societal context is unavoidable in a society that is complex structurally and governed democratically, the response is rarely if ever immediate. Indeed, the accommodation that law makes to societal circumstances seems normally to occur only after a lengthy period. In this regard, a second macrosociological proposition is important, namely, the alteration of social life usually happens slowly. Given the gradual pace at which societal conditions typically change and the appreciable time lapse before the content of law normally responds to the change, prediction of new law pertinent to societal conditions is possible in principle assuming that information on these conditions is available (e.g., from social science research and/or government-compiled time-series data). The predictions, furthermore, will be generally accurate even though they concern law that is forecast to arise many years in the future.[48]

If the reasoning above is correct, the adoption of law enabling no-fault divorce did not occur by chance and cannot be attributed to particular personalities (whether legislators or judges). Instead, my framework for law contends, society-level conditions are in the long run the source of the doctrines and concepts of law applicable to key societal activities, and law in Western nations underwent alteration because sociological, demographic, and economic conditions in these nations had changed.

In the remainder of Part 3, I test the hypothesis that law is a macrosociological phenomenon. In particular, I consider law that permits *unilateral* no-fault

46 As used in this chapter, the word "law" refers to written government rules that have been adopted and implemented pursuant to prescribed procedures. The word does not encompass rules that are followed but are unofficial. *Id.* at 3, 49. The instant chapter thus focuses on law that is de jure rather than on law that is de facto.

47 *Id.* at 118, 142–43 n. 163.

48 *Id.* at 231–32, 430–31.

divorce in countries of Western Europe. Unilateral no-fault divorce is a sociologically important phenomenon, because it embodies the social philosophy of individualism[49] in a relatively pure form.[50] An intensification and substantially expanded prevalence of individualism has been posited as one of the overarching shifts that has occurred in the world since the middle of the twentieth century.[51] Consequently, doctrines of law that embody individualism, instead of being fortuitous, presumably result from the social forces that were responsible for the growth of individualism. If the emergence of these doctrines can be explained by quantitatively measurable social forces, the advent of the doctrines was predictable.

What constitutes unilateral no-fault divorce? The answer requires that unilateral no-fault divorce be distinguished from mutual no-fault divorce. When law allows the unilateral form of no-fault divorce, one spouse in a marriage is able to secure a divorce decree by alleging that the marriage is unworkable, and although the spouses may be required to have separated physically for a minimum length of time, the marriage will be terminated by divorce whether or not the other spouse agrees with the allegation.[52] By contrast, a marriage can be ended immediately by divorce under law that imposes the mutual (i.e., consensual) form of no-fault divorce as long as *both* spouses assert that the marriage cannot be salvaged.[53] If in the latter type of jurisdiction one spouse believes that the marriage can be repaired, the spouses may be required to have separated

49 Individualism is an ideal in which individuals, not groups, are thought to be "the ultimate source of action, meaning, and responsibility." Claude S. Fischer, *Paradoxes of American Individualism*, 23 SOCIOL. FORUM 363, 364 (2008) (italicized in original).

50 *See* Elisabeth S. Scott & Robert E. Scott, *A Contract Theory of Marriage*, *in* THE FALL AND RISE OF FREEDOM OF CONTRACT 201, 209 (F.H. Buckley ed., 1999) (contending that law allowing just one spouse to end her/his marriage through divorce is grounded on the concept of "individual autonomy" and "personal freedom").

51 David John Frank & Elizabeth H. McEneaney, *The Individualization of Society and the Liberalization of State Policies on Same-Sex Sexual Relations, 1984–1995*, 77 SOC. FORCES 911, 912, 914, 916–19 (1999). Until the middle of the twentieth century, the development and spread of the social philosophy of individualism seems to have happened gradually in the Western world over a period of centuries. *Id.* at 917; Jennifer M. Russell, *The Race/Class Conundrum and the Pursuit of Individualism in the Making of Social Policy*, 46 HASTINGS L.J. 1353 (1995). Beginning around the middle of the twentieth century, the pace of the increase in individualism as a social philosophy is believed to have become faster. Frank & McEneaney, *supra*, at 912, 914, 917.

52 Thomas E. Carbonneau, *A Consideration of Alternatives to Divorce Litigation*, 1986 U. ILL. L. REV. 1119, 1188–89 n. 198.

53 Lynn Marie Kohm, *On Mutual Consent to Divorce: A Debate with Two Sides to the Story*, 8 APPALACHIAN J.L. 35, 39 (2008).

for a specified period of time before a divorce decree will be issued to terminate their marriage.[54] Notably, the two forms of no-fault divorce arise from dissimilar social images of marriage. While the mutual form is based on the societal view that marriage is a "constitutive family entity," the unilateral form is based on the societal view that marriage is "a partnership of individuals."[55]

b Research Design

I begin by assuming that the number of law-specified grounds for divorce increases, and the interpretation of legislatively specified grounds for divorce broadens, as marriage furnishes fewer benefits to society. When the institution of marriage becomes less important to a society, in other words, law is more lenient in allowing married couples to divorce.[56] The foregoing assumption, however, does not end our inquiry. Because a social system involves chains of causation with innumerable links, we must identify the factors that are responsible for fostering individualism as a social philosophy and—as a correlate, component, or consequence of that philosophy—reducing the societal importance of marriage.[57] These factors were sought in the study I report below on divorce law in seventeen nations of Western Europe.[58]

For theory to be developed from empirical research, the universe that is chosen for a study must have a specifiable boundary. In the instant study, that universe was situated in Western Europe, which was defined as Austria, Belgium, Denmark, Finland, France, Greece, Iceland, Ireland, Italy, Luxembourg, The Netherlands, Norway, Portugal, Spain, Sweden, Switzerland, and the United Kingdom.[59] The preceding seventeen nations comprised the universe for the study because, as an identifiable region, they were assumed to be

54 Carbonneau, *supra* note 52, at 1183 n. 188.

55 See James Herbie DiFonzo, *Unbundling Marriage*, 32 HOFSTRA L. REV. 31, 44 (2003) (linking each image of marriage as described to its respective form of no-fault divorce law but contending that the former resulted from the latter).

56 The changes in law presumably occur when, as the societal importance of marriage diminishes, thresholds are reached. THE PLACE OF LAW, *supra* note 5, at 231, 465, 468.

57 Social scientists have apparently not yet ascertained whether the lessened societal importance of marriage was a correlate, a component, or a consequence of the growth of individualism.

58 Authoritative sources are not consistent in terms of the nations they include within the region of Western Europe. The nations (listed in the text *infra*) that the instant study assumes constitute Western Europe have been deemed to comprise this region by the National Geographic Society. Wikipedia, Western Europe, http://en.wikipedia.org/wiki/Western_europe (see countries named under "Population of Western Europe").

59 Germany is omitted because it was not a single, continuing sovereignty throughout the period encompassed by the study. The law that concerns the study was adopted during

relatively homogeneous in social, cultural, and economic attributes.[60] Nations outside of Western Europe, if included in the study, could be expected to introduce into the data unknown factors that affect doctrines of law on divorce, and because these factors would be uncontrolled, the statistical analysis could yield findings the accuracy of which was seriously compromised.[61]

i Dependent Variable

Before discussing the independent variables in the study, let me describe the dependent variable. Although by 1997 no-fault divorce was available either de jure or de facto under the law of each of the seventeen nations,[62] most of the nations, when they accepted no-fault divorce, required both spouses to agree that their marriage could not be salvaged, and without such agreement, a decree ending the marriage would not be issued immediately.

---

the period from 1974 to 1993. See the text accompanying *infra* note 63. However, from the end of World War II until 1990, separate sovereignties existed in West Germany (viz., the Federal Republic of Germany) and in East Germany (viz., the German Democratic Republic). The German Democratic Republic was absorbed by the Federal Republic of Germany in 1990 and did not exist after that time. The Federal Republic of Germany was intended to be the surviving law-producing jurisdiction, but from 1990 onward it included the social and cultural conditions that were present in East Germany. These conditions were not the same as the social and cultural conditions that prevailed in West Germany. Jürgen Kocka, *Crisis of Unification: How Germany Changes*, DÆDALUS, Winter 1994, at 173. As a result, the Federal Republic of Germany, after unification of the two geographic areas, was exposed to law-influencing factors that had not affected it in earlier post-war years.

60 The study did not cover every nation that is situated geographically in the western part of Europe. Germany, for the reason given in *supra* note 59, was not included in the study. In addition, small sovereignties such as Andorra, Malta, and Monaco were excluded. Precisely defined, the universe for the study was every major West European nation that exercised sovereignty over a geographic area the boundaries of which did not change during the second half of the twentieth century.

61 Although the nations that comprised the universe for the study are in a distinct geographic region and have intertwined economies, they are not the components of and governed by a single Europe-based sovereign jurisdiction. Consequently, the nations that form the universe for the instant study are not a system that possesses its own law. A universe such as that used here is likely to have methodological implications for studies of the macro-level determinants of the concepts and doctrines of law, and these implications need to be identified in future research. *See* THE PLACE OF LAW, *supra* note 5, at 468–69 (discussing influential outliers in quantitative research on jurisdiction-level characteristics that affect jurisdiction law in a set of jurisdictions that constitute a system and the possible ramifications when a jurisdiction in the system, having been deemed an influential outlier, is excluded from data analyses by such research).

62 Thorstein Kneip and Gerrit Bauer, *Did Unilateral Divorce Laws Raise Divorce Rates in Western Europe?* 71 J. MARRIAGE & FAM. 592, 593 (2009).

However, legislation in five of the nations authorized unilateral no-fault divorce, i.e., allowed a marriage to be terminated by divorce at the request of just one spouse. The five nations having de jure unilateral no-fault divorce were Belgium, Denmark, Finland, Norway, and Sweden; the year in which these nations first had such law was, respectively, 1975, 1989, 1988, 1993, and 1974.[63] In measuring the dependent variable, each of the preceding five nations was coded 1; the other twelve nations were coded 0. The dependent variable in the study, accordingly, was whether or not unilateral no-fault divorce was permitted by statute, with the presence of such a statute identified by the code of 1.

ii Time Frame for Data

The timing of the dependent variable—i.e., the years in which unilateral no-fault divorce law appeared in the law of the five countries—has a major bearing, of course, on the choice of the time period covered by the data on the independent variables in the study. Because law allowing unilateral no-fault divorce materialized in the five nations starting in the mid-1970s and ending in the mid-1990s, the data on the independent variables should ideally cover the period from approximately 1950 to approximately 1995. Why are data for this entire period desirable? Causality involves temporal sequences—i.e., a cause by definition must precede its effect(s)—and given the year when law permitting unilateral no-fault divorce in the seventeen countries last occurred (1993), data on the independent variables ought to extend to the mid-1990s. As the starting point for the data on the independent variables, the year 1950 (or a year shortly thereafter) is desirable for several reasons. First, in most cases macro-level forces probably develop at a gradual pace before they trigger new concepts and doctrines of law, and studies of the macro-level forces that mold law can thus be expected to benefit from employing data on these forces that cover a substantial interval before law changes. Second, such data permit the baseline for each of the explanatory variables to be established. Without a reliable estimate of the baseline of an explanatory variable, an investigator cannot determine whether new law was preceded, and hence may have been produced, by change in the incidence of that variable. Finally, the history of Western Europe justifies 1950 as a starting point for the instant study because

63 *Id.* at 597. The year given for each nation is the first year that unilateral no-fault divorce law was in force in that nation; the specified year is not necessarily the year in which legislation providing for such law was approved. Libertad González & Tarja K. Viitanen, *The Effect of Divorce Laws on Divorce Rates in Europe* 7 n. 5, 26 table 1 (Institute for the Study of Labor, Discussion Paper No. 2023, 2006), http://ssrn.com/abstract=892354.

that year is after the economic depression of the 1930s had ended and World War II had concluded.[64]

Unfortunately, data prior to 1970 that are comparable across all of the countries have evidently not been published on the independent variables. As a result, the study did not pool the meager time series data that were located, but relied instead on a data form that I label "time-spaced cross-sectional data." I use the label to indicate that, in the instant study, the data on the independent variables as well as the data on the dependent variable were each cross-sections of the seventeen nations and that the former data generally were for a point in time that was earlier than the point in time for the latter data.[65] To be exact, the independent variables were, with one exception, measured as of 1970 or 1971,[66] and the data for the dependent variable comprised a cross-section of 1974–1993, i.e., 1974–1993 was treated as a single, undifferentiated period. If (as I assume) law generally is the product of macro-level forces that change slowly, data on the independent variables for years considerably before 1970 would have expanded the analysis and may have yielded helpful insights. That possibility was foreclosed by the lack of such data for years earlier than 1970.

iii Independent Variables

The selection of independent variables for the instant study poses a formidable challenge given the current, ill-developed state of empirically grounded theory[67] on the jurisdiction-level factors that mold doctrines of law.[68] The rudimentary state of such theory should not be surprising, because to date

64 See the discussion in The Place of Law, *supra* note 5, at 464.

65 Because time-spaced cross-sectional data do not measure change over time, they are less able than pooled time-series data to generate conclusions regarding causality that merit a high degree of confidence. Although indicators are often available for a larger number of independent variables when time-spaced cross-sectional data are used, the goal of research in science—viz., the identification of causal agents—makes pooled time-series data generally preferable to cross-sectional data.

66 The independent variables included the societal importance of marriage, which was measured by inter alia the percentage of women 25–29 years old in each country who had never married. *Infra* note 88 and accompanying text. The percentage for Iceland was as of 1974. Iceland was not one of the nations in the study that adopted law permitting unilateral no-fault divorce. Text accompanying *supra* note 63.

67 In the instant chapter, a theory is considered to be a series of general, related principles (i) that attempt to account for the current state of a phenomenon and (ii) that, to the degree they are accurate, allow the prediction of change in the phenomenon. The Place of Law, *supra* note 5, at 24 n. 5.

68 The best-known work to use empirical research in constructing a sociological theory of the institution of law is that by Donald Black, The Behavior of Law (1976).

these factors have been the subject of quantitative studies that are meager in number.[69] As a result, conjecture cannot be avoided when choosing independent variables for a study of macro-level forces that may account for the adoption of law permitting unilateral no-fault divorce.

The instant study relies on two sets of independent variables. Although divided into sets, the independent variables are generally concerned with individualism as a social philosophy and rest on the assumption that individualism molds the concepts and doctrines of law. One set consists of variables that have been posited as determinants of the intensity and prevalence of individualism. The other set consists of two variables that can be (and are considered here to be) indicators of the importance of marriage to a society. Individualism, although not observable itself, has been posited as a factor that affects the societal importance of marriage, a dimension that is presumably measured by inter alia the probability of divorce and the level of childbearing.[70]

The work has been described as the single "most important publication" in the sociology of law, and the theory it proposes has been said to be backed by "[a] broad array of data." Mark Cooney, *Still Paying the Price of Heterodoxy: The Behavior of Law a Quarter-Century On*, 31 CONTEMP. SOCIOL. 658, 661 (2002). However, quantitative studies that have tested the theory have often failed to uncover evidence strongly supporting it. Jody Clay-Warner & Jennifer McMahon-Howard, *Rape Reporting: "Classic Rape" and the Behavior of Law*, 24 VIOLENCE & VICTIMS 723 (2009); Gloria T. Lessan & Joseph F. Sheley, *Does Law Behave? A Macrolevel Test of Black's Propositions on Change in Law*, 70 SOC. FORCES 655 (1992); Linda A. Mooney, *The Behavior of Law in a Private Legal System*, 64 SOC. FORCES 733 (1986); Martha A. Myers, *Predicting the Behavior of Law: A Test of Two Models*, 14 LAW & SOC'Y REV. 835 (1980). More importantly, the theory developed by Professor Black is not concerned, as I am, with the *content* of doctrines and concepts of law and with the reasons this content persists or changes. Instead, his theory deals with the volume and application of law in a society. THE PLACE OF LAW, *supra* note 5, at 22. As a result, the theory advanced by Professor Black supplies no guidance in selecting independent variables for the instant study.

69 Regrettably, the number of such studies will probably increase slowly due to resource constraints. To overcome these constraints, (i) nations must produce a much larger volume of high-quality time-series statistical data that are comparable across jurisdictions and across time; and (ii) many more scholars who are based in law schools must acquire expertise in quantitative research methods. In terms of the speed with which the foregoing problems will be overcome, (ii) seems likely to happen more rapidly than (i), which can be expected to require a multi-decade commitment of substantial amounts of time and large sums of money.

70 *See* Jens Ehrhardt & Martin Kohli, *Individualisation and Fertility*, 36 HIST. SOC. RES. 35, 48–52 (2011) (contending that, in Western nations, greater individualism during the last half of the twentieth century raised divorce rates and reduced childbearing).

The first set of independent variables derives from my prior research on the society-level forces that determine the content of law.[71] In this research, I hypothesized that increases in educational attainment, urban residence, and economic wealth in a society bring about changes in law by inter alia increasing the strength and expanding the prevalence of individualism. The instant study offers an opportunity to test these hypotheses, and educational attainment, urban residence, and economic wealth were accordingly each an independent variable in the data analysis.

- *Education* was measured by the gross enrollment ratio at the university level in each country. The data are for males and females combined and are for 1971.[72] The gross enrollment ratio is the "[n]umber of students enrolled in a given level of education, regardless of age, expressed as a percentage of the official school-age population corresponding to the same level of education. For the tertiary level, the population used is the 5-year age group starting from the official secondary school graduation age."[73]
- *Urban residence* was measured by the percentage of the total population in each nation that resided in an urban agglomeration in 1970.[74] An "urban agglomeration" is "the de facto population contained within the contours of a contiguous territory inhabited at urban density levels without regard to administrative boundaries. It usually incorporates the population in a city or town plus that in the sub-urban areas lying outside of but being adjacent

71 The Place of Law, *supra* note 5, at 200–01, 267–68, 307–10, 342–44, 371–72, 453 n. 223.

72 The data are from UNESCO Institute for Statistics, Gross Enrolment Ratio by Level of Education, http://www.uis.unesco.org/DataCentre/Pages/BrowseEducation.aspx (under "Browse by theme," expand seriatim "Education," "Participation," and "Enrolment ratios") (data for 1971) (last visited May 3, 2015).

The data cover ISCED levels 5 and 6. ISCED level 5 is comprised of "tertiary programmes with academic orientation (type A) which are largely theoretical and tertiary programmes with an occupational orientation (type B)," while ISCED level 6 is comprised of "tertiary studies that lead to an advanced research qualification (Ph.D. or doctorate)." European Comm'n, Glossary: International Standard Classification of Education (ISCED), http://ec.europa.eu/eurostat/statistics-explained/index.php/Glossary:International_standard_classification_of_education_%28ISCED%29 (last visited May 3, 2015).

73 UNESCO Institute for Statistics, Glossary, http://glossary.uis.unesco.org/Glossary/en/Term/2048/en (last visited May 4, 2015).

74 The data are from U.N. Population Div., World Urbanization Prospects: The 2009 Revision Population Database, Panel 2: Urban Agglomerations (2010) [hereinafter Panel 2]. The data were obtained in 2011 from the 2009 Revision Population Database, which is no longer available online.

to the city boundaries."[75] Although the data are for 1970, an area was designated by the agency that compiled the data as an urban agglomeration if, *in 2009*, the area had a population of at least 750,000.[76] However, even if some particular locales that were urban agglomerations in 2009 were not such in 1970, the percentages residing in 2009-defined urban agglomerations were presumably a measure of relatively high population density in 1970.

- *Wealth* was measured by the gross domestic product per person in each nation. The data on wealth are for 1970, are expressed in exact number of U.S. dollars, and are adjusted for differences in price levels between nations.[77]

In addition to the three factors above, the first set of variables includes a fourth factor—culture and language. Culture can account for concepts and doctrines of law because it consists of the fundamental, but often unconsciously held, assumptions that are common to a group and that shape the perceptions and reactions of the members of the group.[78] Language is a factor that potentially explains the content of law because the words of a language, and the ideas that are represented by the words, affect whether a phenomenon

75 U.N. Population Div., Glossary of Demographic Terms, http://esa.un.org/unpd/wup/General/GlossaryDemographicTerms.aspx (last visited May 3, 2015).

76 Panel 2, *supra* note 74. The United Nations Population Division reported that no data were available on urban agglomerations for either Iceland or Luxembourg. However, each of these countries had a population of fewer than 750,000 from 1970 to 2010. U.N. Population Div., *supra* note 74, at Panel 1. Because Iceland and Luxembourg had no urban agglomerations during this period, each was coded in the instant study as having 0.0% of its population in an urban agglomeration in 1970.

77 The data are from Organization for Economic Co-operation and Development, *Gross Domestic Product: GDP Per Head, U.S. $, Current Prices, Current PPPs* (2011), http://stats.oecd.org/Index.aspx (expand seriatim the tree for "National Accounts," for "Annual National Accounts," for "Main Aggregates," and for "Gross domestic product") (last visited May 4, 2015). Differences in price levels between nations were eliminated by using data on gross domestic product per person that were calculated with purchasing power parities. EUROPEAN COMMUNITIES, EUROSTAT—OECD METHODOLOGICAL MANUAL ON PURCHASING POWER PARITIES 261 (2006) (see definition of "PPP or PPPs"), http://ec.europa.eu/eurostat/en/web/products-manuals-and-guidelines/-/KS-BE-06-002 (last visited May 6, 2015)..

78 Edgar H. Schein, *Culture: The Missing Concept in Organization Studies*, 41 ADMIN. SCI. Q. 229, 236 (1996); paragraphs accompanying notes 25 & 26 in *supra* Chapter 2.

is perceived and, when perceived, how it is perceived and interpreted.[79] Notably, although language is distinguishable from culture,[80] no culture-independent quantitative measure of language seems to have been used to date in research on the jurisdiction-level factors that may affect the concepts and doctrines of law.[81]

Because the present study could not empirically separate language and culture, it measured the two phenomena as a single independent variable. Specifically, the variable distinguished the three countries of Scandinavia—Denmark, Norway, and Sweden[82]—from the other fourteen countries in the study. Denmark, Norway, and Sweden were regarded as forming Scandinavia because (i) their populations view themselves as Scandinavian and (ii) they are similar to each other in culture as well as language.[83] The variable was measured as a dummy: Denmark, Norway, and Sweden were each coded 1; the other countries in the study were each coded 0.

At this point, it may be appropriate to point out an aspect of the first set of independent variables. Specifically, all of the variables in the first set are

---

79 Benjamin Lee Whorf, *An American Indian Model of the Universe, in* LANGUAGE, THOUGHT, AND REALITY: SELECTED WRITINGS OF BENJAMIN LEE WHORF 57 (John B. Carroll ed. 1956) [hereinafter LANGUAGE, THOUGHT, AND REALITY]; Benjamin Lee Whorf, *Science and Linquistics, in id.* 207, 212–13; Lera Boroditsky et al., *Sex, Syntax, and Semantics, in* LANGUAGE IN MIND: ADVANCES IN THE STUDY OF LANGUAGE AND THOUGHT 61, 75–77 (Dedre Gentner & Susan Goldin-Meadow eds., 2003) [hereinafter LANGUAGE IN MIND]; John A. Lucy & Suzanne Gaskins, *Interaction of Language Type and Referent Type in the Development of Nonverbal Classification Preferences, in* LANGUAGE IN MIND, *supra*, at 465, 481–82.

80 Indeed, language may exercise a larger influence than culture on perception and interpretation. Lucy & Gaskins, *supra* note 79, at 482–83.

81 Differences between thirty-three languages in the number of sex-differentiated personal pronouns have been found to be inversely related to differences between approximately eighty countries in the length of law-mandated maternity leave. Yehonatan Givati & Ugo Troiano, *Law, Economics, and Culture: Theory of Mandated Benefits and Evidence from Maternity Leave Policies*, 55 J.L. & ECON. 339, 341, 354–55, 362 (2012). The Givati-Troiano study, however, did not separate the effect of language from the effect of culture.

82 14 OXFORD ENGLISH DICTIONARY 575 (2nd ed. 1989) (def. A.1. of "Scandinavian").

83 *Scandinavia*, NEW WORLD ENCYCLOPEDIA, http://www.newworldencyclopedia.org/entry/Scandinavia; *Scandinavia*, WIKIPEDIA, http://en.wikipedia.org/wiki/Scandinavia. While culture unifies the five Nordic nations (Denmark, Finland, Iceland, Norway, and Sweden), language does not. Only in the three Scandinavian nations (Denmark, Norway, and Sweden) are the primary languages part of the Indo-European family; the primary languages of the Scandinavian countries are understandable to the users of one by the users of the others. Einar Haugen, *Semicommunication: The Language Gap in Scandinavia*, 36 SOCIOL. INQUIRY 280, 281 (1966).

likely to alter law indirectly, i.e., by affecting other variables that work through political variables to shape the content of law.[84] Because of these intervening phenomena—e.g., societal changes in sex roles from which politically focused groups arise to alter law bearing on gender—the magnitude of the impact of each of the four factors above may be underestimated in data analyses.

In addition to acquiring data for the independent variables in the first set, the study gathered data for another, and distinct, set of independent variables. The latter set consisted of two empirical measures of the degree to which the institution of marriage is important or central to a society. These measures, which were admittedly crude rather than precise indicators of the societal importance of marriage,[85] were (i) the total fertility rate[86] in each nation in 1970[87] and (ii) the percentage of women in each country who, at age 25–29, had never been married.[88] As to (ii), marriage is presumed to be weaker,

---

84 The degree of religiosity in a jurisdiction has primarily an indirect impact on law in the jurisdiction. Christopher P. Scheitle & Bryanna B. Hahn, *From the Pews to Policy: Specifying Evangelical Protestantism's Influence on States' Sexual Orientation Policies*, 89 Soc. Forces 913, 929–30 (2011). Religiosity is a correlate or consequence of culture. Samuel H. Reimer, *A Look at Cultural Effects on Religiosity: A Comparison Between the United States and Canada*, 34 J. Sci. Stud. Religion 445, 446–47 (1995).

85 Other indicators of cross-country differences in the societal centrality of marriage that might have been used include the mean age at first marriage and birth rates by marital status. Unfortunately, data on these measures could not be found for the early years of the 1970s for all of the countries in the study.

86 The concept of the total fertility rate is explained in the text that accompanies *supra* notes 18 & 19 and in *supra* note 19. The utility of the total fertility rate as an indicator of the societal importance of marriage is explained in the text that accompanies *supra* note 20.

87 Data on the total fertility rate are from U.N. Population Div., World Fertility Data 2008 (2008), http://www.un.org/esa/population/publications/WFD%202008/Main.html (follow, under "World Fertility Data 2008," "Data" hyperlink; then under "Period Fertility Indicators" select "Total fertility") (last visited May 6, 2015).

88 The percentage of women who at age 25–29 had *ever* married was obtained for every country from U.N. Population Div., World Marriage Data 2008 (2008), http://www.un.org/esa/population/publications/WMD2008/Main.html (follow "Data" hyperlink; then, under "Marital Status," follow "Ever married women and men" hyperlink) (last visited May 4, 2015). For an explanation of the procedure used by the United Nations Population Division to calculate the percentage of ever-married persons, see *id.* (follow "Metadata" hyperlink; then follow "Ever married women and men" hyperlink).

The percentage of women in each country who at age 25–29 had *never* married was computed by subtracting from 100.0 the percentage of women who at age 25–29 were ever married.

ceteris paribus, in a country where the percentage is high than in a country where the percentage is low. Age 25–29 was believed to be a more accurate than age 20–24 as a measure of the societal centrality of marriage, because marriage might be important in a society but deferred due to the demands of, inter alia, schooling.[89] In all countries, the percentages comprising (ii) were for 1970 with the following exceptions: In the case of Austria, Greece, Ireland, Italy, and the United Kingdom, the data are for 1971; in the case of Iceland, the data are for 1974.

c *Data Analysis: Preliminary Matters*

Maximum-likelihood logistic regression was employed to estimate the relationship of each independent variable to the dependent variable.[90] In doing so, every indicator was assigned a mnemonic label. Table 4.2 provides a synopsis of the measurement of each variable/indicator and lists its mnemonic label.

Table 4.2 furnishes a reminder that two variables in the study were dummies—the dependent variable UNILAT and the independent variable SCAND. On each of these variables, therefore, every nation was assigned either a 0 or a 1. The coding of UNILAT should be underscored because it must be kept in mind when interpreting the odds ratios that are reported below. For UNILAT, nations whose legislation authorized unilateral no-fault divorce were coded 1; nations not having such legislation were coded 0.

As I considered models for analyzing the data, it became clear that, because of collinearity, one possible indicator of the societal importance of marriage should not be included. The percentage of women 25–29 years old who had never married and the percentage of men in that age range who had never married were found to be substantially correlated with each other ($r = 0.86$),[91] which argued for retaining just one sex in the data analysis. Given that women

89 An age group older than 25–29 was not used because the percentage of persons who have never married generally changes much less between adjacent age groups after age 25–29 than it does from age 20–24 to age 25–29.

90 A helpful explanation of logistic regression is provided by, inter alia, FRED C. PAMPEL, LOGISTIC REGRESSION: A PRIMER (Sage University Papers, Quantitative Applications in the Social Sciences Series No. 132, 2000).

In the instant study, regression analyses were done with the LOGISTIC and LOGIT commands of Stata Release 12.1. STATACORP, STATA BASE REFERENCE MANUAL RELEASE 12 (2011), at 932–82.

91 The correlation coefficients in the discussion that follows were computed with the CORRELATE command in Stata 12.1. STATACORP., *supra* note 90, at 393–400.

TABLE 4.2 *Summary of variables and indicators*

Variable	Measurement	Mnemonic label
Dependent variable		
Law on divorce	Binary (0 or 1)	UNILAT
Independent variables/indicators		
Culture-language	Binary (0 or 1)	SCAND
Education	Percentages	EDUC
Societal importance of marriage		
Never married women 25–29 years old	Percentages	NMW2529
Total fertility rate	Numbers (births per woman)	TFR
Urban residence	Percentages	URBANAGG
Wealth	Numbers (dollars per person)	GDP

evidently experienced more change in sex roles than men during at least a portion of the historical era on which the instant chapter focuses,[92] resistance to marriage among women was believed to be a more appropriate indicator of the societal centrality of marriage, and men were omitted when analyzing the data. By its inclusion of indicators of multiple independent variables—SCAND, EDUC, NMW2529, TFR, URBANAGG, and GDP—the final regression model raises a question of major theoretical importance. If each of the independent variables affects the dependent variable, do they operate concurrently or in sequences? Work to date[93] suggests the sequence diagrammed below ("Diagram 1").

Ideally, the set of paths in Diagram 1 should be tested statistically so that direct effects can be distinguished from indirect effects and the magnitude of each can be estimated reliably. However, such a test requires structural equation modeling, and the number of cases (nations) in the instant study (viz., seventeen) is far below the minimum needed for such modeling.[94]

92 David Cotter et al., *The End of the Gender Revolution? Gender Role Attitudes from 1977 to 2008*, 117 AM. J. SOCIOL. 259, 272 (2011).

93 THE PLACE OF LAW, *supra* note 5, at 369–72.

94 *See* Ming Lei & Richard G. Lomax, *The Effect of Varying Degrees of Nonnormality in Structural Equation Modeling*, 12 STRUCTURAL EQUATION MODELING 1, 16 (2005) (suggesting that the number of cases for structural equation modeling be larger than 100 and recommending the use of more than 500 cases).

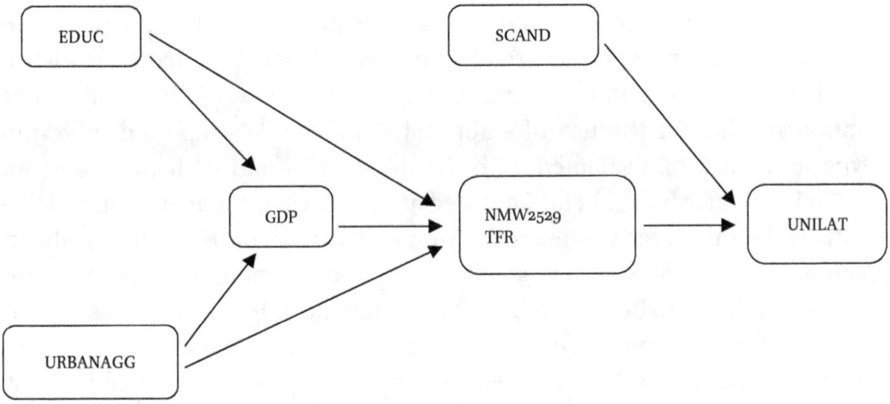

Diagram 1

Consequently, all of the independent variables will be assumed to operate concurrently on UNILAT, and no independent variable will be assumed to work through another. The posited relationships are portrayed in the diagram below ("Diagram 2"). Given the present state of social science knowledge, these assumptions are not unreasonable. Of course, if and to the degree the assumptions are inaccurate, the regression coefficients and odds ratios that are estimated in the data analysis may erroneously estimate the magnitude of the impact of one or more of the independent variables on the dependent variable. Caution, accordingly, is warranted when drawing conclusions from the data.

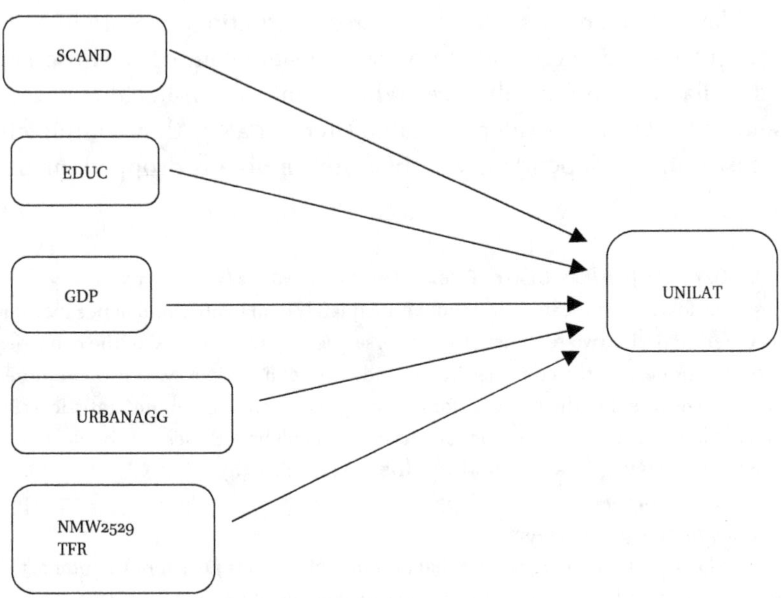

Diagram 2

The number of nations for which data were acquired, as well as the procedure for selecting the nations, also renders inadvisable any reliance on statistical significance as a criterion for decisions on null hypotheses. Although the information needed for the use of statistical significance is reported *infra*, null hypotheses will be evaluated with the odds ratios and with the regression coefficients measured in standard deviations of each independent variable. Statistical significance was not a criterion for two reasons. First, the number of nations in the study was very small, and an incorrect null hypothesis, therefore, was unlikely to be rejected.[95] Second, statistical significance presupposes that (i) the data come from cases selected out of a larger, unambiguously defined universe[96] and (ii) the selection procedure satisfies the requirements of random sampling.[97] The aim of social science is to estimate characteristics of a universe from the characteristics of a sample, but such estimation is possible only when the cases supplying the data were chosen with a random procedure in which the probability of selecting each case was known and not zero.[98] In the instant study, sampling was not employed, and as a result, tests of statistical significance are inappropriate.[99]

d *Data Analysis: Findings*

When UNILAT was regressed on SCAND, EDUC, GDP, URBANAGG, NMW2529, and TFR,[100] coefficients and odds ratios for SCAND could not be estimated, because the nations that were coded 1 on SCAND—Denmark, Norway, and Sweden—were also coded 1 on UNILAT. As measured in the present study, in other words, law on divorce was the same across the nations of Scandinavia: All of the countries that were coded 1 on SCAND were countries whose law authorized unilateral no-fault divorce. When a maximum-likelihood estimate is sought for an independent variable (here, SCAND) that completely separates cases on the dependent variable, the variable is dropped, or the

---

95 RONALD CZAJA & JOHNNY BLAIR, DESIGNING SURVEYS 152 (2d ed. 2005).

96 The universe for the instant study may not be adequately demarcated, and hence may not satisfy criterion (i), for two reasons—the universe does not represent all of the countries in Western Europe, and the countries in the study are not a distinct system. *Supra* notes 59–61. To the degree that the universe for the study is rendered indefinite, statistical significance is less justified as a criterion for decisions on null hypotheses.

97 EARL BABBIE, SURVEY RESEARCH METHODS 303 (2d ed. 1990).

98 CZAJA & BLAIR, *supra* note 95, at 126–27.

99 BABBIE, *supra* note 97, at 301–02.

100 For the reasons given in the paragraph that accompanies note 59 in *supra* Chapter 2, the intercept was omitted when estimating regression coefficients and odds ratios.

coefficient and odds ratio estimated for it are implausible.[101] Given the inability to calculate maximum-likelihood estimates for SCAND, the three Scandinavian countries were omitted when the regression coefficients and odds ratios were calculated for the other independent variables. The latter calculations were thus based on fourteen cases, i.e., the fourteen countries in the study that are not Scandinavian.

Before proceeding, however, a key assumption on which the regression analysis is based should be discussed. Specifically, the analysis assumes that there was no interaction between independent variables.[102] The concept of interaction can be illustrated with three independent variables, two of which (X1 and X_2) are measured in continuous quantities and the third of which (X_3) is measured with qualitatively distinct, unranked categories.[103] Interaction exists when X_1 and X2 together have an effect on the dependent variable (Y) that, in magnitude and/or direction, differs from the effect that would be observed for X1 alone and for X_2 alone.[104] Interaction also exists when the impact of X_1 on Y differs in magnitude and/or direction between two (or more)

101 DAVID W. HOSMER & STANLEY LEMESHOW, APPLIED LOGISTIC REGRESSION 138–39 (2d ed. 2000).

102 A further assumption is that collinearity among independent variables was not sufficiently strong to affect the results. None of the remaining independent variables—EDUC, GDP, URBANAGG, NMW2529, and TFR—had a Variance Inflation Factor ("VIF") at or above 10.0, the threshold that is typically used to indicate the presence of excessive collinearity. *E.g.*, DAMODAR N. GUJARATI & DAWN C. PORTER, BASIC ECONOMETRICS 340 (5th ed. 2009); Jeff Tayman et al., *Evaluating Population Forecast Accuracy: A Regression Approach Using County Data*, 30 POPULATION RES. & POL'Y REV. 235, 256 (2011); Tse-Chuan Yang et al., *Social Capital and Human Mortality: Explaining the Rural Paradox with County-Level Mortality Data*, 76 RURAL SOCIOL. 347, 363 (2011). Indeed, for each of these independent variables, the VIF score was no higher than 3.06, indicating that collinearity was not problematic. The VIF scores of the independent variables were computed without an intercept and excluded the Scandinavian countries. The VIF scores were obtained with the COLLIN command for Stata. UCLA Institute for Digital Res. & Educ., Logistic Regression Diagnostics, http://www.ats.ucla.edu/stat/stata/webbooks/logistic/chapter3/statalog3.htm (last visited May 4, 2015).

103 In this example, X1 and X2 are being measured with an interval or ratio scale, while X3 is being measured with a nominal scale. Anwer Khurshid & Hardeo Sahai, *Scales of Measurements: An Introduction and a Selected Bibliography*, 27 QUALITY & QUANTITY 303 (1993).

104 JAMES JACCARD & ROBERT TURRISI, INTERACTION EFFECTS IN MULTIPLE REGRESSION 21 (Sage University Papers, Quantitative Applications in the Social Sciences Series No. 72, 2d ed. 2003).

of the categories of X_3.[105] When interaction is present between X_1 and another independent variable, in other words, X_1 and the other independent variable act jointly rather than separately on the dependent variable. As I explain below, the regression analysis in this chapter assumes that interaction between independent variables was not present in the data.

Before statistically testing for interaction, an investigator should have a reason to believe that particular explanatory variables may be interacting. That reason is most appropriately derived from theory on the phenomenon under study,[106] because the goal of social science is to explain comprehensively (as well as parsimoniously) the components of the social world and because the efficiency of searches for such explanations will be improved to the extent they are guided by theory. Without theory, pursuit of the causes of a phenomenon will be haphazard. Moreover, if a data analysis that is not driven by theory finds interaction between certain independent variables, there will be no justification for believing this interaction occurs outside the dataset that yielded the finding. Theory, therefore, should be the reason for choosing specific independent variables and checking the data to ascertain whether they interact.

In terms of the instant research, current macro-level theory pertinent to the concepts and doctrines of law furnishes no suggestion that interaction occurs between any of the independent variables in the regression model for the non-Scandinavian countries. As a result, the data being used here will not be examined for interaction. On the other hand, readers should keep in mind that the rudimentary state of macrosociological theory on the content of law may be responsible for the absence of direction regarding possible interaction. In other words, there may indeed be interaction between independent variables in the study. This interaction, moreover, may have an important bearing on understanding the institution of law but has escaped attention due to the meagerness of theory.

e *Examination and Assessment of Findings*

What conclusions can be drawn from the data regarding the macro-level causes of law allowing unilateral no-fault divorce? Three conclusions, I believe, are warranted.

---

105 *Id.* at 3.

106 JAMES JACCARD, INTERACTION EFFECTS IN LOGISTIC REGRESSION 12–13 (Paper No. 135, Sage University Paper Series on Quantitative Applications in the Social Sciences, 2001); F. David Schoorman et al., *The Role of Theory in Testing Hypothesized Interactions: An Example from the Research on Escalation of Commitment,* 21 J. APPLIED SOC. PSYCHOL. 1338, 1338, 1349, 1353 (1991).

First, culture-language is evidently a powerful predictor of the existence of law enabling unilateral no-fault divorce. Such law was found in all of the three nations (Denmark, Norway, and Sweden) that form Scandinavia, but it was found in just two nations (Belgium and Finland) that lie outside of Scandinavia.[107] The disproportionate presence of law allowing unilateral no-fault divorce in a geographic area that is distinctive in culture and language is unlikely to be coincidence, and it underscores the potential importance of these societal attributes to the content of law.

Second, the regression model fit the data exceedingly well as measured by the rate at which the model correctly predicted the non-Scandinavian countries that would have, and the non-Scandinavian countries that would not have, law permitting unilateral no-fault divorce. The five independent variables of EDUC, GDP, URBANAGG, NMW2529, and TFR correctly predicted the law that would be found in every non-Scandinavian nation in the study.[108] However, perfect prediction was achieved because the independent variables completely separated the cases on the dependent variable, and as a result, the odds ratios obtained for the independent variables are untrustworthy. This outcome may well be due to limitations of the study. In particular, the nations in the study are few in terms of number and relatively homogeneous in terms of sociological, demographic, and economic characteristics. Moreover, only two of the fourteen non-Scandinavian nations in the study have adopted law that authorizes unilateral no-fault divorce.[109] While the regression model was correct in every prediction it made, it may be much less accurate when applied to a substantially larger set of nations that are more diverse in their characteristics and in their law on divorce.

But what is the nature of the relationship to the dependent variable of each of the independent variables? In the search for regularities, the direction and magnitude of relationships are important. One approach when a set of independent variables completely separates cases on the dependent variable is to analyze the data with a carefully selected univariate regression model, i.e., with a model that uses a single independent variable.[110] Such an approach, however, does not hold constant any factor that might be contaminating the

---

107 Text accompanying *supra* note 63.

108 Such a percentage is one measure of model fit. J. SCOTT LONG & JEREMY FREESE, REGRESSION MODELS FOR CATEGORICAL DEPENDENT VARIABLES USING STATA 104, 110–11 (2d ed. 2006). The percentage was obtained using the ESTAT CLASSIFICATION command for LOGISTIC and its default cutoff. STATACORP., *supra* note 90, at 503, 932.

109 Text accompanying *supra* note 63.

110 HOSMER & LEMESHOW, *supra* note 101, at 138–40.

relationship of a particular independent variable to the dependent variable. Consequently, a thoughtfully chosen model having fewer than the five independent variables in the initial model may be preferable. A model with two, three, or four independent variables may yield information that can guide future research on a larger number and variety of jurisdictions.

To develop such a model, I rely on Diagram 1 above. The model includes the three variables—EDUC, GDP, URBANAGG—that are at the start of the sequence portrayed in the diagram, and no variable fully separated the fourteen non-Scandinavian nations. Predictions of the law in twelve of the fourteen nations were correct. The results of the data analysis with the three-variable model (estimated without an intercept) are reported in Table 4.3.

The odds ratios reported in Table 4.3 indicate that, among the three independent variables, educational attainment had the largest influence per measurement unit on the odds that a non-Scandinavian country would have law authorizing unilateral no-fault divorce. As the next-to-the-last column in Table 4.3 shows, the odds that such law was present rose 20.7% when EDUC increased by one percentage point, declined by 0.1% when GDP increased by one dollar per person, and fell 7.9% when URBANAGG went up by one percentage point.[111] The foregoing odds ratios, however, may not accurately rank the independent variables in terms of the strength of their relationships to UNILAT, because these variables do not utilize the same unit of measurement.[112] Table 4.3, consequently, presents an alternate way to compare independent variables having different measurement units and ascertain the relative degree to which each is related to the dependent variable. Specifically, the odds ratio of each independent variable was based on the *standard deviation* of the independent variable. While the measurement unit is dissimilar across the independent variables in the instant study, the standard deviation unit is not—one standard deviation of variable X_1 and one standard deviation of variable X_2 include the same fraction of the distribution of each of these variables around their respective means. When the relationship strengths of two or more independent variables are expressed in terms of the standard deviation unit, therefore, they can be compared.

The last column of Table 4.3 shows the percent by which the odds change that UNILAT = 1 when each independent variable increases by one standard

111 The percent change in the odds that a nation will be coded 1 on UNILAT is computed for each independent variable by subtracting 1.000 from the odds ratio for the independent variable and multiplying the outcome of the subtraction by 100.

112 The measurement units of EDUC, GDP, and URBANAGG are described in the text accompanying *supra* notes 72–77.

TABLE 4.3 *Results from regression of* UNILAT *on* EDUC, GDP, *and* URBANAGG: *fourteen non-Scandinavian West European nations*

Variable	Odds ratio	z	p > |z|	Percent change in odds for an increase of	
				One unit	One S.D.
EDUC	1.207	0.84	0.399	20.7%	149.6%
GDP	0.999	-0.97	0.334	-0.1	-59.2
URBANAGG	0.921	-1.02	0.306	-7.9	-59.8

Note: S.D. = standard deviation

deviation. According to the column, the odds that a non-Scandinavian nation had legislation accepting unilateral no-fault divorce rose approximately 150% with an advance of one standard deviation in EDUC and declined roughly 60% with an increase of one standard deviation in either GDP or URBANAGG.[113] As measured in standard deviations, therefore, the prevalence of tertiary-level educational attainment was the primary explanation of UNILAT in non-Scandinavian nations, and the impact on UNILAT of the extent of urban residence and the level of wealth per person was much smaller, though not inconsequential.

4 Review of the Study and Its Implications

Perhaps the most notable finding to emerge from the instant study is the apparent influence of culture-language on law governing the dissolution of marriage. The finding, however, emanates from a study in which culture and language were measured by a single indicator rather than by separate indicators even though they are distinct elements of a society. Because culture and language were not distinguished empirically, the impact that each one may have had could not be differentiated from the impact of the other. Did both factors have a material effect on law bearing on divorce, or did only one of them do so? We simply do not know.

113 With each of the other two independent variables held constant, EDUC had a standard deviation of 4.9 percentage points, GDP had a standard deviation of $1,154, and URBANAGG had a standard deviation of 11.0 percentage points.

There is nothing novel in the hypothesis that culture broadly affects the concepts and doctrines that a jurisdiction has in its law,[114] but the hypothesis that language, too, has a major impact on the content of law has not been widely entertained or prominently considered.[115] However, reason exists for expecting differences in language to contribute to differences in law. The words of a language are applied to stimuli emanating from the physical and social world, but words do more than simply label the stimuli. According to research in linguistics, the words applied to stimuli direct the attention of their users to certain aspects of the stimuli, and the perceptions arising from a particular word exclude alternative perceptions; additionally and more importantly for law, the perceptions that flow from the application of a given word shape the reactions of the users of the word to the phenomenon addressed by the word.[116] As labels, then, words affect the behavior of the labelers, and differences between languages at a particular point in time, as well as changes in a language over time, are likely to shape the concepts and doctrines of law.[117]

An example of the above points may be helpful, and for the example, I use words relevant to the biological attribute of sex inasmuch as that attribute and the different roles associated with it are often considered when the topic of divorce is examined. Distinctions grounded on the sex of human individuals inhere in many words (e.g., "woman," "man," "son," "daughter," "hers," "his"), and these words, in classifying on the basis of sex, convey information that

---

114 *E.g.*, Bernhard Grossfeld & Edward J. Eberle, *Patterns of Order in Comparative Law: Discovering and Decoding Invisible Powers*, 38 TEX. INT'L L.J. 291, 295 (2003) (suggesting that, while culture and law have reciprocal effects, culture affects law to a greater degree than law affects culture).

115 THE PLACE OF LAW, *supra* note 5, at 459–60. The first quantitative study to supply evidence of a relationship between language and law with a direct measure of language seems to have been by Givati & Troiano, *supra* note 81.

116 Benjamin Lee Whorf, *Science and Linquistics, in* LANGUAGE, THOUGHT, AND REALITY, *supra* note 79, at 212–13; Benjamin Lee Whorf, *Language, Mind, and Reality, in id.*, at 246, 247; Lera Boroditsky, *Linguistic Relativity, in* 2 ENCYCLOPEDIA OF COGNITIVE SCIENCE 917 (Lynn Nadel ed., 2003); Boroditsky et al., *supra* note 79, at 75–77; Lucy & Gaskins, *supra* note 79, at 481–82; Barbara C. Malt et al., *Speaking versus Thinking about Objects and Actions, in* LANGUAGE IN MIND, *supra* note 79, at 81, 102–03.

117 Because data on changes in language over time are difficult to compile, research directed at uncovering the impact of language on the content of law will undoubtedly be dominated by comparisons of different languages in a single time period. In these comparisons, the impact of language is likely to be clearest from comparisons of languages that belong to different families, or to different branches of a single family, than from comparisons of languages that are members of the same family or the same branch.

influences responses to and by the persons who have been so classified. In particular, sex roles partly involve, and are backed by, sex-specific words, i.e., words that are based on the sex attribute and that are associated with socially approved conduct toward and by the members of the referenced sex.[118] With the passage of time, however, sex-specific words may develop new meanings and/or come to be regarded as unwarranted or undesirable in some societal contexts where earlier they were espoused for these contexts.[119] Once such a change happens, the application of sex-specific words in the foregoing contexts will generate social disapproval—a necessary (if not sufficient) condition for the application to be rendered unlawful by the enactment of legislation, the interpretation by courts of provisions of statutes and constitutions, and/or the promulgation of rules by administrative agencies of governments. Thus, when applied by an employer in hiring job applicants and rewarding employees, the sex-specific word-categories "male" and "female" have become generally unacceptable in law in the United States since the middle of the twentieth century[120] even though sex-specific labels continue to be widely used by parents when naming their children (e.g., "Paula" for a girl and "Paul" for a boy) and when referencing their children ("my son," "my daughter").[121] In the latter situations, the labels are routinely deemed to be lawful as evidenced by the actions of government—government entities accept the sex-linked labels for and references to persons when, inter alia, recording birth certificates, registering voters, and probating wills.

---

118 Robin Lakoff, *Language and Woman's Place*, 2 LANGUAGE IN SOC'Y 45 (1973). *See* Jennifer R. Johnson, *Preferred by Law: The Disappearance of the Traditional Family and Law's Refusal to Let It Go*, 25 WOMEN'S RIGHTS L. REP. 125, 140–41 (2004) (observing that the word "mother" is "stereotypically feminine" and contending that it strengthens conventional sex roles with regard to caregiving). *See* THE PLACE OF LAW, *supra* note 5, at 400 (positing that social interaction has been aided by the societal practice of assigning sex-linked names to individuals).

119 *See* Jillian Todd Weiss, *Transgender Identity, Textualism, and the Supreme Court: What is the "Plain Meaning" of "Sex" in Title VII of the Civil Rights Act of 1964*, 18 TEMP. POL. & CIV. RTS. L. REV. 573, 597–608 (2009) (describing the evolution of the meaning of the word "sex"). A change in the meaning of a word may occur prior to or concurrently with a change in the societal belief regarding the suitability of the word for certain situations. If the change in word meaning and the change in societal belief happen at the same time, they may, of course, be empirically inseparable. Whether or not the changes occur sequentially or contemporaneously, both may be prerequisites for a revision of law on the subject that is the referent of the word.

120 THE PLACE OF LAW, *supra* note 5, at 268–69 (federal statutes).

121 *Id.* at 400.

Let me turn to the nations outside of Scandinavia and the factors that evidently help to explain whether unilateral no-fault divorce law is present in those nations. Before reviewing the results of the data analysis, however, some preliminary remarks are in order. I begin with the critical point that the number of nations in the instant study was insufficient to permit identification of the paths that exist among the independent variables and between each independent variable and the dependent variable.[122] The inadequate number of cases is a major limitation of the study, because these paths and the magnitude of the impact of each variable on another must be known in order to understand the mechanisms (including feedback loops) that are involved in the development, persistence, and succession of concepts and doctrines of law.

Once every variable and variable-to-variable path has been identified and the sign as well as the magnitude of each effect has been ascertained, time-series data on the factors that are fundamental to the content of law can be used to anticipate whether existing concepts and doctrines of law for a given type of activity or entity will remain or be replaced. All predictions will not be accurate, of course, but a majority of them undoubtedly will be. Moreover, predictions of new concepts and doctrines of law will be possible years in advance, because the attributes of a society—sociological, economic, and demographic—typically undergo change at a slow, gradual pace,[123] and time-series data will allow the direction of change to be observed. The key to such predictions, however, is the acquisition of complete information on the factors that have a bearing on the content of law, the temporal arrangements (sequences) of the factors, and the exact impact of each factor on another in every sequence. Only after this information is in hand will we comprehend the deeply embedded societal conditions that are responsible for the concepts and doctrines of law. To the extent that these conditions are not the immediate antecedents of law, they will probably not attract attention, but they will be the factors fundamental to whether existing law continues or is replaced.

In examining the findings of the instant study, I return to Diagram 1 and Diagram 2 *supra*, which suggest two possible arrangements of the factors I have posited to explain law authorizing unilateral no-fault divorce. If the explanatory factors operated as portrayed in Diagram 1, they acted sequentially rather than simultaneously in the non-Scandinavian countries of Western Europe, and the initial conditions—i.e., the "root causes"—determining whether law permitted unilateral no-fault divorce were (i) the prevalence and

---

122 The set of paths I have posited is in Diagram 1, which accompanies *supra* note 93.

123 THE PLACE OF LAW, *supra* note 5, at 231–32.

length of college attendance, (ii) the share of the population subject to an urban way of life,[124] and (iii) average wealth per person. I discuss each of these factors in turn.[125]

With respect to (i), the relationship reported in Table 4.3 between EDUC and UNILAT is not unexpected given the findings of other studies of the impact of education on law.[126] However, increments in tertiary-level education probably were not important per se in producing law allowing unilateral no-fault divorce. Rather, such law is likely to be attributable to the force that, I believe, was mainly responsible for tertiary-level schooling, namely, growth in the quality and quantity of knowledge.[127] If the stock of knowledge lies behind the size of tertiary-level school enrollments, the proposition becomes plausible that rationality intensifies and spreads in a population when and because its body of knowledge is expanding. Inasmuch as rationality is a correlate (or perhaps a component) of individualism and individualism is at the heart of unilateral no-fault divorce, there should be no surprise that advances in knowledge—and, in turn, increases in tertiary-level education—raise the odds that jurisdictions will adopt law accepting unilateral no-fault divorce.

Knowledge, however, is unlikely to have acted alone in affecting the odds that unilateral no-fault divorce will be authorized by law. Urbanization was found to do so as well, but an increase in urban residence *lessened* the odds of such law. The latter finding is inconsistent with sociological theory, which contends that in areas of high population density the relatively large number of stimuli and the relatively fast pace of change in stimuli foster rationality[128] and that rationality promotes individualism.[129] If sociological theory is correct, urbanism can be expected to raise the odds that law will accept unilateral no-fault divorce.

A second finding in Table 4.3 also conflicts with sociological thinking. In particular, GDP was found to be inversely related to UNILAT—growth in wealth per capita, according to Table 4.3, reduced the odds that a country would have law allowing unilateral no-fault divorce. Even though wealth is not at the start

124 Factors (i) and (ii) are not intended to be a complete list of the factors at the start of the causal sequence. Additional originating factors are likely to be identified in the future through advances in empirical research and theory.

125 In Diagram 1, NMW2529 and TFR are each deemed to be an immediate antecedent, not a "root cause," of UNILAT.

126 THE PLACE OF LAW, *supra* note 5, at 292, 366, 371–72.

127 *Id.* at 267, 308–09; notes 109–10 and 123, and their accompanying text, in *supra* Chapter 2.

128 THE PLACE OF LAW, *supra* note 5, at 201, 344.

129 *Id.* at 433, 453 n. 223.

of the causal sequence I posited earlier to account for the emergence of law on unilateral no-fault divorce,[130] wealth merits discussion because it is relatively early in the sequence and has sociological properties. Despite the apparently popular belief that wealth is simply an economic matter, wealth has social dimensions. A strictly economic framework for law thus differs from a macrosociological framework for law. The economic framework would focus on the monetary aspects of wealth—e.g., the volume of all goods and services, or the volume of certain types of goods and services, that are purchased as the level of wealth changes in a nation. The macrosociological framework, on the other hand, directs attention to the social aspects of wealth—specifically, the broad patterns of social behavior and facets of culture that are influenced by, and that influence, the level of wealth in a society. To elaborate on the latter, wealth has measurable consequences for forms of social life,[131] and in a macrosociological framework, these consequences will include concepts and doctrines of law. Operating through social activities, then, wealth has the potential to shape the content of law. Moreover, the social activities may through feedback loops affect the operation of the economy and the level of wealth.

As a component of a society, law is a societal institution that exists within a system of institutions. Given that society as a system is comprised of components that are interconnected and must keep disorder below the threshold that triggers system dissolution,[132] substantial change in one institution may generate change in another institution; or both institutions, because they are linked, may change in response to shifts in a common antecedent. Thus, when the institution of the economy in a society produces more wealth per capita as well as when it produces less wealth per capita, alterations may occur in the institution of law. Indeed, an effect on law of a wealth-producing social force has been postulated, and this force (viz., the growth of knowledge) is thought to have a set of consequences that affect law in general.[133] Since these

---

130 See Diagram 1 in the text accompanying *supra* note 93.

131 *E.g.*, John R. Hipp & Andrew J. Perrin, *The Simultaneous Effect of Social Distance and Physical Distance on the Formation of Neighborhood Ties*, 8 City & Community 5, 19–20 (2009); Vegard Skirbekk, *Fertility Trends by Social Status*, 18 Demographic Res. 145 (2008), http://www.demographic-research.org/volumes/vol18/default.htm.

132 Kenneth D. Bailey, Sociology and the New Systems Theory: Toward a Theoretical Synthesis 44 (1994). See note 23 in *supra* Chapter 1 and its accompanying text.

133 The Place of Law, *supra* note 5, at 267–68, 453 n. 223 (tracing alterations in the content of law to the expansion of knowledge and the results of this expansion, including gains in wealth); text accompanying note 37 in, and Part 3-b and Part 3-c of, *supra* Chapter 2 (tying

consequences are believed to include the spread of individualism,[134] the odds that the law of a society would authorize unilateral no-fault divorce can be expected to rise with gains in average per capita wealth.

The results in Table 4.3, in short, are contrary to propositions of theory regarding the relationship to law of urbanism and of wealth. Could the inconsistency be due to a problem in the design of the study or to incorrect assumptions on the ways the independent variables are related to each other and to the dependent variable? Two aspects of the former (research design) deserve attention. First, the regression model in Table 4.3 did not include culture among its independent variables and hence did not control for variations in culture across the non-Scandinavian nations of Western Europe. With such a control, however, the theory-anticipated relationships of urbanism and wealth to law allowing unilateral no-fault divorce may have been found. Second, the independent variables in the study were generally measured at points in time that preceded the measurement of the dependent variable, but the data were essentially cross-sectional because the data on each independent variable for a given nation were for a single time point while the data on the dependent variable were also for a single time point.[135] Time-series data for the independent variables would have been preferable, but for each nation and each independent variable, such data were unavailable at multiple time points (years) during the relevant historical period. Because cross-sectional rather than pooled time-series data were used, the design of the study cannot be eliminated as a potential source of error, and Table 4.3 may be incorrect in the relationships it reports between GDP and UNILAT and between URBANAGG and UNILAT. Simply put, the study may have failed to test accurately sociological thinking on wealth and on urbanism.

Let me turn now to the assumptions I made at the start of the study. Was I wrong about the links among the independent variables and between each of the independent variables and the dependent variable? An affirmative answer cannot be ruled out. With the benefit of hindsight, an alternate—and plausible—conception of the links is possible, and the alternate conception is consistent with the results in Table 4.3. The alternate conception begins with the point that by roughly the mid-1990s, law allowed divorce without evidence of spousal fault in all of the fourteen non-Scandinavian countries in the study.[136] The point that,

---

the liberalization of law-specified grounds for therapeutic abortion in the United States to the growth of knowledge).

134 Text accompanying *supra* note 127.

135 Text accompanying *supra* notes 65 and 66.

136 Kneip & Bauer, *supra* note 62, at 594 figure 2, 597; González & Viitanen, *supra* note 63. Until 1997, the law of Ireland did not allow a married couple to divorce and remarry in

at approximately the end of the period for UNILAT, every non-Scandinavian nation in Western Europe had legislation accepting no-fault divorce suggests that law *not* authorizing unilateral no-fault divorce should be examined relative to law authorizing unilateral no-fault divorce. The latter, of course, has been the focus of the data analysis thus far.

As Table 4.3 shows, increases in the prevalence of tertiary-level education raised the odds that the law of a non-Scandinavian nation in Western Europe would accept unilateral no-fault divorce, but in a separate analysis of the data, increases in each of the other independent variables in the table were found to raise the odds that the law of such a nation would *not* accept unilateral no-fault divorce. Specifically, the effects of the independent variables were estimated for the non-Scandinavian nations in the study by computing the odds ratios for EDUC, for GDP, and for URBANAGG in terms of the score of 0 on UNILAT.[137] When those computations were made for an increase of one measurement unit of each independent variable, the odds ratio for GDP was 1.001 and the odds ratio for URBANAGG was 1.086.[138] Among the non-Scandinavian nations in the study, consequently, the percent changes in the odds that law would not permit the unilateral form of no-fault divorce were raised 0.1% for a unit increase of GDP and 8.6% for a unit increase of URBANAGG. However, in terms of an increase of one standard deviation of GDP and of URBANAGG, the odds ratios were 2.449 and 2.489, respectively, and the odds rose 145% and 149%, respectively. By this yardstick, the impact of wealth did not appreciably differ from the impact of urban residence when predicting a score of 0 on UNILAT.

In short, among the non-Scandinavian nations of Western Europe, law that accepted unilateral no-fault divorce became more common with gains in tertiary-level education. By contrast, law that did not permit this type of no-fault divorce—but that allowed another form of no-fault divorce—became more common with rises in average wealth and with growth in the percentage of the

Ireland. No-fault divorce with the right to remarry became possible by law in Ireland starting in 1997. Lindsay L. Abbate, Comment, *What God Has Joined "Let" Man Put Asunder: Ireland's Struggle Between Canon and Common Law Relating to Divorce*, 16 EMORY INT'L L. REV. 583, 598–99, 613, 623 (2002).

137 When estimating the effects, the intercept was excluded. To estimate the relationships of the independent variables to the score of 0 on UNILAT, the odds ratios were obtained for the relationships of these variables to the score of 1, and the results were then subjected to the LISTCOEF command for Stata using the REVERSE option for the command. LONG & FREESE, *supra* note 108, at 464–65.

138 When related to the score of 0 on UNILAT, the odds ratio for a measurement unit of EDUC was 0.829. For one standard deviation of EDUC, the odds ratio was 0.401.

population that resided in urbanized areas. Although the foregoing effects on divorce law are compatible with a sociological rationale,[139] the jurisdiction-level causes of law authorizing unilateral no-fault divorce may differ from the jurisdiction-level causes of law authorizing no-fault divorce of a different type. If this is confirmed by future research, a macrosociological framework for law will need to consider the former apart from the latter, and theory will need to account for the difference between law allowing one type of no-fault divorce and law allowing another.

5 Law as a Societal Institution

With rare exceptions, science builds its stock of knowledge on a subject in small increments and at a gradual pace. That pattern will probably characterize the understanding that quantitative social science studies will eventually provide regarding the society-level factors and processes that shape the content of law. Presently available evidence clearly indicates that, in a jurisdiction having a complex societal structure and democratic government, concepts and doctrines of law on society-central activities do not occur randomly but stem from sociological, economic, and demographic conditions in the jurisdiction. Future research can be expected to bolster the quality and quantity of this evidence. However, quantitative studies on possible links between the attributes and law of jurisdictions arise from a premise that does not comport with currently dominant views of law as an institution in society. These studies and

---

A dependent variable that is measured in binary form with the numbers 0 and 1 has no meaningful standard deviation, and the relationship of a given independent variable to it cannot be precisely calculated for one standard deviation of the dependent variable. In the case of different dependent variables (Y_1 and Y_2), each of which is measured in binary form with the numbers 0 and 1, the relationship of a particular independent variable to Y_1 cannot be compared to the relationship of the same or another independent variable to Y_2 because the dependent variables cannot be measured in terms of their respective standard deviations. PAMPEL, *supra* note 90, at 32–33. Even though substantively different dependent variables are not involved in the data analysis here, the preceding point is pertinent because the independent variables are being used to predict a score of 1 on UNILAT and, in addition, are being used to predict a score of 0 on UNILAT. Neither of these two estimations could measure UNILAT in standard deviations. Consequently, no comparison should be made between, and no ranking should be attempted for, the ability of EDUC to predict a score of 1 on UNILAT vis-a-vis its ability, or the ability of GDP and/or of URBANAGG, to predict a score of 0 on UNILAT.

139 *Supra* note 71 and accompanying text.

their contribution to understanding law, therefore, may not be widely appreciated for a long time.

All scholars have and rely on key assumptions about the phenomena they study, and they are slow to abandon assumptions they have been using, especially if the assumptions that will be substituted are incompatible with the assumptions being replaced. In law schools in the United States, scholarship has for decades been dominated by an approach to law that differs markedly from the approach inherent in the macrosociological framework for law propounded in the instant book. Unfortunately, scholars in U.S. law schools are unfamiliar with sociological concepts and research procedures that are necessary to place and study law in its societal context. As a result, their embrace of a macrosociological framework is unlikely to be quick. Notably, law school scholarship has been resistant to change even when it has received criticism from within law schools. This criticism has a long history. It began three-quarters of a century ago with caustic comments about the nature of scholarly works that appear in the most common forum for these works, namely, journals published by U.S. law schools,[140] but despite such expressed dissatisfaction,[141] law school scholarship remains reluctant to incorporate alternative perspectives on the concepts and doctrines of law. That scholarship has thus undergone little, if any, visible change over time in its fundamental approach to law.

Admittedly, for much of the last half of the twentieth century the disregard in law school scholarship of the quantitative social sciences was not entirely unreasonable, because the social sciences suffered from limitations in data availability and statistical techniques. The continuing neglect of the quantitative social sciences, however, has now become foolhardy given the impressive advances that have been made by these disciplines during the last four decades.[142] The inertia that has characterized law schools, leading them to

140 Fred Rodell, *Goodbye to Law Reviews*, 23 VA. L. REV. 38 (1936).

141 Additional and more recent criticisms of law review scholarship by faculty members at U.S. law schools are found in: Rachel J. Anderson, *From Imperial Scholar to Imperial Student: Minimizing Bias in Article Evaluation by Law Reviews*, 20 HASTINGS WOMEN'S L.J. 197, 234 (2009) (noting a possible lack of impartiality by U.S. law reviews in the choice of articles for publication and recommending that law review editors receive training for their positions "because bias for safe scholarship has been institutionalized"); Joseph P. Tomain & Paul L. Caron, *The Associate Dean for Faculty Research Position: Encouraging and Promoting Scholarship*, 33 U. TOL. L. REV. 233, 243 (2001) (noting that articles published by "the major law reviews" favor certain topics and disfavor other topics).

142 The belief that quantitative social science methods and data need to be used in scholarship on law has been expressed by others. Lee Epstein & Gary King, *Empirical Research*

assign a low priority to the law-relevant advances in knowledge that the social sciences have made possible, is hampering the contribution that these schools can make to the operation of the institution of law and the skills of its practitioners.[143]

Inertia, however, is a concept that primarily describes rather than explains, i.e., inertia does not reveal *why* scholars who work within the institution of law have not become familiar with the resources of sociology and why they avoid a macrosociological framework for the institution. Inertia probably characterizes all institutions, but its main explanation with regard to the institution of law is likely to be an aspect of American society. In the United States, culture is permeated by an ideal of individualism: Americans, more than citizens of many other nations, believe that individuals are and should be paramount to groups[144]; in addition, Americans erect their social reality on a foundation formed by, inter alia, the belief that actions originate with individuals rather than groups.[145] As an ideal, individualism denies the existence and/or the importance of group-level phenomena, and in doing so, it retards recognition of such phenomena. Being an institution—a socially endorsed pattern of activities that possesses a structure and fulfills societal needs[146]—law is a component of a societal system and exists apart from individuals, even the individuals (e.g., lawyers, judges, and police officers) who at a particular point in time staff the positions through which the institution operates. Because a macrosociological treatment of law directly conflicts with a social ideal that is widely endorsed in the United States and hence is embedded in the institution of law, that treatment encounters substantial resistance, and a delay—indeed, a lengthy delay—should not be surprising before a macrosociological framework is generally accepted in U.S. law schools. A new model for understanding a phenomenon will not be quickly embraced when it threatens a prized cultural value.

In the end, I believe, the concepts and doctrines of law will come to be seen as responses to jurisdiction-level conditions, at least when the concepts

---

and the Goals of Legal Scholarship: The Rules of Inference, 69 U. CHI. L. REV. 1, 4 n. 10 (2002).

143 *See* RICHARD SUSSKIND, TOMORROW'S LAWYERS 113 (2013) (predicting that in the future more lawyers will require and receive formal training not only in law but also in one or more other disciplines).

144 Frank B. Cross, *Law and Trust*, 93 GEO. L.J. 1457, 1526 (2005) (comparing residents of the United States to residents of twenty-four other nations).

145 Fischer, *supra* note 49, at 364–66, 369.

146 THE PLACE OF LAW, *supra* note 5, at 78 n. 37, 195 n. 171.

and doctrines concern society-important activities and the society has a democratic form of government, a technologically advanced economy, and a complex social structure. Acceptance of such a framework for law will be unavoidable because ties between the properties of jurisdictions and the content of law in the jurisdictions will continue to be unearthed by quantitative social science research. In social life, the expansion of knowledge erodes beliefs that conflict with what has been learned and eventually renders the beliefs untenable. Studies have documented ties of jurisdiction properties to the law of nations and to the law of U.S. states and local governments.[147] As that knowledge mounts and improves theory, a macrosociological perspective on the content of law can be expected to join the paradigm for law that is presently dominant in the United States and its law schools.

147 Known studies are listed in Appendix A to *supra* Chapter 1.

CHAPTER 5

Mutual Fund Regulation in Europe

Abstract

The instant chapter rests on the thesis that the concepts and doctrines of law are macrosociological phenomena. The chapter illustrates the thesis by presenting data on the societal context of a change that occurred in the interpretation of a section of the United States Investment Company Act. In addition, the chapter reports a test of the thesis using data on the twenty-six European countries having a national organization of investment funds or asset managers that in 2010 was a member of the European Fund and Asset Management Association. The dependent variable in the study was the attractiveness to funds of the fund-applicable law of the twenty-six nations; on the assumption that increases in such attractiveness produce more funds, ceteris paribus, the empirical indicator of the dependent variable was the number of funds located in each nation as of mid-2010. The independent variables were country-level attributes of the nations as of 2005 or 2006. A negative binomial regression model applied to the data suggested that the attractiveness of fund-applicable law (i) declined with increases in the percentage of the population that was under age 65, (ii) rose with the percentage of the population that was age 65 or older, and (iii) declined with increases in the percentage of 20–24 year old persons who were enrolled in tertiary-level education. Methodological limitations of the study are discussed.

1 Mutual Funds and Law in the United States

Mutual funds have become an important component of the financial system of the world, but their sociological aspects have not commanded much attention from scholars. In the United States, the neglect of a sociological perspective on mutual funds is curious because, inter alia, U.S. funds with investments in stock can mold the social policies, and not just the economic policies, of the operating companies that issued the stock. The funds are able to do so because, as shareholders of these operating companies, they vote on matters that are presented to the shareholders,[1] and in casting these votes, U.S. law expects the

1 Sean Collins, Inv. Co. Inst., *Proxy Voting by Registered Investment Companies: Promoting the Interests of Fund Shareholders*, Res. Persp., July 2008, at 4 fig. 3, *available at* http://www.ici.org/pdf/per14-01.pdf.

 | DOI 10.1163/9789004281219_006

funds to protect the welfare of their investors.[2] Notably, the frequency with which the funds have voted in favor of proposals for socially responsible business policies has increased in recent years,[3] and the frequency may rise further in the future.

What is a mutual fund? In broad terms, a mutual fund is a vehicle for collective investments in securities (and is thus labeled an "investment fund" in some nations). Under the U.S. Investment Company Act ("Act"),[4] a mutual fund possesses two key characteristics. Specifically, an entity is a mutual fund if it (i) issues redeemable securities[5] and sells them to investors and (ii) pools the assets it obtains from these sales and invests the assets in securities issued by other entities.[6] The issuers of the securities in the portfolios of mutual funds are typically corporations, governments, and government agencies. Under the Act, a mutual fund is able to invest in a variety of securities and is not limited to the most common types of securities, viz., stocks and bonds. Regardless of the types of securities in its portfolio, however, a fund must abide by a set of Act-imposed requirements that seek to protect the investors in the fund, including investors of modest wealth who are unsophisticated regarding

---

2 Disclosure of Proxy Voting Policies and Proxy Voting Records by Registered Management Investment Companies, Investment Company Act Release No. IC-25922, 68 Fed. Reg. 6564, 6565, 6574 (Feb. 7, 2003).

3 FUND VOTES, MUTUAL FUND VOTING SURVEY, 2004–2008 (Sept. 2008), at 3 (comparing "mainstream mutual fund" families to "socially responsible investing" mutual fund families and finding that, among the former, votes in support of resolutions presented to the shareholders of operating companies for socially responsible business policies doubled from a mean of 5.7% in 2004 to a mean of 11.5% in 2008), http://www.fundvotes.com/manvsshr_2010.php (last visited May 8, 2015).

4 15 U.S.C. §§ 80a-1 to 80a-64 (2014), http://uscode.house.gov/download/download.shtml.

5 The securities issued by a mutual fund to an investor are "redeemable" when the investor is entitled to sell the securities back to the fund and receive from the fund the market value of the securities. 15 U.S.C. § 80a-2(a)(32) (2014), http://uscode.house.gov/download/download.shtml. The Act requires a fund to redeem the securities within seven days after the investor submits the redemption request, but allows a fund to postpone redemptions beyond seven days with the approval of the Securities and Exchange Commission. 15 U.S.C. §§ 80a-22(e), -37 (2014), http://uscode.house.gov/download/download.shtml.

6 Even though the term "mutual fund" is common, it is not in the Act. The Securities and Exchange Commission has taken the position that, under Sections 4 and 5 of the Act, a "mutual fund" is an open-end management investment company. 15 U.S.C. §§ 80a-4(3), -5(a)(1) (2014), http://uscode.house.gov/download/download.shtml. *E.g.*, Enhanced Disclosure and New Prospectus Delivery Option for Registered Open-End Management Investment Companies, Release No. IC-28064 (Nov. 21, 2007), 2007 SEC LEXIS 2716, at *5 & n.12.

securities and investments in securities.[7] Investor protection is important because, inter alia, almost half of all households in the United States own shares of mutual funds[8] and many of those that do have relatively low incomes.[9] A further factor in the need for investor protection is that a large fraction of Americans lack the intellectual skill necessary to understand the risks of mutual funds.[10]

2 Assets and Numbers of Mutual Funds Worldwide

Because the mutual fund sector of the world financial system is often overlooked, a brief review of its dimensions may prove helpful. The review begins with Figure 5.1, which traces the change that has occurred during the last decade-and-a-half in the total net assets of all mutual funds in the world.[11] The

7 *In re* Mutual Fund Sales Antitrust Litigation, 374 F. Supp. 95, 106 (D. D.C. 1973) (quoting testimony to the U.S. Senate Committee on Banking and Currency by the then-chairman of the Securities and Exchange Commission). This objective is also evident in the congressionally specified purposes of the Act. 15 U.S.C. § 80a-1(b) (2014), http://uscode.house.gov/download/download.shtml.

8 Approximately forty-five out of every 100 U.S. households have had an investment in at least one mutual fund in each year from 2000 through 2013. Household ownership of mutual-fund shares during this period included direct ownership of shares as well as ownership of shares through employer-sponsored retirement plans. Kimberly Burham et al., Inv. Co. Inst., *Ownership of Mutual Funds, Shareholder Sentiment, and Use of the Internet, 2013*, ICI RESEARCH PERSPECTIVE, Oct. 2013, at 3 fig. 1, *available at* http://www.ici.org/research/perspective.

9 During the period from 2000 to 2013, between one out of five and one out of four fund-owning households in the United States had a yearly income below $50,000. By comparison, roughly half of all U.S. households had an annual income under $50,000. Calculated from *id.* at 32–33 fig. A5. Among all households in this income range, consequently, fund-owning households are proportionally underrepresented, but households having a yearly income less than $50,000 are nonetheless a sizeable fraction of all households that invest in mutual funds.

10 LARRY D. BARNETT, THE PLACE OF LAW: THE ROLE AND LIMITS OF LAW IN SOCIETY 164–66 (2011) [hereinafter THE PLACE OF LAW].

11 The data in Figure 5.1 were obtained from INVESTMENT COMPANY INSTITUTE, 2006 INVESTMENT COMPANY FACT BOOK 114 (46th ed. 2006) (data for 1998 through 2005) and from INVESTMENT COMPANY INSTITUTE, 2011 INVESTMENT COMPANY FACT BOOK 201 (53rd ed. 2013) (data for 2006 through 2012) [hereinafter 2013 INVESTMENT COMPANY FACT BOOK]. Change in total net assets by geographic region is graphed in Christopher Plantier, Inv. Co. Inst., *Globalization and the Global Growth of Long-Term Mutual Funds*,

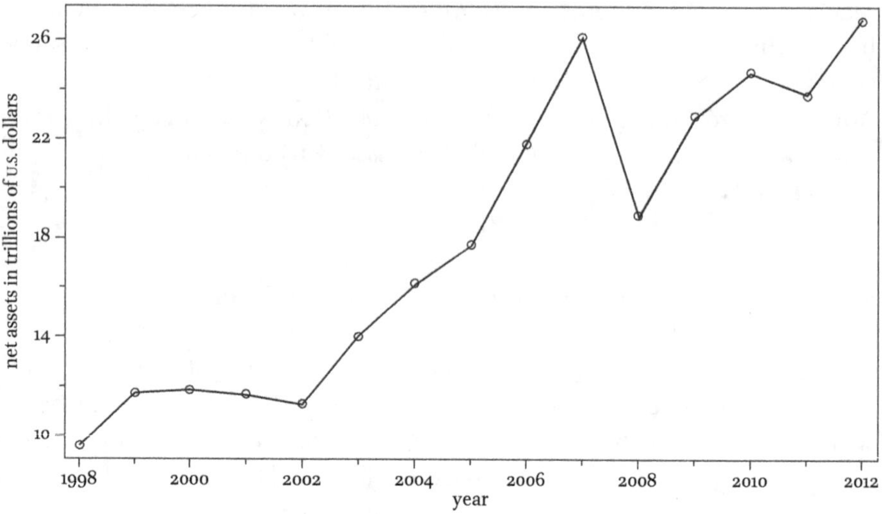

FIGURE 5.1 *Net assets of mutual funds worldwide by year*
SOURCE: SEE FN. 11 IN THIS CHAPTER.

total net assets shown are for each year during the period from 1998 through 2012, are measured as of year-end, and are in trillions of U.S. dollars. As the Figure reveals, the wealth in the hands of mutual funds was significantly larger in 2012 than in 1998. If an upward secular trend in net assets inheres in the 1998–2012 difference, the amount of wealth that mutual funds manage will substantially rise in the future.

At the end of 2012, the assets managed by mutual funds worldwide had a market value of approximately 26.8 trillion U.S. dollars, and the number of mutual funds worldwide exceeded 73,200.[12] However, worldwide totals mask significant differences in the geographic location of mutual funds. Accordingly, the two pie charts that follow deal with the geographic home of mutual funds at year-end 2012.[13] The first pie chart (Figure 5.2) separates the total net assets (in U.S. dollars) managed by mutual funds worldwide into four regions—the United States ($13.0 trillion), Europe ($8.2 trillion), Asia and the Pacific

ICI GLOBAL RESEARCH PERSPECTIVE, March 2014, at 2 fig. 1. Recent publications of the Investment Company Institute are available at www.ici.org/pubs.

12 2013 INVESTMENT COMPANY FACT BOOK, *supra* note 11, at 201–02.

13 The data in the pie charts are from *id.* at 201–02.

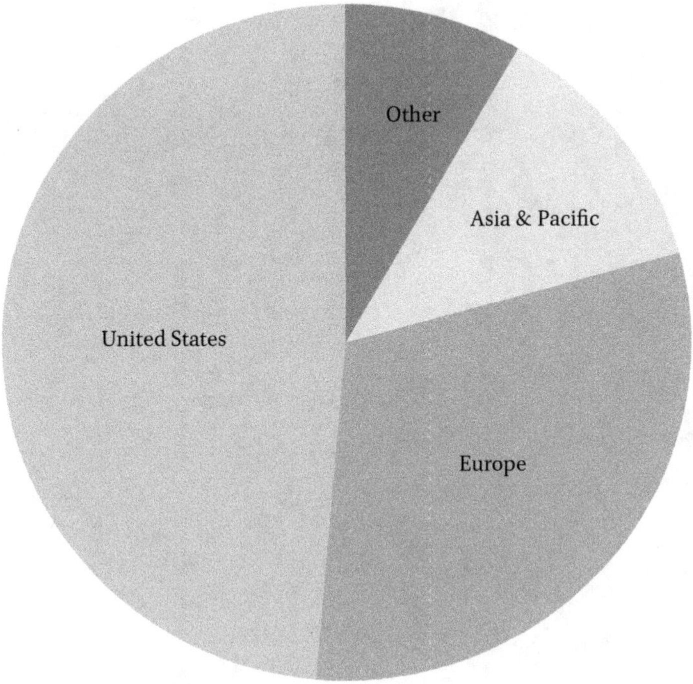

FIGURE 5.2 *Net assets of mutual funds in 2012 by world region*
SOURCE: SEE FN. 12 AND 13 IN THIS CHAPTER.

($3.3 trillion), and other areas ($2.2 trillion).[14] The share of the total in each region (rounded to the nearest whole number) was 49%, 31%, 12%, and 8%, respectively.

The second pie chart (Figure 5.3) depicts the number of mutual funds at year-end 2012 in each of the same four geographic regions. Of the 73,243 mutual funds in the world at that point in time, approximately 47% were in Europe, 23% were in Asia and the Pacific, 10% were in the United States, and 20% were in other areas.[15]

However, the pie charts furnish an incomplete picture of the region-specific prominence of mutual funds, because mutual funds located in one region may purchase and sell securities of issuers located in other regions. To illustrate, as of the end of 2012, more than 1,500 U.S. mutual funds could invest in stocks or

14 Mutual funds in two countries (Brazil and Canada) accounted for 86% of the $2.2 trillion in net assets of mutual funds situated in areas labelled "other." Computed from *id.* at 201.

15 Of the number of mutual funds that were in areas labelled "other," roughly half were in Brazil. Computed from *id.* at 202.

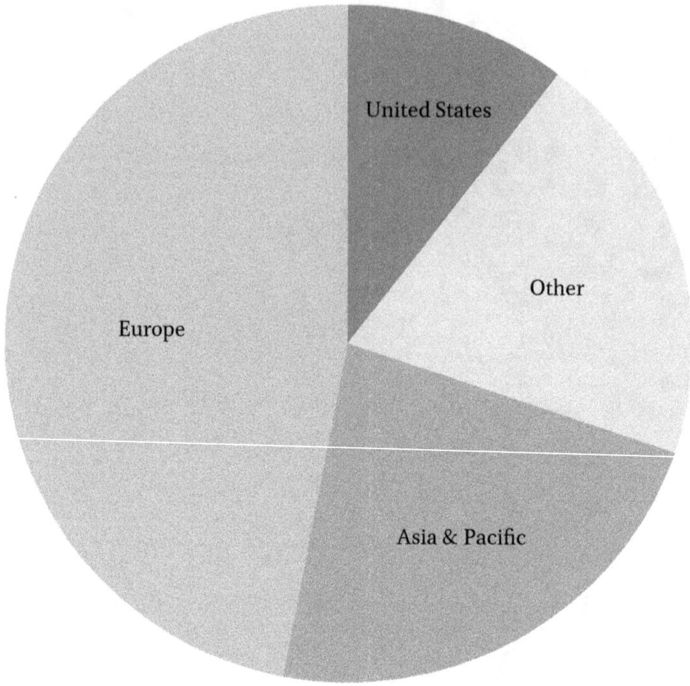

FIGURE 5.3 *Number of mutual funds in 2012 by world region*
SOURCE: SEE FN. 12 AND 13 IN THIS CHAPTER.

bonds issued anywhere in the world, and the market value of their net assets amounted to \$1.9 trillion U.S. dollars.[16] The mutual fund sector thus has a worldwide reach, giving every nation a stake in the operation and regulation of the sector—even a nation having few or no domestic funds.

3 A Macrosociological Perspective on Law

Because vehicles for investing in securities are typically regarded as being in the economic sector of a society, scholarship to date has focused on economic aspects of mutual funds and of the law applicable to them. Not surprisingly, this emphasis on economic matters has been accompanied by a lack of appreciation of the macrosociological nature of law on mutual funds. The present chapter, I hope, will help to foster recognition in scholarship of the multifaceted character of the concepts and rules of law pertinent to mutual funds. In

16 *Id.* at 145, 147 (data for "world" funds).

particular, the chapter advances the thesis that a *social* domain lies below the surface of the funds and their regulation, and contends that this domain must be fully studied if the funds and the law applicable to them are to be understood.

On the assumption that social things are substantively distinguishable from economic things, the instant chapter considers the following three macrosociological aspects of mutual fund regulation in its attempt to counter the tilt toward economics in studies of fund-relevant law:

- Societal benefits of law that regulates mutual funds. Part 3-a *infra* of the chapter suggests what I believe are the principal benefits.
- Societal factors that influence the interpretation of existing provisions of law on mutual funds. Part 3-b *infra* supplies an illustration.
- Societal factors that affect the content (especially the stringency) of statutes and administrative-agency rules that are designed to regulate mutual funds. A quantitative study of factors that may do so is presented in Part 4 *infra* of the chapter.

a *A Macrosociological Framework*

Every discipline that can advance knowledge about a subject will in the long run be employed in scholarship on the subject, and sociology has a place in the study of law to the extent it can contribute to understanding law. What is sociology able to add to scholarship on law? Because sociology includes numerous specialties, many of which are likely to further knowledge about law, the question cannot be answered by a single work or a single sociologist. In the instant chapter, the focus is on one specialty, viz., macrosociology. As the scientific discipline that studies the society-level causes and consequences of phenomena in social life, macrosociology is based on the premise that a society is a system comprised of broad patterns of behavior (i.e., institutions) and that, as a system, a society exists independently of the human beings who populate it at any single point in time. In a macrosociological framework, therefore, a society is a whole that is more than the sum of its parts. A corollary of this premise is that individual human beings are not and cannot be a source of major, permanent change in the concepts and doctrines of law on social activities. Macro-level forces, rather, are believed responsible for the content of law in the long run.[17] Such a thesis, however, is

17 The macrosociological framework that I propose for law is described in Part 1-b of *supra* Chapter 1.

incompatible with the ideal of individualism,[18] and because that ideal is central to American culture,[19] a major obstacle exists in the United States to recognizing that society-level forces mold the social order and its law. Not surprisingly, the macrosociological framework I advance lacks wide appeal in American scholarship on law.

The apparent universality of law as a societal institution (at least in nations that have a complex structure and a democratic government) indicates that law is a necessary condition for social life. What, however, accounts for the universal presence of law? What advantages does a society obtain from law that makes law essential to the social order? Unfortunately, the exact benefits that a society receives from regulatory law have yet to be established by empirical research, but a number of benefits have been hypothesized from law on mutual funds.[20] For example, the agency of the U.S. government that interprets and enforces the Investment Company Act—the Securities and Exchange Commission ("Commission")[21]—regulates the names of mutual funds subject to its jurisdiction for the apparent purpose of maintaining or building public trust in the funds.[22] The same motive evidently contributed to a recent decision by the Commission to adopt a rule under the Investment Advisers Act that bars an investment adviser for two years from being compensated to manage a mutual fund for a government pension plan after the adviser contributes to, or solicits a contribution for, the election campaign of an official of the government; the prohibition applies if the amount of money contributed/solicited exceeds a designated sum and the official is in a position to influence the choice of the investment adviser for the fund.[23] In addition to preserving or restoring trust in mutual

18 In *supra* Chapter 4, the concept of "individualism" is defined in note 49, and the growth of individualism as a phenomenon is the subject of note 51 and its accompanying text.

19 Text accompanying notes 144 and 145 in *supra* Chapter 4.

20 THE PLACE OF LAW, *supra* note 10, at 120–22.

21 15 U.S.C. § 80a-37(a) (2014), http://uscode.house.gov/download/download.shtml.

22 Larry D. Barnett, *The Regulation of Mutual Fund Names and the Societal Role of Trust: An Exploration of Section 35(d) of the Investment Company Act*, 3 DEPAUL BUS. & COM. L.J. 345, 355–58 (2005).

23 Political Contributions by Certain Investment Advisers, Investment Advisers Act Release No. 3043, 75 Fed. Reg. 41,018, 41,019, 41,069-41,071 (July 14, 2010) (codified at 17 C.F.R. § 275.206(4)-5). The amount of a contribution to an election campaign cannot exceed $350 when made to an official for whom the contributor/solicitor was entitled to vote and cannot exceed $150 when made to an official for whom the contributor/solicitor was not entitled to vote. 17 C.F.R. § 275.206(4)-5(b)(1) (2013).

funds, regulation is thought to aid the reputation of funds and to be a symbol that bonds individuals to their society.[24]

A macrosociological framework for law takes account of the societal benefits of the concepts and doctrines of law because the framework must furnish an understanding of the *consequences* of law. However, there is another, equally important concern of a macrosociological framework—viz., the societal *causes* of law. Some quantitative social science studies have been done on whether differences in the characteristics of jurisdictions (e.g., the percentage of the population that has completed a given number of years of schooling) are related to differences in regulatory law between the jurisdictions (e.g., states and nations). Although the studies are limited in number and have mainly involved societies that are socially complex and economically advanced, they provide cogent evidence that jurisdiction-level conditions affect the content of law on rights of individuals.[25] If doctrines of law do not occur at random, as these studies indicate, jurisdiction-level variables are also likely to produce differences between jurisdictions in statutory provisions and administrative-agency rules that bear on the internal structure and business operations of entities, including mutual funds. While the question of whether jurisdiction conditions affect the content of law on these aspects of entities has yet to be studied rigorously—i.e., with a multivariate statistical technique applied to jurisdiction-level data on a system of jurisdictions—such an effect is certainly plausible. Because evidence of that effect may help to end the current disregard of macrosociology in scholarship produced in law schools, it is the subject of the remainder of the instant chapter.

b *Section 3(c)(1) of the Investment Company Act*

My attempt to overcome the reluctance of scholarship to embrace a macrosociological framework for law begins with a pair of interpretations of a section of the Investment Company Act. The interpretations are found in two documents from the Securities and Exchange Commission, and although the documents provide just a simple illustration, they are useful for conveying the potential contribution of a macrosociological framework for law on entity structure and operation. Before I turn to the section, however, I briefly summarize fundamental elements of the Act. The summary is needed if the reader is to discern the statutory function of the section.

---

24 The Place of Law, *supra* note 10, at 120–22.

25 Known studies in this line of research are listed in Appendix A to *supra* Chapter 1.

An investment company exists under Section 3(a)(1) of the Act[26] when a "person"[27] is mainly in the business of (1) issuing securities[28] and (2) using the cash received from the sale of these securities to acquire the securities of other issuers in the hope of profiting from the latter securities. Before an investment company can use mail or interstate commerce in the United States to offer, sell, or deliver the securities it issues,[29] however, the company must register with the Commission. Of course, registration is unnecessary for an entity[30] that is not an investment company. Thus, an entity that qualifies for an exclusion from investment company status need not register[31]; i.e., an entity that is within the terms of Section 3(a)(1) will not be classified as an investment company if it qualifies for an exclusion provided by the Act. One of these exclusions is in Section 3(c)(1) of the Act.[32] The portion of Section 3(c) that is relevant to the present discussion states:

---

26 15 U.S.C. § 80a-3(a) (2014), http://uscode.house.gov/download/download.shtml.

27 A person can be either a human being or an entity. 15 U.S.C. § 80a-2(a)(28) (2014) (defining a person as "a natural person or a company"), http://uscode.house.gov/download/download.shtml; in addition, see 15 U.S.C. § 80a-2(a)(8) (2014) (definition of "company"), http://uscode.house.gov/download/download.shtml. The extension of the word "person" to an entity is consistent with the macrosociological thesis that the key concepts employed by law stem from the society in which the law exists. THE PLACE OF LAW, *supra* note 10, at 256–57. The English language included an entity within the word "person" during the fourteenth century. *Id.* In the fifteenth century, the law of England used the word "person" to cover an entity, and by the first half of the nineteenth century, the law of the United States was doing so. *Id.*; Louisville, Cincinnati & Charleston Rail-Road Co. v. Letson, 43 U.S. 497, 558 (1844) ("a corporation created by and doing business in a particular state, is to be deemed to all intents and purposes as a person, although an artificial person"). *Accord*, Runyan v. Lessee of Coster, 39 U.S. 122, 129 (1840) (describing a corporation as "an artificial being" and "an artificial person").

28 A person can be an investment company only if it is an "issuer." 15 U.S.C. § 80a-3(a)(1) (2014), http://uscode.house.gov/download/download.shtml. The term "issuer" is defined as "every person who issues or proposes to issue any security, or has outstanding any security which it has issued." 15 U.S.C. § 80a-2(a)(22) (2014), http://uscode.house.gov/download/download.shtml.

29 15 U.S.C. §§ 80a-7(a), -7(b), -7(c), -8 (2014), http://uscode.house.gov/download/download.shtml.

30 Because securities are rarely issued by a human being who acts alone, i.e., by an individual, the discussion in the text will be confined to an entity.

31 Section 3(b), for example, excludes from paragraph C of subsection 3(a)(1) an issuer whose primary business is inter alia "other than that of investing, reinvesting, owning, holding, or trading in securities." 15 U.S.C. § 80a-3(b) (2014), http://uscode.house.gov/download/download.shtml.

32 15 U.S.C. § 80a-3(c)(1) (2014), http://uscode.house.gov/download/download.shtml.

> "Notwithstanding subsection (a), none of the following persons is an investment company within the meaning of this title: (1) Any issuer whose outstanding securities (other than short-term paper) are beneficially owned by not more than one hundred persons and which is not making and does not presently propose to make a public offering of its securities...."[33]

Under Section 3(c)(1), accordingly, an entity that satisfies Section 3(a)(1) can avoid being an investment company if two conditions exist: a maximum of 100 persons beneficially own the outstanding securities issued by the entity, *and* these securities are offered for sale privately. If either condition is absent, an entity engaged in the activities specified by Section 3(a)(1) is an investment company, and hence subject to regulation, because it is thought to be capable of jeopardizing the welfare of the public.[34] Thus, when the securities issued by an entity have more than 100 beneficial owners, Section 3(c)(1) does not furnish the entity with an exclusion from the status of investment company,

---

33 15 U.S.C. § 80a-3(c) (2014), http://uscode.house.gov/download/download.shtml.

In this chapter, I omit paragraphs (A) and (B) of Section 3(c)(1). 15 U.S.C. §§ 80a-3(c)(1)(A), -3(c)(1)(B) (2014), http://uscode.house.gov/download/download.shtml. Paragraph (A) is applicable to the numerical test of Section 3(c)(1) when a *company*, as defined in Section 2(a)(8), owns shares of an issuer of securities and the company either is an investment company or, although meeting the criteria of Section 3(a)(1), has escaped the status of an investment company through Section 3(c)(1) or Section 3(c)(7). 15 U.S.C. §§ 80a-2(a)(8), -3(c)(1), 3(c)(7) (2014), http://uscode.house.gov/download/download.shtml. Known as the "look-through" provision, paragraph (A) specifies when the shareholders of the company will be counted individually as beneficial owners of the shares of the issuer even though the shares of the issuer that are held by the company are in the name of the company. The "look-through" provision, when applied, increases the number of shareholders of the issuer and may prevent the issuer from satisfying the numerical test of Section 3(c)(1). Paragraph (B), on the other hand, is relevant when securities (or interests therein) are transferred as the result of "legal separation, divorce, death, or other involuntary event." Under paragraph (B), the transferor rather than the transferee is regarded as the beneficial owner of the securities involved. I exclude both paragraphs from my review because they do not affect *who* or *what* is a "person." Paragraphs (A) and (B) simply designate the "person" that is to be counted toward the numerical limit on beneficial owners imposed by Section 3(c)(1); neither paragraph directly implicates *whether* a particular party is a "person." The latter is the question to be discussed in the text.

34 Nemo Capital Partners, L.P., SEC No-Action Letter, 1992 SEC No-Act. LEXIS 856 (July 28, 1992) (staff reply), at *2.

even if the securities have been offered and sold privately.[35] Only an entity that has privately offered the securities it has issued *and* that has not exceeded the maximum number of shareholders imposed by the section is regarded as not implicating the public interest and as not requiring regulation by the federal government.[36]

While U.S. law on investment companies supplies multiple examples of the utility of a macrosociological framework, I will concentrate on the word "person" in Section 3(c)(1) of the Investment Company Act and the interpretation of the word by the Commission.[37] If a macrosociological framework accurately characterizes law, the ideals of society are embodied in the construction by the Commission of the word "person." Indeed, the framework contends, the interpretation by the Commission of words in the Act must be consistent with—or at the very minimum must not conflict with—the character of American society because otherwise the Commission will be unable to maintain its credibility and legitimacy as a governmental body. Therefore, the interpretation of a particular word will shift over time to the extent a shift is necessary to recognize a significant change in social life.

Let me now furnish an example of the preceding proposition. In 1980, the staff of the Commission concluded that when a married couple possesses an ownership interest in a security and the interest is in both names—i.e., the name of the husband and the name of the wife—the security is beneficially owned by two persons, not one, under Section 3(c)(1).[38] Each spouse must be

---

35 For a discussion by the Commission of the factors determining whether an offering is public or private, see Non-Public Offering Exemption, Securities Act of 1933 Release No. 4552, 27 Fed. Reg. 11,316 (Nov. 6, 1962).

36 H.R. REP. NO. 1341, 96th Cong., 2nd Sess. 35, 36 (1980), *reprinted in* 1980 U.S.C.C.A.N. 4800, 4817.

37 The discussion that follows includes both interpretations by the staff of the Securities and Exchange Commission and interpretations by the commissioners themselves. In this discussion, I use the term "Commission," but I do so loosely because a position taken by the staff in a "no-action" letter does not automatically become a position of the commissioners and, hence, of the Commission. *See* Amalgamated Clothing & Textile Workers Union v. Wal-Mart Stores, 54 F.3d 69, 72 (2d Cir. 1995) ("an SEC no-action letter does not constitute a "rule, regulation, or order" of the SEC; the letters merely provide informal advice of the SEC staff"). A no-action letter is a response by the staff to a request that the staff recommend no action by the Commission under federal securities law for a proposed activity or arrangement. A general discussion of no-action letters is in Donna M. Nagy, *Judicial Reliance on Regulatory Interpretations in SEC No-Action Letters: Current Problems and a Proposed Framework*, 83 CORNELL L. REV. 921 (1998).

38 Wasserman, Chinitz, Giffner & Green, SEC No-Action Letter, 1980 SEC NOACT LEXIS 3834 (Oct. 13, 1980) (staff reply), at *1.

counted, according to the staff, even though the couple acquired the security as joint tenants; enumerating each joint tenant individually under Section 3(c)(1) when the tenants are spouses is not confined to situations where a husband and wife initially owned securities separately and then converted ownership of these securities to joint tenancy.[39] In 1997, however, the commissioners overturned the position of the staff and ruled that a married couple is to be counted as just one person when the husband and wife "jointly" own a security issued by an entity that claims to be exempt from registration with the Commission under Section 3(c)(1).[40]

---

39 *See* Kleinberg, Kaplan, Wolff & Cohen, P.C., SEC No-Action Letter, 1981 SEC NOACT LEXIS 3649 (May 29, 1981) (staff reply) ("We consider a husband and wife as two 'persons'... whether they own a share or several shares of securities separately or as joint tenants").

40 Privately Offered Investment Companies, Investment Company Act Release No. 22,597, 62 Fed. Reg. 17512, 17518 n.69 (April 9, 1997).

The Release does not eliminate the possibility that a security owned by both parties to a marriage as tenants in common will be deemed to have two beneficial owners. In the Release, the commissioners write that, in the context of Section 3(c)(1), a security "jointly owned by both spouses" will be deemed to have one beneficial owner. *Id.* The commissioners do not mention and distinguish the forms of property ownership, viz., joint tenancy, tenancy by the entirety, and tenancy in common. The commissioners may have intended the word "jointly" to apply just to spouses (i) who are joint tenants or (ii) who are tenants by the entirety. The former arrangement contains the word "joint" in its name, and while the latter does not, a tenancy by the entirety is similar to a joint tenancy. Hoag v. Hoag, 213 Mass. 50, 99 N.E. 521 (1912) ("[w]hile it is sometimes said that an estate by entirety is not a simple joint tenancy (as indeed it is not), still the two very much resemble each other, the only practical difference being the inability of either spouse to sever the joint tenancy"). On the other hand, spouses who are tenants in common each have a "separate and distinct," albeit undivided, ownership interest in their property. JOHN E. CRIBBET & CORWIN W. JOHNSON, PRINCIPLES OF THE LAW OF PROPERTY 111 (3d ed. 1989). Counting each spouse in a tenancy in common as a beneficial owner might therefore be justified. However, the commissioners are likely to have used the word "jointly" in a nontechnical sense to cover any situation where both spouses are named as owners of a security. Since the commissioners could not have been unaware of the technical forms of property ownership, the fact they did not discuss these forms suggests they wished to follow the definition by the general public of "jointly," i.e., wished to refer to property owned "in common; together." AMERICAN HERITAGE DICTIONARY 971 (3d ed. 1992) (definition of "jointly"). The view of the commissioners, in short, is probably that a "jointly owned" security exists whenever ownership is in the name of two persons who are married to each other. If so, a security owned by a wife and her husband in the name of both will have just one beneficial owner even when the spouses are tenants in common.

If the words and rules employed in law emanate from and are molded by the society in which they exist, as a macrosociological framework posits, can evidence be adduced that the two Commission constructions of the word "person" in cases of joint spousal ownership—the 1980 construction by the staff and the 1997 construction by the commissioners[41]—were responses to the social milieu? In answering the question, it may be helpful to put the two interpretations in perspective. The 1980 interpretation of the word "person" embodies the belief that marriage does not alter the identities of its participants (wife and husband) and that marriage is in essence a living arrangement. In this view, the individual is primary and the whole is simply the sum of its parts. The 1997 construction of the word "person," on the other hand, embodies the belief that marriage produces something new, viz., the marital relationship; that this relationship has a reality of its own; and that the individuals in a marriage to some degree are subordinated to the marital relationship. The 1997 construction, in short, manifests the belief that the whole is more than the sum of its parts.

In a situation where two individuals who are married to each other are both named as owners of a security and their ownership is "joint," what societal determinants account for the doctrinal shift from 1980 to 1997 on the number of beneficial owners of a security? I believe that an indicator of such a determinant can be found in rates of marital breakdown in the United States. Accordingly, Figure 5.4 shows, for every fifth year from 1950 through 2005, the number of divorces that occurred in the United States per 1,000 married females who were 15 years of age and older.[42] This measure of the divorce rate

---

41 That the staff and the commissioners adopted different interpretations of the word "person" under Section 3(c)(1) is important for showing only *how* the content of law changed; it does not explain *why* the change occurred. The commissioners, of course, possess the authority to overrule the staff, but their decision is of no moment in the theoretical framework that I advance to explain the words and rules of law. Until the commissioners acted, prevailing doctrine on the word "person" under Section 3(c)(1) was the rule announced by the staff. The *source* of a prevailing doctrine of law is not a critical consideration in my framework, which focuses on the substantive content of doctrine. If a society is to function effectively, I argue, *some* source of law will bring doctrine into line with the ideals of the society.

42 The data in Figure 5.4 were obtained from: U.S. CENSUS BUREAU, STATISTICAL ABSTRACT OF THE UNITED STATES: 1982–83, at 82 tbl. 124 (103d ed. 1982) (data for 1950 through 1965), http://www.census.gov/prod/www/statistical_abstract.html; U.S. CENSUS BUREAU, STATISTICAL ABSTRACT OF THE UNITED STATES: 2001, at 87 tbl. 117 (121st ed. 2001) (data for 1970 through 1995), http://www.census.gov/prod/www/statistical_abstract.html; NAT'L MARRIAGE PROJECT, UNIV. OF VIRGINIA, THE STATE OF OUR UNIONS, MARRIAGE IN

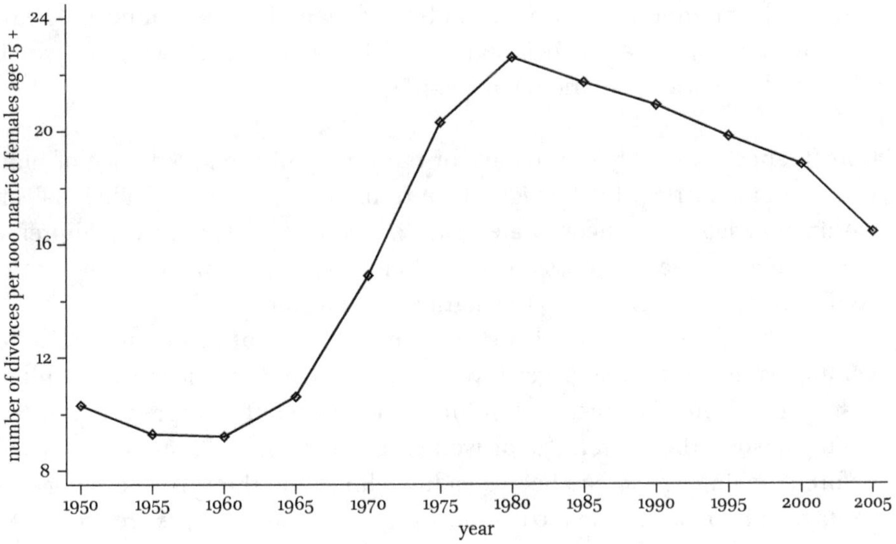

FIGURE 5.4 *Divorce rate in the United States by year*
SOURCE: SEE FN. 42 IN THIS CHAPTER.

is more accurate in gauging long-term trends in the likelihood of marital dissolution than the number of divorces per 1,000 inhabitants of a jurisdiction because the latter measure (the number of divorces per 1,000 inhabitants) is sensitive to changes in the birth rate and the death rate. Changes in rates of births and deaths alter the numerical size of the population and hence affect the denominator when calculating the number of divorces per 1,000 inhabitants. On the other hand, the number of divorces per 1,000 married females not only is unaffected by changes in birth and death rates, but it has the added advantage of measuring the likelihood of divorce only among persons who are at risk of a divorce, namely, individuals who are married.

What does Figure 5.4 reveal? Between 1960 and 1980, a dramatic rise is evident in the rate at which marriages ended. In 1980, of course, the staff decided that, when a married couple had an ownership interest in a security, each spouse would be counted as a separate beneficial owner. The cohesiveness of marriage had thus materially abated during the two decades that preceded the 1980 decision. In this regard, it is relevant that in 1972—just a few years before the staff construed the word "person"—the U.S. Supreme Court recognized an ideology of individualism within marriage:

AMERICA 2010: WHEN MARRIAGE DISAPPEARS 69 fig. 5 (W. Bradford Wilcox ed., 2010) (data for 2000 and 2005), *available at* http://nationalmarriageproject.org/reports/.

> "[T]he marital couple is not an independent entity with a mind and heart of its own, but an association of two individuals each with a separate intellectual and emotional makeup."[43]

Coincidence is unlikely to account for the timing of the acceptance of individualism in marriage by the highest court in the United States. Individualism within marriage was incorporated into a doctrine of law by the Supreme Court—and by the Commission staff—following a substantial decline in the commitment of Americans to the marital relationship.

Notably, greater individualism[44] was manifested not just in an increased willingness to leave a marriage; it was manifested, too, in a decreased willingness to enter one. For instance, prior to the 1980 staff interpretation of the word "person," the percentage of women in the United States who married before reaching age 30 had been steadily falling, and the corresponding percentage of men had started to decline as well. The percentages are presented in Table 5.1, which shows the calendar years when each of seven cohorts were born (first column), the calendar years when each birth cohort had its thirtieth birthday (second column), and the percentages of men (third column) and of women (fourth column) in each birth cohort who had married prior to their thirtieth birthday, whether or not they were currently married. Thus, among women whose thirtieth birthday was in 1955–1964 (i.e., among women who were born in 1925–1934), 91.5% had already married, but among women whose thirtieth birthday was in 1975–1979 (i.e., among women who were born in 1945–1949), 85.4% had married, a decrease of 6.1 percentage points. During the same time interval, men experienced a decline of comparable magnitude, although the decline did not occur gradually among men as it had among women. Instead, the decline among men happened suddenly—from the birth cohort attaining age 30 in 1970–1974 to the birth cohort attaining age 30 in 1975–1979. In short, marriage was less attractive to women and men in the United States during the last half of the 1970s than it had been earlier, and the reduced societal importance of the marital relationship is likely to explain the actions of both the Commission staff and the United States Supreme Court incorporating individualism into American jurisprudence on marriage.

---

43 Eisenstadt v. Baird, 405 U.S. 438, 453 (1972).

44 Note 51 and its accompanying text in *supra* Chapter 4.

TABLE 5.1 *Percentage of men and women born in specified years who had married before 30 years of age: United States*[45]

Birth cohort	Calendar years in which cohort reached age 30	Percentage of cohort that had married prior to age 30	
		Men	Women
1925 to 1934	1955 to 1964	84.7	91.5
1935 to 1939	1965 to 1969	85.3	88.7
1940 to 1944	1970 to 1974	85.3	87.6
1945 to 1949	1975 to 1979	79.7	85.4
1950 to 1954	1980 to 1984	74.0	80.7
1955 to 1959	1985 to 1989	68.8	78.1
1960 to 1964	1990 to 1994	65.6	74.4
1965 to 1969	1995 to 1999	65.2	74.3

During the period that follows 1980, Figure 5.4 discloses a clear but modest reduction in the rate at which marriages dissolved,[46] and Table 5.1 shows that the percentages marrying by age 30, while continuing to decline after 1980, reached a plateau during the 1990s among men as well as among women. Notably, marriage seems to have become more important at this time in the

45 The data are from: Rose M. Kreider & Jason M. Fields, U.S. Census Bureau, *Number, Timing, and Duration of Marriages and Divorces: 1996*, CURRENT POPULATION REP., Feb. 2002, at 4 tbl. 1 (data for birth cohort of 1925–1934), *available at* http://www.census.gov/prod/2002pubs/p70-80.pdf; Rose M. Kreider, U.S. Census Bureau, *Number, Timing, and Duration of Marriages and Divorces: 2001*, CURRENT POPULATION REP., Feb. 2005, at 3 tbl. 1 (data for birth cohorts of 1935–1939 to 1965–1969), *available at* http://www.census.gov/prod/2005pubs/p70-97.pdf.

46 The number of divorces per 1,000 married females age 15 and older rose by 12.0 from 1965 to 1980 and fell by 2.8 from 1980 to 1995. *Supra* note 42. Thus, during the fifteen years that preceded the 1980 interpretation of the word "person" by the Commission staff, the absolute increase in the divorce rate was approximately four times larger than the absolute decrease during the fifteen years that preceded the 1997 interpretation by the commissioners. The absolute difference between the two fifteen-year periods may be evidence of a general proposition. Specifically, the change in social life required to produce a doctrine of law that rejects traditional social values may need to be substantially larger in magnitude than the change in social life required to produce a doctrine of law that once again accepts traditional social values.

social values of Americans. In two surveys of national samples of adults in the United States, interviewees were asked whether they "agree or disagree" with the statement that "personal freedom is more important than the companionship of marriage."[47] In 1988, 59 percent of the respondents expressed disagreement with the statement, but in 1996, 72 percent disagreed with it,[48] a rise of about one-fifth. The surveys thus furnish support for the conclusion that, from 1988 to 1996, marriage came to be more valued by Americans, a change consistent with the view that a married couple should be regarded as a single unit and treated as just one owner of a security. Unfortunately, the question was not included in surveys conducted prior to 1988, and the level of disagreement with the statement at earlier time points is unknown. Nonetheless, the 1988–1996 change is consistent with the position adopted by the commissioners in 1997 and indicates that the ideal of marriage was strengthening before the commissioners ruled that a security in the names of a wife and husband will be considered to have only one owner. The revision of a doctrine of law, in short, was evidently prompted by change in social life.

4 Jurisdiction Characteristics and Law on Mutual Funds in European Nations

In order to develop additional evidence on the thesis that the content of law is molded by society-level conditions, I undertook a study of law on entities. The study covered twenty-six European countries[49]—specifically, those countries

47 NAT'L OPINION RESEARCH CTR., GENERAL SOCIAL SURVEYS, 1972–2008: CUMULATIVE CODEBOOK 1709 (question 1413B) (2009), *available at* http://www3.norc.org/GSS+Website. The mnemonic label of the variable is MARFREE. Interviewees could "strongly agree," "agree," "neither agree or disagree," "disagree," or "strongly disagree" with the statement. Some respondents were coded as "can't choose" or "no answer." *Id.*

48 Computed from http://www3.norc.org/GSS+Website (follow "Data Analysis using SDA (1972–2008)" hyperlink, enter MARFREE as the variable for "Row," and enter YEAR as the variable for "Column"). The percentages in the text were calculated with the composite weight (COMPWT), combine the responses "disagree" and "strongly disagree," and include adults of all ages (i.e., 18 and older). Among respondents who were 18 through 39 years of age, 53% expressed disagreement with the statement in 1988 and 69% expressed disagreement in 1996. *Id.*

49 The twenty-six nations (in alphabetical order) were: Austria, Belgium, Bulgaria, Czech Republic, Denmark, Finland, France, Germany, Greece, Hungary, Ireland, Italy, Liechtenstein, Luxembourg, Netherlands, Norway, Poland, Portugal, Romania, Slovakia, Slovenia, Spain, Sweden, Switzerland, Turkey, and United Kingdom.

in which mutual funds and/or asset managers belonged to a national organization that in 2010 was a member of the European Fund and Asset Management Association ("EFAMA").[50] The study employed data on nation-level characteristics of the twenty-six countries to ascertain whether the characteristics differentiate the countries on an indicator of the stringency of fund-applicable law.

Readers should keep in mind that the current study is just one test of a macrosociological framework for law and that no single study is able to prove or disprove definitively whether a framework correctly portrays the essential aspects of the institution of law. If law—or, for that matter, any complex phenomenon—is to be understood, a framework, and ultimately a theory, must be built from a body of evidence supplied by numerous empirical studies. To that end, the current undertaking furnishes evidence—which I believe is the first evidence—that society-level conditions shape doctrines of law on the internal structure and operation of business entities.

a *Variables and Data*

The framework proposed in this chapter posits relationships between variables and thus requires the selection of (i) a suitable dependent (outcome) variable, (ii) promising independent (explanatory and control) variables, and (iii) at least one quantitative indicator of every variable. The variables and their indicators that were chosen for the present study are summarized *infra* in Table 5.2.

i Dependent Variable

If the content of law is a macrosociological phenomenon, as I contend, logic suggests that an appropriate dependent variable is the relative attractiveness to entities of the law of different jurisdictions, i.e., the degree to which entities favor or are comfortable with the provisions of applicable law. In terms of the instant study, the *comparative* content—especially the comparative stringency—of regulatory law presumably determines the attractiveness to funds of the fund-applicable law in a particular nation. If so, differences in the

50 EFAMA members are "national associations the main objective of which is the representation of the investment fund industry and/or the asset management industry within a European state." EFAMA Constitution art. 5, § 1, http://www.efama.org (in "search this site" window, enter "Constitution"). The names and addresses of the national organizations that are members of EFAMA are available at *id.* on the "About EFAMA" page (follow the "National Member Associations" hyperlink). A summary of the criteria applicable to member national organizations is available at *id.* on the "About EFAMA" page (follow the "Applying for Membership" hyperlink).

content of law between jurisdictions need to be explained, and in the quest to understand these differences, a macrosociological framework directs attention to variation in society-level properties.

Notably, the regulatory requirements imposed on funds are not the same in all of the nations of Europe. While some uniform standards for mutual funds are set by the European Union for nations that are European Union members, the standards serve only as a minimum and individual member-nations can impose stricter requirements.[51] Thus, the nations of Europe as a whole vary in their regulatory requirements for mutual funds with respect to, inter alia, diversification in the investments made by funds, the ability of funds to borrow money, the content and approval of a contract between a fund and an outside management entity, and the maximum number of funds that one management entity can direct.[52]

As the empirical indicator of the relative attractiveness of law on mutual funds, the instant study used the number of funds that existed in each of the twenty-six EFAMA nations at the end of June 2010.[53] All else being equal, nations whose law is appealing to funds can logically be expected to have a larger number of funds than nations whose law is not appealing. The attractiveness of law pertinent to mutual funds should thus be positively and strongly correlated with the number of funds. Although numbers of funds just indirectly measure the relative appeal of applicable law, they seem to be valid *a priori* as a proxy for it.

---

51 David A. Kanarek, Legislative Developments, *Directive 2001/107/EC on the Coordination of Laws, Regulations and Administrative Provisions Relating to Undertakings for Collective Investment in Transferable Securities* (UCITS) *with a View to Regulating Management Companies and Simplified Prospectuses*, 8 COLUM. J. EUR. L. 557, 558–559 (2002); David T. Schubauer, Note, *The Inadequacy of the* UCITS *Directive in a Global Marketplace*, 21 N.Y.L. SCHOOL J. INT'L & COMP. LAW 323, 328 (2002).

52 Matthew J. Hagopian, *The Engines of Privatization: Investment Funds and Fund Legislation in Privatizing Economies*, 15 NW. J. INT'L L. & BUS. 75, 90, 95–98, 101 (1994); Patrick J. Paul, Note, *The European Community's* UCITS *Directive: One Model for United States Regulatory Change in a Globalized Securities Market*, 25 VAND. J. TRANSNAT'L L. 61, 85–86 (1992).

53 Numbers of funds are for the "Overall Fund Industry" and are from European Fund and Asset Management Association, *Worldwide Investment Fund Assets and Flows: Trends in the second Quarter 2010*, INT'L STAT. RELEASE, Oct. 21, 2010, at 9 tbl. 6 (on file with author). The numbers of funds reported by EFAMA for the nations EFAMA covers are believed to include all or almost all funds in these nations. E-mail from Jonathan Healy, European Fund and Asset Management Association, to Larry D. Barnett (Nov. 23, 2010, 04:41:21 EST) (on file with author).

ii Independent Variables

What factors may produce cross-country variation in the dependent variable? Logic and/or research on mutual fund investors in the United States suggest the following country-level independent variables—(a) size and age structure of the population, (b) degree of social modernity, (c) level of social solidarity, (d) degree of societal complexity, and (e) amount of wealth. The data used for the indicators of these variables were for 2005 or, if unavailable for all twenty-six nations that year, for 2006. The indicators of the foregoing independent variables, therefore, were measured at a time point that was several years prior to June 2010, when the dependent variable was measured. The substantial interval between the time point for the independent variables and the time point for the dependent variable is based on the assumption that a multi-year time lag normally occurs before societal conditions have their full effects on the content of law.

Besides the five independent variables above—which were regarded as factors that singly may explain differences between countries on the dependent variable—two other independent variables were included in the regression model for the study. One of the variables was an interaction term created from the indicator of social modernity and the indicator of social solidarity; an interaction term for these two independent variables was added because, as discussed in *infra* Part 4-a-ii, a plausible sociological rationale exists for expecting that the two variables act in combination, not separately, in affecting the number of mutual funds. The second independent variable was a dummy for whether and when a nation became a member of the European Union. Specifically, a country was coded 1 if it was a European Union member no later than calendar year 2004; otherwise, the country was coded 0.[54] The latter

54 The nations that were members of the European Union by 2004 are listed at European Union, How the EU Works, http://europa.eu/about-eu/index_en.htm (follow the "Countries" hyperlink) (last visited May 4, 2015).

Of the twenty-six nations covered by EFAMA in 2010, all but six were members of the European Union as of 2004. The six EFAMA nations that were not European Union members as of 2004 were:

- Bulgaria and Romania, which became members of the European Union in 2007.
- Liechtenstein, Norway, Switzerland, and Turkey, which have not joined the European Union.

The preceding six nations were each coded 0 on the dummy variable; the other twenty EFAMA nations were coded 1.

Five nations that became members of the European Union in 2004—Cyprus, Estonia, Latvia, Lithuania, and Malta—were not covered by EFAMA in 2010. *Id.* None of these five nations, therefore, was included in the study.

variable was employed not as an explanatory factor but as a control to check on whether relationships uncovered between explanatory variables and the dependent variable characterized all EFAMA nations without regard to membership in, and the timing of membership in, the European Union.

- Population size and age structure

Two demographic variables—the size and the age structure of the population of a nation—were included in the instant study. On logical grounds, the number of mutual funds in a nation can be expected to increase with the number of its inhabitants, because all else being equal, there are more potential investors in a large population than in a small population. In addition, the number of funds in a nation may be affected by the relative presence of different age groups in the population of the nation—i.e., by the age structure of the population—because the financial incentive and resources to invest in mutual funds is likely to change as individuals grow older. In this regard, it is relevant that the proportion of households in the United States that had an investment in at least one mutual fund increased noticeably from the mid-1990s to 2010 when the financial decision maker for the household was 45 to 54 years old, 55 to 64 years old, or 65 years or older, but the proportion declined when the financial decision maker for the household was younger than age 45.[55] Although comparable data for Europe are lacking, these trends are presumably not confined to the United States.

Both population size and age structure, consequently, seemed to be promising independent variables, and data on them were included in the study. For each of the countries covered by the study, population size was the total population on July 1, 2005,[56] and age structure was the percentage of the total population in 2005 that was in each of three age ranges for which data were available, viz., age 25 through 49, age 50 through 64, and age 65 and older.[57] Because three

---

55 Michael Bogdan et al., Inv. Co. Inst., *Ownership of Mutual Funds, Shareholder Sentiment, and Use of the Internet, 2010*, RESEARCH FUNDAMENTALS, Sept. 2010, at 22 fig. A4, *available at* http://www.ici.org/pdf/fm-v19n6.pdf.

56 Data on population size are from the United Nations Population Division, World Urbanization Prospects: The 2009 Revision Population Database—Panel 1: Urban and Rural Areas. The data were obtained in 2011 from the 2009 Revision Population Database, which is no longer available online.

57 European Commission, Eurostat, People by Age Classes: Share of Total Population, http://ec.europa.eu/eurostat/data/database (expand seriatim "Data Navigation Tree" menu, "Tables by themes" menu, "Population and social conditions" menu, "Population (t_populat)" menu, "Demography (t_pop)" menu, "Population (t_demo_pop)" menu;

age ranges were the indicators of age structure, three age-structure variables were present in the data analysis.

- Social modernity

Change in patterns of social behavior is probably continuous in a nation that is a democracy and that has a complex societal structure and a technologically advanced economy. If so, social patterns evolve in all Western countries. Between nations, however, the pace of social change undoubtedly differs, and these differences logically can be expected to affect the willingness of nations and their law to welcome novel organizations and arrangements. Specifically, a nation that is socially more modern—a nation that has undergone greater social change—may be more disposed than a less-modern nation to embrace new types of entities such as mutual funds. Social modernity, in other words, may be accompanied by, or may include, openness to innovation.

In order to assess the possibility that degree of social modernity is related to stringency of fund-applicable law, the instant study measured social modernity in each country as of 2006 using (i) the percentage of 20–24 year old females who were enrolled in tertiary education and (ii) the percentage of 20–24 year old males who were enrolled in tertiary education.[58] The indicator of social modernity was the ratio of (i) to (ii). According to this indicator, the social status of women vis-à-vis men is positively correlated with the magnitude of the ratio, and a nation is completely egalitarian with respect to the biological attribute of sex when its ratio is 1.00. If the ratio accurately captures the extent of a gender gap in social status, a country with a high ratio is characterized by less-traditional sex roles than a country with a low ratio, and between-country differences in the ratio measure differences in the degree of social modernity.[59]

---

follow "Tables, Graphs, and Maps interface" for "Population by age group"). The percentage of the population age 65 and older in Turkey was computed by (i) summing the percentages for Turkey in age ranges under 15, 15–24, 25–49, and 50–64 and (ii) subtracting the sum obtained in (i) from 100.0.

58 European Commission, Eurostat, Participation/Enrolment in Education by Sex, http://ec.europa.eu/eurostat/data/database (expand seriatim "Data Navigation Tree" menu, "Database by themes" menu, "Population and social conditions" menu, "Education and training (edtr)" menu, "Education (educ)" menu, "Education indicators—non-finance (educ_indic)" menu; follow "Participation/Enrolment in education by sex (educ_ipart_s)" hyperlink; for TIME, select "2006," for "INDIC_ED" select "PS03_10: Students (ISCED 5–6) by sex aged 20–24—as % of corresponding age population," and for SEX, select seriatim "Male" and "Female" and UPDATE).

59 The range of the ratio for the twenty-six nations in the study was 0.56 to 1.54.

Over the last half-century, Americans have increasingly accepted equality between the sexes.[60] Notably, this change in social values has been manifested in the evolution of U.S. law on gender, an evolution that was anticipated by change in an indicator of the status of women vis-à-vis men that is similar to the indicator described in the preceding paragraph.[61] Shifts over time in the education gap between females and males, in short, are useful as measures of social modernity. Moreover, during the last half of the twentieth century, shifts in the views of Americans regarding sex-based distinctions were paralleled by shifts in the views of Americans regarding distinctions grounded on sexual preference,[62] marriage and childbearing,[63] and race and ethnicity[64]; concurrently, shifts occurred in the concern of Americans with distinctions arising from age.[65] Gender egalitarianism, therefore, developed in conjunction with alterations in other social values, and the changes in combination placed emphasis on individual qualifications and rights. Indeed, it is not happenstance that the preceding changes occurred in the United States during the period in which they did, because (i) during a given period a nation normally seems to experience a *set* (or sets) of related changes rather than isolated, disconnected changes[66] and (ii) after the middle of the twentieth century, nations worldwide evidently moved in the same direction as the United States, namely, toward the acceptance of a philosophy of individualism.[67] Accordingly, the movement toward egalitarianism in sex roles was just one aspect of a general

---

60 Leonie Huddy et al., *Support for the Women's Movement*, 64 PUB. OPINION Q. 309, 319, 322 (2000); J. Scott Carter et al., *The Interaction of Race and Gender: Changing Gender-Role Attitudes, 1974–2006*, 90 SOC. SCI. Q. 196, 203–04 (2009).

61 LARRY D. BARNETT, LEGAL CONSTRUCT, SOCIAL CONCEPT 50–55 (1993) [hereinafter LEGAL CONSTRUCT, SOCIAL CONCEPT]; THE PLACE OF LAW, *supra* note 10, at 225–29.

62 Jeni Loftus, *Attitudes toward Homosexuality, 1973 to 1998*, 66 AM. SOCIOL. REV. 762 (2001).

63 PEW RES. CTR., THE DECLINE OF MARRIAGE AND RISE OF NEW FAMILIES 1, 4, 8, 9, 64, 70 (2010), http://pewsocialtrends.org/files/2010/11/pew-social-trends-2010-families.pdf.

64 PEW RES. CTR., MARRYING OUT 1, 9, 11–12, 21–23, 30 (2010), http://pewsocialtrends.org/files/2010/10/755-marrying-out.pdf.

65 LEGAL CONSTRUCT, SOCIAL CONCEPT, *supra* note 61, at 78–90.

66 Contemporaneous, related changes in a society seem to be common because the English language has devised a word—viz., "era"—to denote them. The word "era" has long been understood to mean "a portion of historical time marked by the continuance throughout it of particular influences, social conditions, etc." 5 OXFORD ENGLISH DICTIONARY 362 (2d ed. 1989) (def. 4.a.).

67 David John Frank & Elizabeth H. McEneaney, *The Individualization of Society and the Liberalization of State Policies on Same-Sex Sexual Relations, 1984–1995*, 77 SOC. FORCES 911, 919 (1999).

shift in social values, and differences between countries in the female-to-male enrollment ratio in tertiary-level education can be assumed to have a strong correlation with (if they are not a component of) between-country differences in overall social modernity.

. Social solidarity

Social solidarity—the degree of unity in a society—presumably includes the willingness of the population of a nation to trust, and hence rely on, entities. However, while generalized trust (i.e., trust in others) is a central component of social solidarity, the level of generalized trust may have a curvilinear relationship to the rate of economic growth.[68] As a result, increases in generalized trust in the nations in the present study may raise economic growth and then, once past a threshold, lower it. If so, a plausible basis exists for expecting that in each country the level of social solidarity will be related to the number of mutual funds. However, the exact nature of the relationship is uncertain, because in addition to its possible curvilinear character, (i) the magnitude of economic growth in a country does not necessarily match the amount of wealth in the country (e.g., a country that is experiencing relatively rapid economic growth may possess relatively little wealth) and (ii) wealth is more likely than economic growth to affect the number and assets of mutual funds.

Sociological studies have examined social solidarity as a possible factor accounting for crime[69] and suicide,[70] and in these studies, the level of social solidarity has been gauged by the divorce rate. Because the foregoing studies have found that the likelihood of divorce affects the incidence of both types of behavior (crime and suicide), divorce likelihood (i.e., divorce risk) is a worthwhile indicator of social solidarity, and it is used as such in the present investigation.

---

68 Felix Roth, *Does Too Much Trust Hamper Economic Growth?*, 62 KYKLOS 103, 111 nn. 4 & 5, 112, 120–21, 121 n.9, 123–24 (2009). The dependent variable in the Roth study was the rate of growth in gross domestic product per capita. *Id.* at 114.

69 *E.g.*, Olof Dahlbäck, *Modelling the Influence of Societal Factors on Municipal Theft Rates in Sweden: Methodological Concerns and Substantive Findings*, 41 ACTA SOCIOLOGICA 37, 38, 50 (1998); Augustine J. Kposowa & Kevin D. Breault, *Reassessing the Structural Covariates of U.S. Homicide Rates: A County Level Study*, 26 SOCIOL. FOCUS 27, 35, 39–40 (1993); William Alex Pridemore, *What We Know About Social Structure and Homicide: A Review of the Theoretical and Empirical Literature*, 17 VIOLENCE & VICTIMS 127, 138–42 (2002).

70 *E.g.*, Hwei-Lin Chuang & Wei-Chiao Huang, *A Re-Examination of the Suicide Rates in Taiwan*, 83 SOC. INDICATORS RES. 465, 467, 476, 479 (2007); Christopher G. Ellison et al., *Religious Homogeneity and Metropolitan Suicide Rates*, 76 SOC. FORCES 273, 282 (1997).

The likelihood of divorce, however, can be measured in more than one way. In the data analysis in Part 4-b *infra*, the likelihood of divorce in each country is the number of divorces in 2005 per 1000 inhabitants who were at least 15 years old.[71] By excluding persons younger than age 15, the instant study employs a measure of the risk of divorce that is more accurate than the crude divorce rate, i.e., than the number of divorces per 1000 total population. The denominator of the crude divorce rate includes *all* persons in the population, even those who are ineligible to marry because of age, and as a result, the crude divorce rate varies with age structure, i.e., with the distribution of age. However, even though the data employed in the present study have an advantage over the crude divorce rate, they can incorrectly gauge differences between countries in the likelihood of divorce, because the denominator in the calculation is not confined to married persons, i.e., to persons who are currently exposed to the possibility of divorce. All else being equal, a nation in which married persons are a large percentage of the population will have a higher incidence of divorce than a nation in which married persons are a small percentage of the population. A measure of the likelihood of divorce that is not calculated from data on the segment of the population that is married can thus incorrectly portray the risk of divorce, and cross-country assessments of the macro-level effects of divorce risk can yield erroneous conclusions if (i) the percentage of the population that is married differs substantially between the countries and (ii) divorce risk was ascertained for an age range rather than for married persons. Unfortunately, divorce rates computed with a denominator confined to married persons were not available and hence could not be used in the instant study.

- Societal complexity

For more than a century, a distinct secular trend in the United States (and presumably in other Western nations) has been the expansion of knowledge, and the trend is hypothesized to have had widespread repercussions for American

---

71 The number of divorces in each country in 2005 was obtained from European Commission, Eurostat, Divorce Indicators, http://ec.europa.eu/eurostat/data/database (expand seriatim "Data Navigation Tree" menu, "Database by themes" menu, "Population and social conditions" menu, "Demography and migration (pop)" menu, "Marriages and divorces (demo_nup)" menu; select "Data explorer" for "Divorce indicators (demo_ndivind)"; select "Divorces" for INDIC_ED and "2005" for TIME, and UPDATE). The data from this source was used to calculate the divorce rate per 1000 persons age 15 and over in each country. In this calculation, the data for the denominator (the number of persons age 15 and over) were computed from information supplied by the source in *supra* note 57.

social life and law.[72] Among the likely effects of additions to knowledge has been increasing societal complexity as growth in knowledge enlarged the number of occupations.[73] An aspect of this enlargement is the emergence of entities having relatively narrow areas of expertise. As occupational segmentation and specialization advances in a social system, then, participants in the system increasingly come to employ other persons (entities and individuals) for the skills possessed by these persons. One such skill is investing in securities, and because the managers of mutual funds are presumed to be experienced with and knowledgeable about securities as investments, mutual funds can be expected to become more numerous as growth occurs in the quantity of knowledge. Notably, the extent to which there is reliance on others to make recommendations regarding investments in securities, as well as the nature of the others consulted, is affected by sociological variables.[74]

Unfortunately, for the nations and time period covered by the instant study, data standardized across countries could not be located on the number of persons in each (or any) of a set of occupational categories. However, if the quantity of knowledge is a key factor driving societal complexity, an accurate indicator of the quantity of knowledge will serve as an accurate indicator of the degree of societal complexity. In the United States, increases in school enrollments at the tertiary level as well as at the secondary level have evidently been due largely to the growth of knowledge.[75] On the twin assumptions that university-level education is key to occupational specialization and that occupational specialization is central to societal complexity, the present study uses

---

72 THE PLACE OF LAW, *supra* note 10, at 264–70.

73 Data on the number of occupations in the United States during the twentieth century are in the following sources: Gregory Williams, *The Changing U.S. Labor Force and Occupational Differentiation by Sex*, 16 DEMOGRAPHY 73, 79 tbl. 2 (1979) (reporting the total number of occupations covered in the decennial censuses of 1900 through 1970); THOMAS S. SCOPP, THE RELATIONSHIP BETWEEN THE 1990 CENSUS AND CENSUS 2000 INDUSTRY AND OCCUPATION CLASSIFICATION SYSTEMS 5 (U.S. Census Bureau Technical Paper #65, 2003) (reporting the number of occupations covered in the decennial censuses of 1960 through 1990). Given the inconsistencies that exist between the two sources in their counts of occupations in the years covered by both, each source obviously used a different criterion and/or procedure for counting occupations. However, although the counts are not comparable between the two sources, the data supplied by each source show a secular rise in the number of occupations over the time period covered by that source.

74 Mariko Lin Chang, *With a Little Help from My Friends (and My Financial Planner)*, 83 SOC. FORCES 1469 (2005).

75 Pamela Barnhouse Walters, *Occupational and Labor Market Effects on Secondary and Postsecondary Educational Expansion in the United States: 1922 to 1979*, 49 AM. SOCIOL. REV. 659, 668 (1984).

as its indicator of societal complexity in each EFAMA country the percentage of all persons 20 to 24 years old who were, as of 2006, enrolled as students at the tertiary level of education.[76]

- Wealth

The economic wealth of a nation is logically an important factor in the number and assets of mutual funds in that nation. A priori, an economically rich nation can be expected to have more funds than an economically poor nation, and the average fund in the former can be expected to have more assets than the average fund in the latter. The data that I analyze in Part 4-b *infra*, therefore, include a quantitative indicator of the wealth of each EFAMA nation, namely, gross domestic product per capita in U.S. dollars as of 2005.[77] The indicator is imperfect, however, in that it lacks an adjustment for price differences between countries, which differences are likely to have an impact on the amount of money available for investing. Regrettably, an indicator with such an adjustment could not be found for all of the countries in the study for a year that would be appropriate.

- Interaction of social modernity and social solidarity

To this point, the discussion of explanatory variables has assumed that the relationship of an independent variable to the dependent variable is unaffected by any other independent variable. If this assumption is correct, the

---

76 European Commission, Eurostat, Participation/Enrolment in Education by Sex, http://ec.europa.eu/eurostat/data/database (expand seriatim "Data Navigation Tree" menu, "Database by themes" menu, "Population and social conditions" menu, "Education and training (edtr)" menu, "Education (educ)" menu, "Education indicators—non-finance (educ_indic)" menu; follow "Participation/Enrolment in education by sex" hyperlink; for TIME, select "2006," for INDIC_ED, select "PS03_10: Students (ISCED 5–6) by sex aged 20–24—as % of corresponding age population," and for SEX, select "Total" and then UPDATE).

77 World Bank, http://data.worldbank.org (select seriatim "Data Catalog," "World Development Indicators," and "databank"; follow "databank" hyperlink; under "Country" tab, choose countries; select "Series" tab, expand seriatim "Economic Policy & Debt" menu, "National accounts" menu, and "US$ at current prices" menu; choose "Aggregate indicators" and "GDP per capita (current US$)"; select "Time" tab and choose year(s); to view data, select "Download"). The country-specific estimates of gross domestic product per capita in 2005 that were used in the data analysis were estimates available from the World Bank as of April 2014.

independent variables, in whether and how they influence the dependent variable, act separately from one another, but if the assumption is incorrect, they do not. In the latter case, independent variables X_1 and X_2 have a joint impact on the dependent variable (Y) that is not the same as the impact that X_1 and X_2 alone would be observed to have. X_1 and X_2, in a word, interact.[78] An illustration of interaction is an impact of X_1 on Y that differs in magnitude and/or direction between levels or categories of X_2. The failure to uncover the foregoing interaction between X_1 and X_2, of course, will lead to an incorrect conclusion regarding the impact of X_1 on Y.

Is there a basis for believing that interaction exists between any of the independent variables in the instant study? Support for an affirmative answer to the question is provided by sociological theory[79] and empirical research[80] pertinent to social solidarity and societal change. To be exact, the strength of social bonds affecting at least some types of activity in a society can weaken as the society undergoes change. When this happens in the modernization of a society, a plausible argument can be advanced that the size of the decline in the potency of social bonds will be altered by thresholds in social modernity and that the effect of social solidarity on an activity thus varies from one range of quantitative values of social modernity to another. If the argument is correct, the magnitude of the impact of social solidarity on an activity is not the same across levels of modernity. Otherwise stated, social solidarity and social modernity interact—the impact on the activity of the former is contingent on the latter.

To assess the possible presence in the data of interaction between social modernity and social solidarity, an interaction term was created from these variables. In regression, the existence of interaction between two independent variables is typically ascertained by generating a new independent variable

---

78 James Jaccard & Robert Turrisi, Interaction Effects in Multiple Regression 3–7 (Paper No. 72, Sage University Paper Series on Quantitative Applications in the Social Sciences, 2d ed. 2003).

79 Ernest R. Mowrer, *Social Crises and Social Disorganization*, 15 Am. Sociol. Rev. 60, 60–61 (1950); Cecil L. Willis, *Durkheim's Concept of Anomie: Some Observations*, 52 Sociol. Inquiry 106, 109–11 (1982). Theory is the key criterion for identifying independent variables that may interact. Jaccard & Turrrisi, *supra* note 78, at 3–4; James Jaccard, Interaction Effects in Logistic Regression 12–13 (Paper No. 135, Sage University Paper Series on Quantitative Applications in the Social Sciences, 2001); F. David Schoorman et al., *The Role of Theory in Testing Hypothesized Interactions: An Example from the Research on Escalation of Commitment*, 21 J. Applied Soc. Psychol. 1338, 1338, 1349, 1353 (1991).

80 Mowrer, *supra* note 79, at 65–66; William Alex Pridemore et al., *An Interrupted Time-Series Analysis of Durkheim's Social Deregulation Thesis: The Case of the Russian Federation*, 24 Just. Q. 271 (2007).

whose measure is the product of the numerical values for the independent variables that might be interacting.[81] The instant study employed the same procedure. To obtain the interaction variable for the study, therefore, the numerical values of the indicators of social modernity and of social solidarity in each of the twenty-six nations were multiplied.

b *Data Analysis*

As Table 5.2 shows, between-nation differences in the dependent variable (measured by ALLFUNDS) may respond to ten independent variables—EU2004, POP, AGE2549, AGE5064, AGE65PLUS, EDRATIO, EDALL, DIVRATE, GDP, and INTERACT. Before turning to the results of the data analysis, however, two statistical matters must be considered. The matters, which derive from different aspects of the data compiled for the study, involve (i) the type of regression that is appropriate for analyzing the data and (ii) the suitability of statistical significance as a criterion for deciding whether a relationship exists between an independent variable and the dependent variable.

With regard to (i), the indicator of the dependent variable in the present study is the *number* of mutual funds located in each of twenty-six countries.[82] Counts, therefore, comprise the data for the dependent variable. While the coefficients of the independent variables can be computed from such data with linear (least-squares) regression, coefficients that are unbiased, consistent, and efficient are more apt to be obtained with negative binomial regression.[83] The relationship between each independent variable and the dependent variable in the present study was estimated, therefore, with negative binomial regression.[84]

As to (ii), the results of the data analysis that are reported below include not only each regression coefficient but also its standard error and level of statistical significance. The information will permit readers who are so inclined to use statistical significance when deciding whether a relationship exists between an independent variable and the dependent variable. However, I do not regard statistical significance as an appropriate basis for such decisions in this study, because the jurisdictions (nations) in the study were not chosen by sampling

---

81 JACCARD & TURRISI, *supra* note 78, at 17; JACCARD, *supra* note 79, at 14.

82 *Supra* note 49 and accompanying text.

83 J. SCOTT LONG & JEREMY FREESE, REGRESSION MODELS FOR CATEGORICAL DEPENDENT VARIABLES USING STATA 349 (2d ed. 2006).

84 The coefficients were estimated with the NBREG command in Stata release 12.1. 2 STATACORP., STATA BASE REFERENCE MANUAL: RELEASE 12, at 1253–64 (2011).

TABLE 5.2 *Variables and their mnemonic labels and empirical indicators*

Variable	Mnemonic label	Empirical Indicator
Dependent variable		
Attractiveness of law on mutual funds	ALLFUNDS	The number of funds at the end of June 2010 in each nation covered by the European Fund and Asset Management Association.
Independent variables		
Member of European Union in 2004 or earlier	EU2004	A country was coded 1 if it was a European Union member no later than calendar year 2004; if a country was not an E.U. member by 2004, it was coded 0.
Population size	POP	The total population of each nation on July 1, 2005 measured in thousands of inhabitants.
Age structure		
Age 25 to 49	AGE2549	The percentage of the total population of each nation in 2005 that was 25 through 49 years old.
Age 50 to 64	AGE5064	The percentage of the total population of each nation in 2005 that was 50 through 64 years old.
Age 65 and older	AGE65PLUS	The percentage of the total population of each nation in 2005 that was 65 years of age and older.
Social modernity	EDRATIO	The ratio in each nation of (i) the percentage of 20–24 year old females in 2006 who were enrolled in tertiary-level education to (ii) the percentage of 20–24 year old males in 2006 who were enrolled in tertiary-level education.

TABLE 5.2 *Variables and their mnemonic labels and empirical indicators* (cont.)

Variable	Mnemonic label	Empirical Indicator
Social solidarity	DIVRATE	The number of divorces in each nation in 2005 per 1000 inhabitants in 2005 who were at least 15 years old.
Societal complexity	EDALL	The percentage of all persons 20 to 24 years old in each nation who were, as of 2006, enrolled as students in tertiary-level education.
Wealth	GDP	The gross domestic product per capita in each nation in 2005 expressed in U.S. dollars and measured in thousands of U.S. dollars.
Interaction term	INTERACT	The product of EDRATIO and DIVRATE.

from a larger universe of jurisdictions.[85] Statistical significance is concerned with using data on a sample to learn about attributes of the universe from which the sample was drawn.[86] The justification for statistical significance was eliminated, therefore, when data were collected for all of the nations covered by EFAMA and sampling was rendered unnecessary.[87]

Leaving statistical matters, we turn to substantive issues. The first such issue is the interaction term that was developed for the regression model. When INTERACT was in the model and used in analyzing the data, between-nation differences in ALLFUNDS were explained to the same extent as when INTERACT was not in the model.[88] Social solidarity, therefore, evidently had an

85 Earl Babbie, Survey Research Methods 292 (2d ed. 1990) (noting that a test of statistical significance requires data on cases obtained by simple random sampling).

86 *Id.* at 303.

87 *Id.* at 301–302.

88 A comparison of the explanatory power of a regression model with and without an interaction term is commonly used to ascertain whether interaction exists between the

impact on the number of funds that occurred independently of the impact of social modernity. Because INTERACT did not matter, it was omitted when computing the results that are reported below.

The regression of the indicator of the dependent variable (ALLFUNDS) on the indicators of the nine independent variables (i.e., the independent variables with the exception of INTERACT) yielded the results in Table 5.3.[89]

---

independent variables that form the interaction term. JACCARD & TURRISI, *supra* note 78, at 18. In the instant study, pseudo-R^2 was found to be 0.120 when INTERACT was included and 0.119 when INTERACT was omitted. Pseudo-R^2 is explained in JOSEPH M. HILBE, LOGISTIC REGRESSION MODELS 243–46 (2009).

89 The data were not examined to determine if any of the twenty-six nations in the study distorted the results, i.e., was an influential outlier. The measure that LONG & FREESE, *supra* note 83, at 151–52, recommend for detecting an influential outlier requires the use of the Stata post-estimation command PREDICT with its DBETA option, but the DBETA option is unavailable when count data are analyzed with negative binomial regression. Notably, LONG & FREESE, *supra* note 83, do not mention a procedure for identifying influential outliers in data that are counts and analyzed with negative binomial regression.

It is pertinent to point out here that, when studying a set of entities that comprise a system, an investigator should presume that each component, i.e., each entity, is *not* an influential outlier. *See* THE PLACE OF LAW, *supra* note 10, at 468–69 (discussing the ramifications of a decision whether a component jurisdiction of a system is an influential outlier when conducting macro-level research on a system of jurisdictions). The presumption is especially important when the number of components of a system is small—an adjective that, in research on the impact of jurisdiction-level attributes, unquestionably depicts a system with just twenty-six components. For a particular system component, this presumption should be overcome only by persuasive evidence that the component deviates from the other components in the system in one or more relevant, significant ways. THE PLACE OF LAW, *supra* note 10, at 422 (concluding that California is an influential outlier in data on state-level characteristics that may affect the application to lawyers of the appearance-of-impropriety standard for conduct). A system is defined in my macrosociological framework as "[a] group of interacting, interrelated, or interdependent elements forming a complex whole." AMERICAN HERITAGE DICTIONARY 1823 (3d ed. 1992).

EFAMA, which covers the countries on which data were compiled for the instant study, is a voluntary organization of national associations, each located in a different country, that satisfy the criteria for membership in EFAMA and that agree to be bound by the standards established by EFAMA for its members. Constitution of the European Fund and Asset Management Association, http://www.efama.org (in "search this site" window, enter "Constitution"). When investigating the impact of macro-level attributes of jurisdictions on the content of law—the type of study undertaken here—the decision to designate or not designate a particular jurisdiction as an influential outlier depends partially on whether the set of jurisdictions under investigation is a system.

In logistic regression, however, a regression coefficient itself has no practical interpretation and is thus not useful for deciding whether an independent variable has an important effect on the dependent variable. On the other hand, a measure that is meaningful and pragmatic can be obtained for a regression coefficient by mathematically transforming the coefficient. The transformations for the independent variables in the instant study are found in Table 5.4, and they will be the basis for decisions on the existence and magnitude of a relationship between each independent variable and the dependent variable.[90]

Because Table 5.4 will occupy our attention, an understanding of its columns is essential. That understanding will be helped by comparing columns in the table.

The first comparison is between columns 2 and 3, on the one hand, and columns 4 and 5, on the other. Readers should note that columns 2 and 3 report the model-predicted impact of each independent variable on the dependent variable when every other independent variable is statistically held constant. Columns 2 and 3 accordingly show the expected relationship that exists

---

The twenty-six countries encompassed by EFAMA are not coextensive with the countries that belong to the European Union. *Supra* nn. 49 & 54. Even though the countries covered by EFAMA do not form a system that is recognized by and embodied in law, the member associations of EFAMA can plausibly be regarded as being components of a system. In pursuing the goals of EFAMA, representatives of the various national associations that are EFAMA members work with one another through EFAMA in pursuing their common interests. *See* European Fund and Asset Management Association, About EFAMA, http://www.efama.org/about/SitePages/Home.aspx (describing the functions of the EFAMA administrative office to include "acting as coordinator and facilitator for its members"); EUROPEAN FUND AND ASSET MANAGEMENT ASSOCIATION, ANNUAL REPORT: 2010, at 45 [no date] (referencing "EFAMA's Working Groups" and "the close cooperation between EFAMA members"), *available at* http://www.efama.org/about/SitePages/Annual%20Reports.aspx. While a national association is able to terminate its membership in EFAMA, the existence of EFAMA indicates that national associations of funds and asset managers belong to EFAMA because EFAMA is thought to advance their common interests to a degree that the national associations acting individually could not. EFAMA, therefore, constitutes more than the sum of its parts, a prominent feature of a system. If EFAMA is a system, the countries whose national associations of funds and asset managers have joined EFAMA can justifiably be combined into a set for study if the purpose of the research is to isolate jurisdiction conditions that affect the law of these jurisdictions.

90 The intercept was included when estimating the regression coefficients in Table 5.3, because without it, the numerical changes that are reported in columns 4, 5, and 6 of Table 5.4 could not have been calculated.

TABLE 5.3 *Negative binomial regression of* ALLFUNDS *on independent variables*

Independent variable	Regression coefficient	Standard error	z	p>|z|
EU2004	1.601052	0.3335864	4.80	0.000
POP	0.000015	0.0000007	2.22	0.026
AGE2549	−0.189824	0.0872462	−2.18	0.030
AGE5064	−0.392666	0.1175464	−3.34	0.001
AGE65PLUS	0.190582	0.0722490	2.64	0.008
EDRATIO	0.230895	1.0561740	0.22	0.827
DIVRATE	0.119115	0.2074783	0.57	0.566
EDALL	−0.042346	0.0215005	−1.97	0.049
GDP	0.038355	0.0069327	5.53	0.000
INTERCEPT	15.643110	4.3054710	3.63	0.000

between a given independent variable and the dependent variable regardless of the amounts of the other independent variables. Columns 4 and 5, however, report the model-predicted impact on the dependent variable when (a) every independent variable except one stays at its own arithmetic mean and (b) the one independent variable that does not remain at its mean rises (i) from one-half of a unit below to one-half of a unit above its mean (column 4) or (ii) from one-half of a standard deviation below to one-half of a standard deviation above its mean (column 5). Columns 4 and 5 thus reveal the change in the dependent variable that is expected to be brought about by a change around the mean of each independent variable when the other independent variables are held at their respective means.

The second comparison—which focuses on a difference between columns 2 and 4, on the one hand, and columns 3 and 5, on the other—involves the type of change that occurs in the independent variables. Specifically, column 2 and column 4 report the model-predicted impacts on the dependent variable that stem from a rise of one *unit* in the measure of each independent variable, while columns 3 and 5 report the model-predicted impacts on the dependent variable that stem from a rise of one *standard deviation* in the measure of each independent variable.[91] The difference between these sets of columns is important in that independent variables can be ranked in terms of the magnitude of their

91 Because EU2004 is a dummy variable, i.e., measured as either 0 or 1, it has no meaningful standard deviation. Columns 3 and 5 for EU2004, consequently, are left blank in Table 5.4.

impact on the dependent variable when change in the independent variables is computed in standard deviations, as it is in columns 3 and 5. Such a ranking is not possible, however, when change in the independent variables is computed in units, because as Table 5.2 shows, the amount and character of one unit—the subject of columns 2 and 4 in Table 5.4—differ between independent variables. For example, one unit of population size (POP) is 1,000 people; one unit of wealth (GDP) is 1,000 U.S. dollars; one unit of social solidarity (DIVRATE) is one divorce per 1,000 inhabitants age 15 or older; and one unit of societal complexity (EDALL) is one percentage point in the percent of all 20 to 24 year-old persons who are currently students in tertiary-level education.

The third comparison in Table 5.4 is between columns 2 and 4, on the one hand, and column 6, on the other. All of these columns deal with the model-predicted change in the dependent variable from a change in each independent variable measured in units rather than in standard deviations. However, columns 2 and 4 report the model-predicted change in number of funds from a rise of just *one* unit of an independent variable, while column 6 reports the model-predicted change in number of funds from a rise across the full *range* of units (from the minimum to the maximum) in the data for each independent variable.[92] Because the results in columns 2 and 4 will tend to be smaller as the range enlarges, columns 2 and 4 will be given less weight than column 6 when evaluating the results of the data analysis.

The fourth and final comparison focuses on a distinction between (i) columns 2 and 3 and (ii) columns 4, 5, and 6. While all of these columns supply model-predicted changes in the indicator of the dependent variable (viz., numbers of funds), columns 2 and 3 supply the predictions of the regression model in *percentages*. Columns 4 through 6, on the other hand, supply the predictions of the regression model in *absolute numbers*. Accordingly, the two sets of columns provide different types of information for the impact of each independent variable—viz., percentage changes versus numerical changes in number of funds.

---

92 The minimum numerical value and the maximum numerical value of the indicator of each independent variable in the regression model was:

	EU2004	POP	AGE2549	AGE5064	AGE65PLUS
Minimum	0	35	33.4	10.6	5.9
Maximum	1	82,409	40.0	20.8	19.5

	EDRATIO	DIVRATE	EDALL	GDP
Minimum	0.556250	0.9336976	5.8	3.513
Maximum	1.535411	3.6062930	44.5	105.380

TABLE 5.4 *Change in the predicted number of mutual funds from an increase of one unit or one standard deviation of an independent variable*[93]

Independent variable (column 1)	Percent change in the predicted number of funds when, with the other independent variables held constant, the given independent variable increases by		Numerical change in the predicted number of funds when, with the other independent variables held at their respective means, the given independent variable increases by		Numerical change in the predicted number of funds when, with the other independent variables held at their respective means, the given independent variable increases in number of units from the minimum to the maximum of its range (column 6)
	One unit (column 2)	One standard deviation (column 3)	One unit (column 4)	One standard deviation (column 5)	
EU2004	395.8%	†	1,500	†	1,000
POP	<1.0	46.0%	<1	331	1,600
AGE2549	−17.3	−26.7	−170	−270	−1,200
AGE5064	−32.5	−54.1	−340	−690	−15,000
AGE65PLUS	21.0	71.6	166	475	1,900
EDRATIO	26.0	4.8	201	41	189
DIVRATE	12.6	9.5	104	79	269
EDALL	−4.1	−29.9	−37	−310	−1,700
GDP	3.9	152.1	33	833	13,000

Note to Table 5.4: † = change not reported because EU2004 is a dummy variable; see Table 5.2.

Before we delve into the findings in Table 5.4, a reminder may be warranted. The goal of the study is to identify sociological forces responsible for the differential attractiveness to mutual funds of applicable country law, but of the nine independent variables for which transformations of regression

93 The data in columns 2 and 3 were calculated with the LISTCOEF command. LONG & FREESE, *supra* note 83, at 94–98, 464–467. The data in columns 4, 5, and 6 were calculated with the PRCHANGE command and its REST(MEAN) option. *Id.* at 118–120, 363–364, 483.

coefficients are reported in Table 5.4, three variables are not treated as such forces. The three variables were placed in the model to remove extraneous influences on between-country variation in the indicator (ALLFUNDS) that was chosen for the dependent variable so that sociological causes of law could be unearthed. One of the three (EU2004) is strictly a control variable.[94] The other two (POP and GDP) eliminate differences between nations in the basic ingredients in mutual funds.

Let me elaborate on the last point. The necessities for mutual funds are investors and investable assets. All else being equal, the number of mutual funds will vary with the size of the pool of potential investors and their economic assets—variables that the instant study measured with POP and GDP, respectively. However, POP and GDP are assumed to establish just a numerical *range* of funds for a nation, with other factors producing the exact number found in the nation. Otherwise stated, POP and GDP are each thought to set a floor as well as a ceiling for the number of funds that a country will have. In doing so, they act as contextual conditions for the sociological determinants of the specific number of funds in a country.

What sociological factors generate differential attractiveness of law on mutual funds? The possible factors—the explanatory variables—in the instant regression model are age structure (AGE2549, AGE5064, and AGE65PLUS), social modernity (EDRATIO), social solidarity (DIVRATE), and societal complexity (EDALL). While age structure may seem to be a purely demographic variable, it is a sociological factor because it has notable social aspects. For example, the distribution of age in a population has an obvious effect on the fraction of the population that is married (since minors cannot marry) and on the fraction of the population that is enrolled in school (since formal education occurs largely at certain ages). In addition, the frequency of many types of social activities is age-related.[95] In short, all of the explanatory factors in the instant study have roots in sociology and, by affecting social life, may have a bearing on the content of law.

In deciding whether a particular explanatory variable had a relationship to the dependent variable that was sufficient in magnitude to regard the explanatory variable as an important causal agent, I will initially consider column 6, which reports the predicted change in number of funds from a rise in each

94 Text accompanying *supra* note 54.

95 Trine Bille, *Cohort Effects, Age Effects, and Period Effects in the Participation in the Arts and Culture in Denmark, 1964–2004*, 14 INT'L J. CULTURAL POL'Y 113, 126, 130 (2008); Stephen J. Cutler & Jon Hendricks, *Age Differences in Voluntary Association Memberships: Fact or Artifact*, 55 B J. GERONTOLOGY: SOC. SCI. S98, S105 (2000).

explanatory variable across its full range, i.e., from its minimum to its maximum in the data. (Columns 2 and 4, by contrast, show the predicted change in number of funds due to an increase of a single measurement unit of each explanatory variable.) Because column 6 gives the total predicted impact of every explanatory variable,[96] it will provide the first basis, though not the sole basis, for identifying explanatory variables that are noteworthy causes of the differential attractiveness of law on mutual funds.

Column 6, however, cannot be used without a criterion for judging whether a variable is an important influence on the dependent variable. To formulate such a criterion, I begin with the number of funds in the nations in the study. Because the largest number of funds in a single country (Luxembourg) was 12,628 and the smallest number was 72 (Romania), the countries in the study differed by as many as 12,556 funds. When examining column 6, this range should inform the conclusion as to whether a particular explanatory variable had a material effect, and an explanatory variable will be deemed to have such an effect if, in column 6, the numerical change in the number of funds associated with the variable is at least 10% of 12,556, i.e., at least 1,250 funds. Although the criterion of 10% is arbitrary, it is intuitively meaningful.

Three of the explanatory variables—AGE5064, AGE65PLUS, and EDALL—satisfy the criterion that has been adopted for column 6, and a fourth—viz., AGE2549—almost satisfies it. Among the former variables, AGE5064 had by far the largest impact shown in column 6. In searching for explanatory variables that had a substantial impact on the dependent variable, however, columns 3 and 5 must also be taken into account, because in these columns, impact is estimated for each explanatory variable when the variable rises by one standard deviation. While the measurement units of the explanatory variables are not the same, as seen in Table 5.2, the standard deviation unit is. As a result, one standard deviation of each explanatory variable furnishes a consistent yardstick for comparing the explanatory variables in terms of the magnitude of their impacts on the dependent variable.[97] According to columns 3 and 5, the impact on ALLFUNDS of AGE5064 was not markedly dissimilar in magnitude to the impact of AGE65PLUS, though the effects of the two variables were in opposite directions.

Let us now consider AGE2549 and EDALL. Of the three explanatory variables (viz., AGE5064, AGE65PLUS, and EDALL) that met or exceeded the

---

96 Readers should note that the estimated impact in column 6 for each independent variable was computed by keeping every other independent variable at its mean.

97 FRED C. PAMPEL, LOGISTIC REGRESSION: A PRIMER 32–33 (Paper No. 132, Sage University Paper Series on Quantitative Applications in the Social Sciences, 2000).

criterion applied to column 6, EDALL had the smallest influence, but its impact differed minimally from that of AGE2549 and was in the same direction. Notably, when measured in terms of one standard deviation of the explanatory variable (column 3 and column 5), the relationships to ALLFUNDS by EDALL and by AGE2549 are not trivial. Given these relationships, both EDALL and AGE2549 should be included among the factors that affected the dependent variable.

If the age variables and EDALL had a bearing on the attractiveness to mutual funds of the law adopted by a nation for the funds, what are the reasons they did so? An answer to the question is unavoidably conjectural, but a search for plausible answers can begin with the direction of each effect. The attractiveness of law, we see in Table 5.4, *diminished* with increases in AGE2549, in AGE5064, and in EDALL, but it *rose* with increases in AGE65PLUS. Gains in the relative size of age groups 25–49 and 50–64 may have reduced the attractiveness of fund-applicable law partly because few members of these groups were retired.[98] In other words, the need of both age groups for mutual funds is in the future, which may reduce their members' sensitivity to and awareness of unwanted effects of strict fund regulation. Moreover, age groups younger than 65 may contain the largest percentage of employed persons who have recently experienced, or through exposure to mass-media reports have become aware of, the problems that arise from self-serving behavior. Adults under age 65, therefore, may be inclined to accept, if not advocate, relatively strict regulation of funds, and in nations where adults under age 65 are more common, this experience/awareness may lead to the adoption of safeguards that are designed to prevent such behavior and to increase accountability. On the other hand, retirement-age persons (age 65 and over) may be more interested in the availability of mutual funds because these persons are especially concerned with potential as well as existing sources of current income. When persons age 65+ become a larger share of the population, then, the result would be a relaxation of law-based regulatory demands on mutual funds. In short, the degree to

98 The Organization for Economic Cooperation and Development (OECD) has found that, in fifteen of the twenty-six nations in the instant study, men retiring in 2005 had to be at least 65 years old to receive full benefits or guaranteed minimum benefits from legislatively mandated pension plans. In several of the fifteen countries, however, a lower age applied to women and, under designated conditions, to all workers. For ten of the other eleven countries in the study, the OECD did not supply information on the retirement age specified by legislation. ORGANISATION FOR ECONOMIC CO-OPERATION AND DEVELOPMENT, LIVE LONGER, WORK LONGER 55–56 (2006).

which the law of a nation appeals to funds depends in part on the prevalence in the population of both the age groups that have not yet, and the age group that has already, reached the threshold for retirement.

Different reasons, however, may be responsible for the finding in Table 5.4 that gains in EDALL caused law to become less attractive to mutual funds. Specifically, growth in enrollment rates in tertiary-level education signals not only increased occupational specialization[99] but also increased rationality.[100] The growth of occupational specialization may enhance the stringency of law-based regulatory requirements for mutual funds, because through the funds, investors in the funds participate in the business of buying and selling securities issued by operating companies and governments. In relying on specialists (funds) to invest in these securities, fund investors are dependent on the funds to invest prudently, and given the significant risks that accompany investments in securities, fund investors presumably want assurance that the funds are acting in the investors' interest. Law can soothe this concern. The spread of rationality may foster the regulation of mutual funds, too, because rationality demands that decisions by individuals and entities be based on the merit of each available alternative. In a rational society, factors other than potential financial return and risk have no place in the choice of mutual funds by investors or in the choice of securities by the mutual funds that hold the assets of investors. Rationality can thus foster regulation that is encompassing and detailed, but for mutual funds, the presence of such regulation in a jurisdiction can reduce the attractiveness of the jurisdiction.

5 Conclusion

The instant study involves a quantitative social science approach to comparative law, a field that today resists quantitative studies. In time, however, comparative law can be expected to embrace quantitative research because a closely allied field—international law—has started to accept it.[101] In comparison to a non-empirical study and an empirical study employing qualitative methods, an empirical study that utilizes quantitative methods can achieve greater precision in its measurements of variables and the relationships between variables. Of course, even a quantitative study is characterized

99 See text accompanying *supra* notes 73, 74 & 76.

100 THE PLACE OF LAW, *supra* note 10, at 267, 308, 433, 453 n.223.

101 Gregory Shaffer & Tom Ginsburg, *The Empirical Turn in International Legal Scholarship*, 106 AM. J. INT'L L. 1, 7–8 (2012).

by limitations and subject to qualifications. In that regard, I turn to an examination of the study reported in Part 4.

Empirical research is based on observation, and in research seeking causal connections, observation can determine only whether one factor temporally preceded another factor. Because causation itself is not observable, some uncertainty is inherent in every conclusion that an antecedent factor is a cause of a subsequently occurring factor. An important corollary of this point is that conclusions differ in the degree of assurance they provide regarding causality, and more confidence can be placed in some conclusions than in others. The likelihood that a specific conclusion is correct depends on the design and data of the study that is the basis of the conclusion.

If the explanatory variables that were found in Part 4-b *supra* to be related to the dependent variable were causal agents in the relationships, the findings of the instant study provide support for the thesis that law is a macrosociological phenomenon, i.e., that important doctrines of law do not occur randomly but are responses to societal conditions.[102] Readers should bear in mind, however, that the instant study was exploratory and that its findings are necessarily tentative. The reasons for the provisional character of the study and its findings can be understood through a brief review of key aspects of the study.

To date, the macro-level forces that may shape the concepts and doctrines of law have been the subject of theory that is based largely on impression and of empirical research that, due to its recent origin,[103] is not large in quantity. All of the forces affecting the content of law are unlikely to have been enumerated, therefore, and the instant study undoubtedly missed many of the forces that account for law. In addition, the study used crude, and almost certainly incomplete, indicators of its explanatory variables and its dependent variable. Future research will thus yield more credible results to the extent it is able to (i) cover more of the forces that determine concepts and doctrines of law, (ii) improve the precision and comprehensiveness of the indicators measuring each of these forces, and (iii) directly measure the prescriptions and proscriptions of law.

Another aspect of the instant study that must not be overlooked is the type of data employed. Specifically, the study relied on time-spaced cross-sectional data, i.e., cross-sections of data on the independent variables that were prior in time to the cross-section of data on the dependent variable. While such data

102 For a general discussion of methodological issues in studies of the impact of jurisdiction characteristics on the concepts and doctrines of law, see THE PLACE OF LAW, *supra* note 10, at 458–69.

103 *Id.* at 458 & 469 n.8.

presumably allow causal relationships to be identified more readily than data from a single time point for all variables, time-spaced cross-sectional data are less likely to reveal causal connections than pooled time-series data on the independent variables and the dependent variable. Unfortunately, adequate time-series data are currently unavailable for the variables in the present study, a situation that can be expected to persist for many years.

In sum, the current study is at most a small step toward understanding the jurisdiction-level causes of law. These causes are of exceptional importance, however, and as such they warrant further investigation. History indicates that law has been an enduring institution in Western nations, and the permanence of law as an institution is evidence that law has deep roots in society. Because scholarship should not shy away from any topic, the societal roots of law on society-central activities deserve to be understood even though the discovery of these roots is likely to shatter the assumption in the popular paradigm for law that lasting concepts and doctrines of law are the product of individual personalities and politically inspired ideology. The macrosociological framework that is the foundation for the instant study thus mounts a challenge to the presently accepted view of law, and by focusing on basic conditions and large-scale shifts in societal systems, it will redirect the search for the determinants of the content of law. The challenge, I hope, will not be brushed aside. If it is summarily dismissed, it will not prompt the additional empirical research that is necessary to ascertain the utility of the proposed macrosociological framework, and an opposing view of a prominent institution will not have its day in court.

PART 2

Macrosociology, Law, and Societal Problems

CHAPTER 6

The Social Footing of the Great Recession

Abstract

In the instant chapter, I hypothesize that the recent economic contraction in the United States was due to the spread of social values favoring hedonism, materialism, and short-term rewards, i.e., social values emphasizing consumption and enjoyment. If the hypothesis is correct, the "Great Recession," as it is popularly known, was the economic outcome of a *social* change, and the lingering economic effects of the recession will not disappear until this change is reversed. Quantitative evidence indicates that the specified values became much more common in the U.S. population during the last third of the twentieth century. The evidence includes data from direct measures of the values and data on two economic precursors of the recession—human capital and personal debt—whose levels the values are presumed to affect. Further evidence is obtained through the macrosociological framework that was developed in Chapter 1. According to the framework, a substantially expanded or reduced presence of particular values in a society having a complex structure and democratic government alters the incidence of, and in turn the law on, the social behaviors molded by the values. The framework suggests that law is a window on society, and the instant chapter thus examines two social behaviors—premarital sexual intercourse among minors and marijuana use—that are logically a function of, inter alia, the values in the instant analysis. During a post-midcentury period that preceded the recession, the rates of both behaviors are found to have increased, and in line with the framework, the increases were followed by revisions of law designed to accommodate the behaviors or their consequences. The chapter concludes with a discussion of the long-term economic costs that the Great Recession may impose on Americans.

1 The Great Recession, Economics, and Sociology

Recent history has not been kind to the discipline of economics in the United States. Even if the role of macroeconomics in the latest contraction of economic activity—popularly labeled "the Great Recession"[1]—has not given credence to

1 Wikipedia, Great Recession, http://en.wikipedia.org/wiki/The_great_recession#cite_note-16 (last visited May 9, 2015).

 | DOI 10.1163/9789004281219_007

jokes about the discipline,[2] it has cast serious doubts on whether economics in general and macroeconomics in particular is in possession of the expertise required to formulate public policy that will promote, or at least not damage, the prosperity of the country.[3] In spite of its claims to such expertise, macroeconomic theory not only failed to anticipate the recent recession; macroeconomic theory led to public policy that evidently contributed to the onset of the recession.[4] Simply stated, macroeconomic policy was flawed because the theory that inspired it was flawed.

From an historical perspective, of course, the role of macroeconomics in the Great Recession was just one more instance of failure in science, for confidence in and a commitment to mistaken paradigms in science are not rare.[5] Some comfort, therefore, may be derived from history. However, macroeconomic policy, having proven faulty, is likely to benefit from assessments prepared in disciplines other than economics. In particular, there must be recognition of the societal setting in which macroeconomic policy is adopted and operates. An economy is rooted in, not separate from, the society in which it exists,[6] and macroeconomic policy cannot be divorced from its societal context. The macroeconomic policy that was implemented by Americans in the pre-recession period, therefore, would not have arisen fortuitously or

---

2 A collection of these jokes is in JEFF THREDGOLD, ON THE ONE HAND...: THE ECONOMIST'S JOKE BOOK (2001).

3 ANDREA RENDA, LAW AND ECONOMICS IN THE RIA WORLD: IMPROVING THE USE OF ECONOMIC ANALYSIS IN PUBLIC POLICY AND LEGISLATION 5–6 (2011); Robert J. Samuelson, *Macroeconomics Loses Its Magic*, WASHINGTON POST, April 22, 2013, at A17.

4 William K. Black, *Neo-Classical Economic Theories, Methodology, and Praxis Optimize Criminogenic Environments and Produce Recurrent, Intensifying Crises*, 44 CREIGHTON L. REV. 597, 597 (2011); Thomas Palley, *America's Flawed Paradigm: Macroeconomic Causes of the Financial Crisis and Great Recession*, 38 EMPIRICA 3 (2011).

5 George E. Smith, *Revisiting Accepted Science: The Indispensability of the History of Science*, 93 MONIST 545, 574 (2010).

6 Sociological theory has posited a strong economy-society connection. *E.g.*, ALEJANDRO PORTES, ECONOMIC SOCIOLOGY: A SYSTEMATIC INQUIRY 14–26 (2010); Milan Zafirovski, *Economic Sociology in Retrospect and Prospect: In Search of Its Identity within Economics and Sociology*, 58 AM. J. ECON. & SOCIOL. 583, 613–14, 616–17 (1999). Quantitative studies have found that aspects of an economy are responsive to sociological variables. LARRY D. BARNETT, THE PLACE OF LAW: THE ROLE AND LIMITS OF LAW IN SOCIETY 63 (2011) [hereinafter THE PLACE OF LAW] (summarizing the findings of quantitative studies of economic impacts of the level of trust in a society); Isabel Neira et al., *An Empirical Analysis of Social Capital and Economic Growth in Europe (1980–2000)*, 92 SOC. INDICATORS RES. 111, 124, 125–26 (2009) (finding that, in European nations, economic growth was affected by the level of trust and the extent of group memberships).

been imposed by a small group dedicated to advancing their own narrow interests. Rather, this policy was adopted, I believe, because it was consistent with, if not endorsed by, social values that Americans had come to accept. These values, which can account not just for public acceptance of the policy but also for the recession, are the principal focus of the instant chapter.

Looking backward in time, we find a strong, prominent movement during the 1980s to lessen regulation of the U.S. economy by the federal government.[7] Because reduced regulation was expected to increase prosperity,[8] the movement was in line with the emphasis on financial wealth that had been developing among Americans, as will be seen in *infra* Figure 6.2. Accordingly, studies that examine the Great Recession from the perspective of macrosociology, including its concern with social values, can improve our understanding of the recession in the United States and what it left behind.[9] Such studies, of course, will employ concepts and principles that are traditionally foreign to economics, but the studies should not be dismissed (or not undertaken) because they are outside the discipline that is currently entrusted to explain and resolve economic contractions. On the contrary, an approach that has been problematic should be supplemented by any new approach that demonstrates promise, a point that is relevant to macroeconomics whose theory and the policies it inspired need help.

As the instant chapter is being written, the onset of the recession in the United States is almost six years in the past and has been declared by the

---

7 Thomas Vocino, *American Regulatory Policy: Factors Affecting Trends Over the Past Century*, 31 POL'Y STUD. J. 441, 444, 446 (2003). The administration of President Ronald Reagan, which began in 1981 and ended in 1989, is often credited with initiating the movement toward less regulation of economic activity by the federal government in the United States. However, steps toward deregulation were taken earlier. *Id.* at 443–44. An indicator of the importance that President Reagan attached to curtailing regulation of the economy is that, in his inaugural address for his first term, he expressly directed attention to and was critical of extensive government regulation of business. Referring to "[t]he economic ills we suffer," Mr. Reagan said: "In this present crisis, government is not the solution to our problem; government is the problem." Ronald Wilson Reagan, First Inaugural Address (Jan. 20, 1981), *available at* http://millercenter.org/president/speeches (follow "Ronald Reagan" hyperlink). More than thirty years later, President Reagan continues to be known for this statement. *E.g.*, Ramesh Ponnuru, *Reaganism After Reagan*, N.Y. TIMES, Feb. 18, 2013, at A17.

8 Vocino, *supra* note 7, at 443.

9 The present chapter is based on a modified version of the sociological theory of functionalism. THE PLACE OF LAW, *supra* note 6, at 19, 302–07; Part 3, especially Part 3-a, of *supra* Chapter 2. The word "macrosociology" and the word "macrosociological" will be used in the present chapter as shorthand for this theory as modified.

federal government[10] to be over.[11] Nonetheless, a sizeable fraction of the population of the country is in a less-advantageous economic position than it was prior to the recession. In this regard, a survey conducted in January 2013 with a national probability sample of adults in the United States is revealing.[12] Of the approximately one in four survey respondents who had been terminated from a job during the recession,[13] almost one out of ten had been unsuccessful in obtaining a new job, and another one out of three required more than half a year to secure new employment.[14] Among those who lost a job during the recession and acquired another, slightly more than half (54%) were earning less in their new job, and fully a third of the lower-paid, reemployed respondents had taken a reduction in pay that exceeded 30%.[15] When respondents were asked to estimate the amount of time that would be needed for "you and your family to recover financially," about one out of four believed that at least half a decade would be necessary.[16] In looking ahead, therefore, many

---

10 The U.S. Department of Commerce has delegated to the National Bureau of Economic Research the responsibility for pinpointing the inception and termination dates of each business cycle. U.S. Dep't of Commerce, Bureau of Econ. Analysis, Recession: How Is That Defined?, http://www.bea.gov/faq/index.cfm?faq_id=485 (last visited May 9, 2015); Wikipedia, National Bureau of Economic Research, http://en.wikipedia.org/wiki/National_Bureau_of_Economic_Research (last visited May 9, 2015).

11 The National Bureau of Economic Research, through its Business Cycle Dating Committee, concluded that the Great Recession began in December 2007 and ended in June 2009. The period of economic contraction—the period from the highest to the lowest point of economic activity—thus lasted eighteen months, which is slightly longer than the next-longest contractions that have occurred since the late 1930s; two of these contractions each continued for sixteen months. Some contractions that happened before the 1930s, however, were as long as, or longer than, the Great Recession. Nat'l Bureau of Econ. Research, US Business Cycle Expansions and Contractions, http://www.nber.org/cycles.html (last visited May 9, 2015).

12 MARK SZELTNER ET AL., DIMINISHED LIVES AND FUTURES: A PORTRAIT OF AMERICA IN THE GREAT-RECESSION ERA (2013), http://www.heldrich.rutgers.edu/products/diminished-lives-and-futures-portrait-america-great-recession-era (on file with author). The sampling and data-gathering procedures of the survey are described in *id.* at 21–22 app. A.

13 *Id.* at 3 Tbl. 1, 38.

14 *Id.* at 38.

15 *Id.* at 5, 39.

16 *Id.* at 34 QFS14. However, most respondents who had not yet recovered may have substantially underestimated the length of their recovery period, because numerous factors may hold back the future growth of the U.S. economy and hence gains in personal wealth. Robert J. Gordon, *Is U.S. Economic Growth Over? Faltering Innovation Confronts the Six*

Americans do not expect that their current financial difficulties will be quickly overcome.

Aspects of the economic downturn, in short, linger even though the downturn itself has ended, and all of these aspects are unlikely to disappear quickly.[17] Notably, four years after the Great Recession formally ended,[18] the chairman of the Board of Governors of the U.S. Federal Reserve System, while acknowledging

---

Headwinds 15–19 (Nat'l Bureau of Econ. Research, Working Paper No. 18315, 2012). The factors include the debt burden of

i. Households. See the text accompanying *infra* notes 97–101.

ii. The federal government. See *infra* notes 179–85 and their accompanying text.

iii. State governments and local governments. See THE PLACE OF LAW, *supra* note 6, at 163–64.

Increases in personal wealth in the United States may also be hindered in the future by:

i. Demographic changes. Richard V. Burkhauser & Jeff Larrimore, *Median Income and Income Inequality: From 2000 and Beyond* 40–42 (2013), *available at* http://www.s4.brown.edu/us2010/Projects/Reports.htm.

ii. Deficiencies in intellectual skills. MADELINE J. GOODMAN ET AL., EDUC. TESTING SERV., AMERICA'S SKILLS CHALLENGE 4-5, 43 (2015); Gordon, *supra*, at 16–17, 19 Fig. 6.

iii. Income inequality. Barry Z. Cynamon & Steven M. Fazzari, *Inequality, the Great Recession, and Slow Recovery* 4–5 (Soc. Sci. Res. Network Working Papers Series, 2014), *available at* http://papers.ssrn.com/sol3/papers.cfm?abstract_id=2205524.

Although the gross domestic product (GDP) of the United States has increased since the recession, it has remained well below the GDP that would have resulted from a continuation of its pre-recession (2000–2007) course. The post-recession GDP has also been lower than its estimated potential even though this potential is less than the GDP that the pre-recession trend would have yielded. Dave Reifschneider et al., Aggregate Supply in the United States: Recent Developments and Implications for the Conduct of Monetary Policy 2, 8, 51–52, Fig. 1.1 (unpublished paper presented at the 14th Jacques Polak Annual Research Conference, Nov. 7–8, 2013) (on file with author), http://www.imf.org/external/np/res/seminars/2013/arc/pdf/wilcox.pdf. The gross domestic product of the United States represents "the total output of goods and services produced by labor and property located in the United States, valued at market prices." PROQUEST, LLC, PROQUEST STATISTICAL ABSTRACT OF THE UNITED STATES: 2013, at 447 (2013 ed., 2012).

17 *See* CARMEN M. REINHART & KENNETH S. ROGOFF, THIS TIME IS DIFFERENT: EIGHT CENTURIES OF FINANCIAL FOLLY 233–39 (2009). *See* Oddbjørn Raaum & Knut Røed, *Do Business Cycle Conditions at the Time of Labor Market Entry Affect Future Employment Prospects?*, 88 REV. ECON. & STAT. 193, 198 Fig. 3, 205–06 (2006) (finding in Norway that disadvantageous economic conditions at the time of labor-market entry raise the long-term likelihood of unemployment for the entering cohort).

18 The recession is considered to have ended in June 2009. *Supra* note 11.

that the job market was no longer at its bottom, described employment in the United States as "weak overall."[19] A comparison of the course of nonfarm employment following the onset of the Great Recession and the course of nonfarm employment after the onset of four other economic contractions experienced by the United States during the prior forty years demonstrates the unusual character of the Great Recession.[20] Relative to earlier contractions, the Great Recession involved a decline in employment that was larger in magnitude, longer in duration, and followed by appreciably smaller gains in jobs. In the words of the vice chair of the Board of Governors:

> [T]he Great Recession stands out both for the magnitude of the job losses that attended the downturn and for the weak recovery in employment that occurred after the recession ended.[21]

Because the labor market is integral to and has major ramifications for American society,[22] various yardsticks have been devised by the U.S. Bureau of Labor Statistics to gauge its condition at a single point in time and over time. The broadest measure of the extent of unemployment and underemployment in the United States that the Bureau has developed is Series U-6, which begins with calendar year 1994 and covers persons age 16 and older.[23] The unemployment-underemployment rate in Series U-6 includes (i) persons age 16 and older who

---

19 Ben S. Bernanke, Chairman, Bd. of Governors of the Federal Reserve System, Testimony Before the Joint Economic Committee, U.S. Congress: The Economic Outlook (May 22, 2013), http://www.federalreserve.gov/newsevents/testimony/bernanke20130522a.htm.

20 Janet L. Yellen, Vice Chair, Bd. of Governors of the Federal Reserve System, A Painfully Slow Recovery for America's Workers: Causes, Implications, and the Federal Reserve's Response (Feb. 11, 2013), at exhibit 2, http://www.federalreserve.gov/newsevents/speech/yellen20130211a.htm.

21 *Id.* In the United States, the Great Recession produced a large increase in rates of unemployment lasting 27 or more weeks, and the persons who experienced such unemployment encountered an inhospitable job market after the recession ended. Alan B. Krueger et al., *Are the Long-Term Unemployed on the Margins of the Labor Market?* 5, 19, 20 Fig. 4, 29–30, 31 Fig. 7, 37–41, 49–54 (Brookings Papers on Economic Activity, 2014), *available at* http://www.brookings.edu/about/projects/bpea/papers/2014/are-longterm-unemployed-margins-labor-market.

22 Wolfgang Streeck, *The Sociology of Labor Markets and Trade Unions*, *in* THE HANDBOOK OF ECONOMIC SOCIOLOGY 254, 254–56, 260–63 (Neil J. Smelser & Richard Swedberg eds., 2d ed. 2005).

23 Bureau of Labor Statistics, U.S. Dep't of Labor, Data Retrieval: Labor Force Statistics (CPS), http://www.bls.gov/webapps/legacy/cpsatab15.htm (select Series U-6 "Not seasonally adjusted" and "Seasonally adjusted" data).

are unemployed, (ii) persons age 16 and older who unwillingly find themselves at the margin of the labor force, and (iii) persons age 16 and older who are working part-time because the economy does not have full-time jobs for them.[24] From the onset of the recession[25] to date, the calendar-year Series U-6 rate—i.e., rate of unemployment and underemployment by year among persons 16 years of age and older—has been:[26]

Year	Series U-6 rate (%)
2007	8.3
2008	10.5
2009	16.2
2010	16.7
2011	15.9
2012	14.7
2013	13.8
2014	12.0

Unfortunately, the employment situation in the Great Recession, being visibly economic, is generally explained in terms of economics, and policies proposed to remedy the situation (and avoid a future repetition of it) focus on economic

24 The three categories of persons included in Series U-6 are defined by the Bureau of Labor Statistics as follows. Category (i) is comprised of persons who "do not have a job, have actively looked for work in the prior 4 weeks, and are currently available for work. Persons who were not working and were waiting to be recalled to a job from which they had been temporarily laid off are also included as unemployed." Bureau of Labor Statistics, U.S. Dep't of Labor, Labor Force Statistics from the Current Population Survey, http://www.bls.gov/cps/lfcharacteristics.htm (follow "All about unemployment" hyperlink). Category (ii), which is labeled "[p]ersons marginally attached to the labor force," covers persons "who currently are neither working nor looking for work but indicate that they want and are available for a job and have looked for work sometime in the past 12 months. Discouraged workers, a subset of the marginally attached, have given a job-market related reason for not currently looking for work." Bureau of Labor Statistics, U.S. Dep't of Labor, Data Retrieval: Labor Force Statistics (CPS), http://www.bls.gov/webapps/legacy/cpsatab15.htm. Category (iii) is comprised of persons "who want and are available for full-time work but have had to settle for a part-time schedule." *Id.*

25 December 2007 is considered to be the start of the recession. *Supra* note 11.

26 Bureau of Labor Statistics, U.S. Dep't of Labor, Data Retrieval: Labor Force Statistics (CPS), http://www.bls.gov/webapps/legacy/cpsatab15.htm (for measure U-6 in table A-15, select "Not seasonally adjusted" and "Retrieve data") (last visited May 9, 2015).

matters. The discipline of economics, therefore, dominates discussions of the recession and its aftermath, but the overriding concern with economics in general and macroeconomics in particular is, I believe, misplaced. In my view, the origin of the Great Recession in the United States, and the reason for the economic distress that has survived it, is to be found in society-level changes that lie outside the scope of economics. Otherwise stated, the Great Recession was the economic manifestation of an underlying social transformation that had taken place, and cannot be fully understood without an appreciation of the metamorphosis that had occurred in the social fabric. This appreciation, however, will not be possible unless the tools of macrosociology are enlisted for analyses of economic contractions. Regrettably, whether these tools will be accepted for such analyses is uncertain. The main reason for the uncertainty is that macroeconomics has captured the debate, a situation that in principle should change since macroeconomists have claimed much more expertise than the state of their discipline warrants. As one critic wrote eight years before the Great Recession, economists would do well to abandon their immodesty.[27]

A caveat, however, is necessary at this point. If sociology—or, more precisely, macrosociology—is essential to understanding the recession and its consequences, sociology cannot perform this task by itself. One obvious reason it cannot do so is that no single scientific discipline can possess all of the knowledge that is pertinent to a problem as massive as the Great Recession. Sociology, nonetheless, can supply key pieces of the puzzle. Unfortunately, sociology may be prevented from making contributions because serious difficulties, largely created by sociologists themselves, beset the discipline. Specifically, a substantial segment of those who presently label themselves sociologists reject science in favor of social ideology and political activism.[28] An ideology-motivated analysis, of course, begins with the ideology and intentionally selects facts that support the ideology; unlike a science, it does not involve either a careful acquisition of all available facts relevant to a problem or a dispassionate, critical assessment of these facts. Self-styled sociologists who engage in such analyses are thus incapable of explaining the Great Recession. However, these individuals impair not only their own reputation and credibility; through the process that psychologists label stimulus generalization, they

27 Robert Kuttner, *What Do You Call an Economist With A Prediction? Wrong*, BUSINESSWEEK, Sept. 6, 1999, at 22.

28 Jonathan H. Turner, *American Sociology in Chaos: Differentiation without Integration*, 37 AM. SOCIOLOGIST 15, 15, 26 (2006). *Accord*, THE PLACE OF LAW, *supra* note 6, at 149 n.216.

harm the reputation and credibility of all individuals linked to the discipline of sociology.[29] As a result, ideology-driven analyses by some individuals in sociology departments promote an avoidance of the entire discipline and a neglect of its potential contributions, and the individuals in sociology departments who are not politically motivated in their professional activities are less likely to be welcome when occasions arise to add to the explanation of major problems such as the recession. Not surprisingly, the academic reputation of sociology in U.S. universities is problematic.[30]

Given the magnitude of the Great Recession and the overriding importance of identifying its causes, the reputation of sociology should not deter reliance on the tools of the discipline and preclude the contributions they *can* make. Historians of the future may well treat the recession as a turning point in the

29 Sociology is not alone in being tied to political activism and political ideology in U.S. universities. Even more than sociology, "social movement" programs may be involved in such activism and ideology. By design, "Women's Studies, Ethnic Studies, and Queer Studies are subversive in their very nature and prepare their students to be as well." *Women's Studies is Not "Easy,"* Feminist Majority Foundation Choices Campus Blog (June 7, 2010), http://feministcampus.blogspot.com/2010/06/womens-studies-is-not-easy.html (last visited May 9, 2015). Women's Studies programs in particular seem to be devoted to promoting a political message and dominated by ideological bias. DAPHNE PATAI & NORETTA KOERTGE, PROFESSING FEMINISM: EDUCATION AND INDOCTRINATION IN WOMEN'S STUDIES (expanded ed. 2003).

In an examination of the University of California system, political activism and ideology were found mainly in academic departments and programs in the social sciences and humanities. CAL. ASS'N OF SCHOLARS, A CRISIS OF COMPETENCE: THE CORRUPTING EFFECT OF POLITICAL ACTIVISM IN THE UNIVERSITY OF CALIFORNIA: A REPORT PREPARED FOR THE REGENTS OF THE UNIVERSITY OF CALIFORNIA 41 (2012), *available at* http://www.nas.org/publications/reports (on file with author). Sociology, Political Science, Women's Studies, and Ethnic Studies were among the often-named individual departments and programs. *Id.* (various pages). Political activism and ideology, however, pose a greater risk to the status of sociology than to the status of social movement programs, because sociology claims that it is a social *science*; social movement programs seem to make no such claim. More generally, the teaching and research missions of a university as a whole may be damaged when political activism and ideology take hold in the classes of even some departments and programs. *Id.* at § 1.2.

Attributes of U.S. universities that are associated with the presence over time of social movement programs were the subject of a study by Lori A. Turk-Bicakci, The Development of Social Movement Programs and Departments In Higher Education: Women's and Ethnic Studies from 1975 to 2000 (2007) (unpublished Ph.D. dissertation, Univ. of California, Riverside) (on file with author).

30 Dennis J. Downey et al., *The Status of Sociology within the Academy: Where We Are, Why We're There, and How to Change It*, 39 AM. SOCIOLOGIST 193, 197–99 (2008).

history of the United States.[31] Accordingly, even though reticence about sociology is not without a factual basis, it is likely to prove counterproductive. Over the last five decades, sociologists have markedly augmented their data sets and improved their statistical techniques. The result is that today quantitatively oriented sociologists who are not politically motivated have the ability to study a broader array of topics than they could even a few decades ago, and can do so with greater rigor. The concepts and data of sociology thus promise to advance human understanding of a host of problems, including the recession.

Let me turn now to the societal change that I posit as the origin of the Great Recession in the United States. Specifically, I trace the recession to an expanded prevalence of hedonism and materialism and to a more-frequent emphasis on short-term results and rewards.[32] To the extent that these social values[33] spread across the population of a society, personal consumption and the pursuit of enjoyment will presumably become more common. Indeed, these values are thought to be present in and the foundation of the phenomenon known as consumerism,[34] and because there is some empirical evidence that the values are correlated,[35] I will treat them as a set.

---

31 Daniel N. Lipson, *Is the Great Recession Only the Beginning? Economic Contraction in an Age of Fossil Fuel Depletion and Ecological Limits to Growth*, 33 New Pol. Sci. 555, 572, 575 (2011).

32 The recession can be examined in the context of the human demand for fossil fuels, especially petroleum, and the quantities of these fuels that are procurable. *Id.* at 559–60, 562, 569–72. However, the increase in the nationwide prevalence of the specified social values, which I document in the text *infra*, was apparently not restrained by resource limitations or other environmental considerations. Notably, educational efforts that focus on environmental problems do not have a lasting influence on attitudes toward and concern with the problems. Chen-Yin Tung et al., *The Effects of Different Environmental Education Programs on the Environmental Behavior of Seventh-Grade Students and Related Factors*, J. Envtl. Health, March 2002, at 25, 28.

33 Values are the yardsticks by which aspects of social life are judged and their worth is determined. Unlike attitudes, which are preferences for specific outcomes in particular contexts, values have broad application and are moral commands. Values are thus beliefs that serve as touchstones in social life and that are prevalent (even if not universally held) in a society. Stavroula Tsirogianni & George Gaskell, *The Role of Plurality and Context in Social Values*, 41 J. Theory of Soc. Behav. 441, 442 (2011).

34 John O'Shaughnessy & Nicholas Jackson O'Shaughnessy, *Marketing, the Consumer and Hedonism*, 36 European J. Marketing 524, 525, 544 (2002).

35 Helga Dittmar & Rod Bond, *"I want it and I want it now": Using a Temporal Discounting Paradigm to Examine Predictors of Consumer Impulsivity*, 101 British J. Psychol. 751, 763, 768, 771 (2010) (finding that impulsiveness in buying consumer items that convey identity is associated with materialism and hedonism, which were measured by the Scale

The centerpiece of the instant chapter is data on the extent to which the social values of consumption and enjoyment were present in the United States since the middle of the twentieth century. Thus, *infra* Part 4 will report data from large-scale sample surveys whose questionnaires directly measured the values, i.e., measured the values apart from specific behaviors. Part 5 and Part 6 will provide quantitative data on the incidence over time of behaviors that logically are manifestations of, inter alia, the values in the set. No single behavior is a perfect measure of the values, of course; each behavior by itself undoubtedly captures not just the specified values but also other factors operating in social life. Nonetheless, the behaviors on which I focus in Part 5 and Part 6 are plausible gauges of the values, and in combination they and the data in Part 4 strengthen the view that the values became more widespread in the United States during the last third of the twentieth century. If social values favoring consumption and enjoyment spread in the U.S. population at this time, the argument gains credence that the values were key to the onset and aftermath of the Great Recession.

2 Macrosociology and Social Values

From a macrosociological perspective, social values serve as benchmarks that the members of a society use in navigating the many facets of the society. In doing so, social values shape the behavior of the members, and because the values are widely held and persist over time, the behaviors they create are broad and enduring. Social values, in short, impose certain perspectives on the situations that the members of a society encounter[36] and generate continuing patterns of behavior that help to define the society. Some of these patterns will be discussed in *infra* Part 5 and Part 6 of the chapter.

But what does the concept of social values contribute to macrosociology? In a science, a concept is worthwhile only insofar as it improves the ability of the science to predict and explain. If macrosociology benefits from the concept of social values, it presumably does so because, inter alia, changes that occur in social values in a structurally complex, democratically governed society are

discussed in *infra* note 91); Serdar Karabati & Zeynep Cemalcilar, *Values, Materialism, and Well-Being: A Study with Turkish University Students*, 31 J. ECON. PSYCHOL. 624, 630 Tbl. 2, 631 (2010) (finding that materialism increased with hedonism and characterizing materialism as a desire for social status and pleasure).

36 John F. Stolte & Shanon Fender, *Framing Social Values: An Experimental Study of Culture and Cognition*, 70 SOC. PSYCHOL. Q. 59 (2007).

followed at some point by an increased or decreased incidence of important behavioral forms that incorporate the values. In turn, the altered incidence of these behaviors in a society can modify the law that the society applies to the behaviors.

In the instant chapter, Part 5 will examine two *economic* variables in the United States that, I believe, were affected by the shift in the social values with which the chapter is concerned. Because these variables became economic precursors of the Great Recession, Part 5 aims to promote recognition of the role that the social values played in the recession.

Part 6 extends the analysis to the content of law but does so for behavioral variables that are *social* aspects of American society. If that content is macrosociological in its origin and nature, as I believe it is,[37] the concepts and doctrines of law that are applied to society-central behaviors in a modern nation reveal the character of the society in which the law developed and operates. Law, in other words, serves as a window on society. Its ability to do so, however, requires that a society be a system, i.e., a set of components that are interrelated rather than independent.[38] If a society is a system, as my macrosociological approach assumes, the same or similar social values can be expected across the various components of a society. Indeed, a society probably cannot be a system without common social values. The social values shaping the economic behaviors that led to the Great Recession, some of which behaviors will be the subject of Part 5, are thus likely to exist concurrently in certain social behaviors, too. Part 6 examines social activities that arise from these values and the law addressing the activities.

A brief discussion is in order regarding a substantive distinction between Part 5 and Part 6. While both Parts deal with the social values that I have posited as the underlying causes of the recession, the Parts diverge in a notable way—Part 5 is concerned with behaviors that are economic in nature and Part 6 considers behaviors that are social. I separate economic aspects from social aspects because of inherent differences between them.[39] Although the dividing line between the economic sphere and the social sphere may not be simple to locate—perhaps because the line varies across time and contexts—it is generally conceded to exist. Furthermore, the economic-social dichotomy helps to introduce two significant points. First, a major change in the incidence of a

37 *Supra* Chapter 1, at Part 1–b.

38 The components are institutions, which are discussed in The Place of Law, *supra* note 6, at 43–44, 152, 200, 394.

39 Larry D. Barnett, Legal Construct, Social Concept: A Macrosociological Perspective on Law 162–63 (1993) [hereinafter Legal Construct].

behavior is more often considered an exigency by the public when the change involves an economic activity than when it involves a social activity. Sensitivity to economic matters, however, may cause social matters that are equally important in the societal system to receive much less attention. For understanding human affairs, the result is regrettable, because a society is capable of being severely damaged by its social aspects,[40] and these aspects may inflict at least as much damage as changes in the economy. All types of threats to a society, therefore, merit recognition and study. Second, my hypothesis regarding the role of changed social values in the Great Recession is grounded in a macrosociological framework that is focused chiefly on the social aspects of a society.[41] The framework thus involves the assumption that a society is an integrated whole, and further contends that social aspects of the society can shape its economic aspects. To illustrate an economic phenomenon that I believe was driven by a social phenomenon, I focus on the Great Recession. In my view, the recession was an economic problem that developed from a remodeling of the social fabric. In such a case, the tools of macroeconomics are insufficient by themselves. For penetrating the surface of the problem, the tools of macrosociology are also necessary.

3 Macrosociology and Law

In furnishing evidence that the recession was preceded by an expanded prevalence of social values encouraging consumption and enjoyment, I supplement an article that I completed early in the recession.[42] The evidence is presented in *infra* Parts 4, 5, and 6. The three Parts, however, employ different approaches. Part 6 considers the content (concepts and doctrines) of law on society-important social behaviors[43] and relies on a framework for this content that I formalized since completing the earlier article. The framework is pertinent not only to Part 6, however. It is also pertinent to Part 4, because Part 4 sets the stage for

40 Shanker Satyanath et al., *Bowling for Fascism: Social Capital and the Rise of the Nazi Party in Weimar Germany, 1919–33* (Nat'l Bureau of Econ. Research, Working Paper No. 19201, 2013), *available at* http://www.nber.org/papers/w19201.

41 *Supra* Chapter 1.

42 Larry D. Barnett, *The Financial Sector Upheaval of 2008: Sociological Antecedents and Their Implications for Investment Company Regulation*, 5 HASTINGS BUS. L.J. 229, 239–47 (2009). An updated version of this article is in THE PLACE OF LAW, *supra* note 6, at Ch. 4.

43 The propositions that I believe describe the macrosociological nature of the content of law—at least the propositions that can currently be derived from well-designed quantitative studies—are enumerated in *supra* Chapter 1, at Part 1-b.

the social behaviors considered in Part 6 and because the content of law can be expected to respond to, inter alia, social values that are measured directly, i.e., without reference to particular behaviors.[44] Data from such direct measures, as explained in the last paragraph of *supra* Part 1, are reported in Part 4. Accordingly, a brief introduction to the framework is warranted at this point, i.e., before we reach Part 4.

Two lines of quantitative social science research are essential to the framework. The first is concerned with the impact of law on the incidence of the activities that law has targeted for regulation, while the second is concerned with the impact that sociological, economic, and demographic characteristics of jurisdictions (nations and states) have on the concepts and doctrines of law in those jurisdictions. The first line thus deals with the effects of law, and the second line deals with the causes of law. Notably, a sizeable body of well-designed studies in the first line has found that, in jurisdictions whose structure is complex and whose government is democratic, law that is designed to regulate society-important activities generally has no more than a temporary and/or small influence on the occurrence of the activities.[45] This finding suggests that the content of law on society-important activities is (at least under some conditions) a response to change in the incidence of the activities. In doing so, the finding enhances the importance of studies in the second line of research.[46]

Let us turn, then, to the second line of research. An understanding of this line is its premise that the concepts and doctrines of law for society-central activities in a jurisdiction with a complex structure and a democratic government are the product of society-level conditions and attributes. Under the premise, the content of law on society-important activities in a modern nation[47] does not arise fortuitously, cannot be explained by the political process, and is not due to particular (or even prominent) individuals. Instead, large-scale forces (e.g., the long-term growth of knowledge[48]), and the conditions that

44 The Place of Law, *supra* note 6, at 223–30.

45 Citations to the studies are collected in Appendix B to *supra* Chapter 1. The studies supporting this conclusion are now more numerous than the studies that led me to the same conclusion in a much earlier work. Legal Construct, *supra* note 39, at 17, 25, 26–36, 161–66.

46 Known studies dedicated to the second line are listed in Appendix A to *supra* Chapter 1.

47 For convenience, I will use the phrases "modern nation" and "modern society" to refer to a setting in which social life is structurally complex and the government is democratic.

48 Text accompanying notes 109–11 and 123–25 in *supra* Chapter 2. The word "knowledge" is defined in note 109 in *supra* Chapter 2.

these forces create, are the source of law,[49] although the forces usually intensify and spread at a slow pace and hence do not immediately generate the concepts and doctrines of law that a society uses. In the language of social science, the content of law in a modern society is a dependent variable, not an independent variable, and the time lag involved in the response of law to change in the societal setting is typically considerable.

The premise behind the second line of research is, of course, significant for building sociological theory on law, but it also has a practical application. Specifically, if the character and problems of a society are manifested in the content of its law, as the premise contends, the former are detectible in and can be inferred from the latter. Judicial decisions, legislation, and administrative-agency rules can thus disclose the nature of and developments in the society that gave birth to them. Law, in short, can be used to observe conditions in the social system.[50]

4 Pre-Recession Change in Social Values

I will draw chiefly on two yearly nationwide surveys for direct measures of the social values—hedonism, materialism, and an emphasis on short-term results and rewards—that I posit as the underlying cause of the Great Recession. The surveys are the Monitoring the Future (MTF) study and the American Freshman (AF) study. In all or almost all of the years since the inception of each study, the questionnaire in the MTF study has included the same items, as has the questionnaire in the AF study. I will rely on these repeatedly used items, but for a number of reasons (see below), I believe the data from the MTF study are more helpful.

Before turning to the two studies, however, a word of caution is in order. The data from both studies that I present below are in the form of trends, and while the trends are consistent with my hypothesis that an increased occurrence of social values endorsing consumption and enjoyment brought on the Great Recession, the data do not definitively prove the hypothesis. The reason is that the trends in the values have not been linked to the onset of the recession

49 *See* Grant Gilmore, *Products Liability: A Commentary*, 38 U. CHI. L. REV. 103, 107, 116 (1970). To explain inconsistent judicial reasoning in two breach-of-warranty cases that were separated by more than a century and hence arose in different historical eras, Professor Gilmore hypothesized that "what had changed…was not so much the law as the societies which the law reflects" and suggested that "most cases—perhaps all cases—are sensibly, or even 'correctly,' decided as of their own time and place." *Id.* at 107.

50 Illustrations are in Part 6 *infra*.

through a statistical test that controls possible effects of other changes that took place in the United States during the same period. The other changes were undoubtedly having impacts on American society, and these impacts must be statistically removed before the contribution of the shift in social values to the recession can be credibly estimated.

The findings I report here from the MTF study are for high school seniors, i.e., students who expect to receive a high school diploma at the end of the current school year. In every year since 1975, the study has selected a set of public high schools and private high schools through a procedure (multistage cluster sampling) that is designed to produce a representative sample of all high school seniors in the continental United States, and twelfth-grade students in the participating schools have completed the questionnaire for the study in the Spring.[51] However, because the MTF study is confined to currently enrolled students, it omits the 15% to 20% of teenagers who have withdrawn from school prior to their final semester of high school.[52]

In every year, the questionnaire for the MTF study has elicited the views that high school seniors hold toward work and leisure. The views were measured by a set of statements to which respondents were asked to react by choosing one of five alternatives, namely, "Disagree," "Mostly Disagree," "Mostly Agree," "Agree," or "Neither" disagree or agree. With regard to the values on which I am focusing, at least one is plausibly measured by the statement that "To me, work is nothing more than making a living."[53] The wording of this statement, as well as its placement in the questionnaire,[54] makes the statement a credible barometer of hedonism, and responses to the statement are thus the subject of Figure 6.1. Specifically, Figure 6.1 shows the percentage of male high school seniors and of female high school seniors who, in every year from 1975 through 2011,[55] reported that their view on the statement was

---

51 Jerald G. Bachman et al., *The Monitoring The Future Project After Thirty-Seven Years: Design and Procedures* 2, 6–9, 28–31 (Univ. of Michigan Inst. for Soc. Res., Occasional Paper No. 76, 2011), http://monitoringthefuture.org (follow "Publications" hyperlink and then "Occasional Papers" hyperlink). The sample each year includes approximately 14,000 to 18,000 high school seniors in 120 to 140 high schools. *Id.* at 2.

52 *Id.* at 7.

53 The statement is item #8060 in the questionnaire that the study used each year.

54 THE PLACE OF LAW, *supra* note 6, at 185 n.49.

55 Figure 6.1 covers all of the years for which sex-specific data on the statement have thus far been published. Figure 6.1 is an updated and revised version of a graph in each of the following publications and is reproduced with permission of the publisher: Larry D. Barnett, *The Financial Sector Upheaval of 2008: Sociological Antecedents and Their Implications for Investment Company Regulation*, 5 HASTINGS BUS. L.J. 229, 242 Fig. 2

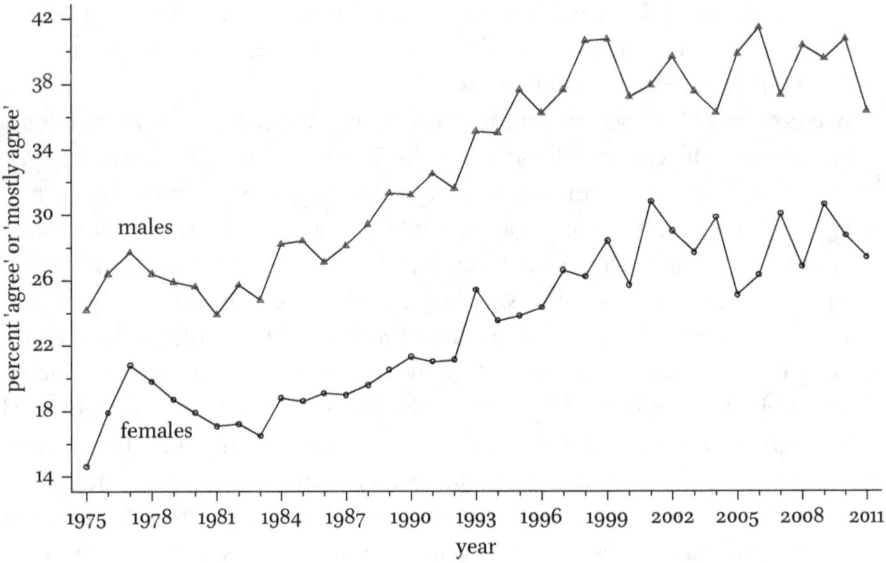

FIGURE 6.1 *Prevalence of hedonism, high school seniors: "To me, work is nothing more than making a living"*
SOURCE: SEE FN. 55 AND 56 IN THIS CHAPTER.

represented by the alternatives "Agree" or "Mostly Agree."[56] Because both alternatives are plausible indicators of hedonism, the vertical axis in the figure combines them. The Figure thus traces across time the percentage of high school seniors of each sex who thought that "work is nothing more than making a living" and, in doing so, gave a response suggestive of hedonism.

As is apparent in Figure 6.1, the trend in the responses of males (top line) corresponds to the trend in the responses of females (bottom line). Although the percentages exhibiting hedonism are consistently higher for males than for females, the Figure shows that both sexes had similar changes over time. Especially notable is the secular expansion of hedonism that begins in the first half of the 1980s and ends in the last half of the 1990s. In addition, after the spread of hedonism came to a halt, the extent of hedonism did not shrink but,

---

(2009) (© 2009 University of California, Hastings College of the Law); LARRY D. BARNETT, THE PLACE OF LAW: THE ROLE AND LIMITS OF LAW IN SOCIETY 160 Fig. 4.3 (2011) (© 2011 Transaction Publishers).

56 The data for Figure 6.1 were obtained from the Reference Volumes of the Monitoring the Future study. The Reference Volumes are listed at http://monitoringthefuture.org/pubs.html#refvols.

instead, leveled off. Over the two-and-a-half decades that preceded the Great Recession, then, the prevalence of hedonism underwent a sustained advance but did not experience a sustained retreat.

We now leave high school seniors and consider students who are enrolled in their first year of tertiary education in the United States. Of course, first-year students in U.S. colleges and universities, although drawn mainly from graduates of U.S. high schools, are not a randomly selected sample of these graduates. Moreover, in terms of their social, economic, and demographic attributes, students in first-year classes in U.S. colleges and universities are likely to have changed substantially over time, because the percentage of high-school graduates who matriculate in a U.S. college or university has undergone a secular increase since the middle of the twentieth century. For instance, while just half of all high-school graduates pursued tertiary education in the mid-1960s, two-thirds did so by the middle of the first decade of the twenty-first century.[57] As a result, the social, economic, and demographic composition of first-year classes in U.S. colleges and universities may not be fully comparable across time,[58] a possibility that should be kept in mind when considering data on trends in the social values expressed by samples of first-year students in tertiary education.

With the preceding caveat in mind, let us consider data from the American Freshman (AF) study. The AF study, which has been conducted almost every year since 1966, samples first-year students in U.S. colleges and universities that (i) grant baccalaureate degrees, (ii) are included in a Fall student-enrollment file maintained by the U.S. Department of Education for a higher education data-collection program operated by the Department, and (iii) had a freshman class of no less than twenty-five full-time first-time (FTFT) students.[59] The data

---

57 Bureau of Labor Statistics, U.S. Dep't of Labor, College Enrollment Up Among 2009 High School Grads (2010), http://www.bls.gov/opub/ted/2010/ted_20100428.htm (follow "[Chart data]" hyperlink) (on file with author) (last visited May 9, 2015).

58 Estimates of change in U.S. high-school completion rates since the middle of the twentieth century are in James J. Heckman & Paul A. LaFontaine, *The American High School Graduation Rate: Trends and Levels*, 92 REV. ECON. & STAT. 244 (2010). Change in overall high-school completion rates is not the sole factor that can affect the composition of classes of first-year classes of students in tertiary education and reduce the comparability of the latter classes across time. Additional factors that can do so are differential change between subpopulations in birth rates and high-school completion rates and change in the volume of, and/or in the countries of origin of, immigrants (lawful and unlawful).

59 JOHN H. PRYOR ET AL., THE AMERICAN FRESHMAN: FORTY YEAR TRENDS 205 (2007), *available at* http://www.heri.ucla.edu/tfsPublications.php (follow "Trends Monographs" hyperlink) (on file with author) [hereinafter FORTY YEAR TRENDS].

reported below are for FTFT first-year students at colleges and universities from which samples could be drawn that were deemed to be representative of the FTFT populations at the colleges and universities,[60] and have been weighted in order to adjust for nonparticipation by students in, and nonparticipation by, colleges and universities.[61] The survey questionnaires were completed by the students very early in their first year, viz., during the registration period, during orientation for first-year students, or during the initial weeks of classes.[62]

Figure 6.2 shows, by year, the percentage of all FTFT male students and the percentage of all FTFT female students who, when presented with a list of goals and asked to "indicate the importance to you personally" of each, rated "being very well-off financially" as either "essential" or "very important."[63] Notably, the statement of this goal includes the word "very" and, in doing so, gives emphasis to financial success. The statement is thus a plausible measure of materialism as a social value. Data on respondents who rated the goal as "essential" or "very important" are available by sex for all but two years from 1966 through 2013.[64]

---

60 FORTY YEAR TRENDS, *supra* note 59, at 208.

61 *Id.* at 210, 212.

62 *Id.* at 208.

63 For every specified goal, the questionnaire asked respondents to choose one of the following four alternatives: "Essential," "Very Important," "Somewhat Important," "Not Important." *Id.* at 220, 224.

64 The missing years are 1973 and 1988. Data for the years 1966 through 2006 (other than 1973 and 1988) are in FORTY YEAR TRENDS, *supra* note 59, at 126–27, 180–81. Data for years after 2006 are in individual-year reports. The latter reports are available at http://www.heri.ucla.edu/tfsPublications.php (follow "Freshman Monographs" hyperlink). The reports are:

2007: JOHN H. PRYOR ET AL., THE AMERICAN FRESHMAN: NATIONAL NORMS FOR FALL 2007, at 58, 80 (2007).

2008: JOHN H. PRYOR ET AL., THE AMERICAN FRESHMAN: NATIONAL NORMS FOR FALL 2008, at 17, 64 (2008).

2009: JOHN H. PRYOR ET AL., THE AMERICAN FRESHMAN: NATIONAL NORMS FALL 2009, at 63, 87 (expanded ed. 2009).

2010: JOHN H. PRYOR ET AL., THE AMERICAN FRESHMAN: NATIONAL NORMS FALL 2010, at 62, 86 (expanded tables) (2011).

2011: JOHN H. PRYOR ET AL., THE AMERICAN FRESHMAN: NATIONAL NORMS FALL 2011, at 65, 91 (expanded ed. 2011).

2012: JOHN H. PRYOR ET AL., THE AMERICAN FRESHMAN: NATIONAL NORMS FALL 2012, at 69, 95 (expanded ed. 2012).

2013: KEVIN EAGAN ET AL., THE AMERICAN FRESHMAN: NATIONAL NORMS FALL 2013, at 66, 92 (expanded ed. 2013).

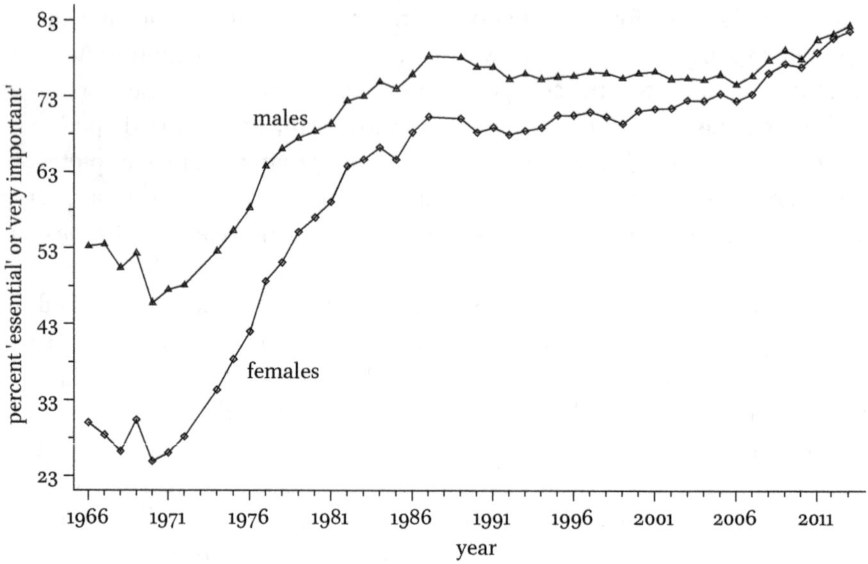

FIGURE 6.2 *Prevalence of materialism, first-year full-time students in tertiary education: "Being very well-off financially"*
SOURCE: SEE FN. 59 AND 64 IN THIS CHAPTER.

What can be gleaned from Figure 6.2? Trends over time are seen in the two lines of the figure—in the top line for males and in the bottom line for females—and clearly the trends do not differ materially by sex. A strong interest in accumulating substantial wealth becomes much more common among males and among females throughout the 1970s, and the increase continues into the 1980s. However, during the last half of the 1980s, the extent of the interest reaches a plateau that continues through the years that preceded the Great Recession.[65] Significantly, after the interest in amassing considerable

65 Some evidence that the "being very well off financially" goal, as it was worded in the questionnaire, was a valid measure of materialism can be gleaned from trends in responses to another questionnaire item. Specifically, the percentages choosing "essential" or "very important" for the "being very well off financially" goal follow a course over time that is the opposite of the course taken by the percentages selecting "essential" or "very important" for the goal of "Developing a meaningful philosophy of life." The latter goal has been included in the AF questionnaire since 1967. For both goals, the alternatives listed in *supra* note 63 were used in the questionnaire. FORTY YEAR TRENDS, *supra* note 59, at 72, 224. The percentage of all respondents who considered a "meaningful philosophy of life" to be an "essential" or "very important" personal goal declined concurrently with increases in the percentage of all respondents who believed that the wealth-accumulation goal was

wealth stops spreading in the late 1980s, its prevalence does not markedly diminish.

The above findings from the AF study are complemented by the conclusion reached in an analysis (a "meta-study") of eighty-five samples of U.S. college students in which narcissism was measured at various time points over a period that covered more than twenty-five years and ended in 2006.[66] Narcissism is relevant to the set of social values that I have posited as antecedents of the Great Recession, because individuals who are high in narcissism seek quick personal and social gratification rather than pursue long-term goals.[67] In each of the eighty-five samples included in the analysis, narcissism was gauged with the forty-item version of the Narcissistic Personality Inventory, a widely used psychological test[68] of, inter alia, the degree to which individuals have an expectation of entitlement as well as an inclination to fulfill personal goals by exploiting other people.[69] The Inventory is also likely to measure impulsiveness, which evidently varies directly with narcissism.[70]

While the samples covered by the analysis were not necessarily drawn randomly from the entire population of U.S. college students, they nonetheless revealed a trend that has some similarities to the trend observed in Figure 6.1. To be exact, the mean narcissism score increased steadily beginning in the 1980s, and continued to rise through the last year in the time series (viz., 2006).[71] The change is illustrated by the larger percentage of college students who had a narcissism score that was at least one standard deviation above the mean score attained in the period 1979–1985. In 1979–1985, this percentage was equal to one out of 6.7 college students, but by 2006, this percentage was equal to one out of 4.2 college students.[72] During the quarter of a century that

---

"essential" or "very important," and the percentages rating the two goals in this way reached plateaus at approximately the same time. *Id.* at 32 Fig. 14.

66 Jean M. Twenge et al., *Egos Inflating Over Time: A Cross-Temporal Meta-Analysis of the Narcissistic Personality*, 76 J. PERSONALITY 875, 880–81 (2008).

67 Simine Vazire & David C. Funder, *Impulsivity and the Self-Defeating Behavior of Narcissists*, 10 PERSONALITY & SOC. PSYCHOL. REV. 154, 160–61 (2006).

68 Twenge et al., *supra* note 66, at 877, 881.

69 Robert A. Ackerman et al., *What Does the Narcissistic Personality Inventory Really Measure?*, 18 ASSESSMENT 67, 70, 82–83 (2011); Nida Corry et al., *The Factor Structure of the Narcissistic Personality Inventory*, 90 J. PERSONALITY ASSESSMENT 593, 594 Tbl. 1, 598 (2008).

70 Vazire & Funder, *supra* note 67, at 157 Tbl. 1, 158, 162.

71 Twenge et al., *supra* note 66, at 882 Fig. 1, 883 Fig. 2.

72 Calculated from *id.* at 884. In both calculations, the reference is the 1979–1985 mean score. Approximately 15% of college students in 1979–1985, and 24% of college students in 2006, had a score that exceeded the 1979–1985 mean by one standard deviation or more. *Id.*

preceded the Great Recession, accordingly, a high level of narcissism became much more frequent among students in tertiary education in the United States.

To summarize, the findings I have presented from the Monitoring the Future surveys, the American Freshman surveys, and the meta-study of narcissism among college students are based on direct measures of the social values that I posited as antecedents of the Great Recession, i.e., are derived from responses to questionnaire items that gauge commitment to hedonism, materialism, and near-term rewards and results without referring to specific behaviors. However, while revealing long-term changes in social values, the trends disclosed by these sources were not temporally in lockstep; rather, the trends diverged with regard to when they started and when they ended. The divergence is perhaps attributable partially to the use of a single indicator for each social value. No indicator, however, can be a perfect measure of a social value. For instance, many social values may have two or more dimensions, and a particular indicator may be an accurate measure of just one of the dimensions. In addition, an indicator may pick up not just the social value it is thought to measure but other social values as well. Consequently, multiple indicators of a phenomenon are needed when drawing a conclusion regarding a trend in a social value. Unfortunately, multiple indicators were unavailable for each of the social values that are of interest here.

Readers should also keep in mind the limitations imposed on the instant chapter by the availability of data. A trend can be depicted only with data that cover a long period of time, but time-series measures of social values that extend back to the 1970s, let alone to the 1960s, are scarce. The foregoing point is critical to a macrosociological examination of the United States during the third quarter of the twentieth century (1950 through 1974). If patterns of social activities and the content of law in a structurally complex, democratically governed society are shaped partially by social values, as I contend,[73] data that cover many decades are essential because social values change at a slow pace. Not surprisingly, then, the numerous gaps and many unknowns in currently available quantitative measures of social values during the third quarter of the twentieth century pose major impediments to depicting changes in values in this historical period and to understanding their societal consequences.

Given the above caveats, can my hypothesis regarding the role in the Great Recession of social values encouraging consumption and enjoyment take any comfort from the data presented? Certainly, the hypothesis is not contradicted by the data from the Monitoring the Future study, the American Freshman study, and the meta-study of narcissism among college students. Indeed, a picture

---

73 Part 1-b and Part 3 in *supra* Chapter 1.

emerges that, although admittedly painted with broad strokes, is compatible with the hypothesis. Specifically, the share of Americans who were desirous of consuming, in the near term, a variety of goods and services was substantially larger when the twentieth century ended than three decades earlier. In an interval that is brief historically, the data disclose, far more Americans came to accept consumption for its own sake and to spurn consumption limited to acquisitions that, after being critically assessed, were chosen for expected long-run economic returns. Among the Americans who adopted these social values, decisions regarding consumption would not have involved cost-benefit analyses, and practicality would not have been regarded as important. Enjoyment, instead, would have been a central motivation. Such broad social changes are capable of inflicting severe damage on the economy.

5 Pre-Recession Economic Manifestations of the Change in Values

To underscore the importance to the Great Recession of social values that endorse consumption and enjoyment, I next examine two economic variables—human capital and personal debt. While the behavior that produces human capital differs from the behavior that produces personal debt, both types of behavior can be considered manifestations of, inter alia, the prevalence of hedonism, materialism, and an emphasis on near-term rewards. As economic forerunners of the recession, the behaviors are helpful in understanding the social foundation of the recession.

a *Human Capital*

Human capital is the ability of labor to be economically productive, and not surprisingly, human capital varies between individuals, between subpopulations in a given population, and between populations.[74] Human capital, however, is not a phenomenon with a single dimension. Rather, types of human capital exist and affect economic productivity. Unfortunately, economists have usually measured human capital by the number of years of schooling completed,[75] i.e., have relied on an overall yardstick of human capital, but the earnings of workers[76]

74 José Lobo & David P. Smole, *Stratification and Spatial Segregation of Human Capital as Determinants of Metropolitan Productivity in the United States*, 39 URBAN STUD. 529 (2002).

75 *Id.* at 531.

76 Eric A. Hanushek & Ludger *Woessmann, The Role of Cognitive Skills in Economic Development*, 46 J. ECON. LITERATURE 607, 638, 657 (2008); Richard J. Murnane et al., *Do Different Dimensions of Male High School Students' Skills Predict Labor Market Success a*

and the economic expansion of nations[77] have been found to depend heavily on type of human capital, including academic skills in science and mathematics.[78] Type of human capital is an especially important matter in the United States, where high skill levels in science and mathematics are much less common than in many other nations.[79] Although not widely appreciated, the deficiency in these skills among Americans has been imposing a substantial cost on the country in the form of foregone economic growth.[80] Moreover, a cohort of individuals that leaves school with a deficiency in an intellectual skill remains in the population for decades[81] and is likely to be followed by other cohorts with the same deficiency. Economic losses thus cumulate over time.

Given the importance of including skill type in any assessment of the human capital of a nation, what is a suitable indicator of human capital in the U.S. population at a single point in time and over time? Obviously, a perfect indicator cannot be devised, and every indicator will be flawed in certain ways. Nonetheless, I believe a useful indicator is offered by the percentage of all Bachelor's degrees each year that are awarded in four fields: (i) earth, atmospheric, and ocean sciences (e.g., geology, meteorology, and oceanography); (ii) physical sciences (e.g., astronomy, chemistry, and physics); (iii) biological sciences (e.g., botany, genetics, physiology, and zoology); and (iv) mathematics (including statistics). Adhering to convention, I label the foregoing fields as the "natural sciences"[82] and mathematics. Although the fields were selected a priori,

---

Decade Later? Evidence from the NLSY, 20 ECON. EDUC. REV. 311, 314, 316 (2001); Yujia Liu & David B. Grusky, *The Payoff to Skill in the Third Industrial Revolution*, 118 AM. J. SOCIOL. 1330, 1367–68 (2013).

77 Hanushek & Woessmann, *supra* note 76, at 638, 657–58; Chun-Li Tsai et al., *Human Capital Composition and Economic Growth*, 99 SOC. INDICATORS RES. 41, 43, 57 (2010).

78 Hanushek & Woessmann, *supra* note 76, at 638, 657–58; Murnane, *supra* note 76, at 314, 316; Tsai et al., *supra* note 77, at 43, 57.

79 Eric A. Hanushek et al., *U.S. Math Performance in Global Perspective: How Well Does Each State Do at Producing High-Achieving Students?* 8, 12 (Harvard Univ. Program on Educ. Pol'y and Governance & Education Next, Report No. 10–19, 2010), *available at* http://www.hks.harvard.edu/pepg (follow "Research" hyperlink); Paul E. Peterson et al., *Globally Challenged: Are U.S. Students Ready to Compete? The Latest on Each State's International Standing in Math and Reading* 5–6, 8 (Harvard Univ. Program on Educ. Pol'y and Governance & Education Next, Report No. 11–03, 2011), *available at* http://www.hks.harvard.edu/pepg (follow "Research" hyperlink).

80 Robert J. Barro, *Human Capital and Growth*, 91 AM. ECON. REV. 12, 16 (May 2001); Peterson et al., *supra* note 79, at 18–19.

81 John H. Bishop, *Is the Test Score Decline Responsible for the Productivity Growth Decline?*, 79 AM. ECON. REV. 178, 179 (1989).

82 Wikipedia, Natural Science, http://en.wikipedia.org/wiki/Natural_sciences#Branches_of_natural_science.

some empirical evidence exists to support the assertion that they are intellectually demanding.[83] If students in these fields are attracted to and willing to learn scholastically rigorous topics, the extent to which the fields are represented among all conferred Bachelor's degrees can logically be expected to decline, ceteris paribus, as social values that favor consumption and enjoyment become more common.[84] The four fields, in short, afford an opportunity to tie human capital to the social values that are the focus of the instant chapter.

Turning to the data for the indicator, Figure 6.3 shows the percentage of all Bachelor's degrees earned by males, and the percentage of all Bachelor's degrees earned by females, that were conferred in the four fields by colleges and universities in the United States. Because the percentages are sex-specific and cover every year in a multi-decade period, they will reveal any trend that occurred in the share of all Bachelor's degrees received by each sex that were in a natural science or mathematics. The Figure begins with academic year 1965–1966 (designated as 1966 on the horizontal axis) and ends with academic year 2009–2010 (designated as 2010).[85] Within this time interval, data are available for every academic year except 1998–1999. For all years, of course, the data involve mainly young adults. However, when considering the data, readers should keep in mind that the behavior of young adults necessarily resulted from values that these young adults acquired several years earlier and that a change in their values is likely to have emanated from, or have occurred concurrently with, a corresponding change in values in older age groups. The indicator in Figure 6.3, therefore, probably understates the prevalence of these values in the population at a given moment. As time passes, moreover, young adults become older, and any trend in social values that continues among succeeding cohorts of young adults will expand the presence of the values in the total population.

---

83 Robert Coe et al., Relative Difficulty of Examinations in Different Subjects 99 Tbl. 29, 100 Fig. 16 (2008), http://www.academia.edu/1289075/Relative_difficulty_of_examinations_in_different_subjects (last visited May 9, 2015).

84 *See* Yuichi Shoda et al., *Predicting Adolescent Cognitive and Self-Regulatory Competencies from Preschool Delay of Gratification: Identifying Diagnostic Conditions*, 26 DEVELOPMENTAL PSYCHOL. 978, 980, 984 Tbl. 4 (1990) (finding in a small sample that the failure of children in preschool to postpone pleasure predicted, eleven to fourteen years later, lower scores on standardized tests of quantitative skills and verbal skills).

85 The percentages in Figure 6.3 were calculated from data in NAT'L SCI. FOUND., NAT'L CTR. FOR SCI. & ENGINEERING STAT., SCIENCE AND ENGINEERING DEGREES: 1966–2010 Tbl. 1, 2, 28, 29, 34, 35 (NSF 13-327) (June 2013), *available at* http://www.nsf.gov/statistics/nsf13327 (last visited May 9, 2015). The specific disciplines that comprise each of the four fields are listed in *id.* at Appendix B.

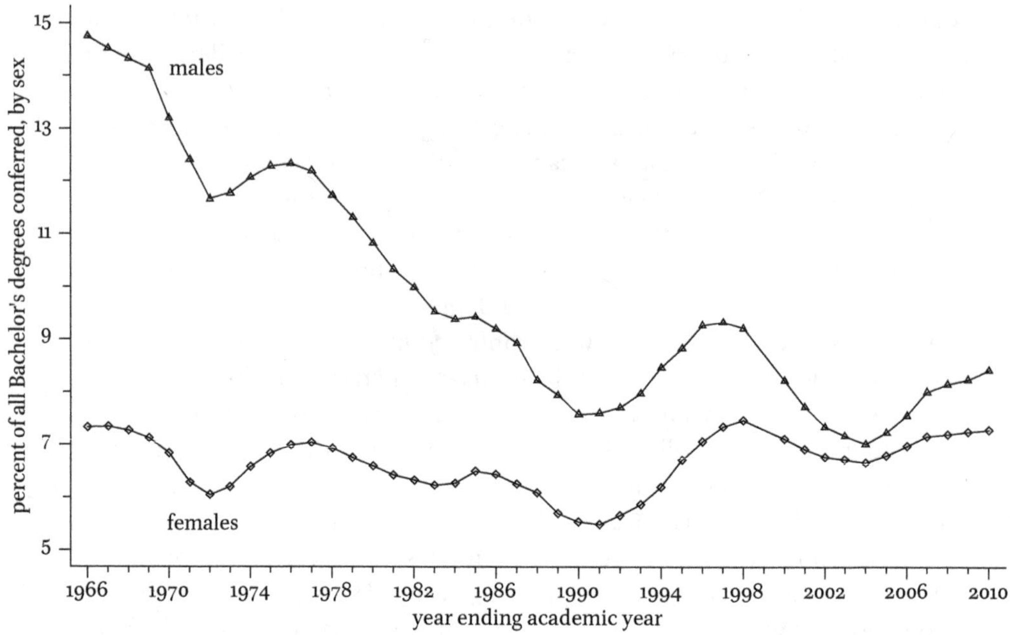

FIGURE 6.3 *Bachelor's degrees in natural sciences and mathematics: by academic year*
SOURCE: SEE FN. 85 IN THIS CHAPTER.

Although Figure 6.3 presents data for each sex, the trend for females will be ignored because it is almost certainly manifesting much more than the change in social values seen in Figures 6.1 and 6.2. An additional, and undoubtedly important, influence on the percentages for females in Figure 6.3 is the substantial transformation in the sex role of females that took place in the United States during the last half of the twentieth century.[86] The two factors would have had opposing effects on the percentages for females in Figure 6.3—the change in social values presumably would have curtailed the percentages, while the change in the societal role of females presumably would have raised the percentages. Because the contribution of each factor to the percentages is likely to have been sizeable but is impossible to ascertain, the trend for females in Figure 6.3 cannot be deciphered. Only the trend for males, whose role in society seems to have experienced relatively little change since the middle of the twentieth century, will be considered.

Before proceeding to the data for males, I should mention that the data used to construct Figure 6.3 are not limited to degree recipients who are United

86 The Place of Law, *supra* note 6, at 226–28, 298–99; notes 87 to 91, and the text accompanying them, in *supra* Chapter 2.

States citizens. Instead, the Figure includes both domestic and foreign students who were awarded Bachelor's degrees. Could change over time in the presence in U.S. colleges and universities of students who come to the United States from other countries have markedly affected the trend for males observed in Figure 6.3? The answer is probably negative, but unfortunately the question cannot be answered definitively because of a lack of longitudinal data that categorize undergraduate students by whether they are U.S. citizens and by their field of concentration. The data in the Figure thus combine domestic and foreign undergraduate students. However, because foreign students have been and continue to be a minuscule percentage of all students in U.S. facilities of higher education,[87] any overrepresentation on their part in the natural sciences and mathematics[88] is unlikely to have skewed the trend for males.

Turning to the data, what conclusions can be drawn from Figure 6.3? In academic year 1965–1966, Bachelor's degrees in the natural sciences and mathematics comprised one out of 6.8 Bachelor's degrees conferred on men, but by academic year 1989–1990, Bachelor's degrees in these fields represented just one out of 13.2 Bachelor's degrees awarded to men. Expressed differently, Bachelor's degrees in the natural sciences and mathematics, as a percentage of all Bachelor's degrees received by men, fell by almost half (from 14.7% to 7.6%) in the space of just a quarter-century. Although over the next two decades the percentage did not exhibit a clear direction, the change during the quarter-century that started in the mid-1960s was material. This change, in evidencing movement away from demanding scholastic subjects, is a plausible indicator of a widening preference for consumption and enjoyment. Not surprisingly, the decline in the prevalence of intellectually rigorous skills had important consequences in the U.S. labor market: During the 1970s and later decades, a sizeable rise occurred in the share of employed persons whose job required fewer years of schooling than the job holders possessed,[89] and the extent of this disparity varied inversely with workers' "functional literacy," i.e., with the degree to which workers possessed the intellectual skills required to comprehend prose, find and utilize pertinent information, and handle numerical data

87 Inst. of Int'l Educ., International Students: Enrollment Trends, http://www.iie.org/en/Research-and-Publications/Open-Doors/Data (2012) (data on undergraduate and graduate students combined) (follow "Enrollment Trends" hyperlink) (last visited May 9, 2015).

88 *See id.* (data on undergraduate and graduate students combined) (follow "Fields of Study" hyperlink).

89 Stephen Vaisey, *Education and its Discontents: Overqualification in America, 1972–2002*, 85 Soc. Forces 835, 843–45 (2006).

in written materials.[90] Social values, through their impact on human capital, thus influenced occupational attainment and labor market functioning.

b *Personal Debt*

We next consider an economic phenomenon that is logically a function of the prevalence of materialism, hedonism, and a commitment to short-term rewards and results. The phenomenon—personal debt—measures the inclination of individuals to consume at the moment rather than defer consumption to the future. Studies by psychologists have linked elevated levels of materialism and hedonism to an exceptionally strong proclivity in individuals to make purchases,[91] a likely consequence of which is debt. Although fewer studies have been done on individuals who do not possess an extreme propensity to buy, such individuals evidently exhibit a greater willingness to purchase and to have larger amounts of debt as their materialism-hedonism increases,[92] to carry a sizeable loan balance when their materialism-hedonism level is high than when it is low,[93] and to assume forms of unsecured debt

---

90 Frederic L. Pryor & David Schaffer, *Wages and the University Educated: A Paradox Resolved*, MONTHLY LABOR REV., July 1997, at 3, 7–8.

91 Laurence Claes et al., *Emotional Reactivity and Self-Regulation in Relation to Compulsive Buying*, 49 PERSONALITY & INDIVIDUAL DIFFERENCES 526, 527–28, 529 (2010); Helga Dittmar, *Compulsive Buying—A Growing Concern? An Examination of Gender, Age, and Endorsement of Materialistic Values as Predictors*, 96 BRIT. J. PSYCHOL. 467, 487 (2005); Helga Dittmar et al., *When a Better Self Is Only a Button Click Away: Associations Between Materialistic Values, Emotional and Identify-Related Buying Motives, and Compulsive Buying Tendency Online*, 26 J. SOC. & CLINICAL PSYCHOL. 334, 348, 355 (2007); Ragna Benedikta Garðarsdóttir & Helga Dittmar, *The Relationship of Materialism to Debt and Financial Well-Being: The Case of Iceland's Perceived Prosperity*, 33 J. ECON. PSYCHOL. 471, 474, 475 (2012); José Manuel Otero-López et al., *Materialism, Life-Satisfaction and Addictive Buying: Examining the Causal Relationships*, 50 PERSONALITY & INDIVIDUAL DIFFERENCES 772, 774, 775 (2011); José Manuel Otero-López & Estíbaliz Villardefrancos, *Five-Factor Model Personality Traits, Materialism, and Excessive Buying: A Mediational Analysis*, 54 PERSONALITY & INDIVIDUAL DIFFERENCES 767, 768, 769, 770 (2013). All of the foregoing studies used a form of the Material Values Scale, which as constructed measures both materialism and hedonism. Marsha L. Richins, *The Material Values Scale: Measurement Properties and Development of a Short Form*, 31 J. CONSUMER RES. 209, 210 (2004). However, because the Scale was developed to assess individuals' degree of materialism, it is labeled the Materialistic Values Scale or the Materialism Values Scale by the investigators in the foregoing studies.

92 Garðarsdóttir & Dittmar, *supra* note 91, at 475–76, 477–79.

93 John J. Watson, *The Relationship of Materialism to Spending Tendencies, Saving, and Debt*, 24 J. ECON. PSYCHOL. 723, 735, 737 (2003) (using the Material Values Scale described in

(e.g., through credit cards) when they want immediate rather than delayed rewards.[94]

Before proceeding further, a definition of the word "personal" in the term "personal debt" will be helpful. In the discussion below, "personal debt" refers to all types of debt that individuals incur and are responsible for paying. Because it has been taken on by individuals, the debt of families as well as the debt of households is deemed to be personal debt,[95] but personal debt does not extend to the debt of entities, which by definition are impersonal in nature. This Part of the chapter, therefore, will not be concerned with debt of the public sector of the economy (i.e., with debt by governments and government agencies) or with debt of the private sector (debt by business firms).

To gauge long-term change in personal debt and the economic burden it imposes, a common measure is household debt in relation to disposable personal income. The measure is especially useful because the data needed to compute it for the United States cover at least fifty years.[96] The measure can

---

supra note 91 and asking respondents about whether they had "loans" other than home-equity loans, mortgage loans, "checking overdrafts, or margin accounts" whose combined total was greater than $1,000). *See* Andrew N. Christopher et al., *Materialism and Attitudes Toward Money: An Exploratory Investigation*, 2 INDIVIDUAL DIFFERENCES RES. 109, 114 Tbl. 2 (2004) (finding an inverse bivariate correlation between the variables of materialism and of conservatism in the personal use of money).

94 Cristina Ottaviani & Daniela Vandone, *Impulsivity and Household Indebtedness: Evidence from Real Life*, 32 J. ECON. PSYCHOL. 754, 755, 759–60 (2011).

95 The distinction between a "household" and a "family" can be gleaned from the definitions of these terms by the U.S. Census Bureau. Briefly, "[a] household consists of all the people who occupy a housing unit.... A household includes the related family members and all the unrelated people, if any, such as lodgers, foster children, wards, or employees who share the housing unit. A person living alone in a housing unit, or a group of unrelated people sharing a housing unit such as partners or roomers, is also counted as a household." On the other hand, "[a] family is a group of two people or more (one of whom is the householder) related by birth, marriage, or adoption and residing together; all such people (including related subfamily members) are considered as members of one family." The term "householder," which is used in the definition of "household," designates "the person (or one of the people) in whose name the housing unit is owned or rented (maintained) or, if there is no such person, any adult member, excluding roomers, boarders, or paid employees. If the house is owned or rented jointly by a married couple, the householder may be either the husband or the wife." U.S. Census Bureau, Current Population Survey (CPS)—Definitions, http://www.census.gov/cps/about/cpsdef.html (last visited May 9, 2015) (follow "Family," "Household," and "Householder" hyperlinks).

96 R. Andrew Bauer & Betty Joyce Nash, *Where are Households in the Deleveraging Cycle?*, ECONOMIC BRIEF (Fed. Res. Bank of Richmond), Jan. 2012, at 1, http://www.richmondfed.org/publications/research/economic_brief/2012. Other yardsticks include the household

thus be followed over an extended period, and an examination of its course is revealing. Household debt as a percentage of disposable personal income in the United States moved within a relatively narrow range from 1960 until the first half of the 1980s, at which point the percentage started a steady climb that continued until the Great Recession.[97] Indeed, during the two-and-a-half decades leading up to the recession, the percentage doubled,[98] and by the time the recession began in December 2007,[99] it had reached approximately 130% of disposable personal income.[100] The increase is telling not only because of its magnitude but also because of its breadth. The percentage rose substantially across almost the entire U.S. population.[101]

Being sizeable and widespread, the pre-recession growth of the debt burden of U.S. households is evidence of a general expansion of social values supportive of consumption and enjoyment. In this regard, I should note that, although the debt burden of households declined after the recession began, little or none of the decline seems to be attributable to a shift in social values. Certainly, recession-generated downward trends in hedonism and materialism are not obvious in Figures 6.1 and 6.2, a situation that is not surprising inasmuch as (i) the post-recession decline in debt burden primarily resulted from debt that was written-off as a consequence of home foreclosures, and (ii) when the reduction of debt from foreclosures is taken into account, consumption by households in the United States during and after the recession continued to be a function of household income and net worth.[102] The decrease in household debt after the onset of the recession, in short, was not apparently due to a modification of social values that led individuals to curtail household financial

debt service ratio and the financial obligations ratio, but they start only in 1980. Fed. Res. Bd., Household Debt Service and Financial Obligations Ratios (2013), http://www.federalreserve.gov/releases/housedebt.

97 Bauer & Nash, *supra* note 96, at 1 Fig. 1.

98 According to Figure 1 in *id.*, the percentage was slightly more than 60% in the early 1980s. In December 2007, the percentage was 129%. *Id.* at 1.

99 *Supra* note 11.

100 *Compare* Bauer & Nash, *supra* note 96, at 1 (reporting the percentage to be 129%) *with* Sandra Pianalto, President, Fed. Res. Bank of Cleveland, Speech at the Rotary Club of Lexington: The Economic Outlook and the Progress of U.S. Households (Nov. 17, 2011) (reporting the percentage to be "over 130 percent in 2007") (on file with author; no longer available online).

101 Cynamon & Fazzari, *supra* note 16, at 13–18.

102 Daniel Cooper, *U.S. Household Deleveraging: What Do the Aggregate and Household-Level Data Tell Us?*, PUB. POL'Y BRIEFS (Fed. Res. Bank of Boston) (No. 12–2) (2012), http://www.bos.frb.org/economic/ppb/index.htm.

liabilities; rather, the decrease occurred because of actions taken by lenders.[103] The foregoing conclusion is consistent with the thesis that social values are an aspect of society and hence embedded in a system.[104] Because a system is characterized by appreciable inertia, change in social values will typically be slow even though in principle social values might be altered quickly by a massive event. Notably, relative to the amounts that would be predicted by their income and net worth, U.S. households may have spent more *after* the recession started and spent less before.[105]

6 Pre-Recession Social Manifestations of the Change in Values

Part 5 *supra* used data on economic behaviors in an attempt to show that hedonism, materialism, and an emphasis on short-term rewards became more common among Americans during the last third of the twentieth century and to support the hypothesis that this sociological change produced the Great Recession. Part 6 will add to the evidence using data on social behaviors.

Part 5 and Part 6 would not be capable of complementing one another, however, without their common roots in macrosociology. In particular, Part 5 and Part 6 are tied together through the macrosociological assumption that (i) a society operates effectively to the extent that, inter alia, its components are compatible with each other and that (ii) this compatibility requires at least that the social values in one component do not clash with the social values in other components. Macrosociology thus deems a society to be an integrated whole, not an assemblage of unconnected elements, and expects that similar social values will be present throughout. In macrosociology, a society is not viewed as a random assortment of individuals who have social, economic, and cultural similarities by mere coincidence.

Part 6 will consider law on particular social behaviors. Why, however, is law a topic relevant to macrosociology? The answer is found in the evident universality of law as an institution in structurally complex, democratically governed societies. Moreover, the concepts and doctrines of law, being key ingredients of the institution, can be expected to accommodate current conditions in their society, albeit with a time lag, as they respond to shifts that occur in societal

---

103 *Id.* at 2, 19 Fig. 7, 21. *Accord*, Karen Dynan, *Is a Household Debt Overhang Holding Back Consumption?*, BROOKINGS PAPERS ON ECONOMIC ACTIVITY, Spring 2012, at 299, 340–41 (2012).

104 *Supra* note 38 and accompanying text.

105 Cooper, *supra* note 102, at 3.

conditions, including social values.[106] In responding to societal conditions, therefore, the content of law portrays these conditions, and the instant chapter will make use of this principle to support its hypothesis that an expanded acceptance of social values endorsing consumption and enjoyment were the underlying agents responsible for the Great Recession. Specifically, Part 6 will describe changes in the incidence of behaviors that are traceable to, inter alia, the societal values in my hypothesis[107] and will review transformations in the content of law on these behaviors. The behaviors that are the subject of Part 6, however, will be social in nature, not economic (as in Part 5). The exercise will not only provide evidence for the hypothesis advanced in the instant chapter but also for the more general contention that a macrosociological perspective is required to understand fully the concepts and doctrines of law on society-important behaviors in a jurisdiction having a complex structure and democratic government.

a *Premarital Sexual Intercourse among Minors*

I begin with a topic—consensual premarital sexual intercourse among minors—that has prompted considerable controversy in the United States.[108] The political contours of the controversy are not my concern, however. Rather, I focus on a social change helping to drive the controversy. That change—an increase over time in the rate at which minors engage in premarital intercourse—is logically attributable in part to a greater acceptance of social values endorsing hedonism and short-term rewards, and it is a source of public concern because premarital sexual intercourse exposes minor females to the possibility of pregnancy. Premarital intercourse involving minors further implicates the public interest, because unless it occurs exclusively within romantic relationships—and it usually does not—premarital intercourse has a general negative effect on the attachment that sexually active minors have to high school and their grade point averages in high school.[109]

---

106 *Supra* Chapter 1, at Part 1-b.

107 Additional evidence for my hypothesis is found in the rise of divorce rates in the United States prior to the adoption of law that allowed divorce without evidence of fault. Data on the trend in divorce likelihood before law authorized "no-fault" divorce are in THE PLACE OF LAW, *supra* note 6, at 10–14. Ceteris paribus, acceptance of social values endorsing hedonism and near-term rewards can be expected to elevate the risk of divorce.

108 Diana Jean Schemo, *Sex Education With Just One Lesson: No Sex*, N.Y. TIMES, Dec. 28, 2000, at A1.

109 Bill McCarthy & Eric Grodsky, *Sex and School: Adolescent Sexual Intercourse and Education*, 58 SOC. PROBS. 213, 218, 220, 222 Tbl. 2, 224 Tbl. 3, 225 Tbl. 4, 227 (2011). The study in the cited article analyzed data obtained from a national probability sample of students in

In the instant chapter, I focus on the rate of premarital intercourse among just females. I confine the discussion to females because pregnancy, being a risk only for females, has more obvious consequences for them than it has for males.[110] Although social science research suggests that minor females who decide to carry pregnancies to term experience few substantial negative consequences in the long run from childbearing and childrearing per se[111] and that

---

grades 7 through 12 at public and private (secular and religious) high schools in the United States that had at least thirty students. The students provided the initial data in their schools during the 1994–1995 school year; subsequent data were obtained through home interviews with the students during 1995 and 1996. *Id.* at 217; Add Health, http://www.cpc.unc.edu/projects/addhealth (from the drop-down menu for "Study Design," follow "Wave I" hyperlink or "Wave II" hyperlink, and "Design Facts at a Glance" hyperlink) (last visited May 9, 2015). Because of the short time interval between the two waves of the study whose data were analyzed, I disregard the change that was estimated to have occurred over this interval in the consequences that premarital intercourse had for the education of participating minors. *See id.* at 217, 226 Tbl. 5.

During the eighteen months prior to the time that respondents provided data for each wave of the study, premarital sexual intercourse that occurred in a nonromantic relationship was nearly twice as common among females, and was exactly three-and-a-half times as common among males, as sexual intercourse that was confined to a romantic relationship. *Id.* at 218, 219 Tbl. 1. Premarital intercourse is deemed to have taken place in a nonromantic relationship during the specified time period if it happened only in such a relationship or if it happened in both a nonromantic relationship and a romantic relationship. *Id.* at 219 Tbl. 1.

110 In concluding that the equal protection guarantee allows a criminal penalty to be imposed on just the male for sexual intercourse with an unmarried minor female, a four-justice plurality of the U.S. Supreme Court reasoned that, "[b]ecause virtually all of the significant harmful and inescapably identifiable consequences of teenage pregnancy fall on the young female, a legislature acts well within its authority when it elects to punish only the participant who, by nature, suffers few of the consequences of his conduct." Michael M. v. Superior Court, 450 U.S. 464, 471, 473 (1981) (Rehnquist, J., joined by Burger, C.J. and Stewart and Powell, J.J.). In *Michael M.*, a minor female had agreed to sexual intercourse with the defendant after being physically hit by the defendant, but even in the absence of violence, she could not have legally consented to the intercourse because she had not reached the age at which state law allowed her to consent. *Id.* at 466, 467.

In the United States, all states and the District of Columbia designate by law an age of consent for nonmarital intercourse. The age varies by state and ranges from 16 to 18, with the most frequent age being 16. Wikipedia, Ages of Consent in North America, http://en.wikipedia.org/wiki/Ages_of_consent_in_North_America#State_laws (last visited May 9, 2015).

111 Melissa S. Kearney & Phillip B. Levine, *Why is the Teen Birth Rate in the United States So High and Why Does It Matter?*, 26 J. ECON. PERSP. 141, 142, 159–61, 163 (2012).

the youthfulness of the mothers may not uniformly harm the children they bear,[112] childbearing and childrearing are not the sole options available to minor females who have conceived. Abortion, too, is an alternative for minor females who are pregnant, and the number electing abortion presumably would not be as large as it is[113] unless the perceived benefits from this course of action were appreciable. Unfortunately, however, little is known about the social and psychological variables that distinguish minors who abort from minors who do not. Pregnant minor females who decide to have a medically induced abortion seem to attend church less often than those who opt not to end their pregnancies.[114] Because involvement in religion takes place in a social setting,[115] unmarried minor females who learn they have conceived and who decide to terminate their pregnancies probably differ on many sociological and psychological attributes from their counterparts who choose to give birth.[116]

---

112 Judith A. Levine et al., *The Well-Being of Children Born to Teen Mothers*, 69 J. Marriage & Fam. 105, 120 (2007).

113 Guttmacher Institute, u.s. Teenage Pregnancies, Births and Abortions: National and State Trends and Trends by Race and Ethnicity 8 Tbl. 2.2 (2010), www.guttmacher.org/pubs/USTPtrends.pdf.

114 Randall H. King et al., *The Demand for Abortion by Unmarried Teenagers: Economic Factors, Age, Ethnicity and Religiosity Matter*, 51 J. Econ. & Sociol. 223, 228, 229 Tbl. 1, 230 (1992) (study of females who were 16 to 19 years old and had never been married). In another study, frequency of church attendance was one of two components of a measure that was found to have no bearing on the likelihood of abortion among never-married females who learned they were pregnant when they were 14 to 26 years old. Amy Adamczyk, *Understanding the Effects of Personal and School Religiosity on the Decision to Abort a Premarital Pregnancy*, 50 J. Health & Soc. Behav. 180, 184, 186, 190 (2009). Notably, the age range in the sample used by the King et al. study and the age range in the sample used by the Adamczyk study were dissimilar. Although the two studies included both females who conceived when they were minors and females who conceived when they were adults, the adults in the study by King et al. had just recently reached the threshold age for majority; the adults in the study by Adamczyk included females who had become adults many years before. *Compare* King et al., *supra*, at 228 *with* Adamczyk, *supra*, at 184. The inconsistency in the findings of the two studies may be due to the different age ranges of the samples. Because my interest is in minors and this age group is more closely approximated by the sample in the King et al. study than by the sample in the study by Adamczyk, I rely on the findings of the King et al. study.

115 Laurence R. Iannaccone, *Religious Practice: A Human Capital Approach*, 29 J. Sci. Study of Religion 297 (1990).

116 For example, tolerance of political protest was found in cross-sectional data to be relatively low when, inter alia, church attendance was relatively high. Amy Katnik, *Religion, Social Class, and Political Tolerance: A Cross-National Analysis*, 32 Int'l J. Sociol. 14, 20, 22, 34 (2002) (using data from sample surveys conducted during 1996 in thirteen countries located in Europe and North America).

These differences are likely to account for the benefits that are anticipated by unmarried minor females who abort pregnancies.

Under what circumstances should law should allow minors to end pregnancies? The question is the focus of a contentious public issue in the United States.[117] However, if the hypothesis advocated in the instant chapter is correct, minor females were engaging in premarital intercourse at an increasing rate before the grounds allowing them access to a lawful abortion were relaxed. Therefore, I examine the rate of premarital sexual intercourse among minors over time, but to identify the time period that is pertinent, I must date the shift that occurred in U.S. law on abortion during the last half of the twentieth century. The review will focus on the law that covered the entire nation rather than on the law of individual states, because time series data on rates of premarital intercourse among minors are available for just the country as a whole.

The U.S. Supreme Court decision in Roe v. Wade,[118] of course, marks the inception of nationally applicable law on abortion in the United States. In that case, which was decided in 1973, the Court concluded that the Constitution provides a pregnant adult female[119] with a personal right to have medically trained personnel terminate the fetus she has conceived, a right on which government cannot significantly encroach unless and until the fetus is viable. Three years later, the Court decided its first case dealing with the conditions under which a minor female has a right to a lawful abortion. In 1976, government was held in breach of the Constitution when it requires an unmarried minor female to secure, either from one of her parents or from her guardian, written approval to abort a pregnancy that is twelve weeks or less in duration.[120] The statute was invalidated because the Court thought that it conveyed to a third party "an absolute, and possibly arbitrary, veto over the decision of the

---

117 *E.g.*, Editorial, *Yet Another Curb on Abortion*, N.Y. TIMES, March 13, 2012, at A24; Katie Zezima, *New Hampshire: Lawmakers Override Veto of Abortion Consent Bill*, N.Y. TIMES, June 23, 2011, at A14.

118 Roe v. Wade, 410 U.S. 113 (1973).

119 The lead plaintiff in Roe v. Wade used a pseudonym (Roe), and while she was never expressly described by the Court as an adult, the Court referred to her as a "woman," implying that she was not a minor. 410 U.S. at 120, 121, 124. Although her age was not publicly revealed until years later, Roe was twenty-one years old when she challenged the constitutionality of the state statute that denied her a lawful abortion. Kevin C. Mcmunigal, *Of Causes and Clients: Two Tales of Roe v. Wade*, 47 HASTINGS L. J. 779, 787 (1996).

120 Planned Parenthood of Central Missouri v. Danforth, 428 U.S. 52, 72–75 (1976). Under the statute that was challenged (and ruled unconstitutional) in this case, written approval by a parent or guardian was not necessary to abort a pregnancy that a physician found was jeopardizing the life of the pregnant female. *Id.* at 58.

physician and his patient to terminate the patient's pregnancy, regardless of the reason for withholding the consent,"[121] but the Court cautioned that some minor females, because of their age or maturity, may be incapable of lawfully agreeing to an abortion.[122] In 1979, the Court, in reviewing a state statute on the circumstances in which a minor female would be allowed to abort a pregnancy, reconciled its concern that all minors not be denied access to abortion with its concern that all minors may not be able to make an informed decision regarding abortion. However, although the statute in the latter (1979) case was held unconstitutional, no majority opinion was written, and the fate of the statute was resolved in two four-justice concurring opinions[123] from which pertinent constitutional standards must be extracted. Notably, the constitutional standards found in the 1976 and 1979 opinions, although formulated a third-of-a-century ago, remain in place and provide the general framework for legislation and administrative-agency rules today on access to abortion by minors.

A brief summary of the statute at issue in the 1979 case will be helpful in identifying the constitutional standards that are shared by the two concurring opinions written by the justices. Under the statute, a pregnant minor female, in the absence of a medical emergency, was compelled to seek permission to end her pregnancy either from her parents or from the surviving, available parent if one of the parents was deceased or had abandoned the family. A minor who was unable to obtain the permission of her parent(s) was allowed to petition a court and seek judicial approval for an abortion, but approval of the petition required the court reviewing it to conclude that the requested abortion was in the best interest of the minor. Notably, the statute provided for the denial of the petition when the reviewing court believed that, even though the petitioning minor was psychologically capable of making an informed choice with regard to abortion, the best interest of the minor would not be served by termination of the pregnancy.[124]

With this background, we can explore the two four-justice concurring opinions that resolved the constitutional challenge to the statute. According to the first of the opinions,[125] government is barred by the Constitution from compelling a pregnant minor female to secure parental approval for an abortion

121 *Id.* at 74.

122 *Id.* at 75.

123 Bellotti v. Baird, 443 U.S. 622 (1979).

124 443 U.S. at 625–26, 630–31 (Powell, J., joined by Burger, C.J. and Stewart and Rehnquist, J.J., concurring).

125 The Court has subsequently labeled this concurring opinion as the "principal opinion" in the case. Lambert v. Wicklund, 520 U.S. 292, 295 (1997).

unless a substitute procedure is made available through which the minor can request, from a court or administrative agency, approval of the abortion.[126] When the substitute procedure is invoked, approval cannot be capriciously denied.[127] In particular, the four justices believed,

> A pregnant minor is entitled in such a proceeding to show either: (1) that she is mature enough and well enough informed to make her abortion decision, in consultation with her physician, independently of her parents' wishes; or (2) that even if she is not able to make this decision independently, the desired abortion would be in her best interests.[128]

If through the proceeding the minor demonstrates that either of the above conditions exists, she must be given permission to terminate her pregnancy.

The constitutional standard in the first concurring opinion is not incompatible with the standard in the second. Indeed, the two opinions exhibit considerable common ground. Specifically, the second concurring opinion focused on the best interests of the minor—condition (2) in the first concurring opinion—but in doing so, it incorporated a concern with the psychological maturity of the minor—condition (1) in the first concurring opinion. When authorizing a court to approve the petition of a minor to abort a pregnancy, the second opinion emphasized, the statute at issue in the case imposed only the criterion of the "best interests of the minor." However, this criterion was deemed to be amorphous,[129] and it was thought to allow the deliberative faculties of the minor to be disregarded. In the words of the second concurring opinion:

> [T]he task of the judge is to determine whether the best interests of the minor will be served by an abortion. The decision is his to make, even if he finds 'that the minor is capable of making, and has made, an informed and reasonable decision to have an abortion.' Thus, no minor in [the state], no matter how mature and capable of informed decisionmaking, may receive an abortion without the consent of either both her parents

126 443 U.S. at 643–44 & 643 n.22 (Powell, J., joined by Burger, C.J. and Stewart and Rehnquist, J.J., concurring).

127 *Id.* at 644.

128 *Id.* at 643–44.

129 *Id.* at 655 (Stevens, J., joined by Brennan, Marshall, and Blackmun, J.J.) (concluding that the statute imposed a criterion that "provides little real guidance to the judge, and his decision must necessarily reflect personal and societal values and mores").

> or a superior court judge. In every instance, the minor's decision to secure an abortion is subject to an absolute third-party veto.[130]

The government procedure by which a minor female can bypass her parents in ending a pregnancy, therefore, cannot ignore whether the minor possesses the psychological capacity to make an informed choice.

The opinions in the 1976 and 1979 cases, when juxtaposed, bar government from denying lawful abortions to all unmarried pregnant minors. Consent to a lawful abortion can be furnished by the parent(s) or guardian of the pregnant minor or by a disinterested third party. When the decision is made by the latter (third party), the minor must be allowed to end her pregnancy if she possesses the ability to understand and rationally choose abortion or, if she lacks this ability, she would benefit from terminating the pregnancy.[131]

From a macrosociological perspective, why are unmarried minors in the United States permitted to abort their pregnancies lawfully? The answer, I suggest, is that pregnancy among unmarried minor females had become sufficiently widespread in the United States by the late 1970s that society needed to permit minors to end their pregnancies, and it acknowledged this need by developing law compatible with the need. The answer garners a degree of plausibility from research in which state statutes requiring that the parents of the minors be involved in the abortion decisions of their unmarried minor daughters were not found to have an effect on either the incidence of abortion among females 15–17 years old[132] or the incidence of sexual intercourse among unmarried females 15–17 years old.[133] If the content of law does not materially alter the frequency or rate of a social behavior—a conclusion that can be drawn from empirical research on many types of behavior[134]—it presumably is a reaction to the incidence of the behavior and/or to whether the behavior poses a threat to the operation of the societal system.

Figure 6.4 supplies evidence that the change in U.S. constitutional law on minors' access to abortion reflected a societal need for such access. The Figure

---

130 *Id.* at 653.

131 Carol Sanger, *Decisional Dignity, Teenage Abortion, Bypass Hearings, and the Misuse of Law*, 18 COLUMBIA J. GENDER & L. 409, 422–23, 429–32 (2009).

132 Marshall H. Medoff, *Estimates of the Abortion Demand of Young and Older Teenagers*, 17 POPULATION RES. & POL'Y REV. 539, 541, 544–45 (1998) (using cross-sectional state-level data for 1992 on females, regardless of marital status, who were 15–17 years old).

133 Bisakha Sen, *Frequency of Sexual Activity among Unmarried Adolescent Girls: Do State Policies Pertaining to Abortion Access Matter?* 32 EASTERN ECON. J. 313, 319, 320, 326 (2006) (data on never-married females who were in the age range 15–17 on December 31, 1966).

134 *Supra* note 45 and accompanying text.

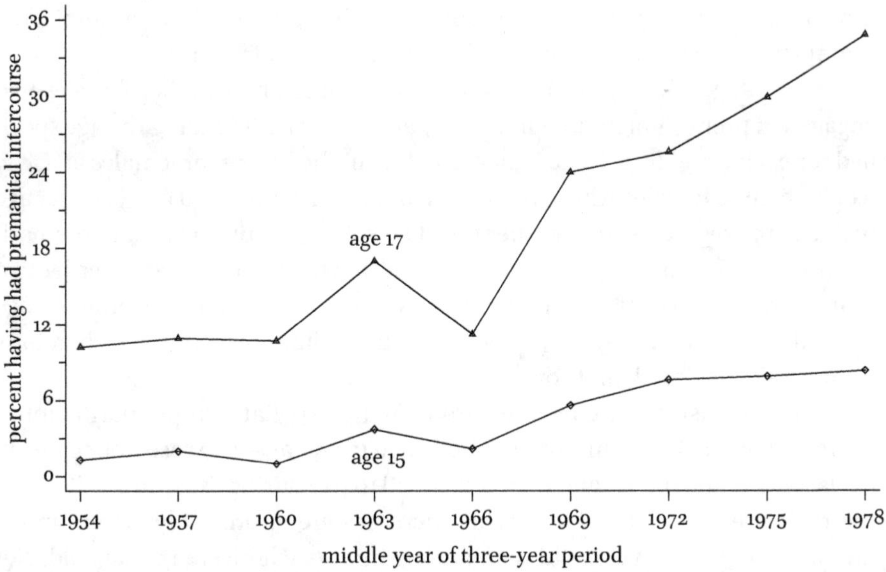

FIGURE 6.4 *Premarital intercourse to age 15 and age 17, white females: cumulative rates by period (1953–1955 to 1977–1979)*
SOURCE: SEE FN. 135 IN THIS CHAPTER.

shows, for each three-year interval from 1953–1955 to 1977–1979, the percentage of White adolescent females in the United States who experienced premarital sexual intercourse up to age 15 and up to age 17.[135] In listing three-year intervals,

135 Figure 6.4 was constructed by converting age-specific data for birth-cohorts into age-specific data for time periods. The birth-cohort data are in Sandra L. Hofferth et al., *Premarital Sexual Activity Among U.S. Teenage Women Over the Past Three Decades*, 19 FAM. PLAN. PERSP. 46, 49 Tbl. 3 (1987). For each birth cohort used by Hofferth et al., the age-specific rates of premarital intercourse were converted into age-specific period rates of premarital intercourse by adding fifteen years to the rate at age fifteen and by adding seventeen years to the rate at age seventeen.

The data in the study by Hofferth et al. were gathered between August 1982 and February 1983 in a nationwide sample survey of women who were 15–44 years old when they were interviewed. Christine A. Bachrach et al., Nat'l Ctr. For Health Stat., *National Survey of Family Growth, Cycle III: Sample Design, Weighting, and Variance Estimation*, VITAL AND HEALTH STATISTICS, Series 2, No. 98 (1985), at 1, *available at* www.cdc.gov/nchs/data/series/sr_02/sr02_098.pdf. The survey was characterized by greater sampling variability for Blacks than for Whites. Hofferth et al., *supra*, at 47. Figure 6.4 is limited to the data on Whites because Whites were subject to less sampling variability than Blacks and because Whites comprised a much larger share of the U.S. population than Blacks. In 1980, according to the decennial census conducted in that year, 83.1% of the population was White and 11.7% was Black. Calculated from BUREAU OF THE CENSUS, 1980 CENSUS

the horizontal axis specifies the middle year of each interval. For example, the year 1957 on the horizontal axis designates the period from 1956 through 1958. The percentages on the vertical axis are determined by whether females had engaged in premarital intercourse at *any* age up to and including the age specified for each trend line. Hence, the trend line in the Figure for females at age 17 would include females whose premarital intercourse occurred at a younger age (e.g., age 15), regardless of whether they had subsequently engaged in premarital intercourse. However, because the ages shown in the Figure differ by two years, females who attained age 15 in a given period may not have attained age 17 until the next three-year period. Each trend line in Figure 6.4, therefore, should be considered on its own.

What conclusions can be drawn from Figure 6.4? Rates of premarital intercourse involving White minor females at age 15 and at age 17 rose noticeably in the last half of the 1960s, and they continued to rise during the 1970s.[136] Because the rates are cumulative by age, the increases are appreciably larger among minors who were 17 years old than among minors who were 15 years old. Not coincidentally, as we have seen, present constitutional jurisprudence constraining government efforts to hamper or deny access to abortion by minors emerged during the last half of the 1970s. The advent of this law is in line with the proposition that concepts and doctrines of law in a modern society respond to change in social conditions[137] and is an illustration of the correlative point

---

OF POPULATION. VOL. 1: CHARACTERISTICS OF THE POPULATION. CH. B: GENERAL POPULATION CHARACTERISTICS. PART 1: UNITED STATES SUMMARY 20 Tbl. 38 (1983), *available at* http://www.census.gov/prod/www/decennial.html (follow "Census of Population and Housing, 1980" hyperlink, then "1980 Census of Population" hyperlink).

136 Although Figure 6.4 does not extend past the 1970s, rates of premarital intercourse among White minor females probably continued to increase during the 1980s. *See* Susheela Singh & Jacqueline E. Darroch, *Trends in Sexual Activity Among Adolescent American Women: 1982–1995*, 31 FAM. PLANNING PERSP. 212, 215 Tbl. 2, 217 Tbl. 4 (1999) (reporting, for 1982, 1988 and 1995, the percentages of females of all races who had engaged in premarital intercourse while in the age range 15–17 and the percentages of non-Hispanic White females who had engaged in intercourse, whether before or within marriage, while in the age range 15–17).

137 The law that emerged during the last half of the 1970s on minors' access to abortion is an indication of a societal need that abortion be available to minors. Evidence of this need is also found in the proportion of pregnancies that were aborted by minor females at this time. Specifically, in the 1970s, induced abortions are estimated to have ended approximately two out of every five pregnancies experienced by females who were 15–17 years old. Stanley K. Henshaw & Kevin O'Reilly, *Characteristics of Abortion Patients in the United States, 1979 and 1980*, 15 FAM. PLANNING PERSP. 5, 6 Tbl. 1 (1983).

that the content of law chronicles such change.[138] More relevant here, however, is that the hypothesis being explored in the instant chapter is strengthened by the combination of the alterations that occurred in social behavior and in law on the behavior, i.e., by the expanded incidence of premarital intercourse among minors and the subsequent reconciliation to this increase of law on the termination of pregnancies by minors.

b *Marijuana Use*

The use of drugs that have been banned by law has long been a prominent public concern in the United States,[139] making the use of illegal drugs a logical topic for the instant chapter. In particular, I will examine the prevalence of and law on marijuana. Three reasons lie behind my choice of marijuana. First, marijuana, when consumed in limited amounts, produces relaxation, intensified sensory awareness, and mild euphoria in the user,[140] and the extent of marijuana consumption can be expected to vary, therefore, with the presence in a population of social values highlighting hedonism and near-term rewards.[141] Second, among drugs prohibited by law, marijuana is the drug most commonly used by Americans,[142] at

138 An explanation of this point is in the text that accompanies *supra* notes 47–50.

139 The concern was expressed in June 1971 by President Richard Nixon when he announced a focused effort by the federal government to engage in an "offensive" against "drug abuse." Richard Nixon, Remarks About an Intensified Program for Drug Abuse Prevention and Control (June 17, 1971), *available at* http://www.presidency.ucsb.edu/index.php (The American Presidency Project) (follow "Documents" hyperlink, then "Public Papers of the Presidents" hyperlink, select "June" and "1971" from the drop-down menus for month and year, and click on "View PPPUS"). The effort came to be popularly known as a "war on drugs." Conor Friedersdorf, *The War on Drugs Turns 40*, The Atlantic, June 15, 2011, http://www.theatlantic.com/politics/archive/2011/06/the-war-on-drugs-turns-40/240472.

140 U.S. Nat'l Library of Medicine, *Drug Abuse*, MEDLINEPLUS (2011), http://www.nlm.nih.gov/medlineplus/ency/article/001945.htm (last visited May 9, 2015); Itai Danovitch, *Sorting Through the Science on Marijuana: Facts, Fallacies, and Implications for Legalization*, 43 MCGEORGE L. REV. 91, 94, 96–97 (2012). However, marijuana also poses long-term health risks to users. Danovitch, *supra* at 101–04; Louisa Degenhardt & Wayne Hall, *Extent of Illicit Drug Use and Dependence, and Their Contribution to the Global Burden of Disease*, 379 THE LANCET 55, 56 (2012).

141 *See* Danovitch, *supra* note 140, at 94 ("Regular users of marijuana typically find these effects pleasurable or reinforcing").

142 LLOYD D. JOHNSTON ET AL., MONITORING THE FUTURE NATIONAL SURVEY RESULTS ON DRUG USE 1975–2012: OVERVIEW, KEY FINDINGS ON ADOLESCENT DRUG USE 10 (2013) ("Because marijuana is much more prevalent than any other illicit drug, trends in its use tend to drive the index of any illicit drug use"), *available at* http://monitoringthefuture.org/pubs.html.

least through age 30.[143] Third, time-series data on marijuana consumption in the United States are available for an extended period. One source of such data is the Monitoring the Future (MTF) study, a main focus of which has been drug use.[144] As explained in *supra* Part 4, the study has gathered data since 1975 from twelfth-grade students in high schools (both public and private) in the continental United States.[145] Because the study has been conducted every year from its inception, it has consecutive-year data on marijuana use.[146]

Figure 6.5 employs data from the MTF surveys and shows, for each calendar year from 1975 through 2012, the percentages of male high school seniors and of female high school seniors who reported using marijuana during the prior twelve months.[147] The Figure covers high school seniors of all races and ethnicities, but it excludes individuals who dropped out of school prior to the twelfth grade[148] as well as twelfth-grade students who were absent when the questionnaire was administered. The omission of "drop outs" and absentees is estimated to have understated the yearly rate of marijuana use in a given cohort by approximately five to seven percentage points,[149] but is thought not to have materially distorted trends over time.[150]

As Figure 6.5 discloses, female high school seniors and male high school seniors experienced remarkably similar trends. Although fewer females than males reported that they had used marijuana within the past twelve months, the usage rates of both groups followed a similar course, peaking in the late 1970s,[151] declining rapidly until 1992 (due to concern that marijuana is injurious

---

143 Lloyd D. Johnston et al., 2 Monitoring the Future National Survey Results on Drug Use, 1975–2012: College Students and Adults Ages 19–50, at 109 Fig. 4–2, 110 Fig. 4–3 (2013), *available at* http://monitoringthefuture.org/pubs.html.

144 Bachman et al., *supra* note 51, at 6.

145 See text accompanying *supra* note 51.

146 Bachman et al., *supra* note 51, at 9.

147 The data in Figure 6.5 are from Lloyd D. Johnston et al., *Demographic Subgroup Trends Among Adolescents for Fifty-One Classes of Licit and Illicit Drugs, 1975–2012* (Monitoring the Future Occasional Paper 79, 2013), at 329–30 Tbl. 12, http://monitoringthefuture.org (follow "Publications" hyperlink and then "Occasional Papers" hyperlink).

148 *Supra* note 52 and accompanying text.

149 Lloyd D. Johnston & Patrick M. O'Malley, *Issues of Validity and Population Coverage in Student Surveys of Drug Use, in* Self-Report Methods of Estimating Drug Use: Meeting Current Challenges to Validity 31, 42, 44 Tbl. 6 (NIDA Research Monograph 57) (Beatrice A. Rouse et al. eds., 1985), *available at* http://archives.drugabuse.gov/pdf/monographs/download57.html.

150 *Id.* at 40, 50.

151 For males, the peak rate (55.9%) was reached in 1978, but in 1979 the male usage rate was essentially the same (55.8%). For females, the peak rate (45.7%) occurred in 1979.

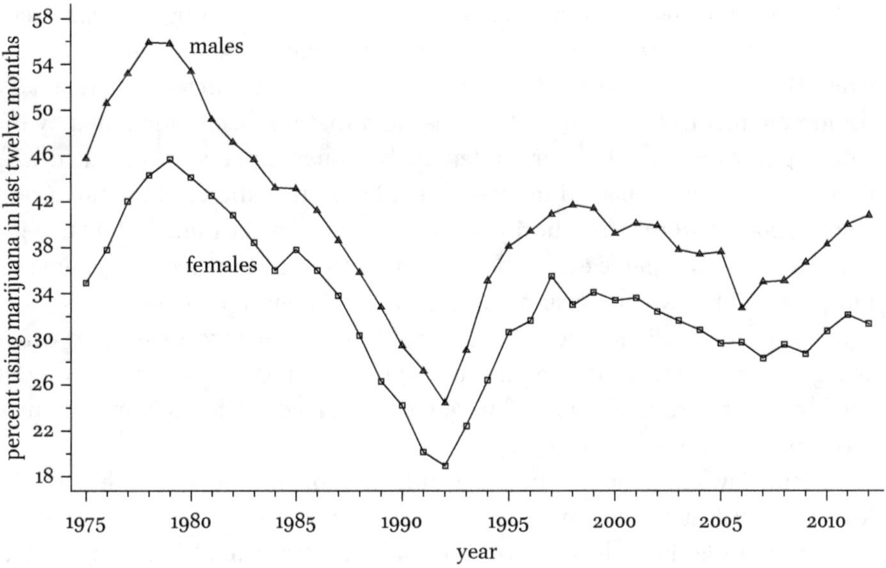

FIGURE 6.5 *Prevalence of marijuana use: high school seniors, 1975–2012*
SOURCE: SEE FN. 147 IN THIS CHAPTER.

to users[152]), and then rebounding sharply for five or six years.[153] Once the rebound was over, a plateau formed (though well below the peaks attained approximately twenty years earlier), and the usage rate of females as well as of males fluctuated within a relatively narrow range. Notably, when measured by first use of marijuana per thousand person-years of exposure during the last decade-and-a-half of the twentieth century, rates display not-dissimilar changes over time both at age 12–17 and at age 18–25, with rates higher in the second half of the 1990s than in the late 1980s.[154] An increase in marijuana use during the 1990s, therefore, was evidently not confined to adolescents. A likely cause of the increase was a more-widespread presence of social values backing consumption and enjoyment.

---

152 Jerald G. Bachman et al., *Explaining the Recent Decline in Marijuana Use: Differentiating the Effects of Perceived Risks, Disapproval, and General Lifestyle Factors*, 29 J. HEALTH & SOC. BEHAV. 92, 97, 107–08 (1988).

153 For males, the rebound lasted until 1998, when the usage rate reached 41.7%. For females, the rebound terminated in 1997 at a usage rate of 35.5%.

154 See the imputed variable time series and edited variable time series in JOSEPH C. GFROERER ET AL., SUBSTANCE ABUSE AND MENTAL HEALTH SERVICES ADMINISTRATION, INITIATION OF MARIJUANA USE: TRENDS, PATTERNS, AND IMPLICATIONS 117 Tbl. A.8 (Analytic Series: A-17, DHHS Publication No. SMA 02–3711) (2002), http://eric.ed.gov/?id=ED468394. Neither time series differentiates females and males.

The spreading use of marijuana in the U.S. population during the last decade of the twentieth century has significance for both federal law and state law. Under federal law, marijuana possession and use are illegal except in research that has a "legitimate medical or scientific" purpose and that has been sanctioned by the federal government.[155] The current federal ban on marijuana[156] originated with legislation that was enacted in 1970,[157] legislation that the U.S. Supreme Court held in 2005 is within the authority granted Congress by the Constitution to regulate interstate commerce even when it is enforced against persons who are permitted by state law to consume and grow marijuana for medical reasons.[158] Federal law on marijuana, accordingly, was in place well before the 1990s when, as Figure 6.5 reveals, a substantial expansion of marijuana use occurred among Americans. The criminal status of marijuana under federal law neither prevented this expansion nor was altered by it.

Federal law, however, is not the only law on marijuana. Although the increased prevalence of marijuana consumption during the 1990s has not prompted a decriminalization of marijuana under federal law, did it affect state law? From the start of the decade through 1995, all states prohibited the possession and use of marijuana,[159] but beginning in 1996, states started to ease or eliminate the prohibition. Today, almost half of the states as well as the District of Columbia have decriminalized the possession of marijuana for medical uses by individuals who qualify and the cultivation of marijuana by these individuals and/or by dispensaries licensed by or registered with the state.[160] In two of the states that have done so, decriminalization has extended to the recreational use of marijuana.[161]

In light of the conflict between current federal law and (some) state law on marijuana, a key point is that enforcement by the federal government of its law on marijuana is "largely toothless" due to constraints imposed on the federal

---

155 Karen O'Keefe, *State Medical Marijuana Implementation and Federal Policy*, 16 J. HEALTH CARE L. & POL'Y 39, 39 & n.3 (2013); 21 U.S.C. § 823(f) (2006).

156 21 U.S.C. § 812 (2006). Marijuana is among the "controlled substances" listed in Schedule I. See Schedule I(c)(10).

157 Comprehensive Drug Abuse Prevention and Control Act of 1970, Pub. L. No. 91–513, 84 Stat. 1236 (1970).

158 Gonzales v. Raich, 545 U.S. 1, 13–14, 22 (2005).

159 Troy E. Grandel, *One Toke Over the Line: The Proliferation of State Medical Marijuana Laws*, 9 U. NEW HAMPSHIRE L. REV. 135, 136, 140–42 (2010).

160 O'Keefe, *supra* note 155, at 39 & n.1; Marijuana Policy Project, Our History, http://www.mpp.org/about/history (last visited June 16, 2015).

161 Sam Kamin & Eli Wald, *Marijuana Lawyers: Outlaws or Crusaders?*, 91 OR. L. REV. 869, 870, 878 (2013).

government by states and their interests and by the availability of funds for enforcement.[162] The marijuana-applicable law of the federal government is thus effectively pro forma at the present time.[163] Moreover, if the movement toward liberalization of state law on marijuana was a response to altered social values, a rewriting and easing of current restrictions in federal law on marijuana can be expected given the macrosociological nature of the content of law.[164]

State law, then, should be the chief focus today when considering law on marijuana. As to this law, the timing of its liberalization during the 1990s is significant. Because liberalization started in the last half of the 1990s, it began after the onset of the substantial increase in marijuana use that is seen in Figure 6.5. The sequence—change in activity incidence followed by change in the content of law—lends credence to the view that concepts and doctrines of law portray social life. This view is further bolstered by quantitative studies of the impact that state law allowing marijuana for medical purposes has had on the incidence of marijuana use. Succinctly summarized, such law has not been found to have a clear and appreciable influence on the extent to which marijuana is consumed for either medical reasons or recreation.[165] The finding buttresses the proposition that, in a nation having a complex structure and democratic government, law on social behavior is a creation of society and a response to, rather than a determinant of, societal conditions. If the content of law emerges from societal circumstances, it offers a window on society.

7 Aftermath of the Great Recession

Parts 4, 5, and 6 were devoted to documenting a shift in social values among Americans during the last third of the twentieth century, a shift that I believe bears responsibility for the Great Recession. The occurrence of the shift, however, raises two important questions—what were the causes of the shift, and what will be the long-term consequences of the recession that it spawned?

162 Robert A. Mikos, *Medical Marijuana and the Political Safeguards of Federalism*, 89 DENVER UNIV. L. REV. 997, 998, 999–1000, 1002–06 (2012).

163 *Id.* at 1002.

164 The macrosociological framework that I believe applies to law on society-important activities in a structurally complex, democratically governed jurisdiction is described in *supra* Chapter 1, at Part 1-b.

165 Sam Harper et al., *Do Medical Marijuana Laws Increase Marijuana Use? Replication Study and Extension*, 22 ANNALS EPIDEMIOLOGY 207, 211–12 (2012); Sarah D. Lynne-Landsman et al., *Effects of State Medical Marijuana Laws on Adolescent Marijuana Use*, 103 AM. J. PUB. HEALTH 1500, 1504–05 (2013).

Regrettably, the reasons for the shift—the subject of the first question—are unknown at the moment. Perhaps they will be unearthed as time passes and additional data become available. Clearly, they are a matter that social scientists ought to investigate.

What are likely to be the long-term consequences of the Great Recession? Until the recession is in the distant past, its effects cannot be fully enumerated. Since the recession began, for instance, the rate of participation in the labor force has appreciably fallen, but whether the abatement in labor force participation will be reversed remains to be seen.[166] Even if there is such a reversal, however, the recession will probably have numerous and varied consequences that persist.[167] In the following pages, I want to explore one category of these consequences. Specifically, I consider certain economic costs of the recession—or, perhaps I should say, certain economic costs of the shift in social values—because these costs will evidently be large in magnitude and may burden the United States for an extended period. When social values change slowly and become deeply embedded in a society, as apparently happened in the United States with values endorsing consumption and enjoyment, the economic costs of the change will not, ceteris paribus, quickly stop mounting, let alone decline. These costs, for example, can logically be expected to include compelled choices between alternatives, and major benefits will undoubtedly be lost

166 Julie L. Hotchkiss & Fernando Rios-Avila, *Identifying Factors behind the Decline in the U.S. Labor Force Participation Rate*, Bus. & Econ. Res., June 2013, at 257, 257–58, 267–68, http://www.macrothink.org/journal/index.php/ber/issue/archive (follow "Vol 3, No 1 (2013)" hyperlink). The Great Recession caused an unusually large decline in labor force participation among persons age 55 and older. Barry Bosworth, *Economic Consequences of the Great Recession: Evidence from the Panel Study of Income Dynamics* 12–15 (Ctr. for Retirement Research at Boston College, Working Paper No. 2012–4, 2012), *available at* http://crr.bc.edu/category/working-papers. The decline is likely to have long-lasting effects on this age group. Matthew S. Rutledge et al., *How Will Older Workers Who Lose Their Jobs During the Great Recession Fare in the Long Run?* 1, 15–16, 19 (Ctr. for Retirement Research at Boston College, Working Paper No. 2013–9, 2013), *available at* http://crr.bc.edu/category/working-papers; Steven A. Sass & Anthony Webb, *Is the Reduction in Older Workers' Job Tenure A Cause for Concern?* 14 (Ctr. for Retirement Research at Boston College, Working Paper No. 2010–20, 2010), *available at* http://crr.bc.edu/category/working-papers.

167 One long-lasting consequence may be that more Americans will be unable financially to continue their pre-retirement standard of living during retirement if they retire at age 65. Among U.S. households in 2010, fully 44% in the age range 50–59 and 55% in the age range 40–49 were projected to be in this situation; both percentages were appreciably increased by the recession. Alicia H. Munnell et al., *The National Retirement Risk Index: An Update* 1–3, 6 & Fig. 8, Tbl. 2 (Ctr. for Retirement Research at Boston College, National Retirement Risk Index Paper No. 12–20, 2012), *available at* http://crr.bc.edu/special-projects/national-retirement-risk-index.

because particular alternatives are not selected. As in most situations, avoidance of a problem is preferable to curing it.

In identifying costs, I concentrate on two policies that were implemented by the federal government to combat the Great Recession in the United States and that are still in place. I have chosen these policies because of the complacency that on the whole exists regarding their potential or actual costs. The first policy is the massive but gradual purchase by the U.S. Federal Reserve System of securities representing debt of the United States or its agencies, i.e., debt securities issued by the U.S. Treasury or its instrumentalities and mortgage-backed securities the payment of whose principal and interest is guaranteed by the U.S. government.[168] The scale of the acquisitions since the onset of the recession, in an undertaking that is popularly labeled "quantitative easing," has been characterized as a move into "uncharted waters,"[169] and has resulted in the System owning approximately $4.2 trillion in debt securities as of February 2015.[170] By comparison, when the recession began in December 2007,[171] the System held less than $800 billion in debt securities.[172] Ownership of debt securities by the Federal Reserve System, accordingly, has quintupled due to the recession.

Given the post-2007 expansion by the Federal Reserve System of its portfolio of debt securities, the possibility exists that the System may incur a sizeable loss when it ends its present policy. The market value of debt securities varies inversely with interest rates, and a marked rise in interest rates—a rise that could stem from developments that the System cannot control—may put the System in the position of selling its securities at an average price that is below the average price at which the securities were acquired. Because repayment of the principal on the debt securities owned by the System generally is not required in the immediate future—i.e., because the debt securities will not

168 Meryam Bukhari et al., *The Fed's Balance Sheet Through Time*, ECONINTERSECT, Aug. 12, 2013, http://econintersect.com/b2evolution/blog1.php/2013/08/12/the-fed-s-balance-sheet-through-time.

169 James Bullard, President, Federal Reserve Bank of St. Louis, President's Message: Quantitative Easing—Uncharted Waters for Monetary Policy (Jan. 2010), https://www.stlouisfed.org/publications/regional-economist/january-2010/quantitative-easing uncharted-waters--for-monetary-policy.

170 Bd. of Governors, Federal Reserve System, Federal Reserve Statistical Release, H.4.1: Factors Affecting Reserve Balances of Depository Institutions and Condition Statement of Federal Reserve Banks (Feb. 26, 2015), http://www.federalreserve.gov/releases/h41. The program of "quantitative easing" ended in October 2014. Press Release, Bd. of Governors, Federal Reserve System (Oct. 29, 2014), http://www.federalreserve.gov/newsevents/press/monetary/20141029a.htm.

171 *Supra* note 11.

172 Bd. of Governors, *supra* note 170 (using the releases in series H.4.1 for December 2007).

mature soon—the prospect of losses is enhanced.[173] If through choice or necessity the System reduced its holdings of debt securities (rather than keep the securities until they matured), the loss to the System could amount to no less than a fifth of a trillion dollars and might exceed a half-trillion dollars.[174] A mechanism will be required to cover such a loss, but neither the mechanism nor the long-term ramifications of a large loss are known.[175]

I turn now to the second policy that the federal government pursued to counter the recession. The policy involved government spending. In fiscal year 2008, the size of the yearly increase in spending by the federal government was noticeably larger than in earlier years; spending jumped by an even greater amount in fiscal year 2009, and remained at an elevated and roughly constant level through fiscal year 2014, the latest for which final data are available.[176] With spending higher, the federal government experienced a dramatically enlarged deficit in its annual budget,[177] and its debt rapidly increased. Figure 6.6 presents a measure that is often utilized to

173 At year-end 2012, the debt securities in the Federal Reserve System Open Market Account had an average duration of approximately six years. FEDERAL RESERVE BANK OF NEW YORK, DOMESTIC OPEN MARKET OPERATIONS DURING 2012, at 15 & Chart 17, 40 n.30 (2013), *available at* www.newyorkfed.org/markets/omo/omo2012.pdf. The average duration of a portfolio of securities is an estimate of the change that will occur in the market value of the portfolio for each rise or fall in interest rates of one percentage-point. A one percentage-point rise in interest rates is expected to decrease by 6.0% the market value of a portfolio that has an average duration of 6.0 years. Morningstar, Inc., The Difference Between "Maturity" and "Duration," http://www.morningstar.co.uk/uk/news/69773/The-Difference-Between-Maturity-and-Duration.aspx (last visited May 9, 2015).

174 Craig Torres et al., Fed Faces Explaining Billion-Dollar Losses in QE Exit Stress, Feb. 26, 2013, http://www.bloomberg.com/news/2013-02-26/fed-faces-explaining-billion-dollar-losses-in-stress-of-qe3-exit.html.

175 *Id.*

176 U.S. OFFICE OF MANAGEMENT & BUDGET, THE BUDGET: HISTORICAL TABLES Tbl. 1.1 (2015), *available at* http://www.whitehouse.gov/omb/budget/Historicals.

177 The yearly deficit was:

Fiscal year	Deficit (billions of dollars)
2008	458.6
2009	1,412.7
2010	1,294.4
2011	1,299.6
2012	1,087.0
2013	679.5
2014	484.6

Id. at Tbl. 1.1.

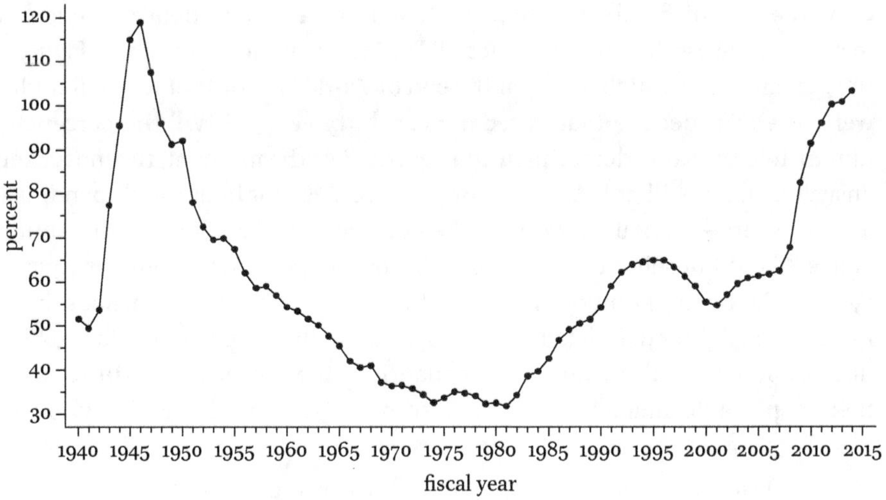

FIGURE 6.6 *U.S. federal government debt burden: federal government debt as a percent of gross domestic product by fiscal year*
SOURCE: SEE FN. 179 IN THIS CHAPTER.

evaluate the magnitude of this debt and gauge the economic burden it imposes on the country.[178] Specifically, the Figure shows gross federal government indebtedness in relation to—expressed as a percentage of—the gross domestic product of the United States in each fiscal year from 1940 through 2014.[179]

---

178 The argument might be made that Figure 6 should include the debt of *all* levels of government—state and local governments as well as the federal government. However, state and local government policies and actions, more than federal government policies and actions, were designed to respond to public needs and demands. D. Wes Sullenger, *Silencing the Blogosphere: A First Amendment Caution to Legislators Considering Using Blogs to Communicate Directly with Constituents*, 13 RICH. J.L. & TECH. article 15, ¶ 15 (2007), http://jolt.richmond.edu (follow "Past Issues" hyperlink). Therefore, state and local government debt can be deemed similar to personal debt, which was discussed in *supra* Part 5-b, and it should be considered in that context, i.e., state and local government debt should be treated as an indicator of the strength of social values underscoring consumption and enjoyment. Data on state and local government debt over time is in THE PLACE OF LAW, *supra* note 6, at 163–64.

179 The percentages in Figure 6 were obtained from U.S. OFFICE OF MANAGEMENT & BUDGET, *supra* note 176, at Tbl. 7.1, and are for "gross federal debt," which consists of federal government debt held by "federal government accounts" and debt held by "the public." The definition of "gross domestic product" is in *supra* note 16.

At the end of fiscal year 2014, U.S. federal government debt was equal to 103% of U.S. gross domestic product.[180] During the period covered by Figure 6, the percentage was higher only at the end of World War II, after which it underwent a secular decline that lasted almost thirty years.[181] Will the percentage diminish to the same degree in future decades? At the moment, the most likely answer is that it will not. A reason for pessimism is that household spending is a large share—roughly 40% to 45%—of economic activity in the United States,[182] but household debt exceeds disposable personal income by roughly 130%.[183] At the midpoint of the twentieth century, by comparison, households had a much lighter debt load: In 1950, household debt represented just 58% of disposable personal income,[184] less than half the current level. In terms of their deployable financial resources, accordingly, households today are far

180 U.S. OFFICE OF MANAGEMENT & BUDGET, *supra* note 176, at Tbl. 7.1.

181 *Id.* at Tbl. 7.1.

182 Michael Mandel, Giving Credit Where Credit is Due: Consumer Spending is *Not* 70% of the Economy 2 (2010), http://innovationandgrowth.wordpress.com/2010/05/01/giving-credit-where-credit-is-due-consumer-spending-is-not-70-of-the-economy (last visited May 9, 2015).

183 *Supra* note 100 and accompanying text.

184 This percentage was calculated using (i) the debt of households and nonprofit organizations at the end of 1950 and (ii) the disposable personal income of consumers during 1950. The numerator (debt in billions of dollars) was the combination of debt from consumer credit instruments and debt from home mortgages. The data on debt were obtained from the Federal Reserve Bank of St. Louis, D.3: Credit Market Debt Outstanding by Sector, http://www.research.stlouisfed.org/fred2/categories/32256 (follow "Households and Nonprofit Organizations: Credit Market Instruments; Liability, Level" hyperlink to "Download Data" and follow "Households and Nonprofit Organizations; Home Mortgages; Liability, Level" hyperlink to "Download Data"). The denominator (disposable personal income in billions of dollars) was obtained from BUREAU OF THE CENSUS, STATISTICAL ABSTRACT OF THE UNITED STATES: 1952, at 256 Tbl. 307 (73d ed. 1952), *available at* http://www.census.gov/prod/www/statistical_abstract.html.

The numerator covered the debt of both households and nonprofit organizations, because data on debt are not reported separately for households and for nonprofit organizations. However, based on a study by the Federal Reserve Bank of New York that employed data for 2010, household debt evidently comprises more than 90% of the debt of households and nonprofit organizations combined. Donghoon Lee & Wilbert van der Klaauw, An Introduction to the FRBNY Consumer Credit Panel 14 (Federal Reserve Bank of New York Staff Report No. 479) (2010) (estimating from a study of individuals in the second quarter of 2010 that the total debt of households was $11.7 trillion, while for the same period, the total debt of both households and nonprofit organizations was reported in the Federal Reserve System flow-of-funds accounts to be $12.6 trillion), http://www.newyorkfed.org/research/staff_reports/sr479.html.

more constrained by debt than were households after World War II, a situation that will curtail the ability of present-day Americans to fuel economic growth[185] that will lower the relative if not absolute amount of federal government indebtedness. In terms of the economy, in short, American history after World War II will probably not be repeated in forthcoming decades. Moreover, the United States could soon suffer a substantial, lengthy rise in interest rates, to the detriment of economic activity, because of the combination of the amount of debt of the federal government relative to the gross domestic product of the country, the portion of federal-government debt that is held by non-government entities, and the current-account deficit of the nation.[186]

At the moment, then, evidence from economics is not comforting with regard to the potential extent, duration, and severity of the aftermath of the Great Recession.[187] Macrosociology, in emphasizing that a society has a life of

185 A factor that may exacerbate the negative impact of household debt on household spending is decreased employment security in the private sector, at least for men. The length of employment tenure among men in the private sector declined from 1973–1983 to 1996–2006. Henry S. Farber, *Employment Insecurity: The Decline in Worker-Firm Attachment in the United States* 23, 25 (Princeton Univ. Ctr. for Economic Policy Stud. Working Paper No. 172, 2008), http://www.princeton.edu/ceps/publications.shtml. In light of the magnitude of the Great Recession, the assumption is reasonable that private-sector job tenure continued to fall after 2006. See the text accompanying *supra* note 20.

186 In a country that has a chronic deficit in its current account, the threshold for such a rise in interest rates is evidently government debt held by non-government entities that is around 80% of gross domestic product. David Greenlaw et al., *Crunch Time: Fiscal Crises and the Role of Monetary Policy* 20, 21, 47, 50–52, 85 (2013), http://research.chicagobooth.edu/igm/usmpf/download2.aspx. The current account balance for a country is "[t]he difference between the nation's total exports of goods, services and transfers and its total imports of them. Current account balance calculations exclude transactions in financial assets and liabilities." Federal Reserve System, Glossary, http://www.federalreserveeducation.org/glossary.

In 2011, United States government debt that was in non-government hands was approximately 80% of gross domestic product. Greenlaw et al., *supra*, at 47. From 1982 to 2012, the current account balance of the United States was negative in all years but one. Federal Reserve Bank of St. Louis, Balance on Current Account (BOPBCA), http://research.stlouisfed.org/fred2/series/BOPBCA (follow "Download Data" hyperlink). More importantly, the mean yearly deficit in the current account of the United States from 2000 to 2012 was approximately 4% of gross domestic product. Greenlaw et al., *supra*, at 51. A simulation with an assumed current-account deficit of 2.5% of gross domestic product has projected that interest rates in the United States will begin a substantial, prolonged increase in the near future. Greenlaw et al., *supra*, at 51, 52 Fig. 3.11.

187 Carmen M. Reinhart & Kenneth S. Rogoff, *Financial and Sovereign Debt Crises: Some Lessons Learned and Those Forgotten* 3–4, 17 (Int'l Monetary Fund, Working Paper No. 266,

its own, adds to the grounds for concern. Specifically, the fabric of U.S. society was altered by the shift in social values that produced the recession, and due to the inertia that characterizes a society with a complex structure and large population, the current prevalence of social values approving consumption and enjoyment may well persist in the United States for a long time. Indeed, neither Figure 6.1 nor Figure 6.2 (*supra* Part 4) offer any clear evidence that these values have been receding in response to the recession.

If any benefit emerges from the Great Recession, it may be the recognition that concepts and data from macrosociology can contribute to understanding the economy. Because the economy is lodged in a societal system,[188] its processes and the policies applicable to them will have social antecedents as well as social consequences.[189] In developing insights into the causes and effects of macroeconomic phenomena, therefore, macrosociology can be expected to make unique contributions, reducing the likelihood that mistaken policies will be adopted in the future for economic problems. To adapt and extend an observation made by Georges Clemenceau,[190] economic events in general, and severe economic contractions in particular, are far too important to be left solely in the hands of economists.[191]

2013) (reviewing the history of financial crises in advanced nations and concluding from the economic consequences of these crises that the Great Recession is likely to have long-term negative effects).

188 *Supra* note 6 and accompanying text.

189 A study whose findings illustrate the social consequences of macroeconomic policy is F. John Mehrtens, III, *Laissez-Faire vs. Regulated Capitalism: A Cross-National Analysis of Social Costs*, 24 SOCIOL. SPECTRUM 341, 359, 361 Tbl. 2, 362–63 (2004).

190 Clemenceau, who was born in 1841 and died in 1929, was prominent in the history of France for approximately sixty years. J. HAMPDEN JACKSON, CLEMENCEAU AND THE THIRD REPUBLIC xi, xiii, 2, 255–56 (1946). He served twice as prime minister of the government of France—from October 1906 to July 1909 and from November 1917 to January 1920. Wikipedia, List of Prime Ministers of France, http://en.wikipedia.org/wiki/List_of_Prime_Ministers_of_France. Clemenceau has been characterized as exemplifying France "as the world has known her" from approximately the middle of the nineteenth century to the middle of the twentieth century. JACKSON, *supra* at xiii.

191 The statement by Clemenceau (as translated into English) was that "War is too serious a matter to leave to soldiers." JACKSON, *supra* note 190, at 228.

PART 3

Final Comments

CHAPTER 7

Moving Forward

Abstract

In jurisdictions that have a democratic government and a complex social structure, according to the macrosociological framework propounded by the instant book, concepts and doctrines of law on society-important activities are a function of society-level conditions. Since these conditions can be studied with different types of empirical evidence, prior chapters of the book have relied on, and hence illustrate, such evidence. Chapter 7 attempts to further the macrosociological framework of the book by offering a hypothesis on societal changes that may have produced Title VII of the U.S. Civil Rights Act of 1964. Because the framework also contends that law has just a small and/or temporary effect on the incidence of society-central activities, social science studies that have estimated the impact of Title VII on race discrimination in employment are reviewed. Finally, Chapter 7 stresses that the framework should not be cabined by disciplinary boundaries, because although grounded in sociology, the framework is likely to be improved by the results of research in other disciplines, including disciplines that are outside the social sciences. As an example, the chapter summarizes and discusses findings of studies in neuroscience that have been conducted on the human brain, and considers the findings in terms of U.S. law on sex-segregated schooling.

1 Introduction

Chapter 7, in winding up the book, is concerned with the future, not with the past, and in looking forward, the chapter suggests some avenues whose pursuit may contribute to the macrosociological framework that is the foundation of the book. In particular, Chapter 7 does not involve a distillation and summary of the six chapters that preceded it. The earlier chapters have delineated the proposed macrosociological framework as fully as now seems possible with the empirical research that is available. Further refinement of the framework, and formulation of a quantitatively grounded macrosociological theory of law, must await the accumulation of additional evidence, especially the evidence required to identify the main society-level forces that affect law in multiple

 | DOI 10.1163/9789004281219_008

historical eras and to pinpoint the sequence(s) in which these forces operate.[1] A condensation of earlier chapters, in short, seems likely to add little that is helpful. Chapter 7 thus pursues other goals.

By way of overview, Chapter 7 follows two distinct paths. The first is designed to underscore the potential breadth of the macrosociological framework that is advanced in the instant book. The chapter applies the framework to a prominent U.S. statute that deals with one aspect (viz., discrimination) of a society-important activity (viz., employment) and, in doing so, discusses a society-level force that, while overlooked to date in the search for macro-level determinants of law, may have been the critical factor leading to the adoption of the statute. The second path taken by Chapter 7 aims to sensitize scholars to the possibility, if not the likelihood, that the framework, although anchored in sociology, will benefit from the findings of research in other disciplines, including disciplines that, on the surface, have no obvious relevance to sociology.

In short, Chapter 7 hopes to attract scholars to the quest for the societal sources of concepts and doctrines of law by directing attention to a society-level force that has not heretofore been considered. At the same time, the chapter hopes to advance the quest by suggesting that the tools of macrosociology may not be sufficient by themselves to paint a complete picture of the roots of law in society. Rather, other disciplines may be required if the societal origins of law are to be fully explained.

Even if the specific paths taken by Chapter 7 prove unproductive, much more can, and in time will, be learned by social scientists about the impact that societal forces and characteristics have on the content of law. Eventually, enough will be known to formulate a comprehensive theory on society-to-law relationships. However, empirical studies of the macro-level factors that mold the concepts and doctrines of law are important not just for theory construction. Such studies have the potential to benefit social life in concrete ways,[2] and should be done for just this reason alone.

Why does research on the societal conditions that determine the content of law hold the promise of practical benefits? The answer requires an understanding of the foundation of the scientific enterprise. Every science assumes that the phenomena it studies are characterized by observable patterns and that the elements of a

---

1 Because the framework is limited to patterns of activity that are important or central to social life in jurisdictions having a complex societal structure and democratic government, the framework must also contain, but presently lacks, criteria to gauge the importance/centrality of activities in such jurisdictions. Efforts to identify the criteria will involve analyses of quantitative data on the various dimensions of social activities.

2 LARRY D. BARNETT, THE PLACE OF LAW: THE ROLE AND LIMITS OF LAW IN SOCIETY 231–32 (2011) [hereinafter THE PLACE OF LAW].

pattern, and change or differences in the elements, can be described qualitatively and/or measured numerically.[3] As a science, sociology is thus grounded on the premise that the social world is not chaotic and that social events do not occur haphazardly. Furthermore, sociology seems generally to make the assumption that the elements of social life can be quantified. Therefore, when an element of society does not last indefinitely or does not exist universally, sociology expects that the change or differences in it can be depicted numerically.

The elements of social patterns, of course, are sociological variables, and hence they supply the grist for the mill of sociological research. Once numeric data on a dependent variable and on a set of independent variables have been assembled, statistical procedures such as multiple regression can uncover the relationship between each antecedent (i.e., independent) variable and the outcome (i.e., dependent) variable. If a particular independent variable has a relationship of substantial magnitude to the dependent variable in more than one historical era in a particular society and/or in more than one society, knowledge of the relationship can be combined with data on the independent variable to forecast the amount of the dependent variable (when the dependent variable is measured in continuous units) or the state of the dependent variable (when the dependent variable is measured with discrete categories). The sociological enterprise thus holds the promise of predicting what has yet to be observed.

Like its parent discipline, macrosociology seeks regularities in social life, but it is solely concerned with *macro*-level aspects of the social world. Consequently, the macrosociological framework that underlies the instant book contends that attributes of society, not the political process[4] or certain individuals, are the source of concepts and doctrines of law on society-important activities. If the framework is correct, our understanding of the society-level variables that temporally precede and are connected to the content of law will reach the

---

3 JOHN G. KEMENY, A PHILOSOPHER LOOKS AT SCIENCE 59–63, 67, 154–55 (1959).

4 Within the political process, proposals of law (bill introductions) must be distinguished from adoptions of law (bill adoptions). Eric A. Whitaker et al., *The Determinants of Policy Introduction and Bill Adoption: Examining Minimum Wage Increases in the American States, 1997–2006*, 40 POL'Y STUDIES J. 626, 632–33, 643–44 (2012) (study of state legislation setting a minimum wage). Notably, the study by Whitaker et al. found that both citizen ideology and a set of variables of a political nature affected the introduction into state legislatures of proposals, i.e., bills. *Id.* at 636–37, 639 Tbl. 2. However, citizen ideology was the sole factor in the regression model that affected adoptions of bills; none of the variables that were of a political character had an impact on whether proposed legislation was approved. *Id.* at 641 Tbl. 3. Citizen ideology is probably an indicator of culture, a factor that was identified in previous chapters as influencing whether states changed their law to expand women's access to medically induced abortion and to impose harsh punishment on persons for repeated criminal convictions. Part 2-c in *supra* Chapter 2 and Part 3 in *supra* Chapter 3, respectively.

point where this content is predictable ahead of time with a known likelihood of error, at least when the predictions are based on accurate measurements of the antecedent variables[5] and the antecedent variables remain the same across historical eras.[6] The advent of concepts and doctrines of law will be capable of prediction long before they are adopted in a jurisdiction, because the antecedent variables evidently exhibit temporally extended trends within jurisdictions and/or large differences between jurisdictions before they trigger new law. An important corollary of the preceding point is that a change in law that upends tradition cannot be permanently blocked or reversed in a complex, democratically governed jurisdiction when the new law originates from one or more fundamental shifts in the social fabric. Simply put, political demonstrations, or even violence and threats of violence, that aim to thwart such a change or restore tradition-endorsed law are futile in the long run. Accordingly, once the macrosociological character of law is widely acknowledged, law can be expected to wane as a source of social conflict.[7]

2 Title VII of the Civil Rights Act of 1964

A concern with rights, especially personal rights, has long been prominent in the American ethos[8] and, hence, in U.S. law,[9] where the concern is aligned with an emphasis on liberty.[10] Indeed, some rights are considered by U.S. law

5 *See* GEORGE A. LUNDBERG, FOUNDATIONS OF SOCIOLOGY 10 (1964).

6 THE PLACE OF LAW, *supra* note 2, at 467–68.

7 *Id.* at 231–32. Besides reducing social conflict, research on the jurisdiction conditions that mold the concepts and doctrines of law may benefit the practice of law. Lawyers who assess risks that law poses for clients are expected to become more numerous in the future. These lawyers, in managing "legal risk" for clients, will be concerned with "anticipating the needs of those they advise, on containing and pre-empting legal problems," a service that is "perhaps the most urgently needed and longest overdue" in the practice of law. RICHARD SUSSKIND, TOMORROW'S LAWYERS 117–18 (2013). Anticipation of law-related client problems, of course, will include predicting changes in law. Predictions will be more accurate, and will be possible farther in advance, to the extent that well-designed studies are available on the jurisdiction-level forces that affect the content of law.

8 Rosemarie Zagarri, *The Rights of Man and Woman in Post-Revolutionary America*, 55 WILLIAM & MARY Q. 203, 205, 228–30 (1998).

9 C. Scott Pryor, *Looking For Bedrock: Accounting for Human Rights in Classical Liberalism, Modern Secularism, and the Christian Tradition*, 33 CAMPBELL L. REV. 609, 611–12 (2011).

10 *See* Planned Parenthood of Southeastern Pennsylvania v. Casey, 505 U.S. 833, 851 (1992) ("At the heart of liberty is the right to define one's own concept of existence, of meaning, of the universe, and of the mystery of human life").

to be indispensable ingredients of liberty.[11] Not coincidentally, then, both the concept of rights and the concept of liberty are referenced by the Declaration of Independence[12] and by amendments to the Constitution.[13] In several of the amendments, furthermore, the U.S. Supreme Court has found assurances of "personal equality and freedom from discrimination."[14] Notably, these assurances have not been confined to the documents on which the Nation was founded. The latter point merits elaboration.

During the last half of the twentieth century, the twin ideas of rights and of liberty have been implicit in statutes that the federal government has adopted to combat discrimination in employment against groups having certain demographic attributes.[15] In particular, the statutes were devised to require that the centerpiece of employment be personal expertise, a goal that was to be achieved in large part by prohibiting the use of stereotypes associated with job-irrelevant

---

11 *E.g.*, Marbury v. Madison, 5 U.S. (1 Cranch) 137, 163 (1803) (stating that "[t]he very essence of civil liberty certainly consists in the right of every individual to claim the protection of the laws, whenever he receives an injury"); Borough of Duryea, Pennsylvania v. Guarnieri, 131 S. Ct. 2488, 2498 (2011) (referring to the rights listed in the First Amendment as "fundamental to liberty").

12 THE DECLARATION OF INDEPENDENCE para. 2 (U.S. 1776).

13 Of the twenty-seven amendments to the U.S. Constitution, the first ten are popularly labeled "the Bill of Rights," and seven of the ten amendments in the Bill of Rights—all except the third, eighth, and tenth amendments—contain the word "right," the word "freedom," and/or the word "liberty." U.S. CONST. amend. I to X. The frequency of these words in the Bill of Rights is not surprising inasmuch as "the Bill of Rights is designed to secure individual liberty." Roberts v. United States Jaycees, 468 U.S. 609, 618 (1984). In addition, seven of the remaining seventeen amendments—viz., the twelfth, fourteenth, fifteenth, nineteenth, twentieth, twenty-fourth, and twenty-sixth amendments—also contain one or more of the aforementioned words. U.S. CONST. amend. XI to XXVII.

14 Oregon v. Mitchell, 400 U.S. 112, 128 (1970).

15 The statutes, not surprisingly, embody the concerns with rights and liberties in employment that are expressed in the federal Constitution. For instance, the U.S. Supreme Court wrote a century ago that: "In so far as a man is deprived of the right to labor[,] his liberty is restricted, his capacity to earn wages and acquire property is lessened, and he is denied the protection which the law affords those who are permitted to work. Liberty means more than freedom from servitude, and the constitutional guarantee [of liberty in the Due Process Clause of the Fourteenth Amendment] is an assurance that the citizen shall be protected in the right to use his powers of mind and body in any lawful calling." Smith v. Texas, 233 U.S. 630, 636 (1914). *See also* Davis v. Passman, 442 U.S. 228, 234–35 (1979) (construing the Due Process Clause of the Fifth Amendment to encompass sex-based employment discrimination by the federal government). In U.S. jurisprudence generally, therefore, unwarranted limitations on employment are regarded as infringements on rights and as curbs on liberty.

demographic attributes. In the words of the U.S. Supreme Court, federal legislation on employment discrimination was an answer to "'inaccurate and stigmatizing stereotypes.'"[16] In disapproving such stereotypes in favor of ability and performance in the workplace, the statutes were built on an endorsement of individual rights and were designed to maintain, if not enlarge, the perimeter of individual freedom. Of the four main statutes at the national level that comprise this line of legislation,[17] Title VII of the Civil Rights Act of 1964[18] has been the most visible, and it has been regarded as the single most useful weapon in the arsenal of federal law that aims to counter socially harmful employment-related discrimination.[19]

a *Title VII and Race Discrimination*

What, precisely, does Title VII cover? Employers, employment agencies, and labor organizations[20] are barred by the statute from using "race, color, religion,

16 Raytheon Co. v. Hernandez, 540 U.S. 44, 54 n.7 (2003).

17 A summary of the principal statutes is in THE PLACE OF LAW, *supra* note 2, at 268–70.

18 Pub. L. No. 88–352, §§ 701–716, 78 Stat. 241, 253–66 (1964) (codified as amended at 42 U.S.C. §§ 2000e to 2000e-17 (2006)).

19 GEORGE RUTHERGLEN, EMPLOYMENT DISCRIMINATION LAW: VISIONS OF EQUALITY IN THEORY AND DOCTRINE 6 (3d ed. 2010) ("in Title VII, the [Civil Rights Act of 1964] created the most important of the statutory prohibitions against employment discrimination and the one that most clearly expanded upon the protection offered by the Constitution").

20 Title VII defines the terms "employer," "employment agency," and "labor organization." 42 U.S.C. § 2000e (2006). In these definitions, the word "person" includes a human individual as well as an entity, i.e., a governmental body or a private-sector organization. 42 U.S.C. § 2000e(a) (2006).

Under Title VII, an employer is "a person engaged in an industry affecting commerce who has fifteen or more employees for each working day in each of twenty or more calendar weeks in the current or preceding calendar year, and any agent of such a person, but such term does not include (1) the United States, a corporation wholly owned by the Government of the United States, an Indian tribe, or any department or agency of the District of Columbia subject by statute to procedures of the competitive service…, or (2) a bona fide private membership club (other than a labor organization) which is exempt from taxation under Section 501(c) of the Internal Revenue Code of 1954…." 42 U.S.C. § 2000e(b) (2006).

An employment agency is "any person regularly undertaking with or without compensation to procure employees for an employer or to procure for employees opportunities to work for an employer and includes an agent of such a person." 42 U.S.C. § 2000e(c) (2006).

A labor organization is "a labor organization engaged in an industry affecting commerce, and any agent of such an organization, and includes any organization of any kind, any agency, or employee representation committee, group, association, or plan so engaged in which employees participate and which exists for the purpose, in whole or in part, of dealing with employers concerning grievances, labor disputes, wages, rates of pay, hours, or other terms or conditions of employment, and any conference, general committee,

sex, or national origin" to discriminate against an individual with regard to employment.[21] Title VII is notable for its reach. The prohibitions of the statute are applicable not only to major, salient aspects of employment (e.g., hiring, discharge and compensation) but also to aspects that are below the surface of employment but are nonetheless significant in the work environment.[22] Illustrative of the latter aspects are recurring oral statements that are recognized as relevant to a covered demographic attribute (e.g., race or sex) and that, because they are offensive, negatively affect the workplace. When "permeated with 'discriminatory intimidation, ridicule, and insult'" that generates "'an abusive working environment,'" the U.S. Supreme Court has concluded, a workplace is in breach of Title VII.[23]

In the instant chapter, a focus on all of the demographic attributes covered by Title VII is not feasible, and I will, therefore, confine the discussion to just one of the listed attributes, namely, race. The attribute of race is a logical choice inasmuch as Congress evidently wanted race discrimination to be the principal target of Title VII.[24] In the words of one U.S. Court of Appeals, "Congress' primary objective in passing Title VII was to eliminate race-related employment criteria."[25] In particular, the statute was prompted chiefly by discrimination against Blacks.[26]

---

joint or system board, or joint council so engaged which is subordinate to a national or international labor organization." 42 U.S.C. § 2000e(d) (2006).

21 42 U.S.C. § 2000e-2 (2006).

22 Harold S. Lewis, Jr. & Elizabeth J. Norman, Employment Discrimination Law and Practice §§ 2.1, 2.20, 2.22 (2d ed. 2004).

23 Harris v. Forklift Systems, Inc., 510 U.S. 17, 21 (1993).

24 The bill that became the Civil Rights Act of 1964 was H.R. 7152. U.S. Equal Employment Opportunity Comm'n, *Part 1—Historical and Legislative Background*, at 1, 11, *in* Legislative History of Titles VII and XI of Civil Rights Act of 1964 (U.S. Equal Employment Opportunity Comm'n ed. [1968]) [hereinafter Legislative History]. The report prepared for H.R. 7152 by the House Committee on the Judiciary includes a statement of seven members of Congress who contended that "this bill can and will commit our Nation to the elimination of many of the worst manifestations of racial prejudice" and that Title VII was part of the bill because "[a]ll vestiges of inequality based solely on race must be removed." H.R. Rep. No. 88–914 (1963), pt. 2, at 2, 30, *as reprinted in* 1964 U.S.C.C.A.N. 2487, 2488, 2517 and Legislative History, *supra*, at 2122, 2123, 2151. *See also* Griggs v. Duke Power Co., 401 U.S. 424, 434 (1971) ("'the very purpose of title VII is to promote hiring on the basis of job qualifications, rather than on the basis of race or color'" (quoting the *Congressional Record*)).

25 Contreras v. City of Los Angeles, 656 F.2d 1267, 1277 (9th Cir. 1981), *cert. denied*, 455 U.S. 1021 (1982). *Accord*, Holloway v. Arthur Andersen & Co., 566 F.2d 659, 662 (9th Cir. 1977); Ulane v. Eastern Airlines, Inc., 742 F.2d 1081, 1085 (7th Cir. 1984), *cert. denied*, 471 U.S. 1017 (1985).

26 United States v. Weber, 443 U.S. 193, 202–03 (1979). In commenting on the bill that was adopted as the Civil Rights Act of 1964, the House Committee on the Judiciary stated:

The racial group of which an individual is a member, however, is not necessarily clear at a particular juncture in time and constant across time. Race is determined not just by the physical features of an individual; it is also a function of social conditions. In the United States, accordingly, the racial category of a particular individual may not be permanently fixed. Indeed, the racial designation of a person can shift over time—both when the designation is made by the person and when it is made by someone else.[27] Furthermore, sociological variables affect the racial category in which an individual is placed at a given moment relative to the category in which the individual was placed previously.[28] Nonetheless, even though a not-inconsiderable percentage of individuals in the United States have moved between racial categories, just a small percentage has changed between the categories of White and Black.[29] The boundary that separates Whites from Blacks, in short, has been largely impermeable in the United States.

b *A Macrosociological Approach to Title VII*

Let us now examine Title VII with the macrosociological framework for law that was outlined in Part 1-b of Chapter 1. Does the framework offer a plausible and useful account of Title VII? I attempt to answer the question by exploring two matters. First, I return to the hypothesis that was the subject of Part 2 in Chapter 1 and ascertain whether the hypothesis, when applied to Title VII, is supported by quantitative data. If the hypothesis is correct, the emergence of Title VII followed substantial improvements in the employment situation of Blacks in the United States. Second, by reviewing social science studies, I assess whether Title VII was responsible for a material reduction in the incidence of employment discrimination against Blacks. Obviously, Title VII would not have received support during the course of its consideration by Congress unless it was expected to bring a major, tangible, and lasting benefit. Even if Title VII was enacted while Blacks were experiencing economic gains, the statute may have appreciably increased the magnitude of the gains and hence resulted in advances for Blacks to a degree that would not otherwise have occurred.

"In various regions of the country there is discrimination against some minority groups. Most glaring, however, is the discrimination against Negroes which exists throughout our Nation. Today, more than 100 years after their formal emancipation, Negroes, who make up over 10 percent of our population, are by virtue of one or another type of discrimination not accorded the rights, privileges, and opportunities which are considered to be, and must be, the birthright of all citizens." H.R. Rep. No. 88–914 (1963), *as reprinted in* 1964 U.S.C.C.A.N. 2391, 2393 and LEGISLATIVE HISTORY, *supra* note 24, at 2001, 2018.

27 Aliya Saperstein & Andrew M. Penner, *Racial Fluidity and Inequality in the United States*, 118 AM. J. SOCIOL. 676, 696 Tbl. 2, 697 Tbl. 3 (2012).

28 *Id.* at 698–701, 720 Tbl. A4.

29 *Id.* at 688, 696–98.

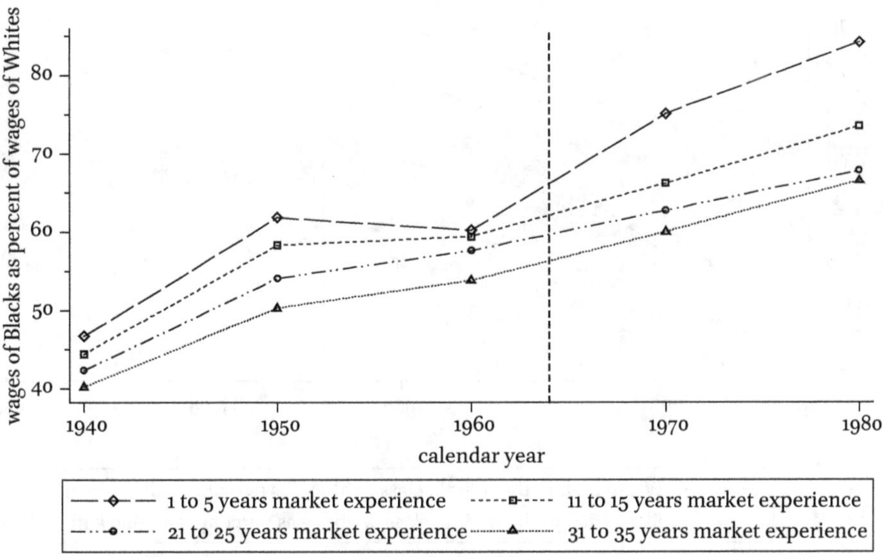

FIGURE 7.1 *Difference in weekly wages between black men and white men: by calendar year and years of market experience*
SOURCE: SEE FN. 30 IN THIS CHAPTER.

Turning to the hypothesis that was tested in Chapter 1, did the passage of Title VII occur after Blacks had started to close the economic gap with Whites in the United States? Evidence pertinent to the question is in Figure 7.1 and Figure 7.2.[30] The data in each Figure are derived from the decennial censuses conducted in the United States in 1940, 1950, 1960, 1970, and 1980. The Figures begin with 1940 because earlier censuses did not gather information on personal income,[31] and they are confined to men because data for women are not reported by the study that supplied the data used in the Figures.[32] Each

30 Figure 7.1 and Figure 7.2 were constructed from data in JAMES P. SMITH & FINIS R. WELCH, CLOSING THE GAP: FORTY YEARS OF ECONOMIC PROGRESS FOR BLACKS 6 Tbl. 2, 12 Tbl. 4 (1986), *available at* http://www.rand.org/pubs/reports/R3330.html.

31 *Id.* at 4.

32 In their study, Smith and Welch do not state their reason(s) for omitting women. A possible explanation is the relatively low rate of labor force participation among civilian women during the period from 1940 to 1980. Combining all races, all marital statuses, and all ages 16 and older, the rate did not rise and remain above one out of three women until the mid-1950s. U.S. CENSUS BUREAU, NO. HS-30: MARITAL STATUS OF WOMEN IN THE CIVILIAN LABOR FORCE: 1900 TO 2002, http://www.census.gov/statab/hist/HS-30.pdf (last visited June 16, 2015). In 1950, furthermore, the labor force participation rate of these women was just two-fifths that of men in the same age range (16 and older); even though the labor force participation rate among women steadily rose

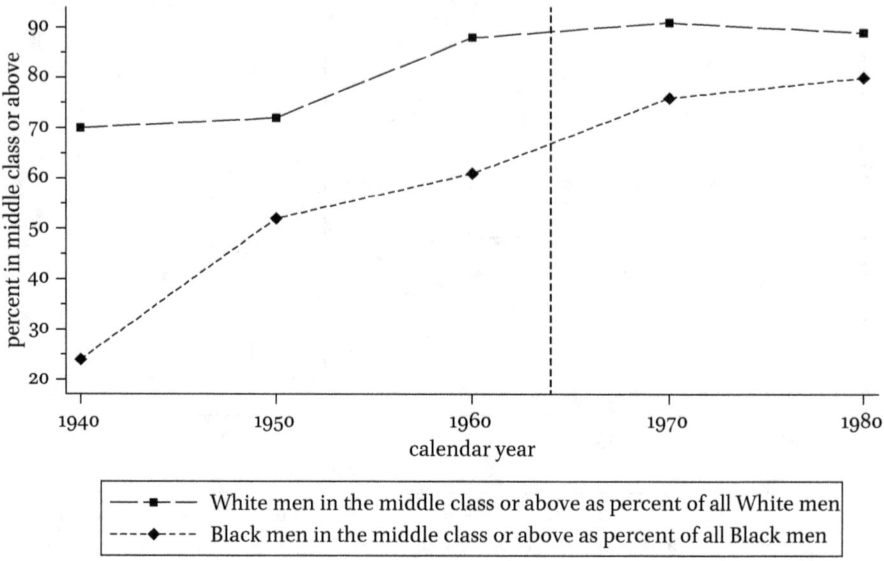

FIGURE 7.2 *White men and black men in the middle class or above: by calendar year and race*
SOURCE: SEE FN. 30 IN THIS CHAPTER.

Figure includes a vertical line that marks 1964, the year in which Title VII became law.[33]

Figure 7.1, which presents the weekly wages of Black men as a percent of the weekly wages of White men, reveals that, prior to Title VII, Black men

between 1950 and 1980 while the rate among men steadily fell, the rate in 1980 was still one-third lower among women than among men. Computed from Mitra Toossi, *A Century of Change: The U.S. Labor Force, 1950–2050*, MONTHLY LABOR REV., May 2002, at 15, 22 Tbl. 4, http://www.bls.gov/opub/mlr/author/toossi-mitra.htm.

An alternative or additional explanation may exist for the focus on men but not women in the Smith-Welch study. Specifically, a rise occurred during the 1950s in the proportion of all U.S. families that were headed by nonwhite females, and this rise may have been due to increased income from government welfare payments rather than from employment. Richard Butler & James J. Heckman, *The Government's Impact on the Labor Market Status of Black Americans: A Critical Review*, *in* EQUAL RIGHTS AND INDUSTRIAL RELATIONS 235, 241–43, 273 (Leonard J. Hausman et al. eds., 1977). If government welfare programs increased income among Black females to a considerably greater degree than among Black men during all or part of the time span being examined, sex-specific explanations exist for the economic position of each sex, and the economic position of women was affected more by a source that did not directly involve economic production, i.e., the manufacture of goods and the provision of services.

33 The Civil Rights Act of 1964 was approved by Congress, and was signed by the President, on July 2, 1964. Ctr. for Legis. Archives, Nat'l Archives, Civil Rights Act, July 2, 1964, http://www.archives.gov/legislative/features/civil-rights-1964/civil-rights-act-1964.html

were generally advancing relative to White men and that the advances were substantial in magnitude. From 1940 to 1950, a pattern of secular declines is apparent in the Black-White wage gap across the four levels of estimated market experience shown in the figure.[34] The declines largely continued from 1950 to 1960. However, the diminishing disadvantage of Black men relative to White men that occurred during this period had its inception decades before. In 1940, in 1950, and in 1960, cohorts of Black men who had joined the labor market more recently suffered generally less of a race-based disadvantage in weekly wages than cohorts of Black men who had joined the labor market earlier.[35] In 1950, for example, the weekly wages of Black men were 61.8% of the weekly wages of White men among men who entered the labor market in 1948, but among men who had entered the labor market in 1913, the percentage was just 46.9%. In short, the 1940-to-1960 reductions in the Black-White wage gap were part of prolonged, gradual change in the social system of the United States.

Figure 7.2 shows the extent of affluence among Black men and White men in the United States and reveals a notable difference between 1940 and 1960 in economic stratification. The difference arose from change that paralleled, and is related to, the reductions during this period in the Black-White wage gap. The most obvious trend disclosed by Figure 7.2 is that, as time went on, progressively higher proportions of Black men and of White men were in affluent strata, i.e., the middle class or above.[36] However, this upward shift is less

---

(last visited May 9, 2015). The provisions of Title VII that are cited in *supra* notes 20 and 21 were in force immediately, but some provisions of Title VII were not in force until one year later. Pub. L. No. 88–352, § 716, 78 Stat. 266 (1964).

34 Market experience (measured in years) was estimated for each person by subtracting (i) the age at which schooling was assumed to have ended from (ii) current age. SMITH & WELCH, *supra* note 30, at 6 n.3.

35 SMITH & WELCH, *supra* note 30, at 17 Tbl. 8.

36 To investigate economic stratification, the study by Smith and Welch initially identified the middle class in the 1940 census. Specifically, the middle class was considered to be White men who reported an income that was at least two-thirds (but no more than four-thirds) of the median income of White men in 1940. In each subsequent census year, the minimum income needed for membership in the middle class was the sum of (i) the minimum income that White males required to be a member of the middle class in the immediately prior census year and (ii) one-half of the rise in the real income of White men between the prior year and the current year. In every census year, men who were in the (one) socioeconomic class above the middle class reported an income that was no less than four-thirds of the median income of White men. For Black men, the two affluent strata (i.e., middle class and above middle class) were determined by the income criteria for the strata of White men. *Id.* at 11 n.6.

pertinent to the macrosociological framework of the instant book than another trend observable in Figure 7.2. Specifically, the disparity between the percentage of Black men and the percentage of White men who were in affluent strata was noticeably smaller in 1960 than it had been in 1940. While the contraction of the disparity occurred entirely from 1940 to 1950,[37] the notable point is that movement in the direction of parity in economic stratification began well before the advent of the Civil Rights Act of 1964.

If Title VII was adopted after the economic position of White men and of Black men had started to converge in the United States, did enactment of the statute materially help Blacks, or were any economic gains made by Blacks in the years following Title VII due to factors other than the statute? Economic position is tied to social position, of course, and if Title VII did not produce meaningful economic advances for Blacks, economic as well as social improvements would presumably have continued for Blacks even without Title VII, and both improvements are likely to have occurred at roughly the same pace. Because the impact of a statute on the problem it targets is pertinent to understanding the role of law in society, studies of the impact will help in assessing the macrosociological framework that was presented in Chapter 1. In this regard, Title VII is important because of its prominence in U.S. legislation on personal rights.

c *The Impact of Title VII on Race Discrimination in Employment*

Studies of the degree to which law curbs societal problems are often plagued by serious mistakes and major limitations. One mistake can occur when dating the advent of new law. The "effective date" of a statute, administrative agency rule, or court decision may not be a single point in time. Rather, two or more dates may need to be tested,[38] but a study of the impact of law may err in using just one. Other aspects of research design may also severely damage the credibility of a study that estimates the influence of law on the incidence of a problem (the dependent variable). Specifically, the ideal study for quantifying the impact of law possesses (i) accurate time-series data on the dependent variable as well as on the variables other than law—the sociological, economic,

37 The ratio of the percentage of White men in affluent strata to the percentage of Black men in affluent strata was 2.92 in 1940, 1.38 in 1950, and 1.44 in 1960. The ratio, although essentially stable from 1950 to 1960, was 1.20 in 1970, suggesting the possibility of a convergence between Whites and Blacks during the years surrounding passage of the Civil Rights Act.

38 A single date may be unsuitable for a number of reasons. For example, while a statute, agency rule, or court decision may be adopted or issued at time 1, compliance with it may not be mandated until time 2, and enforcement may not commence until time 3.

and demographic variables—that may affect the dependent variable; (ii) time-series data on the incidence of the dependent variable that are for short (e.g., monthly) intervals; (iii) time-series data on the incidence of the dependent variable that cover a lengthy period (e.g., a decade) before, and a lengthy period (e.g., a decade) after, the emergence of the new law; and (iv) data on the dependent variable and the independent variables for *both* a jurisdiction that adopted the new law *and* a jurisdiction that did not adopt the new law. A final element (v) is that the jurisdictions in (iv)—the jurisdiction with the law and the jurisdiction without the law—must be similar if not the same in terms of the sociological, economic, and demographic factors that are determinants of the dependent variable.[39] The absence from a study of any of the preceding impairs the credibility of the conclusions reached by the study. Colloquially explained, a study is like a chain—it can be only as strong as its weakest link.

The above standards are applicable, of course, to quantitative social science studies of whether race discrimination in employment was materially and permanently lessened by Title VII.[40] To illustrate departures from the standards, two important studies will be briefly discussed.

The first of the studies is a detailed review of prior research. The authors of the review, which was published in 1991, concluded that Title VII and its enforcement appreciably curtailed race-based employment discrimination in the South (though not elsewhere).[41] However, the authors acknowledged that "this position cannot be readily verified or falsified through standard econometric tests because of the difficulties in measuring Federal [government] pressure."[42] A conclusion that utilizes indirect evidence and hence is reached solely by inference may not be accurate, of course, and reliance on it is imprudent given the possibility that the conclusion is wrong and that continued government regulation justified by the conclusion will have or already has had side-effects that are unwanted. An additional consideration stems from an

39 The ideal research design is discussed and illustrated in Chester L. Britt et al., *A Reassessment of the D.C. Gun Law: Some Cautionary Notes on the Use of Interrupted Time Series Designs for Policy Impact Assessment*, 30 LAW & SOC'Y REV. 361 (1996).

40 Prior to the enactment of Title VII in 1964, numerous states adopted statutes that prohibited job-related race discrimination. LEGISLATIVE HISTORY, *supra* note 24, at 5–6; DUANE LOCKARD, TOWARD EQUAL OPPORTUNITY: A STUDY OF STATE AND LOCAL ANTIDISCRIMINATION LAWS 21–22 Tbl. I, 24 Tbl. II (1968). Several quantitative studies, which will not be considered here, have attempted to estimate whether Blacks benefitted economically from the statutes.

41 John J. Donohue III & James Heckman, *Continuous Versus Episodic Change: The Impact of Civil Rights Policy on the Economic Status of Blacks*, 29 J. ECON. LIT. 1603, 1640 (1991).

42 *Id.* at 1640. The authors also call attention to the quality of the evidence in *id.* at 1604.

observation made by the authors, namely, that many employers in the South used Title VII as a justification to end a practice (race discrimination) that they had already concluded should be stopped.[43] If that was the case, the economic improvement among Blacks that was attributed to Title VII would presumably have taken place, albeit at a slower pace, had Title VII not been enacted. Title VII, in short, may have simply hastened an economic change that societal forces were in the process of bringing about.

In the second study of Title VII to be discussed here, yearly data were drawn from the period 1990 through 2002 on private-sector employers that exceeded specified thresholds in terms of number of employees.[44] Like all research on the impact of Title VII, this study was concerned with a statute that applied throughout the United States and hence was unable to compare a jurisdiction that was subject to the statute with a jurisdiction that was not. A further limitation is that the study included data on employer work establishments for only a portion of the period that Title VII had been law. To be exact, work establishments were studied for a mean of 8.4 years[45] using data obtained from reports that employers filed with the Equal Employment Opportunity Commission, but the reports, which had been submitted since 1966,[46] were evidently available for 37 years when the data were compiled. Unfortunately, the limited time interval of the study may be accompanied by another major problem, viz., the quality of the data contained in the reports may be seriously deficient.[47]

Another aspect of this study is worthy of mention. Based on past studies of the impact of law, research that corrects a problem in the design of a prior study appears more likely to confirm a prior study that found no appreciable, enduring effect than to confirm a prior study that found such an effect. Notably, the study that comprises the second illustration concluded that Title VII had little direct influence on the extent of occupational segregation by race in the work establishments that were covered by the statute. Specifically, the investigator reported that such segregation was unresponsive to enforcement actions by the Equal Employment Opportunity Commission as well as to litigation,

---

43 *Id.* at 1605, 1640.

44 C. Elizabeth Hirsh, *The Strength of Weak Enforcement: The Impact of Discrimination Charges, Legal Environments, and Organizational Conditions on Workplace Segregation*, 74 AM. SOCIOL. REV. 245, 252–53, 258 (2009).

45 *Id.* at 259 Tbl. 2.

46 Donald Tomaskovic-Devey et al., *Documenting Desegregation: Segregation in American Workplaces by Race, Ethnicity, and Sex, 1966–2003*, 71 AM. SOCIOL. REV. 565, 569 (2006).

47 James P. Smith & Finis Welch, *Affirmative Action and Labor Markets*, 2 J. LAB. ECON. 269 (1984).

and while such segregation was reduced by charges of race discrimination by Blacks (and other races), the magnitude of the effect seems to have been small.[48] Summarizing the findings of her study with regard to the impact of Title VII on race discrimination, the investigator observes that "employers are largely indifferent to race charges, settlements, regulatory efforts, and legal environments."[49] Instead, direct effects on the extent of occupational segregation by race stemmed mainly from the organization-level characteristics of employers. Given these findings, future research is unlikely to reveal that Title VII (and equivalent state legislation) has been a substantial, long-term antidote to race discrimination in employment.

d *Societal Causes of Title VII*

Even if Title VII was of little or no long-term assistance to Blacks in securing, retaining, and advancing in employment, it undoubtedly provided societal benefits. A statute as prominent as Title VII would not last unless it aided the social order in some important way(s). In particular, Title VII may have symbolized a commitment to equality, created (or reinforced) trust in the Nation, and bolstered the reputation of the government of the country. In doing so, Title VII would have been socially productive. However, the benefit(s) that American society derived from Title VII does not explain why Title VII was adopted in the 1960s rather than at a much earlier or later point in history. For the explanation, I suggest, we must delve into systemic, long-term changes that had occurred in the United States. While I cannot identify these changes with certainty, I can formulate a credible hypothesis. Like any hypothesis, of course, mine must be empirically tested, and until that happens, its accuracy will be unknown.

Succinctly stated, the hypothesis I propose is that the Civil Rights Act of 1964 is attributable to societal changes that were associated with, if not directly caused by, the migration, over much of the preceding half-century, of large numbers of Blacks from the South to other regions of the country. In a nutshell, my reasoning is that this migration stream markedly intensified society-level stress, and thereby upset the equilibrium of the social systems, in the receiving geographic regions. The increase in race-grounded societal stress, I believe, was in turn responsible for societal pressure to develop means that appeared likely to reduce the stress. Because the institution of law is popularly assumed to offer such means, the result was the enactment of the Civil Rights Act of 1964.

---

48 Hirsh, *supra* note 44, at 263 Tbl. 5, 265, 266–67. Because of the manner in which the dependent variable was measured, the regression coefficient for race-discrimination charges does not have an apparent, intuitively meaningful interpretation. *Id.* at 253, 256.

49 *Id.* at 267.

Let me provide the historical background to my hypothesis. The beginning of World War I in 1914[50] curtailed immigration into the United States from Europe and, by hampering the ability of American industry in non-Southern states to recruit additional workers, acted with other factors to trigger a marked increase starting around 1916 in the movement of Blacks out of states in the South to states in the Northeast, North Central, and Western regions of the United States.[51] Notably, the elevated volume of migration of Blacks in the South to these regions did not end with World War I. Instead, during the decades that followed the war, migration out of the South by Blacks continued at a higher level than before the war, although the migration abated to some extent during the 1930s because the main force behind the migration had been more-attractive economic conditions in the states of destination than in the states of origin.[52] However, in the 1930s as well as in later decades, economics does not fully account for the volume of out-migration by Blacks from the South to other regions. Sociological factors were also important. Specifically, in the 1930s, the curtailment of economic opportunities was partially countered by social infrastructure in Black communities outside the South, and in later decades the availability of economic opportunities was augmented by social ties between newly arriving and earlier migrants.[53]

Accordingly, the enlarged movement of Blacks from the South to other regions outlasted World War I. Indeed, that movement persisted until, as well as into, the period of time—the 1950s and 1960s—when the United States developed its current federal civil rights law on race discrimination.[54] The societal

---

50 Samuel R. Williamson, Jr., *The Origins of World War I*, 18 J. INTERDISC. HIST. 795 (1988).

51 DANIEL M. JOHNSON & REX R. CAMPBELL, BLACK MIGRATION IN AMERICA: A SOCIAL DEMOGRAPHIC HISTORY 71–77, 80–86 (1981); CAROLE MARKS, FAREWELL—WE'RE GOOD AND GONE: THE GREAT BLACK MIGRATION 93–94, 121–22 (1989); DOUGLAS S. MASSEY & NANCY A. DENTON, AMERICAN APARTHEID: SEGREGATION AND THE MAKING OF THE UNDERCLASS 28–29 (1993).

52 JOHNSON & CAMPBELL, *supra* note 51, at 95–96, 108–110, 122–23;

53 Townsand Price-Spratlen, *Between Depression and Prosperity? Changes in the Community Context of Historical African American Migration*, 77 SOC. FORCES 515, 517–19, 533 (1998).

54 The inception of this period can be fixed at May 1954, when the U.S. Supreme Court held that "separate but equal" racially segregated public schools violate the equal protection guarantee of the Fourteenth Amendment to the Constitution. Brown v. Bd. of Educ., 347 U.S. 483, 495 (1954). The ruling in *Brown* not only marks the start of the current era in U.S. law on civil rights for Blacks but is considered to be among the most important rulings by the Court since it first decided a case more than a century-and-a-half earlier. BERNARD SCHWARTZ, A HISTORY OF THE SUPREME COURT 20, 286, 309–10 (1993).

The changes in the U.S. social fabric that preceded and were responsible for *Brown* are probably attributable in large part to the increased migration of Blacks out of the South

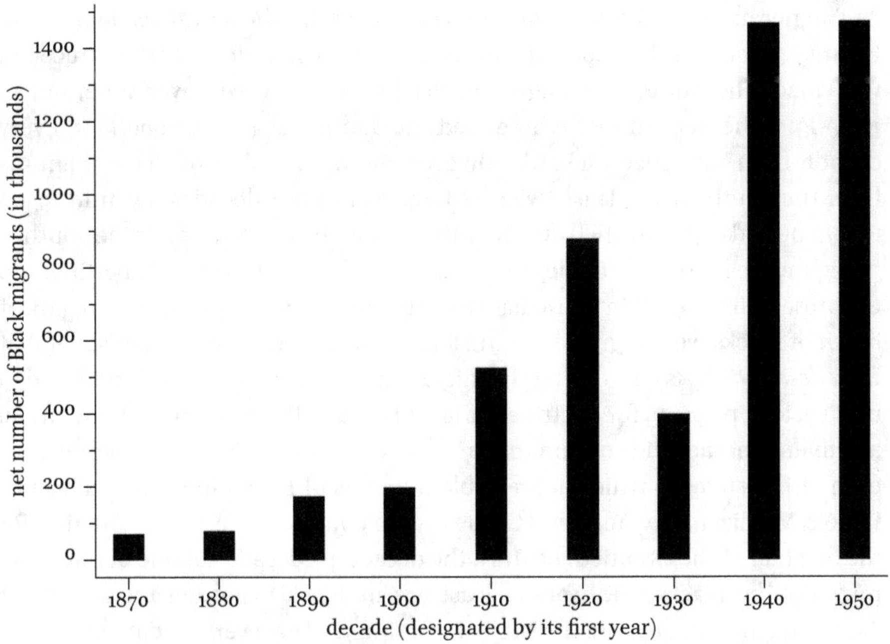

FIGURE 7.3 *Migration of blacks out of the south, by decade: 1870–1880 to 1950–1960*
SOURCE: SEE FN. 55 IN THIS CHAPTER.

pressure that was responsible for this law, in short, was building during the first half of the century and, for some as-yet unknown reason(s), brought about its adoption at mid-century.

To illuminate the narrative above, I provide quantitative measures of the migration that occurred among Blacks in the United States over the course of the time span being considered. Figure 7.3 shows the estimated net number of Blacks who left the South during each decade from 1870–1880 to 1950–1960.[55] The numbers combine males and females and include all ages. The horizontal axis, in designating decades, specifies just the first year of each decade. The decade of 1870–1880, for example, is represented on the horizontal axis by the year 1870.

---

in the decades prior to 1950. My hypothesis is thus not limited to the provisions of the Civil Rights Act of 1964 dealing with race discrimination. Rather, it extends to all of U.S. law that developed after World War II to end race discrimination against Blacks.

55 Figure 7.3 was constructed from data in REYNOLDS FARLEY & WALTER ALLEN, THE COLOR LINE AND THE QUALITY OF LIFE IN AMERICA 113 Tbl. 5.1 (1987). The Farley-Allen estimates diverge somewhat from estimates in DOUG MCADAM, POLITICAL PROCESS AND THE DEVELOPMENT OF BLACK INSURGENCY, 1930–1970, at 78 Tbl. 5.2 (1982). The McAdam estimates, however, lead to the same general conclusions as the Farley-Allen estimates.

The net number of Blacks who moved away from the South, we learn from Figure 7.3, was less than 200,000 during each of the four decades that preceded 1910–1920. The number of migrating Blacks had increased over time, but in 1900–1910, the net number who exited the South was just 197,000.[56] In every decade from 1910–1920 onward, however, the net number of Black migrants from the South was at least twice as large as in prior decades. Even in 1930–1940, a period of diminished out-migration, fully 398,000 Blacks left the South.[57]

Figure 7.3, however, supplies only one part of the context that is pertinent to the present discussion. In particular, the figure provides data on only the region of *origin* of Blacks who migrated; it furnishes no data on the region(s) or state(s) of their *destination*. Assuming that the migration flows created societal stress and in turn societal pressure for doctrines of law to protect Blacks from discrimination, as I maintain, they did so primarily in the states that received the migrants. For each of five states to which appreciable numbers of Blacks moved—California, Illinois, Michigan, New York, and Ohio[58]—Table 7.1 and Table 7.2 thus provide, for the first half of the twentieth century, the decade-by-decade volume of interstate migration by Blacks who were at least age 10. Black males are the subject of Table 7.1; Black females are the subject of Table 7.2. However, the data in neither table disclose the region or state of origin of the migrants, and the counts in each table may include individuals who did not move from another region. Among the latter would be individuals who moved between states in the same region. An unknown number of the persons who were counted in Tables 7.1 and 7.2, accordingly, did not migrate from states in the South.

Each table is divided into two panels, which have been labeled Panel A and Panel B. Panel A shows the net number of Black males age 10 and older (Table 7.1), and the net number of Black females age 10 and older (Table 7.2), who are estimated to have resided in each state at the end of the decade specified but who did not reside in that state at the beginning of the decade.[59] Readers should keep in mind that the net numbers in Panel A, although based on data from decennial censuses, unavoidably involve some amount of error. For instance, the net numbers in Panel A were computed on the assumption that, at each time point, the age-sex composition and mortality rates of the

56 FARLEY & ALLEN, *supra* note 55, at 113 Tbl. 5.1.

57 *Id.*

58 The five states were the destination of approximately seven out of ten Blacks who migrated from one state to another at any time during the five decades 1910–1920 through 1950–1960. Computed from MCADAM, *supra* note 55, at 80 Tbl. 5.4.

59 The net numbers of interstate migrants shown in Panel A of Table 7.1 and Table 7.2 are from 1 EVERETT S. LEE ET AL., METHODOLOGICAL CONSIDERATIONS AND REFERENCE TABLES 116, 136, 158–59, 183–84, 191 (1957) [hereinafter METHODOLOGICAL CONSIDERATIONS].

TABLE 7.1 *Net number of black male interstate migrants to selected states, by decade: 1900–1950*[60]

Decade	California	Illinois	Michigan	New York	Ohio
Panel A:					
1900–1910	5,200	11,700	1,100	16,700	8,600
1910–1920	8,000	35,000	23,200	28,900	39,500
1920–1930	17,300	57,400	43,500	82,300	44,500
1930–1940	20,500	18,300	12,200	50,100	7,600
1940–1950	127,300	87,000	82,300	107,200	52,300
Panel B:					
1900–1910	66.7%	25.1%	13.9%	32.9%	17.4%
1910–1920	56.3	50.9	118.4	39.6	55.0
1920–1930	64.1	49.4	80.6	62.8	38.5
1930–1940	43.9	11.4	13.7	23.8	5.0
1940–1950	105.2	39.9	58.4	35.6	28.3

population of every state matched those of the nation as a whole.[61] The numbers in Panel A also suffer from undercounts of Blacks.[62] Apart from and in addition to errors, the net numbers in Panel A have limitations. In particular, Panel A misses individuals who, during a decade, moved across a state line more than once or who moved across a state line but returned to their state of origin before the end of the decade.[63]

While in both tables Panel A reports absolute numbers, Panel B reports percentages. Specifically, for each table, Panel B shows the net number of Black interstate immigrants in Panel A as a percentage of the *average* number of Blacks of the same sex who were inhabitants of the state during the decade specified and who were at least ten years old. The percentages in Panel B are thus a reasonable measure, though certainly not a perfect measure,[64] of the

60 Panel A and Panel B are explained in the text accompanying *supra* notes 59–62.

61 Everett S. Lee, *Migration Estimates*, in METHODOLOGICAL CONSIDERATIONS, *supra* note 59, at 15–16.

62 Simon Kuznets & Dorothy Swaine Thomas, *Introduction*, *in* METHODOLOGICAL CONSIDERATIONS, *supra* note 59, at 6.

63 Everett S. Lee, *Migration Estimates*, *in* METHODOLOGICAL CONSIDERATIONS, *supra* note 59, at 13.

64 The percentages suffer from all of the errors contained in the counts in Panel A.

TABLE 7.2 *Net number of black female interstate migrants to selected states, by decade: 1900–1950*[65]

Decade	California	Illinois	Michigan	New York	Ohio
Panel A:					
1900–1910	4,600	11,800	800	19,100	7,000
1910–1920	8,100	34,800	15,500	34,200	29,900
1920–1930	19,100	61,900	42,600	90,500	46,200
1930–1940	20,800	31,100	15,800	85,800	13,100
1940–1950	131,700	92,800	81,000	136,400	54,400
Panel B:					
1900–1910	65.7%	28.4%	11.1%	33.8%	15.4%
1910–1920	61.4	54.6	104.0	43.0	47.9
1920–1930	70.5	54.6	93.4	64.0	44.6
1930–1940	43.2	18.4	18.9	35.5	8.9
1940–1950	104.9	39.0	58.3	37.5	28.7

degree to which the Black population of a given sex in a state was augmented by migrants of that sex during each decade. The magnitude of a percentage is a plausible barometer of the amount of societal stress that was created in a state by the arrival of Black interstate migrants.

The juxtaposition of Panel A and Panel B in each table reveals a generally not-insubstantial net migration of Blacks into the five states from 1910–1920 to 1940–1950. In the decades of 1910–1920, 1920–1930, and 1940–1950, the augmentation rate of the Black population (Panel B) ranged from a low of 28.3% to a high of 118.4% among Black males and from a low of 28.7% to a high of 104.9% among Black females. In the five states covered by Table 7.1 and Table 7.2, consequently, the population of Blacks expanded by no less than one-fourth, and in a few cases doubled, in a mere ten years during each of the three decades. Even in the 1930s, the population-augmentation rate, though lower, was considerable. Such demographic changes, in magnitude and speed, are important, if not momentous, sociological events.

However, if the appreciable increase in the migration of Blacks to North Central, Northeastern, and Western states that began in 1916 generated societal stress and eventually societal pressure for civil rights law concerned with race

65 Panel A and Panel B are explained in the text accompanying *supra* notes 59–62.

discrimination, as I have hypothesized, it must have done so by promoting serious, concrete, society-level problems during the half-century that followed 1916. Indeed, these problems have been documented, and they evidently had two distinct aspects. First, the enlarged migration flows directly or indirectly set in motion growth in residential segregation of Blacks in states in the North Central, Northeastern, and Western regions.[66] The growth of segregation was intensified, and its effects exacerbated, by the lower educational attainment of Blacks who migrated than of Blacks who had been born in the areas that received the migrants.[67] Second, the growth in residential segregation was accompanied by a set of interrelated macro-level problems. Specifically, in areas where Blacks were concentrated, the increase in race-based residential segregation was associated with (i) a higher rate of crime,[68] (ii) an enlarged population living in buildings that were in disrepair and in housing that was overcrowded,[69] and (iii) a greater incidence of disease.[70]

Returning to my hypothesis, was the migration flow of Blacks from the South that had its inception in World War I responsible for the advent of civil rights law aimed at suppressing race discrimination? The hypothesis is certainly not contradicted—and actually is made plausible—by the evidence reviewed above because, between the mid-1940s and the adoption of the Civil Rights Act of 1964, all of the states in Tables 7.1 and 7.2 enacted legislation that was designed to combat race discrimination in employment. Specifically, the five states in Tables 7.1 and 7.2, along with sixteen others, adopted statutes authorizing both (i) administrative-agency hearings for instances of alleged race discrimination in employment and (ii) court enforcement of orders issued

---

66 Massey & Denton, *supra* note 51, at 19–24, 26–32, 37–39, 42–48; Stanley Lieberson, A Piece of the Pie: Blacks and White Immigrants since 1880, at 259 Tbl. 9.2, 291 (1980); Stewart E. Tolnay et al., *Race, Regional Origin, and Residence in Northern Cities at the Beginning of the Great Migration*, 67 Am. Sociol. Rev. 456, 471–72 (2002).

67 Stewart E. Tolnay, *Educational Selection in the Migration of Southern Blacks, 1880–1990*, 77 Soc. Forces 487, 502–05 (1998).

68 1 St. Clair Drake & Horace R. Cayton, Black Metropolis: A Study of Negro Life in a Northern City 203–04 (rev. & enlarged ed. 1970); Florette Henri, Black Migration: Movement North 1900–1920, at 122–24 (1976); Marks, *supra* note 51, at 147.

69 Henri, *supra* note 68, at 85; Johnson & Campbell, *supra* note 51, at 110–11; Kenneth L. Kusmer, A Ghetto Takes Shape: Black Cleveland, 1870–1930, at 166 (1976); Marks, *supra* note 51, at 145–46; Gilbert Osofsky, Harlem: The Making of a Ghetto 127–31, 135–36, 140 (1966).

70 Drake & Cayton, *supra* note 68, at 204–05; Henri, *supra* note 68, at 108–09, 111–14; Johnson & Campbell, *supra* note 51, at 111; Kusmer, *supra* note 69, at 221–22; Marks, *supra* note 51, at 147; Osofsky, *supra* note 69, at 141–43.

by the agencies and their officials when such discrimination was found to have occurred.[71] Hence, my hypothesis is sufficiently credible to warrant empirical testing. The test, which can be carried out with a design comparable to the studies in *supra* Chapter 2 and Chapter 3, may be able to use, for its dependent variable, the foregoing state statutes and contemporaneous state legislation of similar content.

3 The Contribution of Other Disciplines to Explaining the Content of Law

Universities are prominent in economically advanced nations, but in spite of their important research and educational contributions to society, they possess drawbacks that critics have noted, sometimes sarcastically. A university has thus been described colorfully as "an aggregation of separate sovereignties 'connected…by a common heating plant.'"[72] Such a characterization, though less than flattering, directs attention to a socially approved, and government-subsidized, aspect of modern society—growth in the quality and quantity of knowledge—and to an unavoidable consequence of this growth. In particular, the expansion of knowledge results in specialization of fields of study and of occupations. Not surprisingly, universities embody this specialization. As the partitioning of knowledge proceeds, a university develops a sizeable number of "sovereignties"—self-administered academic departments and comparable organizational units. The partitions of knowledge are not preordained, however, and hence to some extent are arbitrary.[73] For that reason, the partitions can have undesirable consequences. With a larger number of partitions and sovereignties, "the walls around each departmental cosa nostra"[74] may not only separate more disciplines in a university; they can also be expected to pose formidable barriers for more academic personnel who would like to surmount or penetrate the walls, and would benefit from doing so. Such walls, in short, can hinder the advance of science.[75]

---

71 U.S. Equal Employment Opportunity Comm'n, *Part 1—Historical and Legislative Background, in* Legislative History, *supra* note 24, at 5–6.

72 Milton Mayer, Robert Maynard Hutchins: A Memoir 97–98 (1993) (internal quotation from Robert M. Hutchins), *available at* http://publishing.cdlib.org/ucpressebooks/view?docId=ft4w10061d;brand=ucpress (last visited May 9, 2015).

73 Abraham Kaplan, The Conduct of Inquiry 31 (1964); Douglas W. Vick, *Interdisciplinarity and the Discipline of Law*, 31 J. Law & Soc'y 163, 167 (2004).

74 Mayer, *supra* note 72, at 98.

75 Kaplan, *supra* note 73, at 4, 31.

Sociology with its subspecialties is among the many disciplines that inhabit universities, and in a very large percentage of universities in the United States, sociology is housed in its own academic department rather than in a single administrative unit that includes other disciplines, e.g., anthropology. Of course, sociology is not unique in being placed in a separate department. Nonetheless, the disadvantages of discipline-defined departments should not be overlooked. While the establishment of a department for a discipline may be organizationally desirable or unavoidable in a university once the professional staff of the discipline reaches a certain size, intellectual progress in a discipline can be hampered by the department-defined boundaries of the discipline. Succinctly stated, department boundaries have the ability to inhibit the idea-generating process that occurs in a university, because they tend to limit scholars to within-discipline contacts and deter cross-discipline contacts. No single discipline has a monopoly on truth, however, and by confining each discipline largely to its own intellectual resources,[76] the segregation of disciplines can restrain the advancement of knowledge by inhibiting the emergence of novel ideas and the occurrence of intellectual breakthroughs.

For a number of reasons, the structure of universities may inflict greater harm on sociology than on other social sciences. One reason is that sociology as an academic discipline, having existed for only about a century,[77] is relatively young and hence can benefit from exposure to the widest range of ideas. Another reason is that sociologists, given the course they have followed for several decades,[78] suffer from widespread disagreement over their subject, theory-building procedures, and research methods.[79] In addition to these internal difficulties, sociologists are handicapped by their social standing in universities in the United States; stated in blunt terms, sociology is held in low regard as an academic discipline.[80]

---

76 Vick, *supra* note 73, at 166–70.

77 Jonathan H. Turner, *The Disintegration of American Sociology: Pacific Sociological Association 1988 Presidential Address*, 32 SOCIOL. PERSP. 419, 422–23 (1989). The history of sociology and the history of social thought are different subjects. The history of sociology is concerned with the origin of ideas that have contributed to theory in sociology; the history of sociology is not, and must be distinguished from, the history of social thought, i.e., the history of ideas that have characterized a society. Harry J. Kienzle, *The History of Social Thought and the History of Sociology*, 4 SOCIOL. FOCUS 78, 82–83 (1971).

78 THE PLACE OF LAW, *supra* note 2, at 149 n.216.

79 Jonathan H. Turner, *American Sociology in Chaos: Differentiation without Integration*, 37 AM. SOCIOLOGIST 15, 26 (2006).

80 Dennis J. Downey et al., *The Status of Sociology within the Academy: Where We Are, Why We're There, and How to Change It*, 39 AM. SOCIOLOGIST 193, 198–99 (2008). *Accord*, THE PLACE OF LAW, *supra* note 2, at 53–57.

Nonetheless, sociology has a distinctive subject matter[81] on which empirical data can be gathered and theory can be formulated. Sociology thus qualifies as a science,[82] but being less advanced and less accepted than its companions in the social sciences, sociology has the potential to experience a larger improvement in credibility and quality as a science from major advances in understanding its subject. In light of the benefits that may inure to the development of sociology, scholars who hope to build sociological theory—including a macrosociological theory of law—should consider potential contributions from other fields of science, including fields concerned with subjects that are remote from the subject of sociology. Unfortunately, however, sociological work has thus far generally ignored the promise of disciplines whose content is seemingly distant. Of course, sociologists are not alone in being confined to their own discipline-bounded department in a university, but they may be paying a higher price for doing so.

The discipline-based structure of a university, in short, both isolates sociologists and puts blinders on them. However, sociologists are likely to understand social life more fully if they take into account biological aspects, including genetically influenced aspects, of the human species.[83] These aspects have attracted attention among a few social scientists,[84] and available evidence indicates that the aspects must not be ignored in studies of law.[85] Accordingly, I turn to the discipline of neuroscience. In particular, I point out findings from some of the research that has been done on sex differences in the structure, maturation, and operation of the human brain—findings that may be uncomfortable for persons in sociology departments and "social movement" programs who are driven by political ideology.[86] I then discuss the findings with regard to a societal phenomenon that has become a focus of law in the United States.

---

81 Bruce H. Mayhew, *Structuralism Versus Individualism: Part 1, Shadowboxing in the Dark*, 59 SOC. FORCES 335, 338–39 (1980) (contending that the discipline of sociology is concerned with the structure of social life).

82 Randall Collins, *Sociology: Proscience of Antiscience?*, 54 AM. SOCIOL. REV. 124 (1989).

83 Lisa Wade, *The New Science of Sex Difference*, 7 SOCIOL. COMPASS 278, 287 (2013), *available at* http://www.academia.edu/2042106/The_New_Science_of_Sex_Difference; ANTHONY WALSH, BIOSOCIOLOGY: BRIDGING THE BIOLOGY-SOCIOLOGY DIVIDE 4 (2014).

84 Findings from a recent sociological study indicate that male–female differences in the level of the hormone testosterone can have social consequences. Robb Willer et al., *Overdoing Gender: A Test of the Masculine Overcompensation Thesis*, 118 AM. J. SOCIOL. 980, 1010–11 (2013). *See also* Edward Bell et al., *The Origins of Political Attitudes and Behaviours: An Analysis Using Twins*, 42 CANADIAN J. POL. SCI. 855 (2009) (finding evidence of genetic factors in political attitudes and behaviors).

85 Jason D. Boardman et al., *Population Composition, Public Policy, and the Genetics of Smoking*, 48 DEMOGRAPHY 1517 (2011).

86 In *supra* Chapter 6, see (i) text accompanying note 28 and (ii) note 29.

a *Sex Differences in the Human Brain*

Neuroscience today recognizes that differences exist between the brain of the human female and the brain of the human male.[87] More specifically, research by neuroscientists has found that aspects of brain structure, development, and operation are not, in their mean measurements, the same in each sex[88] due to sex-divergent manifestations of genes and chromosomes.[89] For example, studies of the human brain have reported dissimilarities between women and men in the complexity of the cortex,[90] in the thickness of the cortex,[91] and in the amount and distribution of gray matter.[92] Indeed, according to available research, sex apparently has an impact on the human brain throughout the post-birth life cycle. Thus, studies of pre-adults have found that females and males are not identical in aspects of brain structure and maturation,[93] while studies of adults

---

87 Laura S. Allen & Roger A. Gorski, *Sex Differences in the Human Brain, in* 4 ENCYCLOPEDIA OF THE HUMAN BRAIN 289, 294, 299–300 (V.S. Ramachandran ed., 2002); Margaret M. McCarthy et al., *Sex Differences in the Brain: The Not So Inconvenient Truth*, 32 J. NEUROSCIENCE 2241, 2241, 2246 (2012).

88 Larry Cahill, *Sex- and Hemisphere-Related Influences on the Neurobiology of Emotionally Influenced Memory*, 27 PROGRESS IN NEURO-PSYCHOPHARMACOLOGY & BIOLOGICAL PSYCHIATRY 1235, 1235–36 (2003); Julio M. Duarte-Carvajalino et al., *Hierarchical Topological Network Analysis of Anatomical Human Brain Connectivity and Differences Related to Sex and Kinship*, 59 NEUROIMAGE 3784, 3800 (2012); Gaolang Gong et al., *Age- and Gender-Related Differences in the Cortical Anatomical Network*, 29 J. NEUROSCIENCE 15684, 15691 (2009); Tuck C. Ngun et al., *The Genetics of Sex Differences in Brain and Behavior*, 32 FRONTIERS IN NEUROENDOCRINOLOGY 227, 227 (2011); Society for Women's Health Research, Fact Sheet: Sex Differences in the Brain (2009), http://swhr.org/sex-differences-in-the-brain (last visited May 9, 2015).

89 Daniah Trabzuni et al., *Widespread Sex Differences in Gene Expression and Splicing in the Adult Human Brain*, NATURE COMMUNICATIONS, Nov. 22, 2013, at 1, 2 (finding in post-mortem samples of human brain tissue that "sex-biased gene expression was widespread in terms of the numbers of genes, chromosomes and range of brain regions involved"), http://www.nature.com/ncomms/archive/date/2013/11/index.html.

90 Eileen Luders et al., *Gender Differences in Cortical Complexity*, 7 NATURE NEUROSCIENCE 799 (2004).

91 Kiho Im et al., *Gender Difference Analysis of Cortical Thickness in Healthy Young Adults with Surface-Based Methods*, 31 NEUROIMAGE 31, 37 (2006); Elizabeth R. Sowell et al., *Sex Differences in Cortical Thickness Mapped in 176 Healthy Individuals between 7 and 87 Years of Age*, 17 CEREBRAL CORTEX 1550 (2007).

92 Eileen Luders et al., *Why Sex Matters: Brain Size Independent Differences in Gray Matter Distributions between Men and Women*, 29 J. NEUROSCIENCE 14265 (2009); A. Veronica Witte et al., *Regional Sex Differences in Grey Matter Volume are Associated with Sex Hormones in the Young Adult Human Brain*, 49 NEUROIMAGE 1205, 1207–08 (2010).

93 Jennifer E. Bramen et al., *Sex Matters during Adolescence: Testosterone-Related Cortical Thickness Maturation Differs between Boys and Girls*, PLoS ONE, March 2012, at 1, 3, 5–6;

indicate that females and males may not be identical in aspects of brain aging.[94] Moreover, because of genetic differences between females and males, sex-linked dissimilarities in the human brain are likely to be present before birth as well, i.e., during gestation.[95] Notably, the evidence that has accumulated on sex differences in brain structure, maturation, and functioning is sufficient in quantity and quality that it has contributed to the emergence of a new area of specialization, viz., sex-based biology.[96]

In any consideration of conclusions reached by studies of sex differences in the human brain, however, four points must be kept in mind. First, research on a phenomenon yields the most persuasive findings when that research involves more than one study and either (i) the studies are on the same aspect of the

---

Jay N. Giedd et al., *Review: Magnetic Resonance Imaging of Male/Female Differences in Human Adolescent Brain Anatomy*, BIOLOGY OF SEX DIFFERENCES 3 (article 19), at 1 (2012), *available at* http://www.ncbi.nlm.nih.gov/pmc; Harriet W. Hanlon et al., *Gender Differences in the Development of EEG Coherence in Normal Children*, 16 DEVELOPMENTAL NEUROPSYCHOLOGY 479 (1999); Rhoshel K. Lenroot et al., *Sexual Dimorphism of Brain Developmental Trajectories During Childhood and Adolescence*, 36 NEUROIMAGE 1065 (2007); Tomáš Paus, *Sex Differences in the Human Brain: A Developmental Perspective*, 186 PROGRESS IN BRAIN RES. 13, 21–23 (2010).

94 Patricia E. Cowell et al., *Sex Differences in Aging of the Human Frontal and Temporal Lobes*, 14 J. NEUROSCIENCE 4748, 4752–53 (1994); Joel Salinas et al., *Sex Differences in Parietal Lobe Structure and Development*, 9 GENDER MED. 44 (2012); Madhav Thambisetty et al., *Longitudinal Changes in Cortical Thickness Associated with Normal Aging*, 52 NEUROIMAGE 1215, 1220–21 (2010); Jiang Xu et al., *Gender Effects on Age-Related Changes in Brain Structure*, 21 AM. J. NEURORADIOLOGY 112, 117 (2000). *Contra*, Anders M. Fjell et al., *Minute Effects of Sex on the Aging Brain: A Multisample Magnetic Resonance Imaging Study of Healthy Aging and Alzheimer's Disease*, 29 J. NEUROSCIENCE 8774, 8780 (2009).

95 Jill B. Becker et al, *Strategies and Methods for Research on Sex Differences in Brain and Behavior*, 146 ENDOCRINOLOGY 1650, 1651 (2005). Certain pre-birth differences between females and males in the structure of the human brain may exist because of the X sex chromosome and its genes, while other pre-birth sex-linked differences in human brain structure may be present due to the hormone testosterone. *See* Emilia Lentini et al., *Sex Differences in the Human Brain and the Impact of Sex Chromosomes and Sex Hormones*, 23 CEREBRAL CORTEX 2322, 2330 (2013) (findings from a study of adults).

96 Ngun et al., *supra* note 88, at 240. The emergence of sex-based biology as a distinct specialty in science is evidenced by the formation of:

1. The International Society for Gender Medicine (http://isogem.com/#). The Society is an umbrella entity for professional associations in seven countries (Austria, Germany, Israel, Italy, Japan, Sweden, and the United States).
2. The Organization for the Study of Sex Differences (http://www.ossdweb.org). The Organization has an open-access journal titled *Biology of Sex Differences* that publishes peer-reviewed articles.

phenomenon and their findings are generally in agreement or (i) the studies are not on the same aspect of the phenomenon but their findings reinforce one another, i.e., form a pattern.[97] With regard to research on aspects of the human brain, no male–female difference has been observed in some studies. The weight of evidence, however, is to the contrary. Taken as a whole, the findings of research conducted over the last several decades strongly indicate that aspects of the human brain are not the same in males and females.[98]

Turning to the second point, sex-based differences that studies uncover in the human brain are differences between *means*—a mean for females and a mean for males. Because the female mean and the male mean on an attribute are each calculated from a distribution of measurements of the attribute among the members of the relevant sex, the mean for females as well as the mean for males has a standard deviation. Consequently, some members of the sex that has the lower mean on a particular attribute will possess more of the attribute than some members of the sex with the higher mean; conversely, some members of the sex that has the higher mean on an attribute will possess less of the attribute than some members of the sex with the lower mean.[99]

Third, neuroscience is a discipline within the life sciences,[100] and the findings generated by its research on sex differences in the human brain are within the realm of biology. Female–male brain dissimilarities, consequently, are a matter for science, not for social or political ideology. They certainly do not establish the foundation for a social ranking of the two sexes, and they do not necessarily supply a foundation for distinct gender roles. Otherwise stated, while female–male brain dissimilarities probably contribute to some female–male differences in behavioral patterns, the placement of one sex in a higher societal stratum than the other sex is not thereby fated or warranted,[101] and

97 *See* Cordelia Fine, *From Scanner to Sound Bite: Issues in Interpreting and Reporting Sex Differences in the Brain*, 19 CURRENT DIRECTIONS IN PSYCHOL. SCI. 280 (2010) (discussing the limitations of studies that use the technique of neuroimaging to investigate sex differences in the human brain).

98 Tara Perrot-Sinal, *Sex Differences in the Brain: From Genes to Behavior*, 358 NEW ENG. J. MED. 2189 (2008) (book review).

99 The preceding will occur to the extent that the distribution of individual scores for one sex overlaps the distribution of individual scores for the other sex. The extent of overlap for a particular attribute will depend on the magnitude of the difference between the means of each sex on that attribute and the magnitude of the standard deviation for each mean.

100 Wikipedia, Branches of Science, http://en.wikipedia.org/wiki/Branches_of_science (last visited May 9, 2015).

101 Wade, *supra* note 83, at 280–82, 284–86.

sex-linked social stereotypes are not thereby preordained.[102] One reason to believe that female–male brain dissimilarities do not have predetermined effects on a society is that the effects of the dissimilarities probably depend on, and vary to some extent with, culture and social organization.[103]

The fourth point that, I believe, should not be ignored touches on evolution. Specifically, the sex-linked differences in the human brain can be an advantage for homo sapiens as a species, because the differences evidently improve the ability of the species to respond effectively to major challenges. At the species level, in other words, the differences are an asset. How do the differences favor the human species? Leaving aside conception and reproduction, female–male biological differences, including differences in brain structure and operation,[104] permit the members of one sex to be more proficient on average than the members of the other sex in handling certain types of tasks and problems.[105] In combination, female–male brain differences supply sex-related,

---

102 Fine, *supra* note 97 at 280, 282–83.

103 Jinzhao Wang et al., *Sex Difference in the Processing of Task-Relevant and Task-Irrelevant Social Information: An Event-Related Potential Study of Familiar Face Recognition*, BRAIN RES., Aug. 23, 2011, at 41, 46.

104 In addition to average sex differences in the structure of the human brain, some average differences by sex have been detected in the degree to which certain portions of the brain are used in specific types of situations. Wang et al, *supra* note 103. *Accord*, Georg Grön et al., *Brain Activation During Human Navigation: Gender-Different Neural Networks as Substrate of Performance*, 3 NATURE NEUROSCIENCE 404, 406 table 2 (2000); Alice Mado Proverbio et *al., Face Coding Is Bilateral in the Female Brain*, PLoS ONE, June 2010, at 1, 6. Such differences were reported in the study by Grön et al., *supra*, and in the study by Proverbio et al., *supra*, when, respectively, human beings (i) must rely on their eyesight to navigate spatially a complicated setting with which they are not familiar and (ii) respond to faces. Furthermore, sex differences have been found in the regions of the brain that are involved (i) in memories of emotion-kindling events, Cahill, *supra* note 88, at 1236–38, 1239; (ii) when unpleasant events are expected to occur, Giulia Galli et al., *Sex Differences in the Use of Anticipatory Brain Activity to Encode Emotional Events*, 31 J. NEUROSCIENCE 12364, 12367 (2011); and (iii) with positive emotions and negative emotions, Jennifer S. Stevens & Stephan Hamann, *Sex Differences in Brain Activation to Emotional Stimuli: A Meta-Analysis of Neuroimaging Studies*, 50 NEUROPSYCHOLOGIA 1578, 1588–90 (2012). Differences may also exist between men and women in the degree to which particular locations in the brain and particular components of the brain (white matter versus gray matter) are involved in overall intelligence. Richard J. Haier et al., *The Neuroanatomy of General Intelligence: Sex Matters*, 25 NEUROIMAGE 320, 325 (2005).

105 Miguel Burgaleta et al., *Sex Differences in Brain Volume Are Related to Specific Skills, Not to General Intelligence*, 40 INTELLIGENCE 60 (2012); Doreen Kimura, *Human Sex Differences in Cognition, Fact, Not Predicament*, 6 SEXUALITIES, EVOLUTION & GENDER 45, 46–48, 50–51 (2004); Tim Koscik et al., *Sex Differences in Parietal Lobe Morphology: Relationship to Mental*

function-specific benefits to the species by allowing the species to perform a broader range of tasks and solve a greater variety of problems than would be possible if the differences did not exist.

b *Sex-Segregated Schooling*

How do the sex dissimilarities in the structure, maturation, and operation of the human brain affect concepts and doctrines of law? Because a link between these dissimilarities and social patterns has yet to be empirically proven, a definitive answer to the question is not possible, and any answer that is proposed necessarily entails speculation. Nonetheless, it is not outside the realm of possibility that the male–female brain dissimilarities have an influence on social patterns and, hence, on law. Sex-based distinctions persist in social life in the United States,[106] and males and females in a range of cultures exhibit mean differences in psychological attributes.[107] Such patterns are unlikely to be due to chance and may not be due to human inertia either.

In light of the evidence that was cited in *supra* Part 3-a, one plausible hypothesis is that female–male differences in brain structure and operation affect, in certain ways and/or to some extent, the perception and interpretation of phenomena. If so, the differences can have an influence on social life and, in turn, on the content of law. An illustration may lie in the views that adults hold as to whether morality is a public issue or a private matter. Behavior that implicates morality in a society is less likely to be regulated by law when the behavior is considered to be within the private sphere than when the behavior is assigned to the public sphere. Notably, the odds that morality will be seen as a private matter are much higher among U.S. women than among U.S. men, and the gains that occurred during the last half of the twentieth century in the status of U.S. women may thus account, at least in part, for the shift in U.S. law that resulted in the elimination of prohibitions on consensual, noncommercial, and nonpublic sexual activity.[108] Partially because of differences in brain structure and functioning,[109] females and males may diverge in their social construction and treatment of such activity.

Rotation Performance, 69 BRAIN & COGNITION 451, 455–56 (2009); Lisa Lejbak et al., *The Female Advantage in Object Location Memory Is Robust to Verbalizability and Mode of Presentation of Test Stimuli*, 69 BRAIN & COGNITION 148, 152 (2009). *Accord*, David S. Moore & Scott P. Johnson, *Mental Rotation in Human Infants: A Sex Difference*, 19 PSYCHOL. SCI. 1063 (2008).

106 David S. Cohen, *The Stubborn Persistence of Sex Segregation*, 20 COLUM. J. GENDER & L. 51 (2011).

107 Paul T. Costa, Jr. et al., *Gender Differences in Personality Traits Across Cultures: Robust and Surprising Findings*, 81 J. PERSONALITY & SOC. PSYCHOL. 322, 326–28 (2001).

108 THE PLACE OF LAW, *supra* note 2, at 223–30.

109 Citations to supporting evidence on sex differences in brain functioning are in *supra* notes 104 and 105.

Let me turn to another question that arises from studies of sex-based differences in the human brain and that has implications for law in the United States. The question is whether females and males in U.S. elementary schools and/or secondary schools should be taught in classes that are segregated by sex. The question exists because the maturation of the human brain is not the same in each sex[110] and the divergence in maturation may produce differences in age-specific learning abilities of pre-adult females and males. Perhaps not surprisingly, sex-segregated classes have been controversial.[111]

The number of single-sex classrooms in public schools at the elementary and secondary levels has grown during the twenty-first century,[112] and a chief argument advanced by advocates of same-sex classrooms is that an important variable in learning is female–male differences in brain maturation.[113] This variable, they contend, must be taken into account when designing educational programs in elementary and secondary schools. However, a public school is operated by a governmental body, and it thus must abide by the provisions of the U.S. Constitution.[114] According to the latest pronouncement on the subject by the U.S. Supreme Court, a distinction grounded on the biological attribute of sex, when used by a public school, does not invariably breach the ban on classifications that is imposed by the equal protection guarantee of the Constitution.[115] However, a sex-based distinction by a governmental body will conform to the requirements of equal protection only if the distinction

---

110 Supporting evidence is cited in *supra* note 93.

111 Rosemary C. Salomone, *Feminist Voices in the Debate Over Single-Sex Schooling: Finding Common Ground*, 11 MICH. J. GENDER & L. 63, 63, 70 (2004); Galen Sherwin, *Single-Sex Schools and the Antisegregation Principle*, 30 N.Y.U. REV. L. & SOC. CHANGE 35, 36 (2005).

112 Nat'l Ass'n for Single Sex Public Educ., http://www.singlesexschools.org/schools-schools.htm (last visited May 9, 2015); POL'Y & PROGRAM STUD. SERVICE, U.S. DEP'T OF EDUC., SINGLE-SEX VERSUS COEDUCATIONAL SCHOOLING: A SYSTEMATIC REVIEW ix (2005), *available at* http://www2.ed.gov/rschstat/eval/other/single-sex/single-sex.pdf.

113 Nat'l Ass'n for Single Sex Public Educ., Single-Sex Education, http://www.singlesexschools.org/home.php (last visited May 9, 2015).

114 Kevin Cole, *Federal and State "State Action": The Undercritical Embrace of a Hypercritized Doctrine*, 24 GA. L. REV. 327, 330–31 (1990).

115 The Fourteenth Amendment includes an explicit equal protection provision that is applicable to government at the state and local level, but the Fourteenth Amendment does not apply to the federal government. U.S. CONST. amend. XIV § 1 ("No State shall…deny to any person within its jurisdiction the equal protection of the laws"). The Fifth Amendment, with which the federal government must comply, provides no explicit promise of equal protection, but does contain an express due process guarantee. U.S. CONST. amend. V ("No person shall…be deprived of life, liberty, or property, without due process of law"). As construed by the U.S. Supreme Court, the due process guarantee of the Fifth

was made for an "exceedingly persuasive" reason,[116] i.e., the governmental body had in mind an important goal that the distinction appreciably furthers.[117] Consequently, while female–male biological differences cannot be the basis for placing "artificial constraints on an individual's opportunity" in a public school, these differences may be used by public schools "to advance full development of the talent and capacities of our Nation's people."[118] If research proves that sex-linked average dissimilarities in brain maturation have more than a trivial impact on the ability of each sex to learn certain topics at certain ages—proof that seems not yet to exist but that is not implausible in light of available evidence—public schools can be expected to have a constitutionally acceptable ground for relying on a combination of the sex and age of students when scheduling classes on these topics.

The discipline of neuroscience, in short, may eventually furnish a constitutional footing for policies requiring some single-sex classes in public schools. If it does, the findings of research in the discipline will need to be acknowledged in a macrosociological approach to law. A macrosociological process—expansion of the stock of knowledge[119]—extended the period that females and males devote to schooling,[120] and as the stock of knowledge from research in neuroscience continues to grow, more public schools at the elementary and secondary levels may, without violating constitutional guarantees, add the criterion of sex to the criterion of age when arranging their curricula and assigning students to classes.

4 A Final Word

The advance of every science is a never-ending process that normally involves innumerable small steps, each adding incrementally to the quantity of knowledge. On occasion, however, a science reaches a point where a large step—a leap forward—is possible. Unfortunately for the advance of science, the large step

---

Amendment furnishes an assurance of equal protection that is comparable to the Equal Protection Clause of the Fourteenth Amendment. San Francisco Arts & Athletics, Inc. v. U.S. Olympic Committee, 483 U.S. 522, 542 n.21 (1987).

116 United States v. Virginia, 518 U.S. 515, 532–33 (1996).

117 Engineering Contractors Ass'n of South Florida, Inc. v. Metropolitan Dade County, 122 F.3d 895, 907–08 (11th Cir. 1997), *cert. denied*, 523 U.S. 1004 (1998).

118 United States v. Virginia, 518 U.S. at 533–34.

119 THE PLACE OF LAW, *supra* note 2, at 263–68.

120 Richard Rubinson & John Ralph, *Technical Change and the Expansion of Schooling in the United States, 1890–1970*, 57 SOCIOL. EDUC. 134 (1984).

may not be taken when it becomes feasible. Instead, the step may be delayed for a lengthy period because of inadvertence—the evidence for it is overlooked—or because of resistance—the step threatens deeply entrenched beliefs. Eventually, of course, the large step is made, because individuals and ideologies can only hinder the advance of science; they cannot defeat it. As the past has shown, "[t]he progress of science, like an ancient desert trail, is strewn with the bleached skeletons of discarded theories which seemed once to possess eternal life."[121] In science, a rigid, unthinking acceptance of presently popular paradigms is thus ill-advised.

The history of science provides context to the instant book. In proposing that findings from currently available social science research offer the opportunity to acquire a new understanding of the relationship between a modern society and the content of its law—an understanding that differs sharply from now-dominant ideas regarding law—the book challenges the status quo and provides an alternative to the currently fashionable view of the role of law. The possibility that this leap can be made today is reasonably clear. What remains uncertain is whether the leap will happen soon or whether it will be pushed into the distant future.

---

121 Arthur Koestler, The Ghost in the Machine 178 (1967).

Author Index

Subject Index

www.ingramcontent.com/pod-product-compliance
Lightning Source LLC
LaVergne TN
LVHW010624300926
849162LV00001B/57
* 9 7 8 9 0 0 4 2 8 1 2 0 2 *